J 30
F/7

40320

FORGING MODERN JEWISH IDENTITIES
PUBLIC FACES AND PRIVATE STRUGGLES

Parkes–Wiener Series on Jewish Studies
Series Editors: David Cesarani and Tony Kushner
ISSN 1368-5449

The field of Jewish Studies is one of the youngest, but fastest growing and most exciting areas of scholarship in the academic world today. Named after James Parkes and Alfred Wiener, this series aims to publish new research in the field and student materials for use in the seminar room, to disseminate the latest work of established scholars and to re-issue classic studies which are currently out of print.

The selection of publications will reflect the international character and diversity of Jewish Studies; it ranges over Jewish history from Abraham to modern Zionism, and Jewish culture from Moses to postmodernism. The series also reflects the inter-disciplinary approach inherent in Jewish Studies and at the cutting edge of contemporary scholarship, and provides an outlet for innovative work on the interface between Judaism and ethnicity, popular culture, gender, class, space and memory.

Other Books in the Series

Holocaust Literature: Schulz, Levi, Spiegelman and the Memory of the Offence
Gillian Banner

Remembering Cable Street: Fascism and Anti-Fascism in British Society
Edited by Tony Kushner and Nadia Valman

Sir Sidney Hamburger and Manchester Jewry: Religion, City and Community
Bill Williams

Anglo-Jewry in Changing Times: Studies in Diversity 1840–1914
Israel Finestein

Double Jeopardy: Gender and the Holocaust
Judith Tydor Baumel

Cultures of Ambivalence and Contempt: Studies in Jewish-on-Jewish Relations
Edited by Siân Jones, Tony Kushner and Sarah Pearce

Alfred Wiener and the Making of the Wiener Library
Ben Barkow

The Berlin Haskalah and German Religious Thought: Orphans of Knowledge
David Sorkin

Myths in Israeli Culture: Captives of a Dream
Nurith Gertz

The Jewish Immigrant in England 1870–1914, Third Edition
Lloyd P. Gartner

State and Society in Roman Galilee, A.D. 132–212, Second Edition
Martin Goodman

Disraeli's Jewishness
Edited by Todd M. Endelman and Tony Kushner

Claude Montefiore: His Life and Thought
Daniel R. Langton

Forging Modern Jewish Identities

Public Faces and Private Struggles

Editors

MICHAEL BERKOWITZ, *University College London*

SUSAN L. TANANBAUM, *Bowdoin College*

SAM W. BLOOM, *University of Haifa*

VALLENTINE MITCHELL

LONDON • PORTLAND, OR

First published in 2003 in Great Britain by
VALLENTINE MITCHELL
Crown House, 47 Chase Side, Southgate
London N14 5BP

and in the United States of America by
VALLENTINE MITCHELL
c/o ISBS, 5824 N.E. Hassalo Street
Portland, Oregon 97213-3644

Website: www.vmbooks.com

British Library Cataloguing in Publication Data

Forging modern Jewish identities: public faces and private
struggles. – (Parkes–Wiener series on Jewish studies)
1. Jews – Identity 2. Jews – Cultural assimilation 3. Jews –
History – 20th century
I. Berkowitz, Michael II. Tananbaum Susan L. III. Bloom, Sam W.
305.8'924

ISBN 0-85303-454-0 (cloth)
ISBN 0-85303-455-9 (paper)
ISSN 1368–5449

Library of Congress Cataloging-in-Publication Data

Forging modern Jewish identities: public faces and private struggles / edited
by Michael Berkowitz, Susan L. Tananbaum, Sam W. Bloom.
    p. cm. – (Parkes-Wiener series on Jewish studies, ISSN 1368-5449)
Includes bibliographical references (p.) and index.
ISBN 0-85303-454-0 (cloth) – ISBN 0-85303-455-9 (pbk.)
    1. Jews – Identity. 2. Jews – Cultural assimilation. 3. Social integration.
I. Berkowitz, Michael. II. Tananbaum, Susan L. III. Bloom, Sam W., 1966–
IV. Series.

DS143.F59 2003
305.892'4–dc21   2002074075

Typeset in 11/13pt Palatino by Vitaset, Paddock Wood, Kent
Printed in Great Britain by
MPG Books Ltd, Victoria Square, Bodmin, Cornwall

MB: To my Aunt and Uncle, Betty and Louis Berman, and to my *mekhutonim*, Norman and Barbara Rozansky, with love

SLT: With love to my family for all their support and in memory of my father

SWB: To Anne and Bill for their unwavering support

Reprint Acknowledgements

The authors gratefully acknowledge permission to use previously published material. Sections of the chapter by Daniel Soyer appeared in 'Back to the Future: American Jews Visit the Soviet Union in the 1920s and 1930s', *Jewish Social Studies* (Spring–Summer 2000), pp. 124–59 and 'The Immigrant Travel Agent as Broker Between Old World and New: The Case of Gustave Eisner', *YIVO Annual* (1993), pp. 345–68. The chapter by Mark Levene was published in a slightly different form in *Jewish Culture and History* 2, 2 (2000), pp. 66–95.

Permission for use of L. Pasternak's 'Musikanken' and Herman Struck's 'Polnischer Jude', from Berthold Feiwel (ed.), *Jüdischer Almanach*, II (Berlin: Jüdischer Verlag, 1904), is granted by the Central Zionist Archives, Jerusalem.

Contents

List of Contributors

Michael Berkowitz is Reader in Modern Jewish History at University College London

Sam W. Bloom is Lecturer in the Department of French Language and Literature at the University of Haifa, Israel

Lawrence G. Charap, Independent Scholar, is employed by Digital Learning Interactive

Miriam Dean-Otting is Professor of Religious Studies, Kenyon College, Ohio

Musya Glants is at the Davis Center for Russian Studies, Harvard University

Mark Levene is Reader in Comparative History, the Parkes Centre for Jewish–Non-Jewish Relations and the Department of History, University of Southampton

Michelle Mart is Assistant Professor of History, Pennsylvania State University, Berks Campus

Alice S. Nakhimovsky, is Professor of Russian, Colgate University, New York

Stanislao G. Pugliese is Associate Professor of Modern European History at Hofstra University and a former Visiting Research Fellow at the Italian Academy for Advanced Studies at Columbia University

Glenn Sharfman is Professor of History, Hiram College, Ohio

Daniel Soyer is Associate Professor of History, Fordham University, New York

Susan L. Tananbaum is Associate Professor of History, Bowdoin College, Maine

Péter Várdy is Emeritus Lecturer in Philosophy, Twente University, Enschede, The Netherlands

Introduction:
Anthologizing Jews

There is no question that Jews have become highly acculturated in disparate modern non-Jewish contexts, especially in the west. They have reached such a degree of comfort in America, France and Britain that their presence in almost any niche of these societies is unremarkable. Simultaneously, however, acculturated Jews continue to move in and out of major Jewish religious denominations, voluntary associations and cultural, political and educational endeavours – that often play a part in the persistence, formation and permutations of Jewish identity. Since the inception of Zionism in the late nineteenth century, Jews have had the option of 'returning', for varying lengths of stay, to the Jewish settlement in Palestine, and later, the State of Israel. For most western Jews though, their engagement with the Land of Israel has involved a tour, rather than permanent relocation.[1] Few pull up stakes if they are well entrenched. Perhaps most amazingly, Jews have resuscitated Jewish culture in the former Soviet Union despite the near suffocation of such activity for half a century, and Jewish life, however changed from the pre-war era, has re-emerged in central and eastern Europe. The latter is a consequence of initiatives launched by non-Jewish agencies and individuals, as well as by secular and religious Jewish interests.[2] Especially since 1989, travel and study in former centres of Jewish civilization of Europe is competing with Israel as a means for Jews to explore and recapture aspects of their identity.

To be sure, many of the formerly prominent organizations among Jews, such as trade unions, Zionist societies, fraternal orders and local, national and international groups have experienced a precipitous decline. One of the former chief bonds of solidarity among Jews, the Yiddish language, has atrophied. Yet by other measures, among Jews who appear well mixed in their surrounding milieu, there is tremendous organizational zeal and foment in the early days of the twenty-first century, which may suggest new forms of identity coming into being. It is a central fact of modern history that Jews were the chief victims of Nazi genocide that destroyed the basis of Jewish corporate existence and continuity in most of central and eastern Europe. However, before the Nazi menace became apparent, the threat that traditionally had been seen as potentially fatal in societies that were not rife with anti-Semitism, was self-dissolution.[3]

Despite dire warnings of the impending demise of Jewish communal vitality since the massive movement of Jews westward in the 1880s, the cases where Jewry, in a recognizable manner, have ceased unequivocally to be Jews are few and far between. The consequences of increased rates of intermarriage, from a historical perspective, are far from conclusive, however much self-styled champions of Jewish survival decry the likelihood of 'a world without Jews'.[4] It is true that some Jews have permanently abandoned Judaism;[5] for larger numbers, there is a decisive drift away from long-established Jewish institutions. However, modern Jews tend to seek institutional support and sustenance at critical junctures in private life, such as from synagogues, secular and religious educational institutions, philanthropic organizations, and community centres, even if their Jewish connections are mainly dormant. For the most part, rather than becoming Christians in significant numbers, or formally renouncing their faith, Jews in the west have tended to become different types of Jews. On occasion this has occurred because of, or accompanied by, a great degree of self-awareness. Often, Jews have been oblivious to the transformations epitomized by their own lives. For many, no doubt, the reality is something in between: a sense that there is something historical, and possibly transitional, about their own situation or evolution as a Jew, as well as recognition that the ways they express their Jewishness are not the same as earlier generations.[6]

Jewish history and social science, not surprisingly, have lagged behind Jews themselves in noticing and interpreting Jews' adaptability and complexity.[7] In his caustic essay, 'Eine Krone für Zion' (1898), Karl Kraus predicted that Theodor Herzl's Zionist dream had no future, because Jews, above all, had a genius for improvising to fit their surroundings.[8] He failed to imagine, however, that Zionism might itself become (in the words of historian Ezra Mendelsohn) a sort of 'Aladdin's lamp', promising to fulfil

the wishes of all Jews who were drawn to it.[9] Jews, as opposed to
Jewish historians, sociologists and demographers, have had a
more imaginative sense of what it meant and means to be Jewish
than those who tell their stories, and propose to glean some
significance from their transformations. In other words, modern
Jews have been more creative, in the sense of re-creating themselves, than critics and scholars have perceived.

In a 1982 essay that has accumulated gravitas as a state-of-
the-field reckoning, Paula Hyman surveyed the landscape of
modern Jewish history and found it severely wanting, especially
in light of the developments in historiography outside the
Jewish field.[10] One focus of her remarks was the formidable
and useful primary source anthology of Jehuda Reinharz and
Paul Mendes-Flohr, *The Jew in the Modern World*, which has
since been revised.[11] Although she was generous in praise of its
merits, Hyman found the selections in many respects wedded to
long-held legalistic and male-dominated, religious-organizational
frameworks. Furthermore, she claimed that such tendencies
pervaded the field at large. Hyman did, however, point enthu-
siastically to those works which she saw as pioneering in their use
of newer social-historical methods, such as Todd Endelman's
studies of Anglo-Jewry, and the more nuanced applications of
gender analysis to Jewish history, as exemplified by Marion
Kaplan's history of the *Jüdischer Frauenbund* in Germany.[12] More
recently, Michael John and Albert Lichtblau, contrasting the
regions of Bukovina and Galicia,[13] and Rainer Liedtke and
Stephan Wendehorst, writing on Anglo- and German Jewry,
have produced exemplary comparative social historical studies
that built on Kaplan and Endelman.[14] In a later historiographic
essay, Hyman called for greater historical sophistication in
dealing with Jewry in the west. She questioned the assumption
of many scholars that Jewish history in central and western
Europe has been a variation on overwhelming assimilation processes, which automatically entailed becoming less distinctively
Jewish and more like the majority group in the surrounding
environment.[15]

In a great number of instances, historians have responded to
the lacunae such as those articulated by Hyman. The result
has been a proliferation of works in modern Jewish history that
move beyond mainstream historiography and draw on current
historiographic approaches in European and American history.

George Mosse, Todd Endelman, Marion Kaplan, Aron Rodrigue, David Biale, Michael Brenner, John Efron, James Young, David Myers, Yael Zerubavel, Dietz Bering and others are responsible for invigorating the study of modern Jewry with fresh approaches that have intelligently applied the tools current in the field at large.[16] Fruitful convergence with literary studies which adopt a historical approach and take ethnic differentiation seriously, with explicit attention to perceptions and image-making, has resulted in important studies of Jewish history and anti-Semitism by Linda Nochlin and Tamar Garb, Sander Gilman, Daniel Boyarin, David Brenner, Bryan Cheyette and Marc Weiner.[17] In addition to monographs, the newer trends in Jewish history are evident in a flurry of recently published anthologies; we view this current volume as complementing this burgeoning literature.[18]

If one wishes to survey developments in modern Jewish history, there are several anthologies of scholarly articles that epitomize fresh approaches. Among the most effective, in this regard, are *Profiles in Diversity: Jews in a Changing Europe 1750–1870*, edited by Frances Malino and David Sorkin, which delves into the early emancipatory period mainly through biographies and collective biographies of Jewish elites in contrasting settings,[19] and *Insider/Outsider: American Jews and Multiculturalism*, edited by David Biale, Michael Galchinsky and Susannah Heschel, a cross-disciplinary exploration of the problematic Jewish role and presence in the US, which is increasingly characterized by the assertion of 'ethnic options'.[20] Sometimes an anthology is a way to accentuate a revisionist perspective, such as John Klier and Shlomo Lambroza's volume on pogroms, which seeks to overturn the conviction that the pogroms in Tsarist Russia were largely state-sponsored.[21] Laurence Silberstein's volume, based partly on recently declassified documents, brings the work of the 'New Historians' in Israel to an English-reading public and re-examines the myths of modern Israel's emergence and early years of state-hood.[22] Ada Rapoport-Albert's collection on Hasidism scrutinizes the deterministic social analysis first advanced by Simon Dubnow and accepted by a generation of scholars, that Hasidism mainly arose from the retrograde socio-economic status of Jewry in the south-eastern region of the Pale of Settlement.[23] *Jewries at the Frontier: Accommodation, Identity, and Conflict*, edited by Sander Gilman and Milton Shain, focuses on Jewries usually defined as 'peripheral' as its main framework of analysis.[24]

This is not to say, however, that all these anthologies are, or are

meant to be, ground-breaking. One of the first, and still formidable, products of an attempt to provide a comprehensive overview of Jewish history and scholarship is Judah Goldin's *The Jewish
Expression*.[25] Other anthologies, and entire series concentrating on
topics or periods of Jewish history, have asserted that there exists
a canonical set of scholarly papers that constitute the essence of a
subfield. Among the volumes deemed 'Essential Papers' by New
York University Press, the *Essential Papers on Zionism*, edited by
Jehuda Reinharz and Anita Shapira, favours traditional approaches
to mainstream aspects of Zionism[26]; Marc Saperstein, in his
collection on messianic movements and personalities in the same
series, draws on a wider range of scholarly approaches.[27] Since the
appearance of the volume on *Jewry and the Left*, edited by Ezra
Mendelsohn,[28] work by a new vintage of scholars, including
Sharman Kadish, Anne Kershen, Jeffrey Veidlinger, Michael
Steinlauf, Eli Lederhendler, Naomi Seidman and Joel Berkowitz
has substantially enriched earlier appraisals.[29] Rather than
anthologies with restricted definitions of what properly constitutes Judaism, as opposed to its 'betrayal',[30] a number of collections have emerged that are by self-definition either marginal, or
not yet recognized as generally significant to the field. Such
studies extend the boundaries or means of conceptualization
accepted by teachers and practitioners in the area. Such is the case
for Sander Gilman and Jack Zipes' *Yale Companion to Jewish Writing
and Thought in German Culture, 1096–1996*,[31] which seeks to embed
a wide range of texts in their historical contexts, and Daniel and
Jonathan Boyarin's *Jews and Other Differences*, which situates new
work in Jewish Studies in the burgeoning field of cultural studies,
mainly through the use of cultural anthropology.[32] In *Interpreting
Judaism in a Postmodern Age*, Stephen Kepnes aspires to begin a
dialogue between Jewish Studies and postmodernist discourse.[33]
The collection of Miriam Peskowitz and Laura Levitt[34] uses postmodernism to differentiate it from earlier collections on women
and Judaism edited by Judith Baskin, Maurie Sacks and Tamar
Rudavsky.[35] The books edited by Gilman and Zipes, the Boyarins,
Kepnes, and Peskowitz and Levitt are self-consciously theoretical,
in the sense that they embrace approaches that have long influenced literary, religious and gender studies before coming into the
domain of Jewish Studies.

One of the distinguishing characteristics of this book, as well,
is that many of the pieces draw on approaches that have not been
widely embraced or exploited in treatments of modern Jewish

history. Theory, while less overt, has influenced the episodes and individual case studies under consideration. In addition, they deal with a wider selection of Jewry than is often examined, and these pieces tend toward a 'thick' description of discrete topics. Included in this collection are studies of American, British, French, Russian, Hungarian, Italian and German Jewry. We look at Jewish identity as more open-ended, less predictable and teleological than those stemming from stances that prize a specific outcome – whether it be the emergence of a particular political or religious stream, such as Reform, Conservative or Orthodox Judaism, or Jewish statehood.[36] Jewish identity, as complicated, fragmented and multi-faceted as it is, invites anthologies more than many subjects that might be better served by synthetic treatments. Overall, the essays here contribute to a point better said collectively: Jewish identity has taken on numerous guises, and historical investigation and critical interrogation of its lesser known forms results in a greater understanding of modern Jewish experiences. We do not wish to imply that Jewish identity is protean – infinitely malleable – nor that it is possible to define an essence of the modern Jewish experience.

The following collection of essays emerged from a workshop on modern Jewish history, which was the largest component of the fourth biennial conference of the International Society for the Study of European Ideas held in Utrecht, in the summer of 1996. The organizers of the conference, Ezra and Sascha Talmor of Haifa University, granted permission for the workshop's papers to be published in a different forum. Shorter unedited versions of several papers appeared on a CD-ROM conference volume, compiled by Henry Kunnemann. The essays appearing here are a selection from a group of three dozen which have all been substantially revised. In some cases, these contributions are completely different from the initial conference presentation.

The first chapter illustrates the potential of fusing Jewish history with theory, cultural anthropology and sensitivity to transient states of being – regarding the relationship of tourism to ethnic identity. Daniel Soyer discusses the phenomenon of immigrant Jews travelling to the 'Old Country', including responses to visiting the Soviet Union. Drawing on important theoretical literature about similar group practices, Soyer gives us new insights and interpretations about a little-studied part of the immigrant experience that was often a watershed in an individual's life. Simultaneously, it was a way of affirming, and casting into sharp relief, one's American and Jewish identity. Soyer's analysis extends recent studies of Jewish immigrant culture, such as those of Hadassa Kosak, Steven Cassedy, Susan Glenn and Andrew Heinze, and is especially rich thanks to Soyer's expertise in mining Yiddish sources available for the period.[37]

Using the periodical *American Hebrew* as a template, in the second chapter Lawrence Charap shows how the discourse of 'religious modernism' influenced the development of 'interfaith dialogue', that is, discussion between Jews and Christians. Charap reveals how the discourse played a significant role in inter-Jewish polemics. In one of the stranger and more fascinating instances of intertextuality one might imagine, Charap analyses the ways opponents of the Reform movement – without admitting the practice – appropriated liberal Christian texts to defend the 'modernity' of Orthodox ways. Hence, ironically, modern Orthodoxy in America invented itself, or at least cast its public face, through Christian means. His critical reading of a well-known periodical conveys a complex understanding of the texts and the reality of Jewish–Christian and Jewish–Jewish polemics. Jews used words intended as extensions of friendship to Jews, by Christians, as a weapon to delegitimate fellow Jews.

Also in the realm of historical approaches to popular culture, in chapter three Michelle Mart analyses the interrelationships between best-selling novels, films and changing views of American Jewish identity. Rather than accepting the dictum that art or popular culture 'reflect' life, Mart demonstrates, through her perceptive reading of well-known authors such as Saul Bellow, Jerome Weidman and Herman Wouk, that sometimes culture helps create or mould the ensuing attitudes and facts on the ground. American Jewry, according to Mart, was surprisingly self-confident in articulating the tensions in their personal lives, poised as they were between remnants of the immigrant generation and the worlds that began opening up to Jews from the 1930s to the 1950s.

The fourth chapter, by Mark Levene, shifts the focus to a slightly later period, and across the Atlantic to Britain. Levene shows that the British experience in World War I, and its immediate legacy, is quite different from and more varied than the official record suggests, and includes 'hostility and resistance to military service'. His close reading of two war-related memoirs of British Jews shows that young men's choices and attitudes were not necessarily predictable from one's social situation. Levene brings to these documents a knowledge of the wider events in the Anglo-Jewish and general political spheres. He reveals much more than the life stories of two individuals and speaks to Jewish men's identity in the beginning of the twentieth century, which includes struggles with nationalist or patriotic feelings towards one's home nation, the embrace of some form of Jewish nationalism, or the rejection of all nationalist alternatives completely. One of Levene's main achievements is a better understanding of those who did not fit into any self-justifying camp.

Susan Tananbaum, in chapter five, analyses the concepts of Jewish identity advanced by Jewish social welfare institutions, in Britain and America, focusing on their attempts to respond to and control what they perceived as deviant behaviour of disadvantaged youth. This interpretation shows the interplay between traditional Jewish philanthropic stances, which were in a process of flux, with late Victorian ideologies. It offers a remarkably clear view of the anxieties of 'established' Jews that were behind their endeavours to restrain and mould their troubled youths. At the same time it opens a window to social realities in Britain and the US that the Jewish communities preferred to hide, while showing how overwrought were Jewish fears about perceptions of their part in crime and delinquency.

Moving from the Whitechapel street to the Parisian salon, in chapter six, Sam Bloom examines the work of Marcel Proust and Jewish humour. Bloom traces the connections between Proust, Jewish jokes, clown-like behaviour and thought about Jewish identity. Jewish jokes within the Proustian narrative, Bloom argues, make it identifiably and perhaps comfortably (or uncomfortably?) Jewish to its Jewish readers. One can read both self-hatred and disdain for assimilation into these jokes, whose very telling and retelling with commentary, Harold Bloom would label as an obvious Jewish characteristic.[38] Drawing on Sander Gilman's incisive reading of bodily aspects of literature related to Jews, the author shows that the growth or shrinkage of Swann's nose was a humorous bell-wether of his proximity to his 'flock'. The Jewish humour of Proust, according to Sam Bloom, elicits eruptions of Jewishness which nevertheless remain open to a wide range of interpretations.

Continuing with the motif of humour within Jewish identity, in chapter seven, Alice Nakhimovsky's study of Jewish comedian Mikhail Zhvanetskii, explores a vital Jewish dimension in Soviet Russian culture which helps to answer the question: how was

Jewish identity preserved and nurtured in a general atmosphere in which Soviets expected Jewishness to disappear? Nakhimovsky argues that both the content and forms of Zhvanetskii's humour made it recognizable as something 'Jewish'. As the late twentieth century has witnessed the increasing influx of Jews from the former Soviet Union into central Europe, North America and Israel,[39] it is important to see their Jewish legacy for what it was – as it was different from that of their contemporaries, but unquestionably part of their identity. Nakhimovsky recovers the significance of this variety of popular culture, which is mostly inaccessible to non-Russian speakers and applies her interpretive acumen to tease out Soviet-Jewish identity, which was more complex than a reaction to crass anti-Semitism and anti-Zionism. She is one of few westerners able to convey and elucidate, dispassionately but sensitively, the Soviet Jewish scene.

Turning to the pre-Soviet period, examining a group of Russian-Jewish artists who rarely receive notice for their distinct Jewish contributions, Musya Glants, in chapter eight, argues that there was something of a family resemblance among them. Using published and unpublished letters and memoirs, Glants relates that there was a tendency for this cohort to affirm their connection to Judaism and Jewry at late stages of their lives, and that their careers consistently merged Christian and Jewish imagery, which might be read as suggestive of their aspirations for Jewish perseverance and continuity. Glants also shows, ironically, that their intense passion for Russian culture, almost an unrequited love, separated them from their fellow artists. Such a study complements the increasing scrutiny given to the place of Jews, which typically has been overlooked, in modern art history.[40]

Chapter nine, by Glenn Sharfman, confronts an explicit attempt to grapple with Jewish identity in 'Between Identities: The German-Jewish Youth Movement Blau-Weiss, 1912–1926'. The author especially notes how pressures on Jewish adolescents in an increasingly hostile environment resulted in the emergence of the *Bund deutsch-jüdischer Jugend*. As Marion Kaplan and Frank Nicosia have argued, historians should not be blind to Jewish political and cultural activity in the early years of the Nazi regime, simply because of hindsight.[41] Sharfman, basing his work on journals, memoirs and interviews, reconstructs the efforts of these young people who faced hatred and recriminations not just from anti-Semites, but from Zionists who perceived them as foolhardy or traitorous. For those who emigrated, Sharfman argues, the quest of the organization was not in vain. Although the *Bund deutsch-jüdischer Jugend* has received little attention from most historians of German Jewry, and especially of German Zionism, Sharfman convincingly argues that given the tiny Jewish community, the 5,000-member organization deserves consideration on its own terms.

Miriam Dean-Otting, in chapter ten, works with largely unpublished archival sources; her contribution juxtaposes the attitudes toward Jewish identity in two generations of Czech Jewish women: Berta Fanta and Else Fanta Bergmann. Berta Fanta, a leading salon hostess of her generation, while not renouncing Judaism, was by contrast more eclectic and pluralistic in her intellectual loyalties than was her daughter, who was keen to explore and celebrate her Jewish heritage. In this instance, therefore, we are presented with a generational shift that is not far removed from traditional Judaism, but a transformation from the ecumenical to the Jewishly specific. The daughter evinced a desire to reclaim a Jewish past and live in the midst of a Jewish present, eventually settling in Palestine with her husband, philosopher S.H. Bergmann.

Péter Vàrdy's study, chapter eleven, illuminates relations between Jews and non-Jews in Hungary, before, during and after the Holocaust; it is the product of collaborative research that includes over 100 interviews. One of the more fascinating aspects of these accounts is the window they provide on the fate of the deportees who returned to their homes. They encountered a vast spectrum of unpredictable responses, from compassion to violence. Following Lawrence Langer's prescription to avoid imposing an order or meaning on stories which are, in fact, fragmentary, Vàrdy's findings resist a neat packaging and conclusions, for the individual stories are too starkly varied to allow for generalizations about Jewish and non-Jewish interaction.[42]

Stanislao Pugliese, in chapter twelve, considers the historical legacy of Italian Jewry in the age of Fascism in historical perspective. Concentrating on the Jews among the anti-Fascist intelligentsia, he asks why they were over-represented in this group. Pugliese challenges Renzo De Felice's assertion that there was no 'Jewish anti-Fascism' – just Jews who happened to be among them. Pugliese concludes that there was a more pronounced Jewish identity and subculture than typically assumed, however much the Jews might have been oblivious to what constituted their bonds of solidarity. Like other examples in Jewish history, but unlike anything that had ever occurred in Italy, politics and literature combined as a main focus of identity. Pugliese sees them as co-equally Italian, Jewish, and anti-Fascist – as a shared 'cultural memory', discernible among Jewish intellectuals.

Similar to the way that David Sabean has called into question the notion that kinship ties automatically weaken when confronted with modernization,[43] this body of scholarship infers that Jews' immersion in modernity is not necessarily synonymous with gradually relinquishing Jewish identity. Nevertheless, the self-conscious maintenance of Jewishness and Judaism necessarily involves processes of negotiation, and often arguments with oneself, intimates and fellow Jews. The analysis of historian David Gross may help in this regard: he suggests that the very discussion of traditional practices – even if they have been thrown off – is a way of preserving tradition that need not be seen as inadvertent. Gross writes that:

> The demise of tradition, though real, can easily be exaggerated. Many traditions continue in the nooks and crannies of modern life. They exist privately where they have eroded publicly. Some survive by going underground, others by reconstituting themselves in such a way as to live on in new forms and guises.[44]

Jews continue to define themselves in relation to their complex past and versions of their pasts that they see as embodied by other Jews around them. All of this is not to deny the continuing significance of acculturation and assimilation to non-Jewish societies of which Jews are a part, but to suggest that Jews' self-fashioning, in many important respects, continues to derive from working through what it means to be Jewish.

NOTES

1. Michael Berkowitz, *Western Jewry and the Zionist Project, 1914–1933* (Cambridge: Cambridge University Press, 1997), pp. 125–46; Glenn Bowman, 'The Politics of Tour Guiding: Israeli and Palestinian Guides in the Occupied Territories', in David Harrison (ed.), *Tourism in Less Developed Countries* (London: Bellhaven, 1992), pp. 121–34.
2. Sander L. Gilman and Karen Remmler (eds), *Re-emerging Jewish Culture in Germany: Life and Literature Since 1989* (New York and London: New York

University Press, 1994); Michael Steinlauf, *Bondage to the Dead: Poland and the Memory of the Holocaust* (Syracuse: Syracuse University Press, 1997).

3. This may be found most explicitly in the writing of Zionist philosopher Jacob Klatzkin in *Tehumim* (Boundaries) (Berlin: Rimon, 1925).

4. See Alan Dershowitz, *The Vanishing American Jew: In Search of Jewish Identity for the Next Century* (Boston, MA: Little, Brown, 1997).

5. See Todd M. Endelman, *Radical Assimilation in English Jewish History, 1656–1945* (Bloomington and Indianapolis, IN: Indiana University Press, 1990), pp. 4, 6.

6. See Michael Marrus, 'European Jewry and the Politics of Assimilation: Assessment and Reassessment', *Journal of Modern History*, 49, 1 (1977), pp. 89–109.

7. See Mitchell Hart, *Social Science and the Politics of Modern Jewish Identity* (Stanford, CA: Stanford University Press, 2000).

8. Karl Kraus, 'Eine Krone für Zion', in Johannes J. Braakenburg (ed.), *Frühe Schriften*, volume two (Munich: Kösel, 1979), pp. 293–314.

9. Ezra Mendelsohn, *On Modern Jewish Politics* (New York: Oxford University Press, 1993), p. 109.

10. Paula Hyman, 'The History of European Jewry: Recent Trends in the Literature', *Journal of Modern History*, 54, 2 (June 1982), pp. 303–19.

11. Paul Mendes-Flohr and Jehuda Reinharz, *The Jew in the Modern World* (New York: Oxford University Press, 1982), 2nd rev. edn, 1995. For a more bibliographic approach, see Jack Wertheimer (ed.), *The Modern Jewish Experience: A Reader's Guide* (New York and London: New York University Press, 1993); on the Holocaust see Yitzhak Arad, Israel Gutman and Abraham Margaliot (eds), *Documents on the Holocaust* (Lincoln, NE and London: University of Nebraska Press, 1999); on Zionism, Arthur Hertzberg (ed.), *The Zionist Idea: A Historical Analysis and Reader* (New York: Atheneum, 1986) and Jehudah Reinharz (ed.), *Dokumente zur Geschichte des deutschen Zionismus 1882–1933* (Tübingen: Mohr, 1981).

12. Todd Endelman, *The Jews of Georgian England, 1714–1830: Tradition and Change in a Liberal Soceity* (Philadelphia, PA: Jewish Publication Society of America, 1979); Marion A. Kaplan, *The Jewish Feminist Movement in Germany: The Campaigns of the Juedischer Frauenbund, 1904–1938* (Westport, CT: Greenwood, 1979).

13. Albert Lichtblau and Michael John, 'Jewries in Galicia and Bukovina, Lemberg and Czernowitz: Two Divergent Examples of Jewish Communities in the Far East of the Austro-Hungarian Monarchy', in Sander L. Gilman and Milton Shain (eds), *Jewries at the Frontier: Accommodation, Identity, Conflict* (Urbana and Chicago, IL: University of Illinois Press, 1999), pp. 29–66.

14. Rainer Liedtke, *Jewish Welfare in Hamburg and Manchester, c. 1850–1914* (Oxford: Clarendon Press, 1998); Rainer Liedtke and Stephan Wendehorst (eds), *The Emancipation of Catholics, Jews and Protestants: Minorities and the Nation State in Nineteenth-Century Europe* (Manchester and New York: Manchester University Press and St Martin's, 1999).

15. Paula Hyman, 'Was There a "Jewish Politics" in Western and Central Europe?', in Zvi Gitelman (ed.), *The Quest for Utopia: Jewish Political Ideas and Institutions Through the Ages* (Armonk, NY and London: M.E. Sharpe, 1992), pp. 105–17.

16. George L. Mosse, *Confronting the Nation: Jewish and Western Nationalism* (Hanover, NH and London: Brandeis University Press, 1993); Marion A. Kaplan, *The Making of the Jewish Middle Class: Women, Family, and Identity in Imperial Germany* (New York: Oxford University Press, 1992); Aron Rodrigue, *Images of Sephardi and Eastern Jewries in Transition: The Teachers of the Alliance Israelite Universelle* (London and Seattle, WA: University of Washington

Press, 1993); David Biale, *Eros and the Jews: From Biblical Israel to Contemporary America* (New York: Basic, 1992); Michael Brenner, *The Renaissance of Jewish Culture in Weimar Germany* (New Haven, CT: Yale University Press, 1995); John Efron, *Defenders of the Race: Jewish Doctors and Race Science in Fin-de-Siècle Europe* (London and New Haven, CT: Yale University Press, 1994); Yael Zerubavel, *Recovered Roots: Collective Memory and the Making of Israeli National Tradition* (Chicago, IL: University of Chicago Press, 1995); James E. Young, *The Texture of Memory : Holocaust Memorials and Meaning in Europe, Israel, and America* (New Haven, CT: Yale University Press, 1993); David Myers, *Re-Inventing the Jewish Past: European Jewish Intellectuals and the Zionist Return to History* (New York: Oxford University Press, 1995); Dietz Bering, *The Stigma of Names: Antisemitism in German Daily Life, 1812–1933*, trans. Neville Plaice (Ann Arbor, MI: University of Michigan Press, 1992).

17. Linda Nochlin and Tamar Garb (eds), *The Jew in the Text: Modernity and the Construction of Identity* (London: Thames and Hudson, 1995); Sander Gilman, *Jewish Self-Hatred: Anti-Semitism and the Hidden Language of the Jews* (Baltimore, MD and London: Johns Hopkins University Press, 1986), Gilman, *Kafka, the Jewish Patient* (New York: Routledge, 1995); Daniel Boyarin, *Unheroic Conduct: The Rise of Heterosexuality and the Invention of the Jewish Man* (Berkeley and Los Angeles, CA: University of California Press, 1997); David Brenner, *Marketing Identities: The Invention of Jewish Ethnicity in Ost und West* (Detroit, MI: Wayne State University Press, 1998); Bryan Cheyette, *Constructions of 'the Jew' in English Literature and Society: Racial Representations, 1875–1945* (Cambridge: Cambridge University Press, 1993); Marc A. Weiner, *Richard Wagner and the Anti-Semitic Imagination* (Lincoln, NE and London: University of Nebraska Press, 1995).

18. In addition to the volumes mentioned in the text and notes, significant edited volumes in modern Jewish history include Nancy L. Green (ed.), *Jewish Workers in the Modern Diaspora* (Berkeley, Los Angeles, CA and London: University of California Press, 1998); Michael Brenner, Rainer Liedtke and David Rechter (eds), *Two Nations: British and German Jews in Comparative Perspective* (Tübingen: Möhr Siebeck, 1999); Michael Brenner and Derek Penslar (eds), *In Search of Jewish Community: Jewish Identities in Germany and Austria, 1918–1933* (Bloomington, IN: Indiana University Press, 1998); Jonathan Frankel and Steven J. Zipperstein (eds), *Assimilation and Community: The Jews in Nineteenth Century Europe* (Cambridge: Cambridge University Press, 1992); Nicholas DeLange (ed.), *The Illustrated History of the Jewish People* (New York, San Diego and London: Harcourt Brace, 1997); Geoffrey H. Hartman (ed.), *Holocaust Remembrance: The Shapes of Memory* (Oxford and Cambridge, MA: Basil Blackwell, 1994); Arthur A. Cohen and Paul Mendes-Flohr (eds), *Contemporary Jewish Religious Thought: Original Essays on Critical Concepts, Movements and Beliefs* (New York: Free Press and London: Macmillan, 1987); Pierre Birnbaum and Ira Katznelson (eds), *Paths of Emancipation: Jews, States, and Citizenship* (Princeton, NJ: Princeton University Press, 1995); Hana Wirth-Nesher (ed.), *What is Jewish Literature?* (Philadelphia, PA and Jerusalem: Jewish Publication Society, 1994); Kamal Abdel-Malek and David C. Jacobson (eds), *Israeli and Palestinian Identities in History and Literature* (London: Macmillan and New York: St Martin's, 1999); David Theo Goldberg and Michael Krausz (eds), *Jewish Identity* (Philadelphia, PA: Temple University Press, 1993); Dagmar Lorenz and Gabrielle Weinberger (eds), *Insiders and Outsiders: German-Jewish, Yiddish and German Literature and Culture in Contact* (Detroit, MI: Wayne State University Press, 1994); Jehuda Reinharz and Walter Schatzberg (eds), *The Jewish Response to German Culture* (Hanover, NH and London: University Press of New

14   *Forging Modern Jewish Identities*

England, 1985). Important articles continue to appear in Festschrifts: see John Efron, Elisheva Carlebach and David Myers (eds), *Jewish History and Jewish Memory: Essays in Honor of Yosef Hayim Yerushalmi* (Hanover, NH: University Press of New England [for] Brandeis University Press, 1998); Seymour Drescher, David Sabean and Allan Sharlin (eds), *Political Symbolism in Modern Europe: Essays in Honor of George L. Mosse* (New Brunswick, NJ: Transaction Books, 1982); *Totalitarian Democracy and After: International Colloquium in Memory of Jacob L. Talmon, Jerusalem, 21–24 June 1982* (Jerusalem: Magnes Press, 1984); *Religion, Ideology and Nationalism in Europe and America: Essays Presented in Honor of Yehoshua Arieli* (Jerusalem: The Historical Society of Israel and the Zalman Shazar Center for Jewish History, 1986).

19. David Sorkin and Frances Malino (eds), *Profiles in Diversity: Jews in a Changing Europe, 1750–1870* (Detroit, MI: Wayne State University Press, 1998); originally published as *From East and West: Jews in a Changing Europe, 1750–1870* (Oxford: Basil Blackwell, 1991).

20. See Mary C. Waters, *Ethnic Options: Choosing Identities in America* (Berkeley, CA: University of California Press, 1990).

21. John L. Klier and Shlomo Lambroza (eds), *Pogroms: Anti-Jewish Violence in Modern Russian History* (Cambridge: Cambridge University Press, 1992).

22. Laurence J. Silberstein (ed.), *New Perspectives in Israeli History: The Early Years of the State* (New York and London: New York University Press, 1991).

23. Ada Rapoport-Albert (ed.), *Hasidism Reappraised* (London: Vallentine Mitchell, 1996).

24. Sander L. Gilman and Milton Shain, *Jewries at the Frontier: Accommodation, Identity, Conflict* (Urbana and Chicago, IL: University of Illinois Press, 1999).

25. Judah Goldin (ed.), *The Jewish Expression* (New York: Bantam, 1970).

26. Jehuda Reinharz and Anita Shapira (eds), *Essential Papers on Zionism* (New York: New York University Press, 1995).

27. Marc Saperstein (ed.), *Essential Papers on Messianic Movements and Personalities in Jewish History* (New York: New York University Press, 1992).

28. Ezra Mendelsohn (ed.), *Essential Papers on Jews and the Left* (New York and London: New York University Press, 1997).

29. Sharman Kadish, *Bolsheviks and British Jews: The Anglo-Jewish Community, Britain and the Russian Revolution* (London: Frank Cass, 1992); Anne J. Kershen, *Uniting the Tailors: Trade Unionism Amongst the Tailors of London and Leeds, 1870–1939* (London: Frank Cass, 1995); Jeffrey Veidlinger, *The Moscow State Yiddish Theater: Jewish Culture on the Soviet Stage* (Bloomington, IN: Indiana University Press, 2001); Michael Steinlauf, *Bondage to the Dead*; Eli Lederhendler, *Jewish Responses to Modernity: New Voices in America and Eastern Europe* (New York and London: New York University Press, 1994); Naomi Seidman, *A Marriage Made in Heaven: The Sexual Politics of Hebrew and Yiddish* (Berkeley and Los Angeles, CA: University of California Press, 1997); Joel Berkowitz, *Shakespeare on the American Yiddish Stage* (PhD dissertation: Graduate Center of the City University of New York, 1995).

30. Jack Wertheimer (ed.), *The American Synagogue: A Sanctuary Transformed* (Hanover, NH and London: Brandeis University Press, 1995); Wertheimer (ed.), *The Uses of Tradition: Jewish Continuity in the Modern Era* (New York and Jerusalem: The Jewish Theological Seminary of America, 1992); Jonathan D. Sarna (ed.), *The American Jewish Experience*, second edition (New York and London: Holmes and Meier, 1997).

31. Sander Gilman and Jack Zipes (eds), *Yale Companion to Jewish Writing and Thought in German Culture, 1096–1996* (London and New Haven, CT: Yale University Press, 1997).

32. Jonathan and Daniel Boyarin (eds), *Jews and Other Differences: The New Jewish Cultural Studies* (Minneapolis, MN: University of Minnesota Press, 1997).

33. Stephen Kepnes (ed.), *Interpreting Judaism in a Postmodern Age* (New York and London: New York University Press, 1996).

34. Miriam Peskowitz and Laura Levitt (eds), *Judaism Since Gender* (New York: Routledge, 1997).

35. Judith R. Baskin (ed.), *Jewish Women in Historical Perspective* (Detroit, MI: Wayne State University Press, 1991); Maurie Sacks (ed.), *Active Voices: Women in Jewish Culture* (Urbana and Chicago, IL: University of Illinois Press, 1995); Tamar Rudavsky (ed.), *Gender and Judaism: The Transformation of Tradition* (New York: New York University Press, 1995).

36. See especially Jack Wertheimer (ed.), *The Uses of Tradition: Jewish Continuity in the Modern Era*.

37. Hadassa Kosak, *Cultures of Opposition: Jewish Immigrant Workers, New York City, 1881–1905* (Albany, NY: State University of New York Press, 2000); Steven Cassedy, *To the Other Shore: The Russian Jewish Intellectuals Who Came to America* (Princeton, NJ: Princeton University Press, 1997); Andrew Heinze, *Adapting to Abundance: Jewish Immigrants, Mass Consumption, and the Search for an American Jewish Identity* (New York: Columbia University Press, 1990); Susan Glenn, *Daughters of the Shtetl: Life and Labor in the Immigrant Generation* (Ithaca, NY and London: Cornell University Press, 1990).

38. Harold Bloom, Foreword to *Zakhor* by Yosef Yerushalmi (Seattle, WA: University of Washington Press, 1996), p. xxv.

39. See Fran Markowitz, *Coming of Age in Post-Soviet Russia* (Urbana, IL: University of Illinois Press, 2000); Markowitz, *A Community in Spite of Itself: Soviet Jewish Emigres in New York* (Washington, DC: Smithsonian Institution Press, 1993).

40. See Richard I. Cohen, *Jewish Icons: Art and Society in Modern Europe* (Berkeley, CA: University of California Press, 1998); Catherine Sousloff (ed.), *Jewish Identity in Modern Art History* (London, Berkeley and Los Angeles, CA: University of California Press, 1999); Mark H. Gelber, *Melancholy Pride: Nation, Race, and Gender in the German Literature of Cultural Zionism* (Tübingen: Max Niemeyer Verlag, 2000); Michael Stanislawski, 'Vom Jugendstil zum "Judenstil": Universalismus und Nationalismus im Werk Ephraim Moses Liliens', in Michael Brenner and Yfaat Weiss (eds), *Zionistische Utopie – israelische Realität: Religion und Nation in Israel* (Munich: Verlag C.H. Beck, 1999), pp. 68–101.

41. Marion Kaplan, 'Jewish Women in Nazi Germany: Daily Life, Daily Struggles, 1933–1939', in Peter Freimark, Alice Jankowski and Ina S. Lorenz (eds), *Juden in Deutschland: Emanzipation, Integration, Verfolgung und Vernichtung* (Hamburg: H. Christians Verlag, 1991), pp. 406–34; Frank Nicosia, 'Resistance and Self-Defence: Zionism and Anti-Semitism in Inter-War Germany', in *Leo Baeck Institute Year Book XLII* (1997), pp. 123–34.

42. Lawrence L. Langer, *Holocaust Testimonies: The Ruins of Memory* (New Haven, CT: Yale University Press, 1991).

43. See David Warren Sabean, *Kinship in Neckarhausen, 1700–1870* (Cambridge: Cambridge University Press, 1998).

44. David Gross, *The Past in Ruins: Tradition and the Critique of Modernity* (Amherst, MA: University of Massachusetts Press, 1992); Gross, *Lost Time: On Remembering and Forgetting in Late Modern Culture* (Amherst, MA: University of Massachusetts Press, 2000), p. 4.

1

Revisiting the Old World: American-Jewish Tourists in Inter-war Eastern Europe

DANIEL SOYER

On his way to visit his hometown of Lublin, Poland, in 1934, the New York Yiddish poet, Jacob Glatstein, found he was not alone. The closer he got to his destination, the more it seemed as if all of his fellow travellers were American immigrant Jews going to their places of origin in eastern Europe. Approaching their old homelands, the poet noticed, these Jews seemed to revert to their pre-migration ways of being:

> Where are you going, one Jew asks another. To Poland, to Romania, to the Soviet Union, to Lithuania. Where have all the other passengers gone, those who travel simply for the sake of pleasure to Paris, Italy, England, Ireland, Switzerland, Spain? Where are you going, one Jew asks another … Where are you going? A Romanian Jew, a Polish Jew, a Russian Jew, a Lithuanian Jew. They are all going home. They have all suddenly been Romanianized, Polanized, Lithuanianized.[1]

As Glatstein realized, such travel had profound implications for the personal and ethnic identities of the travellers, particularly for the former immigrants' evolving sense of themselves as eastern European Jews, as immigrants, and as Americans. After all, Glatstein's observation implies that in order to become 'Romanian-ized', etc., on their return, these former eastern European Jews must have changed significantly – perhaps become Americanized – in the years since they emigrated. Moreover, although Glatstein does not mention the Soviet Union, it too received its share of

return visitors. And also since travel to the USSR almost necessarily entailed political judgements on the part of the travellers
(indeed politics motivated much of the travel there), accounts of
visits to Russia also illuminate some of the issues of place and
identity that animated Jewish politics in the inter-war period.

In fact, Jewish travel to eastern Europe was closely bound up
with politics as well as questions of personal identity. In this
respect, of course, Yiddish-speaking Jews were not alone. As
Matthew Jacobson has pointed out, old homelands remained
central to the collective self-definitions and communal politics of
many immigrant groups in the US.[2] Travel and travel accounts
figured prominently in inter-war Jewish controversies concerning
the various homelands that presented themselves as candidates
for Jewish allegiance, in particular the Soviet Union, Poland,
Palestine and (implicitly) the US. This chapter focuses on the
Soviet Union and Poland, two parts of Jewish eastern Europe that
had only recently separated. Travellers could not help but
compare the two countries, generally favouring revolutionary
Russia. Those who visited both the Soviet Union and Poland on
the same trip found the contrast especially striking, and their
reports home helped to fuel debates over the nature of the
transformation that had taken place in Russia.[3]

Whether they were going to newly independent Poland or to
Soviet Russia, the travellers felt that they were, in some sense,
going home. However, their visits often threw into stark relief just
how complicated the notion of 'home' was for these well-settled
immigrant Jews. The historian of travel Eric Leed has argued that
'tourism assumes a return to the home, and a change of attitude
toward it, in which the home becomes chosen rather than a fate
and is seen from the outside rather than from the inside'.[4]
However, in which direction did home lie for these travellers? Did
they choose eastern Europe or America? For many, including
almost all who travelled to Poland and some who went to Russia,
visits to their places of origin brought a shocking realization of the
degree to which they had become estranged from their native
environments and transformed by their years in America. Ironically, these travellers' visits brought not the reversion posited by
Glatstein from Americanized former immigrant to Polish Jew, but
a new realization of their foreignness to Jewish Poland. Visits to
the 'old home' helped them come to grips with the fact that their
'new home' in America had become their true home to a greater

extent than they had previously recognized. On the other hand, many who went to the Soviet Union identified with Russia in a way that they never could have done under the tsarist regime. For them, the Soviet Union became not just a native land, but a spiritual homeland.

The degree to which travellers could identify with a country as their true home (as well as the political stance they took in debates about the Soviet Union), revolved in large part around whether they saw that particular country as an 'old country' or a 'new country'. The verdict on Poland was relatively clear. Poland represented all of the negative characteristics associated with the Old World: poverty, backwardness and oppression. The nature of the Soviet Union was less clear. Some visitors, especially those who concentrated on the older regions of Jewish settlement, saw it in much the same light as they saw Poland. Others, however, preferred to see Russia as a new 'New World', with all the attributes that such a place should have – youth, vigour, independence and social innovation. No wonder they eagerly sought a renewed sense of personal identification with their former homeland.

Travel often signifies a change in personal status, and this was certainly true of those Jews who travelled to their old homes in eastern Europe. The very ability to undertake such a journey indicated that the travellers had achieved some success in their new home. They had entered into the middle class, broadly speaking, and had time and money to spare. Indeed, the growth of Jewish tourism in eastern Europe corresponded with a general increase in tourism worldwide in the 1920s, a boom that depended on the appearance of a middle class with the means and the inclination to spend money on leisure activities rather than tangible goods. Americans, drawn to Europe partly by the strong position of the dollar after World War I, were in the vanguard of this trend. The number of US citizens departing American seaports for points abroad grew throughout the 1920s, from 278,331 in 1922 to 461,254 in 1930. The number of travellers fell off with the onset of the Depression, but the crisis had more effect on the amount of money each traveller spent abroad. In addition to citizens, 100,000 resident aliens made trips each year in the late 1920s, as one observer noted, 'mainly to visit their friends and relatives in the "old country"'. Some countries, including Poland, made special efforts to promote visits by emigrants and their descendants.[5]

Although overseas tourism was a quintessentially middle-class activity, even many former immigrants and others in modest circumstances by American standards had the resources to make a trip abroad by the 1920s. Jacob Glatstein admitted that he felt 'like a provincial' for having delayed his own trip for 20 years 'at a time when any schoolteacher can afford the luxury of taking a little trip each summer'.[6] Knowledgeable travel agents like Gustave Eisner helped to put this kind of activity within the reach of even skilled blue-collar workers by coming up with special package tours. During the Depression Eisner sold mostly tourist or third-class tickets, but on at least one occasion he persuaded a ship's crew to allow his third-class customers to use second-class facilities.[7]

Nevertheless, such a journey took not only money but time as well, since travel to and from eastern Europe took two or three weeks in itself. Altogether a visit to one's old home in Poland or Russia therefore necessitated that the traveller set aside at least four weeks; trips of seven or more weeks were probably even more common. One punctilious traveller, who visited his hometown of Velizh, in the Soviet Union, in 1929, kept a careful account of both money and time spent. He figured that he had spent a total of $675, including $425 for direct travel expenses, $100 for other expenses and $150 for gifts for family in Russia on going and in New York on returning. He lost $250 in wages during his nine-week-and-two-day absence from work, but saved $75 in ordinary expenses, for a net cost of $850. Of his nine weeks away from home, he spent 23 days going (via Britain and Germany) and coming (via Germany and France). During his six-week stay in the Soviet Union, he visited with family in Velizh for 19 days, and made side trips to Moscow, Leningrad and elsewhere.[8]

Although the Jewish tourist movement to eastern Europe formed only a small part of a much broader phenomenon, it created a large enough niche to support at least one specialized travel agent, and to draw the attention of shipping lines, which advertised in the Yiddish press. Gustave Eisner, a former Yiddish journalist from Lodz, Poland, set up shop as a travel agent in 1926, six years after arriving in New York. Much of his business consisted of facilitating trips to the eastern European homelands of his mainly Jewish clientele, or to Palestine. Eisner and others sought to combine the appeal of travel 'home' with the attractions of general tourism. One Eisner advertisement thus included illustrations of well-known tourist sights in Venice, Vienna, Prague, Cracow, Warsaw, Moscow, Paris and Milan. However, its headline in Yiddish made clear where the emphasis lay: 'Soviet Russia, the Land of Israel, Poland, Romania, Lithuania, Latvia, and other countries'. This particular announcement cited specific prices for round trips to Warsaw and Bucharest.[9]

Eisner and other travel agents skilfully exploited the positive social sanctions, including prestige, that travel brought to the traveller. Despite its increasing accessibility to the masses, foreign travel retained its aura of a high-toned activity to Jews, who had pioneered domestic vacationing in the era before World War I.[10] Some travellers combined visits home with more conventional tourism. Rose Fuchs, one of Eisner's clients, for example, spent two weeks in Paris before making her way via the Alps, Milan, Venice, Trieste and Vienna, to her native city of Lodz, Poland. (She also toured the Soviet Union.[11]) Even as he emphasized the affordability of his package tours, Eisner sought to associate travel to Europe (even eastern Europe) with the cachet of an elite activity. He advertised the prominence of his clients from among the Yiddish cultural elite in New York, tailoring each list to a specific audience. In one advertisement, he featured the 'Famous Actors and Artists' who had availed themselves of his services, urging readers to 'follow the example of the above-mentioned celebrities'. Advertising in the Communist daily *Freiheit*, Eisner noted the prominent activists he had helped go to the Soviet Union. Finally, Eisner's radio spots featured declamations of Yiddish poetry, and associated travel with the 'spiritual enjoyment' afforded by great literature. As Eisner's ads all demonstrate, the opportunity to emulate important personalities within the Jewish community could be one of the appeals of travel abroad.[12]

Just as the upsurge in Jewish travel abroad paralleled a similar movement among other members of the rising middle class, so the motivations of Jews returning home were in many respects similar to those of most tourists. The theorist and anthropologist of tourism, Dean McCannell, argued that the tourist was the ultimate embodiment of modern personhood. Moderns, in this view, for all their sophistication and cosmopolitanism, perceived in their lives a lack of rootedness in a solid reality. Travel became for them a search for authenticity, which, they believed, could only be found in other societies: 'For moderns, reality and authenticity are thought to be elsewhere: in other historical periods and in other cultures, in poorer, simpler lifestyles'.[13] This search for the authentic helps to explain the appeal of travel to exotic locales, found in the late twentieth century mainly in remote parts of the Third World.[14] However, it also helps to explain why Yiddish speaking American Jews returned to their native lands in eastern Europe – whether these now lay in Poland or the Soviet Union.

As residents of New York and other great American cities, the Jewish travellers found themselves at the heart of modernity, with which they had an ambivalent relationship. Some, like the writer and communal activist Z. Tygiel, seemed to revel in the dynamism of urban America. 'Came to love this land', he wrote. 'Love the big-city bustle. But what really exerts a magnetic attraction is that which has not yet happened in this country. I have the impression that it's only the beginning here'. Nevertheless, on the eve of his own trip home, Tygiel expressed the other side of modern urban outlook – a feeling of rootlessness and a longing for a simpler, more authentic way of life. Like many immigrants he associated this idyll with the life he had known as a youth in eastern Europe. Despite his love for the modern metropolis, Tygiel has to admit that 'a deliciously sweet feeling envelopes you when you make a trip home. Even the sour, the bitter, aspects of your youth are concocted into a sweet dish. Every little place, for another the worst, the ugliest, is dear to you, because it is connected to your youth'.[15]

As Tygiel realized, the urge to go home was fundamentally a desire to reconnect with one's youth, and therefore arose at a particular stage of the life cycle – the crisis of middle age. This crisis may have been especially acute for immigrants, who associated the authenticity of the old country with their own authentic selves. The Yiddish journalist and English-language novelist, Abraham Cahan, recognized this phenomenon in his saga of New York Jewish life, *The Rise of David Levinsky*. Even those who enjoyed more modest success than Cahan's fictional garment manufacturer might have empathized with Levinsky when he concluded, 'David, the poor lad swinging over a Talmud volume in the Preacher's Synagogue, seems to have more in common with my inner identity than David Levinsky, the well-known cloak-manufacturer'.[16] Moreover, identity is closely linked with memory, and, as the anthropologist of religion Robert Orsi has pointed out, immigrants were people of 'severed memories', who 'remembered a time and place they no longer remotely inhab-ited'.[17] Visiting their parents and hometown promised to help overcome the acute sense of disruption between memories of childhood in the old country and memories of life in the New World.

Jacob Glatstein acknowledged the ways in which both the crisis of middle age and the problem of reconnecting the various parts of his remembered life informed his trip home in 1934. In one of the surrealistic reveries that characterized the novelistic account of his journey, Glatstein pictured himself as a boy in Poland and as a young newly arrived immigrant in New York. However, the two personas were so detached from each other that they could actually observe each other's movements. Although the young man kept watch over the boy, and the boy found himself navi-gating the streets of New York with surprising familiarity, there is little sense of continuity between the two. Glatstein mentioned only briefly a third persona, that of the modern urban sophisti-cate, the one who actually made the voyage to Poland. At the end of his trip, Glatstein saw that he had 'reached the autumn of my life', a shadowy season that he linked to the world economic and political crisis as well as to the specific crisis of Polish Jewry.[18]

Jewish travel home in the 1920s and 1930s thus differed in one important respect from other touristic searches for authenticity. Rather than the exotic, the Jewish travellers sought the *heymish*, the familiar. This was true of visitors to both Poland and the Soviet Union, despite the great differences between the two societies and between their appeals to observers from abroad. In either case, unlike other modern visitors to underdeveloped regions, the Jewish tourists believed that they belonged to these places, and conversely, that these cultures were part of them. In fact, of course, they were in large part right. Going home in a literal sense, these tourists went to visit parents, friends and relatives.

Both Poland and Russia were sites of pilgrimage in that the travellers viewed them in some sense as their real spiritual homes. Each promised visitors a large share of authenticity.[19] But the nature of each pilgrimage, and the authenticity sought, could be starkly different. Those going to their hometowns in Poland often expected to find places much as they had left them decades earlier, unaffected by the forces of history and unsullied by the modern world. Travellers to the Soviet Union, on the other hand, were divided. Some had expectations similar to those of the Polish travellers. Others hoped to see a new kind of society, though the fact that it was taking shape on familiar territory formed a large part of its appeal even for them. While the pilgrims to Poland went to visit *keyver oves*, the graves of their ancestors, in an unambiguous Old World, many of those who entered the Soviet Union saw it as a new holy land of messianic redemption, an expression of some of their deepest aspirations for the future.

Even as they resembled each other in some ways, the journeys to Poland and to the Soviet Union thus also diverged. Hoping to find themselves at home, the travellers to Poland often discovered that their encounters with their places of origin alienated them more than ever. After ten or twenty years abroad, the emigrants had become much more American than they realized. Indeed, they were often surprised at how exotic their old homes had come to seem to them. Photographs of American visitors to their own former hometowns testify to this fact: well-groomed and well-dressed in their straw boaters and white spats, the Americans contrasted strongly with their families and friends in traditional, often tattered, garb. Even the expressions on their faces seemed to reflect different cultures.[20] Though the visits helped on one level to reconnect the emigrants to their hometowns – indeed some visitors went with the aid of *landsmanshaft* organizations in the US – the trips served even more to convince them that they had made the right choice in becoming American. The dismal economic conditions they often encountered simply served to emphasize this conclusion.

Rose Schoenfeld, for example, had been born in the town of Drohobycz, Galicia, and come to the US in 1912. Twenty years later she returned to her hometown for a visit. Schoenfeld, a Yiddish writer, already believed strongly that she had done well by migrating to the US, a decision that had been opposed by her family. Everything she saw in Drohobycz confirmed her faith in America, and her self-identification as an American. 'The entire city besieged me when the people found out that an American had come. They all cried and begged for help. It was very heart-breaking to see the poverty so plainly on everyone's face'. Even her brother, who had been quite wealthy, had lost everything. 'When I came *home* [emphasis added]', she concluded, 'I thanked God properly for the first time for leading me on the right path to America, the land of freedom where I could make decent people of my children'.[21]

Narratives by Schoenfeld and other individual travellers vividly illustrate the mix of emotions felt by visitors to hometowns many of them had not seen for decades. Such accounts demonstrate especially clearly the travellers' shifting definitions of 'home'. Jacob Glatstein began the first of his two books recounting his trip to Poland by describing his thoughts as he fell asleep on his first day aboard ship. 'I am going home, home, home', he thought, in clear reference to Lublin. By the end of the second book, which took place in Poland, he recorded an exchange between his character and the son of a Hasidic rebbe:

> – I really must start to pack for my journey, because I begin my trip back home tomorrow at dawn.
> – Home, home. If you only knew how fine and how proud that sounds. Would that all Jews had your home.

By now, home was the US, and the Polish Jews themselves reminded him that he should be grateful for that fact.[22]

Likewise, Sidney Herbst visited his hometown of Sedziszow in 1935 after 15 years in America. He left New York on 3 January, arriving at his destination 11 days later. Boarding the train for Sedziszow in Warsaw, he noted excitedly in his diary that he was glad to leave the capital 'for home'. However, disillusionment set in almost as soon as he arrived. He refused to return the kiss his brother-in-law gave him at the station, causing embarrassment to both men. (Did this indicate a cultural difference, or differing understandings of the intimacy of their relationship? It is not clear.) He found the dismal main street of the town to be a 'horrible sight' and his family's home to be 'very shabby, neglected'. Within a day, after arriving 'home', he could write, 'Sedziszow is very cold. I am freezing day and night ... Can't wait 'til I leave. Counting days like in a prison'. Significantly, the only occasion during his trip to Poland at which he felt 'sort of at home' was a visit to the American consul in Warsaw.[23]

Polish Jewry's abject poverty and, above all, its dependence on American assistance deeply disturbed the travellers. These signalled that Poland was indeed the 'Old World', and that it held little promise for the future. Some visitors actually travelled as delegates of their *landsmanshaftn*, American organizations made up of immigrants from the same eastern European towns, with the explicit mission of distributing aid. Sidney Herbst, for example, represented the First Sedziszow Galician Society during his trip. However, even he tired of the long lines of 'beggars in unspeakable poverty'. 'Endlessly they come', he wrote the day before he left, 'asking for relatives in Baltimore, Cleveland'.[24] Similarly, Glatstein devoted an entire chapter to the succession of Polish Jews who pleaded with him to intercede with their neglectful relatives and friends in America. The supplicants included a poor porter, a widowed stepmother, a starving autodidact, an old maid in need of a dowry, the writer's old Hebrew teacher, the town cantor, a former man of wealth and an unemployed rabbi with an ancient letter from Herbert Hoover. All complained bitterly of uncaring relatives in America who had the means to help them, but did not. Even more pathetic than the hunger itself, Glatstein wrote, was the 'one-sided certainty that salvation would yet come from there, the other side of the sea'.[25]

Even when they were not commenting directly on the poverty and dependence of Polish Jewry, the American travellers indicated their alienation from their former compatriots by commenting on the backwardness evident in both the community and the country as a whole. In the films he made to show at society meetings in America, for example, Gustave Eisner often focused on sights that made even Warsaw seem old-fashioned in comparison with New York – cows and horse-drawn vehicles in the middle of the city, for example, or people in archaic dress.[26] Herbst found but one house in Galicia that he could describe as 'civilized' by American standards.[27] Glatstein depicted a meeting with the burial society in his home city of Lublin, in which the members appeared to him to have stepped out of the Bible. Significantly, a number of travellers recounted scenes in which they failed to recognize old friends and relatives. Again, Glatstein commented on the moment he met his cousins, who appeared to him to have aged unnaturally:

> I had never so thought of the intervening twenty years in terms of war, hunger, pogroms, fear, poverty and want as I did now as I looked at the three yellowed faces. Never had it occurred to me to think of the twenty years even in simple terms as a bit of time that had passed, as it did now as I stood riveted to the spot and looked at the three faces.[28]

Incidentally, Glatstein may have been the only traveller to have had a friend of his youth not recognize him! However, the effect is the same, a sense of distance from people and places previously assumed to be very near.[29]

Chune Gottesfeld, a well-known Yiddish humourist, incorporated many of these themes in his book-length account of his visit to his birthplace of Skala in East Galicia, after an absence of nearly 30 years. Gottesfeld proclaimed his obscure hometown 'the most important place in the world', and wrote that he embarked for Skala 'full of curiosity and longing'. As he made his way from New York via Berlin and Warsaw, Gottesfeld reminisced about typical scenes from the past, prominent local personalities, and about his own close relatives. However, even Gottesfeld could not forget that he no longer unambiguously belonged to Skala or to Poland. As he neared the town, locals constantly reminded him of his status as an outsider. In Tarnopol, a young man immediately recognized him as an American by his shoes. In a train a passenger asked him where he was coming from, and Gottesfeld was forced to identify himself as an American, an admission that caused quite a stir:

> – I am coming from America.
> – From America! the young man cried.
> – From America! the old woman echoed.
> – From America! the youth repeated.

In Skala, the townspeople awaited his arrival as if for the messiah. As an American, they figured, he must be rich and in a position to save them from the economic ruin into which the whole region had fallen. As old friends and relatives called on him one by one, Gottesfeld failed to recognize any of them. He was shocked by the deep darkness that enveloped the town at night and by the mud that covered its streets. The local inhabitants, the physical environment, and his own inability to recognize old friends all conspired to remind him of the degree to which he had become estranged from his roots.[30]

The political context in which Gottesfeld's account was published, however, meant that estrangement could not be the entire story. The book served an explicit organizational imperative, having been published by the United Galician Jews in America to raise funds for its overseas relief efforts. In order to encourage readers to lend their support to the campaign, therefore, the book had both to report on the dire poverty of Galician Jewry and establish a connection between Galician Jews in Poland and those in the US. Accordingly, the tone of Gottesfeld's account changed midway through the narrative. When he managed to convince the townspeople that he was not wealthy, they became friendlier. 'Since you are a pauper', they told him, 'you are one of us'.[31] He was then allowed access to the inner life of the community in a way that he was not when his hosts thought he had money. Visiting his relatives and friends, meditating at his father's grave, and attending a banquet in his honour, Gottesfeld was once more able to feel that he belonged to the community of Skala Jews.

Despite Gottesfeld's partial redemption, however, visiting Poland proved a depressing experience for many Jewish travellers. After all, it was a place that seemed increasingly inhospitable to its own Jewish citizens, never mind its Jewish visitors. Adolph Held, president of the association that published the *Jewish Daily Forward*, called his seven days in Poland in 1936, 'the saddest I have ever lived through'.[32] The bad impression began right at the border. Entering Poland from Germany, Herbst noted a 'very unpleasant border inspection, worse than [on entering] Germany'.[33]

Those who also saw the Soviet Union on the same trip often made explicit comparisons between the two societies. In contrast to Poland, with its faltering economy, corrupt officialdom, and growing anti-Semitism, the Soviet Union seemed all the more enticing. Again, the contrast began at the frontier between the two countries. As Yiddish writer Moyshe Nadir exclaimed in 1926, 'Crossing the Polish border into Russia is like leaving a stuffy room full of medicinal odours for the bright outdoors. For the time being I am a bit blinded and can't see a thing'.[34] Likewise, Gustave Eisner visited the Soviet Union in 1931 and 1935, both times after longer stays in Poland. Depressed by the poverty and persecution he witnessed in Poland, Eisner saw 'folks with happy faces and full of hope as soon as we crossed the Polish border'. The building projects that seemed to proceed everywhere he looked contrasted favourably not only with Poland, but even with Depression-era America and certainly contributed to his friendly feelings toward the Soviet Union.[35]

Nevertheless, opinion on Soviet Jewish society was divided. Those who were already inclined to be critical of the Soviet experiment, and who insisted on visiting the small towns of the former Jewish Pale of Settlement, tended to see the same sort of old-worldly conditions that their counterparts in Poland saw.

Mendel Osherowitch, an editor of the New York socialist Yiddish daily *Forward*, found his hometown of Trostinets, Ukraine, in ruins in 1932, the local factory closed, and the market barely functioning. Emblematically, he failed to recognize many of his childhood friends, who seemed to him 'aged and miserable'. The only sign of the new order lay in the destruction of the town's many synagogues and study houses.[36] Moreover, the townspeople envied his ability to return to America, and would have gone with him if they could. Conspicuous for their mobility as well as for their fine clothes, Osherowitch and others like him came away with the peculiar feeling of having become foreigners in their native lands.

However, for many travellers, the Soviet Union was an entirely New World, newer and more vibrant even than the US itself. Indeed, their enthusiasm for the new order depended in large part on this perception. Some resorted to the language of metaphysics to describe the transformation through which Russia had passed. Writer Borekh Glazman believed the Soviet Union to be 'not only ... a new country, but actually ... a new world – a new world just born, standing for the time being alone in the cosmos, surrounded by watery wilderness'.[37] Reuben Brainin, the old Hebraist who converted to the Soviet cause in the late 1920s, went further. 'Contemporary physics is very concerned with the problem of time and space', he proclaimed in a speech in Moscow in 1930. 'There it is a matter of metaphysics. Here in the Soviet Union, these problems have a practical character. The Five Year Plan (Piateletka) in four years; a week in five days. I feel as if I have fallen onto a new planet. A new conception of time and space is being created'.[38] Various rituals reinforced this expectation, from the moment the travellers reached the Soviet border, where red flags and banners met them with calls for the workers of the world to unite.

Significantly, pro-Soviet writers also used the language of immigration to describe their reactions. Only now, they implied, the traditional relationship between America and Russia, had been reversed. Even those who hailed originally from the old Russia were greenhorns in the Soviet Union. As poet Moyshe Nadir put it, 'The greenhorns in America are, what? – 99 per cent less green than the greenhorns here in Soviet Russia ... Even those who spent years here earlier, even those who were born here from the start and went to the local tsarist schools – even they, when they return from abroad, are so deathly green that one must pity them'.[39] So much had the Soviet Union supplanted America as the New World that relatives from 'the other side' clamoured to be 'brought over' and 'allrightnik' immigrants forgot about their families left behind.[40]

However, even as they wrote of the Soviet Union as a New World, the fact that it was located in old Russia formed a big part of its appeal. This was a place to which they could belong, paradoxically, both because of its familiarity *and* because of its transformation. The red flags and socialist slogans at the border appealed especially to former revolutionaries, who now felt that the country they had left decades earlier had been made over in their own image.[41] Even being allowed to visit Moscow and Leningrad excited some Jews who remembered the restrictions of the pre-revolutionary era. Joe Rapoport, a left-wing trade-unionist, recalled of his visit in 1934, 'In my youth, in the tsarist days, a Jew could not enter Moscow without special privileges. But there I was walking on the cobblestones of Red Square … It was fantastic!'[42] Hearing Yiddish spoken openly on the streets of Leningrad impressed another visitor as something 'incredible … an impossible thought in the Russia [he] had left in 1909'.[43]

Unlike Poland, the revolutionary Soviet State seemed prepared to accept the formerly despised Jewish population as equal citizens. Moreover, even within the framework of revolution, there was much that was reassuringly familiar. For example, sympathetic observers believed that new Jewish agricultural settlements in Ukraine and Crimea would remake Russian Jewish life by 'productivizing' the 'declassed' former shtetl occupants. Further, it would heal the wounds left by the pogroms of the civil war, undermine anti-Semitism, and provide a sound material basis for a flourishing Jewish culture.[44] However, here too, it was the familiarity of the setting that helped the visitors identify person-ally with the new order. 'The migrants from surrounding areas certainly feel good in their new homes,' wrote Glazman, 'much, much better than the Jewish migrants to the land in such far away places as Argentina, North America and Palestine … They do not feel torn, uprooted or foreign [surrounded by] familiar mountains and valleys'.[45] It also reassured, at least some of the visitors, that the emerging culture would more closely resemble the Jewish culture familiar to them than would that of the 'new, strange tribe' arising in Palestine. Symbolically, the Yiddish and Hebrew writer Abraham Victor retold a story he heard on one colony of a delegate from Palestine ecstatic over the taste of 'real Jewish sour cream', something apparently unavailable in Tel Aviv.[46]

A great part of the Soviet Union's appeal was thus that it constituted a New World taking shape within the old. However, Russia's claim on the status of New World did not go uncontested. Another test of its newness was the degree to which Soviet Jewry remained dependent on aid from abroad, a trait that helped define the Jewish Old World for its American offspring. Abundance and independence characterized the New World in America. If the Soviet Union was also a New World, it too should have displayed these qualities. Pro-Soviet writers argued that Russian Jews, unlike their Polish counterparts, no longer sought aid from Jews in the United States. Thus, Victor described the case of one old man who returned money to his son in New York with a note saying:

> My dear son, It certainly makes me happy that you are not forgetting your old parents. But we do not need any assistance. Praise God, I am a worker and am still able to do my part, and since I am a member of the union, you do not have to worry about us. Now, about your great American fortune I am not so certain. Better save what you can for yourself and your household.[47]

Soon, suggested Abraham Epstein, national organizer of ICOR, an organization devoted to assisting Jewish agricultural settlements in Russia, Soviet Jews would have to send aid to their American relatives.[48]

However, in the eyes of critical observers such as Nohum Chanin and Osherowitch, Soviet shtetl Jews were as forlorn and dependent on outside aid for survival as were their cousins in Poland or Lithuania. They presented a portrait of Old-World Jewry quite different from that of the proud, productive and self-reliant worker portrayed by Victor, and one that served to emphasize in their own minds the chasm between their own experience and that of their *landslayt* left behind. Chanin recalled that 'whenever I met a Jew and asked him how he lived, I would hear the same response, "My relatives in America send me money"'. In one town, he reported, 60 per cent of the population received regular material assistance from America.[49]

Travel to eastern Europe thus raised all sorts of questions in the travellers' minds about their own identities and about the nature of the societies in which they lived and which they visited. Since Jewish politics revolved around these very questions, accounts of their journeys contributed to contemporary debates within the Jewish community. Indeed, for those who considered themselves to be Jewish opinion makers, travel abroad was nearly obligatory. Whatever their political affiliation, public intellectuals returned home to report their findings in the press, on the radio and at mass meetings. Gustave Eisner, for one, based much of his standing as an immigrant leader on his ability to mediate between his constituency and the Old World. Not only did he help individual travellers reach their destinations in Poland and Russia, but he also travelled to those places himself and returned each time to describe what he had seen. His experiences gave him the authority to play a leading role in a variety of organizations, especially those made up of immigrants from his own home city of Lodz, and from Poland generally.

Indeed, organizations of immigrants from the same town (or country) often used travel and travel accounts to solidify the sense of solidarity among their members and encourage support for their programs. The United Galician Jews' role in publishing Gottesfeld's account has already been mentioned. Movies of visits to the old country drew even otherwise inactive members to meetings, and some society delegates even hired professional cameramen in Poland to produce films of their hometowns. The United Kolbeshever Relief Organization commissioned a film of its town in 1929. The result, 'A Pictorial Review of Kolbuszowa', premiered at the relief organization's annual banquet in 1930, helping to raise $4,500 for relief activities in the town.[50]

In 1930, the Federation of Polish Jews in America even began to organize annual excursions of its members to Poland. The group explained its motivation in the announcement for its second tour in 1931:

> The idea was that it was very important that as many as possible of our American Jews who come originally from Poland should visit the Old Country. When they return they understand better the needs there, and on their return they become more devoted to our work in general, and especially to relief work which must not be stopped for a minute.[51]

Interestingly, organizational agendas also dovetailed with the kinds of reports that came out of Poland and Russia. While the Polish societies depended on a perception of crisis to motivate their members, pro-Soviet groups counted on glowing reports from the USSR to energize theirs.

The potential of tourism to sway the allegiances of the Jewish public was not lost on the governments and movements that vied for its support. Even Poland, which had little hope of gaining much sympathy in the American Jewish community, seems to have made some attempt to do so by encouraging travel. In 1936, Yiddish poet Kadia Molodowsky, who had migrated from Poland to the US shortly before, decried the apparent success of some of these efforts. She complained of a recent article in the Yiddish press that said:

> American tourists have nothing to be afraid of in Poland, that even the Endekes [members of an anti-Semitic political party, the National Democrats] are upstanding people in private ... And so people should go to Poland because Poland wants to develop its tourism. The glibness of the journalistic pens, who can find a thousand ways to pronounce a reptile kosher, is a real misfortune ... But it appears that the Jewish journalists had to pay with something for the hospitality on the Polish ship.

Indeed, the Federation of Polish Jews benefited from a Polish tourist policy that favored group excursions, 'mostly [by] Polish nationals living abroad and foreign visitors of Polish descent'. Participants in such excursions received free visas, as well as steep discounts on train fares. The Polish vice-consul himself discussed with Eisner the 'revitalization of the tourist movement between the United States and Poland'.[52]

Few Jewish travellers, however, seemed to be aware of these efforts, and Poland had little chance of success in gaining a large Jewish constituency abroad. Jewish travellers were more likely to gain a sense of solidarity with Polish Jewry against Polish society at large. As Glatstein put it, 'Russian Poland did not instill in me the consciousness that I was leaving my country. Neither did *Polonia Restituta* reach out to me, her estranged "son", with motherly tenderness'. Entering his Zionist phase, Glatstein compared, with some bitterness, the situation of the Jewish traveller returning home to Poland to that of American journalist Louis

Adamic, who received a hero's welcome during his visit to his native Yugoslavia.[53]

Indeed, Zionists and Communists had a much greater chance of winning over the Jewish public than did the Polish government. As a number of historians have recently noted, Zionist leaders early recognized that tourism to Palestine would encourage Jewish attachment to the country and help to mobilize political and financial support among both Jews and non-Jews. By the inter-war period, Zionist organizations had become adept at carefully orchestrating tours so that travellers would come away with a favourable impression of the reconstructed Jewish spiritual and political homeland. Abraham Cahan's visit to the Land of Israel in 1925 illustrates the efficacy of such trips. The influential editor of the *Jewish Daily Forward* returned with a new regard for the labour Zionist enterprise, helping to further the rapprochement between much of the American Jewish labour movement and Zionism.[54]

Like their Zionist counterparts, Soviet leaders realized that tourism could prove a useful propaganda tool in winning over public opinion abroad. They therefore sought to encourage visitors, and to create an infrastructure to guide the tourists and make sure they came away with the intended impression. One Profintern publication noted in 1932 that workers considered delegates returned from Soviet trips to be 'authoritative' and that the latters' 'social role and influence on the masses are very great'.[55] Other observers agreed with this assessment. Emma Goldman, for example, conceded to her dismay that tourists were the 'travelling salesmen of the Russian revolution … more responsible than the Bolsheviks themselves for the lies and dissipations about Russia'.[56] A variety of contemporaries, from settlement-house leader Lillian Wald to knit-goods worker Joe Rapoport, recalled being influenced by the lectures of returning travellers before making their own trips.[57]

Indeed, when travellers returned to America from Russia, they discussed their impressions of the first socialist state in a variety of public forums, including mass rallies, organizational meetings, the Yiddish press, books and radio programmes. Eager for authoritative reports, large sections of the Jewish public proved to be an attentive audience. However, as noted above, they heard starkly conflicting accounts, as pro- and anti-Soviet factions sought to establish their own credibility and undermine that of the opposing side. Critical observers like Osherowitch ritualistically boasted of their objectivity, denying, not always ingenuously, that they had any preconceived notions of what they would find in the Soviet Union.[58] In response, the Communist press attacked the legitimacy of the travellers who returned with less than positive things to say about the new Russia. In Osherowitch's case, for example, the *Freiheit* released a Soviet statement accusing him of being a 'capitalist lackey' whose eyes were 'sealed shut with dollars'.[59]

A central issue in this ongoing debate was the question of whether Soviet Russia remained part of the Old World or had been transformed into a New World altogether. Moissaye Olgin, a leading Jewish Communist, believed that the USSR possessed a vitality that could only be found in a New World, arguing that travellers 'must derive new courage and new energy from a visit to the socialist fatherland'.[60] Like many pilgrims, Olgin brought home a bit of the charisma of the pilgrimage site itself. After hearing a report of his visit in 1924, many in the audience at a mass rally in New York refused to leave the hall, explaining that 'the *shkhine* [divine presence] rested on this place today'.[61] On the other hand, a poster advertising a lecture by Osherowitch at a branch of the Workmen's Circle summed up such a talk's dual appeal to much of the Jewish public. Osherowitch, declared the poster, had 'looked into the new sort of life' lived in the Soviet Union, but it also urged people to 'come and hear news of the old home'.[62]

In the period between the two World Wars, thousands of increasingly well-settled, foreign-born American Jews returned as tourists to their former homelands in eastern Europe. Going to visit family, friends and the scenes of their youth, these Jewish travellers hoped, like many modern tourists, to find a sense of authenticity and rootedness that eluded them in their everyday lives. Their experiences often threw into stark relief issues related to the travellers' own personal identities, even as they also contributed to general Jewish political debates.

The Old World presented them with two very different faces, and travellers to eastern Europe came away with varied, sometimes unexpected, impressions. Those who travelled to such comparatively unreconstructed countries as Poland expected to encounter the traditional societies familiar to them from their youths. However, they were often shocked to discover just how foreign their old homes had come to seem to them after ten or twenty years in America. Visits to Poland often ended up reinforcing the travellers' identification not with their old homes, but with their new one in America. For those whose former homes had been incorporated into the Soviet Union, on the other hand, a visit to the old home was simultaneously a journey into a new social order thought to be more representative of the future than the past. The Soviet State gave sympathetic emigrants a new basis for identification with their native land. However, whether or not the Soviet Union should be seen primarily as a New World or as part of the old remained an important point of contention.

NOTES

Sections of this article appeared previously in different form in Daniel Soyer, 'The Travel Agent as Broker between Old World and New: The Case of Gustave Eisner', *YIVO Annual*, 21 (1993), pp. 345–68; and in Daniel Soyer, 'Back to the Future: American Jews Visit the Soviet Union in the 1920s and 1930s', *Jewish Social Studies*, 6 (Spring–Summer 2000), pp. 124–59.

1. Jacob Glatstein, *Ven Yash iz geforn* (New York: In Zich, 1938), pp. 182–3.
2. Matthew Frye Jacobson, *Special Sorrows: The Diasporic Imagination of Irish, Polish, and Jewish Immigrants in the United States* (Cambridge, MA: Harvard University Press, 1995); Ewa Morawska, 'Changing Images of the Old Country among East European Immigrants, 1880–1930: A Comparison of Jewish and Slavic Representations', *YIVO Annual*, 21 (1993), pp. 273–341.
3. Following contemporary practice, I use the terms 'Russia' and 'Soviet Union' nearly interchangeably. Poland can represent the other non-revolutionary states of eastern Europe: Romania, Lithuania, Latvia.
4. Eric Leed, *The Mind of the Traveler: From Gilgamesh to Global Tourism* (New York: Basic, 1991), p. 263, quotation on p. 292. See also Nelson H.H. Graburn, 'Tourism: The Sacred Journey', in Valene Smith (ed.), *Hosts and Guests: The Anthropology of Tourism*, 2nd edn (Philadelphia, PA: University of Pennsylvania Press, 1989), pp. 27–8.
5. Herbert M. Bratter, *The Promotion of Tourist Travel by Foreign Countries* (Washington, DC: Department of Commerce, Bureau of Foreign and Domestic Commerce, 1931), pp. 1, 50; F.W. Ogilvie, *The Tourist Movement: An Economic Study* (London: P.S. King and Son, 1933), pp. 140–2, 213–14; quotation on p. 210.
6. Jacob Glatstein, 'Ven Yash iz geforn', *Inzikh*, 6 (new series) (October 1934), p. 109.
7. Eisner to G. Wise, 2 September 1931; client reservation forms, Papers of Gustave Eisner, RG 316, MKM 12.1-5, YIVO Institute for Jewish Research.
8. Ella Davis Mazel, 'First Person, Singular: Impressions and Memories' (1987), pp. 35–7, in Collection on Family History and Genealogy, RG 126, folder 31.4, YIVO Institute for Jewish Research.
9. *Lodzer almanakh* (New York: Lodzer Branch 324, Workmen's Circle, 1934), p. 154. See also similar advertisements placed by Cunard in the same journal

on p. 158, and by Eisner and others in *Der farband* August 1927, p. 27 and back cover; December 1930, n.p.; January 1935, p. 7; April 1935, p. 7; and in Lodzer Young Men's Benevolent Society, *35th Anniversary Jubilee Book* (1937), pp. 54, 76.

10. For Jewish domestic vacation practices, see Andrew Heinze, *Adapting to Abundance: Jewish Immigrants, Mass Consumption, and the Search for American Identity* (New York: Columbia University Press, 1990), pp. 124–32.

11. Client reservation forms, Eisner Papers, MKM 12.4, frame 329.

12. See clippings in the Eisner Papers: 'Barimte shoyshpiler un kinstler opgeforn nokh Eyrope' (undated, source unidentified); 'Prominente khaveyrim opgeforn keyn Eyrope', *Freiheit*, 10 May 1928; undated, unidentified clipping on radio advertisements.

13. Dean MacCannell, *The Tourist: A New Study of the Leisure Class* (New York: Schocken, 1976), p. 3.

14. Valene Smith, 'Introduction', in Smith (ed.), *Hosts and Guests*, pp. 4–5. See also Kathleen M. Adams, 'Come to Tana Toraja, "Land of the Heavenly Kings": Travel Agents as Brokers in Ethnicity', *Annals of Tourism Research*, 11 (1984), pp. 469–85. John Urry takes issue with the idea that a search for authenticity motivates tourism, arguing instead that tourists mainly desire to step out of their normal everyday routines and places. Urry's theory seems most useful in explaining the appeal of local beach resorts and the like, which in fact provide him with his primary models. It is less helpful in explaining the specific appeals of certain faraway countries to certain kinds of very focused travellers. See John Urry, *The Tourist Gaze: Leisure and Travel in Contemporary Society* (London: SAGE, 1990), especially pp. 11–12.

15. Z. Tygiel, 'Ikh for aheym', *Der farband* (July 1928).

16. Abraham Cahan, *The Rise of David Levinsky* (1917; New York: Harper and Row, 1960), p. 530.

17. Robert Orsi, *The Madonna of 115th Street: Faith and Community in Italian Harlem, 1880–1950* (New York: Yale University Press, 1985), p. 153.

18. Jacob Glatstein, *Ven Yash iz gekumen* (New York: M.S. Sklarsky, 1940), pp. 36–54, quotation on p. 284. Literary critic Dan Miron discusses the importance of the crisis of middle age and the disconnection of memory in the postscript to his Hebrew translation of the first volume of Glatstein's account. See Dan Miron, 'Ba-shule ha-sefer', in Jacob Glatstein, *Kshe'Yash nasa* (Tel Aviv: Kibbutz Hameuchad, 1994), pp. 205–21. For a reading of Glatstein's accounts that comes to conclusions different from mine, see Leah Garrett, 'The Self as Marrano in Jacob Glatstein's Autobiographical Novels', *Prooftexts*, 18 (September 1998), pp. 207–23.

19. On pilgrimage, see Simon Coleman and John Elsner, *Pilgrimage: Past and Present in the World's Religions* (Cambridge, MA: Harvard University Press, 1995), p. 10; Shifra Epstein, 'Introduction: Contemporary Jewish Pilgrimages as a Means of Creating Jewish Culture', p. 4, and André Levy, 'Ethnic Aspects of Israeli Pilgrimage and Tourism to Morocco', p. 21, both in *Jewish Folklore and Ethnology Review* (Special issue on Jewish pilgrimage) 17, 2 (1995).

20. See Roberta Newman, 'Pictures of a Trip to the Old Country', *YIVO Annual*, 21 (1993), pp. 223–40; Jack Kugelmass and Jeffrey Shandler, *Going Home: How American Jews Invent the Old World* (New York: YIVO Institute for Jewish Research, 1989).

21. Rose Schoenfeld, manuscript autobiography (#110), p. 30, Collection of American-Jewish Autobiographies, RG 102, YIVO.

22. Glatstein, *Ven Yash iz geforn*, p. 15; Glatstein, *Ven Yash iz gekumen*, pp. 296–7.

23. Diary of Sidney Herbst, entries for 1/14, 1/15, 1/23, Herbst family file,

Collection on Family History and Genealogy, RG 126, YIVO. On the Herbst trip see also Roberta Newman, 'Home Movies and the *Alte Heym* (Old Home): American Jewish Travel Films in Eastern Europe in the 1920s and 1930s', *Jewish Folklore and Ethnology Review*, 15, 1 (1993), pp. 23–4.
24. Herbst diary, 1/15, 1/25.
25. Glatstein, *Ven Yash iz gekumen*, pp. 136–56.
26. Newman, 'Home Movies and the *Alte Heym*', p. 22.
27. Herbst diary, 1/22.
28. Glatstein, *Ven Yash iz geforn*, pp. 227–8.
29. Glatstein, *Ven Yash iz gekumen*, pp. 273–4.
30. Chune Gottesfeld, *Mayn rayze iber galitsie* (New York: Fareynikte Galitsianer Yidn in Amerike, 1937), quotations are from pp. 26, 34.
31. Gottesfeld, *Mayn rayze*, p. 119.
32. 'Adolf Held – bagaystert far Biro Bidzhan', *Nailebn*, September 1936, p. 12.
33. Herbst diary, 1/12.
34. Moyshe Nadir, 'Fun nekhtn biz morgn', *Freiheit*, 4 September 1926, p. 4.
35. Radio speech beginning 'Zeyer khosheve tsuherer un fraynt', 1935; notebook with inscription 'blok atid', 1931, both in Eisner Papers. For other comparisons of the USSR with Poland, see Jacob Rader Marcus, 'Jews in Poland and the USSR', *Nailebn*, November 1936, pp. 6–8; Gina Medem, 'In der alter heym', *Freiheit*, 7 October 1934, p. 6.
36. Mendel Osherowitch, *Vi menshen leben in sovet-Rusland, ayndruken fun a rayze* (New York, 1933), pp. 79–128, quotes on p. 74.
37. B. Glazman, *Step un yishev: bilder fun a rayze iber di yidishe kolonyes fun sovetn-Rusland* (Warsaw: Kultur Lige, 1928), p. 6.
38. 'Di rede fun Reuvn Braynen oyf dem fareyniktn plenum fun "gezerd"', *ICOR*, September 1930, pp. 10–11.
39. Moyshe Nadir, 'Fun nekhtn biz morgn', *Freiheit*, 27 November 1926, p. 4.
40. Pesach Novick, 'Oyslender in Biro Bidzhan', *Freiheit*, 9 November 1936, p. 5.
41. *Der emes*, 1 July 1924, clipping in Marmor Papers, f. 318, YIVO; Robert A. Karlowich, 'Stranger in a Far Land: Report of a Bookbuying Trip by Harry Miller Lydenberg in Eastern Europe and Russia in 1923–1924', *Bulletin of Research in the Humanities*, 87 (1986–1987), p. 198; Robert H. Davis, Jr, '"Something Truly Revolutionary": The Correspondence of Babette Deutsch and Avrahm Yarmolinsky from Russia, November 1923–March 1924', *Biblion*, 2 (Fall 1993), p. 145; H. Leivick, 'Af'n rand fun onheyb', *Freiheit*, 26 September 1926, p. 6; N. Chanin, *Soviet Rusland vi ikh hob ihr gezehn* (New York: Farlag veker, 1929), pp. 3, 5.
42. Kenneth Kann, *Joe Rapoport: The Life of a Jewish Radical* (Philadelphia, PA: Temple University Press, 1981), p. 110.
43. David Goldberg, 'The New Jew in the USSR', *Nailebn*, August 1935, pp. 41–2.
44. Ab. Victor, *In sovetishn geboy: bashraybung un ayndrukn fun a rayze ibern sovetnfarband in harbst fun yor 1929* (New York: Farlag 'Morgn Freiheit', 1931), pp. 36, 78–9; Kann, *Joe Rapoport*, pp. 114–16; Glazman, *Step un yishev*, p. 92; M. Olgin, *Sovetn-Farband* (New York: Morning Freiheit, 1944), pp. 163–8 (1931); Winchevsky, 'Idishe kolonizatsie un idishe klogen', *Freiheit*, 24 November 1924, p. 4; Y.E. Rontch, 'In kolvirt afn nomen Kaganovitsh lebn Kiev', *Nailebn*, October 1935, pp. 18–19.
45. Glazman, *Step un yishev*, p. 207.
46. Glazman, *Step un yishev*, p. 229; Victor, *In sovetishn geboy*, p. 102.
47. Victor, *In sovetishn geboy*, pp. 250–1. For a similar story, see Gina Medem, 'Vi di idishe poyerim lebn in di krimer kolvirtn', *Freiheit*, 7 July 1934, p. 5.
48. 'Kh' Ab. 'Epshteyn un "ikor" turisten-grupe opgeforen in Sovetn-Farband',

ICOR (September 1930), p. 12.

49. Chanin, *Sovet Rusland*, pp. 51, 53; Osherowitch, *Vi menshen leben*, pp. 123, 128. According to Shub, many of those who came in contact with Osherowitch and Chanin were arrested. See Shub, *Fun di amolike yorn*, pp. 768, 797.

50. Dovid Keshir, 'Landslayt', in *Tsvishn vent* (New York: Farlag Signal baym Proletpen and Proskurover Br. 54, IWO, 1939), pp. 121–4; Newman, 'Home Movies and the *Alte Heym*', pp. 22–3.

51. *Der farband*, April 1931.

52. Molodowsky to H. Leivick, 30 June 1936, papers of H. Leivick, RG 315, YIVO; Bratter, *Promotion of Tourist Travel*, 50; 'Di ekskoyrshon keyn Poyln ayngeordnt fun der federeyshon a groyser erfolg', *Der farband* June 1930; Roman Kwiecien to Eisner, 23 September 1933, Eisner Papers.

53. Glatstein, 'Ven Yash iz geforn', p. 108, quotation on p. 110.

54. Michael Berkowitz, *Western Jewry and the Zionist Project, 1914–1933* (Cambridge: Cambridge University Press, 1997), pp. 125–46; Moses Rischin, 'The Promised Land in 1925: America, Palestine, and Abraham Cahan', *YIVO Annual*, 22 (1995), pp. 81–104; Yaacov Goldstein, 'American Jewish Socialists' Attitudes to Zionism and Palestine in the 1920s', *YIVO Annual*, 23 (1996), pp. 419–44; Jeffrey Shandler and Beth Wenger, '"The Site of Paradise": The Holy Land in American Jewish Imagination', in Shandler and Wenger (eds), *Encounters with the 'Holy Land': Place, Past and Future in American Jewish Culture* (Hanover, NH and Philadelphia, PA: University Press of New England, *et al.*, 1997), pp. 13–20.

55. Sylvia Margulies, *The Pilgrimage to Russia: The Soviet Union and the Treatment of Foreigners, 1924–1937* (Madison, WI: University of Wisconsin Press, 1968), p. 25. The Comintern also kept tabs on published accounts. See Harvey Klehr, John Earl Haynes and Kyrill M. Anderson, *The Soviet World of American Communism* (New Haven, CT: Yale University Press, 1998), pp. 217, 315.

56. Zosa Szajkowski, *Jews, Wars, and Communism* (New York: Ktav, 1972), Vol. 1, p. 408.

57. Lewis S. Feuer, 'American Travelers to the Soviet Union 1917–1932: The Formation of a Component of New Deal Ideology', *American Quarterly*, 14, 2 (Summer 1962), p. 128; Kann, *Joe Rapoport*, p. 72.

58. See, for example, 'Ab. Kahan, forverts redaktor, iz nekhtn opgeforn fun Berlin keyn sovetn-Rusland', *Forward*, 4 July 1927, p. 1; Ab. Cahan, 'Vi azoy ikh kum tsu fohren keyn Rusland', *Forward*, 18 October 1927, p. 6; Harry Lang, 'Mayn rayze iber sovet Rusland', *Forward*, 25 November 1933, p. 8; N. Chanin, 'A lezer vegn tsvey bikher', *Der Veker*, 31 March 1933, pp. 9–10.

59. See pamphlet reprint, 'Forverts blofs vegn dem Sovetn Farband oyfgedekt', in US Territorial Collection, RG 117, box 80, YIVO; Shub, *Fun di amolike yorn*, v.2, pp. 768, 797; Lang to Cahan, 6 November 1933, Cahan Papers, f. 88.

60. Olgin, *Sovetn-Farband*, p. 97.

61. 'Arum Kh' Olgin's masnfarzamlung', *Freiheit*, 24 September 1924, p. 4.

62. See poster, 'Vos ikh hob gezehn in sovet-Rusland', folder 259, Osherowitch Papers.

2

'Our Esteemed Christian Contemporaries': Inter-Faith Dialogue in the *American Hebrew*, 1885–1908

LAWRENCE CHARAP

At the end of 1902, the editors of the *American Hebrew*, a leading English-language Jewish magazine in New York, read some recent editorials in the Christian press. One Unitarian weekly, the *Christian Register*, had wished 'a "Merry Christmas" to the Jew' by loftily asserting: 'Now is the time to let up on the Jew. Let us learn to treat him as an individual being on his merits, without regard to ancient antipathies'. The *Hebrew*'s editors took the remark in their stride, and sarcastically responded:

> The Jewish people may paraphrase the compliment and say, 'It is time for the Jewish rabbi to let up on the Christian'; it is time to let each stand for its principle, tolerant of differences. A 'jovial Chanuka' to the Christian![1]

This complicated exchange, with its offer (in condescending, if well-meaning, terms) of Christian goodwill, and its Jewish response of somewhat irritated bemusement, typified a wide range of similar discussions held in the pages of Jewish and Christian weeklies at the turn of the century. Both Christian and Jewish editors reprinted and analysed one another's sermons, poems, prayers, theological discussions, and analyses of contemporary politics and editorials. Most religious journals at some point possessed a special section for such excerpts – often called

'Religious Intelligence' – that allowed Jewish, Protestant, and even Catholic, news and views to be collected together and compared on a single page. The *Hebrew* followed this pattern by reprinting Christian and secular statements along with Jewish ones in its 'Our Contemporaries' and 'Borrowed Gems' sections, as well as in its editorials.

The attempt of religious journalists to gather and discuss inter-faith opinion came alongside more general efforts at face-to-face dialogue. At the turn of the century Jewish and Christian clergy-men engaged in public symposia, spoke in one another's pulpits, mixed at clubs formed for inter-faith discussion, came together at Jewish–Christian conferences, and in rare instances forged personal friendships.[2] The 'religious sentiment' created by such events created a subtle but extremely important backdrop to the more heated and substantive discussions that also took place during these years. The resulting inter-faith discourse about Jews and Judaism helped to create a viable religious pluralism in twentieth-century America.

The *American Hebrew*, which claimed to be the second-largest Jewish periodical in America, played an important part in this inter-faith dialogue.[3] The *Hebrew*'s editorial board – powerful clergymen and lay leaders from New York's Sephardic and German-Jewish elite, including Solomon Solis-Cohen, Cyrus Adler and Cyrus L. Sulzberger – saw the weekly as a champion of Jewish traditionalism opposed to Reform Judaism, but still hoped to make it broad enough to address Christian readers.[4] Editor-in-chief Philip Cowen remembered in his memoirs that the *Hebrew* sought to speak on behalf of the whole Jewish community to 'the best classes of non-Jews' and act as a 'journalistic redeemer' for the entire Jewish community.[5] Although Jewish immigrants from eastern Europe numerically overwhelmed the German-Jewish elite represented by the *Hebrew*'s editors during the years under study, the *Hebrew* ignored the chaos and diversity of America's Jews.[6] For their part, Christian weeklies treated journals like the *Hebrew* as representative of the entire Jewish community, looking to them to provide a consensus of Jewish opinion.[7]

The knowledge that Christians read the *Hebrew* affected its outlook in a number of ways. The weekly resembled Christian journals in tone and format, and Christian endorsements figured prominently in its advertising.[8] Its editors were conscious that a religious journal aspiring to respectability, as measured by Christian standards, could not afford to be seen as too parochial.

In 1889 the *Hebrew*'s editors explained their long-standing opposition to printing Bar-Mitzvah and wedding announcements by saying that '[t]he outside world ... has no fondness for reading detailed accounts of such festivities'.[9]

Most importantly, the *Hebrew*'s editors frequently addressed its 'esteemed Christian contemporaries' in reviews and editorials, and reprinted their articles. For Jews, participation in religious press discourse served two important purposes. First, Jewish editors could involve themselves in important discussions taking place in the pages of their powerful Christian contemporaries. When the *Independent* or the *Outlook* considered issues of direct importance to Jews – like the role of missionaries or anti-Semitism in American life – the *Hebrew*'s editors were able to invite themselves into a public forum and gain a hearing for their views beyond the confines of their own community. Just as important, the Christian position, whether as interlocutor or imagined outsider, played a critical part in shaping the *Hebrew*'s own discussions of American-Jewish identity. Both of these aims show the leaders of the Jewish community searching for new ways to take full advantage of a still-nascent American religious pluralism.

Christians played their most critical role in the *American Hebrew* by virtue of the insight they provided into standards of public religiosity. Between 1889 and 1904 the *Hebrew*'s editors set aside a special section for reprinted articles from the Protestant press entitled 'Our Contemporaries'. This feature culled representative opinion from major Protestant weeklies like the Episcopalian *Churchman*, the Dutch Reformed *Christian Intelligencer*, the Methodist *Christian Advocate* and the non-denominational *Independent*.[10] Although the editors did not often explicitly state their reasons for printing a given article, they sometimes made clear that they expected their Jewish readers to take Protestant ideas seriously. An introduction to a reprinted article on habits of church attendance in 1892 explains the pattern:

> The following note which appeared originally in the *Christian Advocate*, our esteemed Methodist contemporary, was reprinted by the *Christian Inquirer*, our esteemed Baptist contemporary, with the suggestion that 'Baptist' be substituted wherever the word 'Methodist' occurs. We pass the paragraph along the line with the similar suggestion that Jews or Jewish should be inserted wherever needed instead of 'Methodist' and 'Christian'.[11]

In these reprints and editorials, the *Hebrew*'s editors frequently argued that the synagogue had much to learn from the modern church, particularly when it came to generic issues of observance, ritual, piety and decorum. In 1885, for example, one editor, after making 'a visit to our neighbors' churches', told readers that Jews 'have a great deal to alter' if they wished to institute congregational singing, 'the worship of the future'.[12] When a neighbouring Protestant weekly fulminated against an 'abrupt rushing out of the pews' at the conclusion of services, or condemned the use of the bicycle on Sunday, the *Hebrew*'s editors cheered.[13] The editors also reprinted Christian sermons in the hope that rabbis might find ways to make their own sermons more engaging and appealing to the young.[14] These pieces expressed the belief that all American clergymen and lay leaders, regardless of denomination or sect, were united by similar practical concerns: managing a house of worship, energizing congregations and maintaining group identity.

In addition to such practical issues, the *Hebrew*'s editors printed examples of Christian piety and religious fervour they believed would help inspire Jewish readers. The high point of this process was the *Hebrew*'s 'Borrowed Gems' feature (which appeared for a short time in 1894), but in most of the years under study a variety of poems, prayers, extracts from sermons and general expressions of faith made their way into different parts of the journal. Such pieces appeared out of their Christian context and omitted any sectarian christological message: a poem like 'Jehovah Reigneth', reprinted from the *Christian Intelligencer*, expressed a general reverence for God that was perfectly compatible with traditional Judaism.[15] One reprinted sermon from a Protestant source appeared in the *Hebrew* as 'A Gentile's Sermon on the Sedrah', thus fitting its message into the traditional structure of Jewish practice – in this case, a *sedrah* or weekly reading from the Torah.[16] In such ways the *Hebrew*'s editors glossed or translated these articles for Jewish readers, presenting them as models of general, non-sectarian religious sentimentality.

The process of reprinting Protestant expressions of belief and piety in the Jewish press served two different goals. On the one hand, Jewish editors and writers clearly hoped that this form of inter-faith borrowing would be a two-way street, so that Christians would read Jewish journals and find that Jewish opinions and sentiments were worthwhile. Given their familiarity with Christian standards, the *Hebrew*'s editors had no difficulty giving advice to Protestant journals when the latter were discussing rituals or practices. In the midst of an 1893 Christian debate on lay preaching, for example, the *Hebrew* told contemporaries that '[t]he experience of Judaism has been such as to cause wonder why the experiment is not oftener repeated'.[17] Protestant editors did indeed study Jewish weeklies – as well as synagogue services and Jewish books – during these years, and frequently expressed praise for Judaism.[18] The numerous homilies, prayers and poems that made their way from one journal to another created a world of 'religious sentiment' shared by Protestants and Jews, shaped by a common spiritual sensibility.[19]

The *Hebrew*'s editors, however, had more than just inter-faith goodwill in mind when making use of Protestant judgements. Like other advocates of traditionalist Judaism in these years, the *Hebrew* began to perceive important similarities between conservative Judaism and conservative Christianity. Orthodox rabbi (and *Hebrew* editorial board member), H. Pereira Mendes, addressing 'the Christian world' in the *Independent* in 1887, called on Christians to support traditionalist Jewish institutions; it would be a 'decided step', he declared, 'in the direction of stemming the tide of Infidelity which threatens all revealed religion'.[20] At the same time, the *Hebrew*'s editors began to find unacknowledged similarities between Jewish and Protestant brands of observance: the ritual and 'high church' practices of Episcopalianism, they argued, were 'especially instructive' for Jews, 'as that is the nearest approach of any Christian service to the traditional Jewish service'.[21]

Jewish traditionalists pointed out these similarities, and thereby validated Christian opinions, in order to bolster their attacks on Reform Judaism. It was in this vein that the *Hebrew* reprinted exhortations from Protestant sources for Jews to remain steadfast in Judaism.[22] When Protestants made negative assessments of Reform Judaism, the *Hebrew*'s editors gleefully noted that Christian weeklies had 'truly and accurately' understood the situation.[23] The *Churchman*'s 'candid views of an unbiased observer', declared the *Hebrew* in an introduction to one anti-Reform piece from 1888, 'should be heeded by those sincere Israelites who think that the only hope of saving Judaism is in sacrificing one after another, everything that made it what it was'.[24] A 1901 address by Episcopal Bishop Potter to Orthodox Jews at Congregation

Shearith Israel, admonishing them to '[t]ake care how you let go of usages that come down to you from the past', received similar respectful coverage.[25]

The *Hebrew*'s editors also pointed to one of the more unusual aspects of the religious eclecticism of the 1890s: some Christians seemed to be adopting traditional Jewish practices. The *Hebrew* took special notice in 1893 when 'fashionable Christian circles' used the canopy or *chuppah* in weddings, and in 1895 when some churches began building outdoor shacks or *sukkoth* in accord with the biblical holiday of Tabernacles.[26] Such episodes seemed to demonstrate that traditionalist Judaism was more appealing to impartial observers than was Reform; the editors highlighted the irony that 'the very ceremonies that Reform has believed it necessary to discard because antique and meaningless, or worse, in their eyes, should be inaugurated by Christians'.[27]

Yet the *Hebrew*'s use of Christian opinion to justify traditional Judaism contained ironies that were not lost on contemporary observers.[28] Most writers in the Protestant press who rejected Reform Judaism did so because they believed that only Christianity could be a truly modern religion.[29] Depictions of Judaism as hopelessly outdated and narrow – a 'diseased mass of sectarianism and pride' in the words of one *Churchman* writer – abounded in the Christian religious press.[30] However, unlike their colleagues in the Reform weeklies, the *Hebrew*'s writers and editors did not often call attention to such language in editorial polemics. They advised rabbis, for example, that discussions of Jesus had the potential to be 'injurious' to the well-being of the American Jewish community.[31]

The *Hebrew*'s refusal to respond to statements in the Christian press that portrayed Judaism as a faded relic left Jewish traditionalism dangerously exposed. Reform writers claimed to be greater defenders of Jewish authenticity than the *Hebrew*, by boldly declaring that Judaism, in the words of the *American Israelite*, would never 'succumb to Christianity, as reason will never surrender to the products of phantasy'.[32] The *Hebrew*'s genteel interest in cultivating Protestant opinion would not be served by such naked invocations of Jewish triumphalism. For the editors, the best answer was once again to find Christian opinion that would be sympathetic to Jewish concerns and willing to defend traditional Judaism.

One prominent and highly ironic example of this use of

Christian opinion occurred in 1895, as part of the controversy over the ideas of Jewish modernist Josephine Lazarus. Lazarus's plan for Jewish revitalization, as detailed in *Hebrew* columns and her recent book, *The Spirit of Judaism*, called on Jews to shed the 'body' of Jewish law and ceremonials in order to allow the Jewish 'spirit' to flourish in the modern world.[33] The *Hebrew*, like many Christian weeklies, saw in this message a capitulation to the traditional Christian opposition between Jesus's 'love' and narrow Jewish 'law'. To counter Lazarus's apparent call for Jews to merge into Christianity, the *Hebrew* sought a wide variety of hostile Jewish and non-Jewish opinions.[34]

Most notably, the *Hebrew*'s editors used outspoken Christians to attack Lazarus's claims. One issue contained a 'Christian Standpoint' on *The Spirit of Judaism* from Methodist scholar Dr Richard Wheatley, which argued that 'the lesson of history' proved that Jews needed to observe their religious tasks.[35] However, a more thorough attack on the assimilationist ideals that the *Hebrew* felt animated *The Spirit of Judaism* came in an article by John W. Chadwick prominently entitled 'A Unitarian's Point of View'. Chadwick represented a liberal movement that many contemporaries believed would soon merge with Reform Judaism, yet he provided defenders of Jewish identity with a perfect trump card:

> [T]his book by the sister is an impassioned summons to the Jew to merge himself in Christianity. Do you know that, as I read, I found myself reading as a Jew, and well-nigh the words of scornful reprobation and rejection burst from my lips: 'No, no, and no a thousand times! ...' By all the disabilities of my people in the past, by all the insults and injuries they have suffered and are suffering still ...[36]

To the *Hebrew*'s editors, Chadwick, unlike Lazarus, was reading – and *thinking* – like a Jew, conscious of Jewish history and concerned about Jewish survival. In this way, the *Hebrew*'s editors elicited philo-Semitic opinions that fitted into the *Hebrew*'s theological agenda. Yet merely by the act of culling laudable Christian opinion and printing it in their pages, the editors unintentionally demonstrated that such sympathy for Jews was not universal in the American press.[37] The process of borrowing and discussing Protestant opinions to bolster traditional Judaism thus remained unstable and ambivalent, and after 1900 it collapsed into anti-Christian acrimony.

As has previously been mentioned, the *Hebrew*'s editors hoped that by printing material from the Christian press, they would induce Christians to contemplate Jewish positions in return. In particular, the editors were interested in getting their 'esteemed Christian contemporaries' to consider Jewish arguments about social issues that affected Jews in America. The *Hebrew*'s editors drew up pieces that laid out Jewish community positions about the Jewish role in American life, and repeatedly demanded that 'the churches' or 'the Christian press' speak with one voice on issues like anti-Semitism or discrimination. They then took any Protestant refusal to discuss such issues as an insult to the Jewish community.

For the *American Hebrew*'s editors, Christian leaders possessed a particular prominence and authority on social questions that affected American Jews. They argued that the close link in the public mind between Christianity and American values often resulted in an intolerant spirit that hampered Jewish social and civic equality. The end of the nineteenth century saw a number of Christianizing proposals in the public sphere: Sunday closure laws, temperance movements, mission work and changes to the Constitution.[38] Such measures were motivated by the widespread belief, expressed most famously by Supreme Court Justice David Brewer in 1892, that the US was simply a Christian nation.[39] The American-Jewish press therefore constantly sought during these years to find public support for their position – that Christian values should not dominate American laws and institutions.

The *American Hebrew*'s genteel approach to questions of public religion began by granting Protestants primacy on most definitions of American morality. Its editors criticized radicals and atheists, supported anti-vice societies, and even agreed that 'morality' should be taught in the public schools, provided that 'sectarianism' was avoided.[40] Addressing Jews, the *Hebrew* promoted an ideal of 'Americanism' that disclaimed any specific Jewish role in politics, warning that Jewish political clubs were 'fraught with the greatest danger to [our] higher interests'.[41] A similar fear of ethnic assertiveness drove the *Hebrew*'s disapproval of nationalistic Zionism.[42]

Further, by identifying 'Americanism' with the separation of religion from politics, the *Hebrew*'s editors positioned the journal to refute evangelical definitions of the US as a 'Christian nation'. While still affirming the need for public piety, the *Hebrew* warned the Christian press 'to join us in averting the serious danger of introducing religion into our politics'.[43] The most significant practical handicap to Jews was New York's Sunday closure law, which the *Hebrew* called an 'un-American form of legalized persecution'.[44] Christians proved receptive to appeals on the basis of the hardship caused to Sabbath-observant Jews: '[n]o man is a true Christian', declared the *Independent*, 'who will not admit the force of this consideration'.[45]

The *Hebrew*'s editors thus defined 'Americanism' as the tradition of religious pluralism that Protestants themselves had created. Jewish survival, as in the ancient religious revolt of the Macabbees commemorated by Hanukkah, had paved the way for the Protestant commitment to religious liberty found in American history.[46] Nativist movements like the American Protective Association could be attacked ironically as 'Jesuitical' (and thus 'un-American') for their advocacy of Protestant *en bloc* voting.[47]

Jewish editors and writers took a similar approach – agreeing with many aspects of the Protestant position – when trying to get Protestants to disavow the missionaries of the Lower East Side. Pointing out that support for missionaries would undercut the Christian press's stated tolerance for Jews, the *Hebrew*'s writers depicted missionaries as schemers or criminals, 'the quackery of the scum of our people', whose 'botch-work' and 'mercenary motives' disgusted impartial observers.[48] The Jewish press focused on deceptive practices used by missionaries, such as their habit of enticing children with presents into missions, or posing as rabbis.[49]

In taking this approach the *Hebrew*'s editors theoretically opened the door to 'honest' conversion efforts. A typical 1893 editorial pleaded the *Hebrew*'s tolerance of proselytization made in an 'earnest' and 'respectable' manner. However, at the same time it cited the *Independent* as a 'devoutly Christian and eminently representative' journal that condemned mission activities conducted under false pretences.[50] This meant that, in practice, the *Hebrew* could condemn as fraudulent virtually all Jewish missions. In this the editors were to some extent following the strategy historian Jonathan Sarna found among other elite Jewish leaders of the time, who financed professional anti-missionaries while professing their tolerant and progressive attitudes in public.[51] Yet the conflict over missionaries strained inter-faith relations, even for the *Hebrew*: when missionaries' 'bigotry and stupid methods' incited downtown Jews to riot against them in the 1890s, the editors called the immigrants' reactions 'quite natural'.[52]

Once again, the *Hebrew*'s editors sought out Christians who would publicly accept this position. By portraying the missionaries as deceptive and dishonest, they tapped into broader Protestant reservations about the missionary enterprise.[53] The *Hebrew*'s focus on missionaries' financial abuses and their fraudulent appeals to children had some effect on Christian opinion.[54] In 1889, after reading the thoughts of the *Hebrew* on the issue, the *Christian Advocate* conceded that, 'it would not be right to endeavor to induce *small* children of Jewish parents to attend Methodist Sunday-schools without the consent of those parents'.[55] Such successes helped Jews to portray opposition to common missionary tactics as simply an extension of general respectability.[56]

Another major social concern brought up by the *American Hebrew*'s editors in inter-faith dialogue was the rise of anti-Semitism and intolerance in the US and the world during the 1890s and 1900s. The *Hebrew* accordingly sought to combat anti-Semitism by reprinting articles and sermons from the Christian press that condemned anti-Semitism as un-Christian and un-American, and that praised Jewish survival and courage.[57] Happily for Jews, condemnations of anti-Semitism as 'offensive to all right-minded people' were not hard to come by in the religious press.[58] The *Hebrew* relied on journals like the Presbyterian *Observer*, the Baptist *Examiner*, the *Sunday School Times* and the *Christian Union* to condemn specific anti-Semitic actions or statements, and applauded them for doing so.[59] Jews were not unmoved by these expressions of Christian support: one attack on anti-Semitism inspired one writer to hear the 'mighty voice of love between man and man ... resounding through the world, and the spectres of hatred and bigotry ... flee[ing] away before the advancing light of human kindness'.[60]

Yet, while they recognized Christian opposition to anti-Semitism, the *Hebrew*'s editors felt that a more forthright stand by clergymen was needed. In particular, they blamed anti-Semitism on some of the teachings of Christianity itself, like the Crucifixion story laid out in the Gospels, and insisted that ministers repudiate them. In 1885 the editors called the doctrine of supersessionism 'the final cause of all anti-Semitic feeling, all Jewish persecutions'.[61] Christians who accepted this responsibility and explicitly condemned potentially anti-Semitic aspects of Christian teachings were praised and their writings were reprinted in the Jewish press. Once again, it was John Chadwick who set the acceptable tone, in an 1888 sermon printed in the *Hebrew*:

> [T]he truly Christian hatred of the Jewish people ... [has caused] the most outrageous disabilities that one race or class has ever imposed upon another ... The Jews, whom Christians have so hated, and so persecuted for rejecting Jesus, have been much nearer to his thought and life than their persecutors. It is [Christians] who have rejected him, these who have ever crucified his simple truth afresh ...[62]

When episodes of anti-Semitic violence broke out overseas, Jewish editors argued that American Christianity needed to 'absolve itself from the obloquy heaped upon it' by the barbarous actions of nominally Christian nations; expressions of disapproval meant little unless accompanied by a 'recognition of the responsibility devolving upon modern Christianity'.[63]

In gathering Christian sentiment to argue against anti-Semitism, however, the *Hebrew*'s editors often had to acknowledge a difference of interpretation about causes. In 1890, the *Hebrew* sponsored a symposium in which 62 prominent Christians of all persuasions provided a discussion of the meaning and causes of anti-Semitism. Most of these clergymen condemned anti-Semitism in no uncertain terms, but few agreed that the Crucifixion or Christian theology played any role in fostering anti-Semitism.[64] In future years – contemplating the Dreyfus affair, violence against Jews in Russia, and the spread of anti-Semitism to the US – Jews and Christians continued to differ publicly over the root causes of these events, causing a rising frustration among Jewish journalists.[65]

The use of Christian opinion by a Jewish traditionalist journal created both opportunities for Jewish–Christian dialogue and strains on inter-faith relations. These strains and a mistrust of Christian motives seem to have caused the abrupt and unexplained disappearance of Christian views from the *Hebrew* after 1904. A review of 'December Magazines' that year did not mention a single Christian religious periodical. The *Hebrew*'s celebration of its twenty-fifth anniversary in the same issue included only tributes from Jewish figures and other Jewish publications – in marked contrast to the list of Christian testimonials it had advertised with a decade before.[66]

The *Hebrew*'s editors never directly commented on why they stopped printing articles, sermons and other reflections of Christian opinion in their pages. Something of a shift can be discerned, however, in the way that Christians began to appear after 1900 more as hostile outsiders and missionaries than as friendly fellow citizens. In place of dialogue with Christians, the *Hebrew*'s columns increasingly contained discussions of the strained relations that existed between elite German Jews and their immigrant downtown coreligionists, and the beginnings of a *rapprochement* between these two groups.[67]

Perhaps reflecting a new-found sensitivity to immigrant Jews' concerns, the *Hebrew* also devoted more attention to anti-Semitism abroad, especially the ongoing horrific violence faced by the Jews of Russia. The Kishinev pogroms and the anti-Jewish attacks that attended the failed revolution of 1905 attracted considerable Christian sympathy, as well as a willingness on the part of some religious press editors to blame anti-Semitism on Christian teachings.[68] In 1903 the *Hebrew* at first took gracious note of 'so many eminent Christian ministers protesting with vigor and indignation at every opportunity offered them'.[69] But, by 1905, this sentiment had been replaced by anger at Christian complacency. Buried within its coverage of the crisis, the editors made an angry and revealing aside:

> The *Congregationalist* wishes to be excluded from among those Christian religious weeklies, who, as we claimed in a recent issue, have said nothing to indicate their sympathy for the Jews ... But one swallow does not make a summer, and one or two or three religious weeklies do not constitute the entire Christian religious press ... [I]nstead of protesting as Christians against acts committed in Christianity's name, our contemporaries have not, in the main, spoken out against the Church that has been inciting and abetting murder ...[70]

By this point, the idea of pleading for Christian help seemed hopeless and demeaning. Even Josephine Lazarus, prophet of Jewish–Christian convergence in the 1890s, declared in the *Hebrew* that, '[o]nly a Jew, as a Jew, can come to the rescue of the Jew. Let us cease our futile "petitioning" to the Powers that Be'.[71]

These writers used the events in Russia to pass judgement on decades of inter-faith journalistic dialogue with the Christian press, and with Christians in general. They now drew a connection between missionaries on the East Side and pogroms in Russia, and perceived in the weakness of the Christian response to anti-Semitism an indifference to Jewish physical survival. In so doing they admitted a deep sense of bitterness and betrayal that reflected a loss of their earlier optimism about the potential benefits of dialogue. As the Jewish community's focus shifted inward, inter-faith connections were abandoned in order better to safeguard Jewish identity.

Jews rejoined efforts at inter-faith goodwill in the 1920s, but only after they felt certain that Protestants were committed to fighting anti-Semitic bigotry. The institutions for greater understanding that were built during the 1920s made the journalistic dialogue of previous years look tenuous by comparison.[72] Yet the spirit of inclusivity and pluralism among both Protestant and Jewish leaders in these years had emerged from ground prepared by a generation's worth of inter-faith meetings and interaction in each group's religious press.

NOTES

1. 'A Jolly "Chanuka"', *American Hebrew*, 72 (2 January 1903), p. 236.
2. Some of the scope and variety of these contacts can be gathered from Richard Gottheil, *The Life of Gustav Gottheil: Memoir of a Priest in Israel* (Williamsport, PA: Bayard Press, 1936), pp. 115–45; *Jewish Encyclopedia*, Vol. 1 (New York: Funk and Wagnalls, 1906), s.v. 'America, Judaism in', p. 517. On the broader interaction during this period, see Benny Kraut, 'Frances E. Abbott: Perceptions of a Nineteenth-Century Religious Radical on Jews and Judaism', in Jacob A. Marcus and Abraham J. Peck (eds), *Studies in the American Jewish Experience* (Cincinnati, OH: American Jewish Archives, 1981), pp. 90–113; Benny Kraut, 'Judaism Triumphant: Isaac Mayer Wise on Unitarianism and Liberal Christianity', *AJS Review*, 7–8 (1982–83), pp. 179–230; Grant Wacker, 'A Plural World: The Protestant Awakening to World Religions', in William R. Hutchison (ed.), *Between the Times: The Travail of the Protestant Establishment in America, 1900–1960* (Cambridge: Cambridge University Press, 1989), pp. 253–77.
3. For a detailed history of the *American Hebrew*, see Yehezkhel Wyszkowski, 'The "American Hebrew" Views the Jewish Community in the United States' (Ph.D. Diss., Yeshiva University, 1979). See also Jesse T. Todd, 'American Hebrew', in P. Mark Fackler and Charles H. Lippy (eds), *Popular Religious Magazines of the United States* (Westport, CT: Greenwood Press, 1995), pp. 32–5.
4. Yehezkhel Wyszkowski, 'The *American Hebrew*: An Exercise in Ambivalence', *American Jewish History*, 76 (1987), pp. 342–3.
5. Moshe Davis, *The Emergence of Conservative Judaism: The Historical School in Nineteenth-Century America* (Westport, CT: Greenwood Press, 1977 [1963]), pp. 225–8.

6. Gerald Sorin, *A Time for Building: The Third Migration, 1880–1920* (Baltimore, MA: Johns Hopkins University Press, 1992), pp. 32–7. See also Gerald Sorin, 'Mutual Contempt, Mutual Benefit: The Strained Encounter Between German and Eastern European Jews in America, 1880–1920', *American Jewish History*, 81 (Autumn 1993), pp. 34–59.
7. Protestants rarely even noticed the Yiddish immigrant press; one late exception is *Congregationalist and Christian World*, 90 (21 January 1905), p. 77.
8. *American Hebrew*, 52 (23 December 1892), p. 281.
9. *American Hebrew*, 41 (8 November 1889), p. 2.
10. See 'Our Contemporaries: Why Preaching Has Declined', *American Hebrew*, 63 (July 29, 1898), p. 376; 'Purpose of Bible Study', *American Hebrew*, 62 (December 3, 1897), p. 134. On the history and significance of these journals and the American Protestant press in general, see Fackler and Lippy (eds), *Popular Religious Magazines of the US*; Frank Luther Mott, *A History of American Magazines* (Cambridge, MA: Belknap Press of Harvard University, 1957 [1939]), Vol. 3, pp. 63–89; Martin E. Marty, John G. Deedy, Jr, David Wolf Silverman and Robert Lekachman, *The Religious Press in America* (Westport, CT: Greenwood Press, 1972 [1963]).
11. *American Hebrew*, 51 (2 September 1892), p. 563.
12. *American Hebrew*, 23 (19 May 1885), p. 17.
13. *American Hebrew*, 52 (11 November 1892), p. 52; *American Hebrew*, 62 (11 February 1895), p. 443.
14. *American Hebrew*, 33 (30 December 1887), p. 128, quoting the *Sunday School Times*; *American Hebrew*, 42 (28 March 1890), p. 142.
15. A.D.W., 'Jehovah Reigneth', *American Hebrew*, 54 (8 December 1893), p. 195; see also 'Borrowed Gems', *American Hebrew*, 55 (28 September 1894), pp. 679–80ff.
16. Heber Newton, 'A Gentile's Sermon on the Sedrah', *American Hebrew*, 58 (22 November 1895), p. 80.
17. *American Hebrew*, 53 (18 August 1893), p. 493.
18. See 'The Jews' New Year', *Christian Advocate*, 79 (15 September 1904), p. 1492.
19. For a small sample in other contemporary weekly magazines from both Jews and Protestants, see Isaac S. Moses, 'New Year's Eve', *Christian Register*, 65 (30 December 1886), p. 828; *Independent*, 39 (22 December 1887), p. 1655; Emil G. Hirsch, 'Thy Kingdom Come', *Reform Advocate*, 1 (12 June 1891), pp. 279–81; Rabbi Jacob, 'A Parable for Congregations', *Congregationalist*, 78 (8 June 1893), pp. 917–18; 'Joy in Worship', *Congregationalist*, 80 (25 April 1895), p. 534.
20. H. Pereira Mendez [*sic*], 'A Jewish Theological Seminary in New York', *Independent*, 39 (20 January 1887), p. 82. See also 'The Orthodox Jews – Their New Seminary', *Christian Union*, 35 (13 January 1887), p. 20.
21. *American Hebrew*, 54 (November 3, 1893), p. 7.
22. *American Hebrew*, 37 (1 February 1889), p. 215; C.L.C., 'A Gentile on Reformed Judaism', *American Hebrew*, 61 (20 August 1897), pp. 468–9.
23. *American Hebrew*, 51 (29 July 1892), p. 403. Another example is 'Two Views from Outside', *American Hebrew*, 51 (29 July 1892), p. 412.
24. *American Hebrew*, 35 (13 July 1888), p. 149.
25. 'Bishop Potter at Shearith Israel', *American Hebrew*, 69 (15 November 1901), pp. 681–2 (quoted); *American Israelite*, 48 (21 November 1901), p. 4.
26. *American Hebrew*, 53 (5 May 1893), p. 9; *American Hebrew*, 57 (11 October 1895), p. 565.
27. Ibid. See also 'The Old Paths', *American Hebrew*, 72 (2 January 1903), pp. 231–3.
28. These rhetorical invocations of Christian opinion became a frequent source

of irritation for Reform partisans. Emanuel Schreiber, columnist for the Chicago *Reform Advocate*, scoffed at the idea that 'those who deny that Judaism has any mission whatsoever … [can] be considered by us as judges on the merits or demerits of Reform Judaism'. E. Schreiber, 'Views on Current Topics', *Reform Advocate*, 29 (6 May 1905), p. 256.

29. See, for example, 'Christ the Salvation of Judaism', *Independent*, 40 (19 April 1888), pp. 490–1; 'The Jews', *Christian Advocate*, 67 (15 October 1891), pp. 685–6; *Churchman*, 69 (7 April 1894), pp. 412–13.

30. S.L. Hanson, 'The Calling of the Gentiles', *Churchman*, 49 (17 May 1884), pp. 553–4.

31. 'The Discussion Should End', *American Hebrew*, 69 (6 September 1901), pp. 400–1.

32. *American Israelite*, 32 (7 May 1886), p. 4.

33. Josephine Lazarus, *The Spirit of Judaism* (New York: Dodd, Mead and Company, 1895), p. 173.

34. See Solomon Solis-Cohen, 'Miss Lazarus' "Claim of Judaism"', *American Hebrew*, 55 (13 July 1894), pp. 333–5. For a receptive Protestant assessment of Lazarus, see 'A Voice from Judaism', *Independent*, 46 (22 February 1894), p. 235. On the Lazarus affair in general, see discussion in George L. Berlin, *Defending the Faith: Nineteenth-Century American-Jewish Writings on Christianity and Jesus* (Albany, NY: SUNY Press, 1989), pp. 60–4.

35. Richard Wheatley, 'From a Christian Standpoint', *American Hebrew*, 58 (20 December 1895), p. 201. The *Hebrew's* editors nevertheless had to concede reluctantly that '[Wheatley] naturally endorses this book', because he believed that 'Judaism of the divine type cannot be abandoned, except as scholars leave the first principles of any science and go on into perfect knowledge and application'.

36. John W. Chadwick, 'Miss Lazarus's "Spirit of Judaism": A Unitarian's Point of View', *American Hebrew*, 58 (3 January 1896), p. 255.

37. On this, see Irving Weingarten, 'The Image of the Jew in the American Periodical Press, 1881–1921' (Ph.D. Diss., New York University, 1980).

38. Robert Handy, *A Christian America: Protestant Hopes and Historical Realities*, 2nd edn (New York: Oxford University Press, 1984), pp. 64–81. See also Handy, 'Minority–Majority Confrontations, Church–State Patterns, and the US Supreme Court', in Jonathan D. Sarna (ed.), *Minority Faiths and the American Mainstream* (Urbana, IL: University of Illinois Press, 1998), pp. 305–34.

39. Naomi W. Cohen, 'Antisemitism in the Gilded Age', in Naomi W. Cohen (ed.), *Essential Papers on Jewish–Christian Relations in the United States: Imagery and Reality* (New York: New York University Press, 1990), pp. 147–8, fn. 32.

40. On atheism: 'The Certainty of Eternal Punishment', *American Hebrew*, 21 (23 January 1885), p. 162; *American Hebrew*, 44 (10 October 1890), p. 181. On anti-vice societies: F. de Sola Mendes [a member of the *Hebrew's* anonymous editorial board], 'Crime and Its Remedies', *Christian at Work*, 51 (16 June 1892), p. 754; on schools: 'Religion and Public Education', *American Hebrew*, 30 (8 April 1887), p. 134.

41. *American Hebrew*, 57 (1 November 1895), p. 653. See also 'Jews and Politics', *American Hebrew*, 64 (11 November 1898), p. 40.

42. However, in marked contrast to Reform leaders and periodicals, the *Hebrew's* editors allowed ample discussion of the nascent Zionist movement in their pages: see *American Hebrew*, 64 (4 November 1898), p. 7. See also Wyszkowski, 'The "American Hebrew"', pp. 458–68, for a different view on this point.

43. *American Hebrew*, 54 (16 March 1894), p. 581.

44. *American Hebrew*, 55 (24 August 1894), p. 499. See also *American Hebrew*, 56 (14 December 1894), p. 179.
45. *Independent*, 37 (2 July 1885), p. 855. See also 'Brave Christians!', *American Hebrew*, 54 (23 February 1894), p. 486; (9 March 1894), p. 549; 'The Light Spreading', *American Hebrew*, 57 (12 July 1895), p. 231; Malcolm R. Birnie, 'Sabbath Observance', *Christian Intelligencer*, 69 (16 November 1898), p. 738.
46. 'Is Chanuka a Minor Festival?', *American Hebrew*, 58 (13 December 1895), p. 168.
47. 'Very Bad', *American Hebrew*, 55 (13 July 1894), pp. 332–3.
48. *American Hebrew*, 55 (1 June 1894), p. 139.
49. 'A Neglected Duty', *American Hebrew*, 40 (16 August 1889), p. 18. Indeed, the missionaries themselves boasted of similar practices in the Christian press; see 'Observer', 'The Hebrew-Christian Christmas Festival', *Christian Intelligencer*, 58 (12 January 1887), p. 5.
50. 'A Bad Cause', *American Hebrew*, 52 (7 April 1893), p. 736. See also *American Hebrew*, 54 (1 December 1893), p. 153.
51. Jonathan D. Sarna, 'The American Response to Nineteenth-Century Christian Missions', in Cohen (ed.), *Essential Papers*, p. 26.
52. Quoted in Sarna, 'American Response', p. 32.
53. Jonathan D. Sarna, 'American Christian Opposition to Missions to the Jews', *Journal of Ecumenical Studies*, 23 (Summer 1986), pp. 225–38.
54. See, for example, the changing coverage of the Warszawiak mission in the 1890s in different weeklies: 'A Jewish Missionary', *Christian Intelligencer*, 62 (1 April 1891), p. 14; 'A Bad Cause', *American Hebrew*, 52 (6 April 1893), p. 736; 'Philadelphia Letter', *Christian Intelligencer*, 63 (17 May 1893), p. 391; *American Hebrew*, 54 (1 December 1893), p. 153; *Independent*, 47 (24 January 1895), p. 112; 'Jewish Missions in New York', *Independent*, 47 (18 July 1895), p. 963; 'American Mission to the Jews', *Christian Intelligencer*, 67 (18 March 1896), p. 182.
55. 'An Accusation Considered', *Christian Advocate*, 64 (25 September 1889), p. 572. Emphasis in original.
56. *American Hebrew*, 69 (15 November 1901), p. 679. See also 'Our Imperative Duty', *American Hebrew*, 64 (17 March 1899), p. 672; Albert Lucas, 'Communications: The Persistent Missionary Question', *American Hebrew*, 72 (23 January 1903), p. 327.
57. 'Tribute to the Jew', *American Hebrew*, 72 (1 May 1903), pp. 809–10.
58. 'Persecuting the Jews', *Outlook*, 61 (7 January 1899), p. 3.
59. *American Hebrew*, 53 (26 May 1893), p. 109; 'From Childhood Up', ibid. (7 July 1893), p. 302; *American Hebrew*, 52 (30 December 1892), p. 291.
60. Rudolph Grossman, 'Jew and Christian', *American Hebrew*, 45 (9 January 1891), pp. 228–30.
61. *American Hebrew*, 23 (29 May 1885), p. 33.
62. John W. Chadwick, 'The Wandering Jew', *American Hebrew*, 62 (28 January 1898), pp. 394–5. See also *Jewish Messenger*, 64 (1 August 1888), p. 4; Marie Harrold Garrison, 'The Jews and Jesus', *Reform Advocate*, 17 (22 July 1899), p. 639; 'How Christians and Jews Should Treat Each Other', *American Israelite*, 49 (30 April 1904), p. 5.
63. 'The Breaking of the Silence', *American Hebrew*, 49 (11 December 1891), p. 122.
64. 'Prejudice Against the Jew: Its Nature, its Causes and Remedies: A Consensus of Opinions by Non-Jews', *American Hebrew*, 42 (4 April 1890), pp. 165–95. For more on Christian responses to the questionnaire, see Berlin, *Defending the Faith*, pp. 50–1; Louise A. Mayo, *The Ambivalent Image: Nineteenth-Century America's Perception of the Jew* (Rutherford, NJ: Farleigh

Dickenson University Press, 1988), pp. 115–16.

65. For one late and exceptionally acrimonious exchange in late 1908, see Charles S. Bernheimer, 'Prejudice Against Jews in the United States', *Independent*, 65 (12 November 1908), pp. 1105–8; Sydney Reid, 'Because You're a Jew', *Independent*, 65 (26 November 1908), pp. 1212–17; *American Hebrew*, 84 (4 December 1908), p. 130; 'Race Prejudice Against Jews', *Independent*, 65 (17 December 1908), pp. 1450–6.

66. *American Hebrew*, 76 (2 December 1904), p. 163.

67. The controversy between the groups finally intruded onto the pages of the *American Hebrew*, in 1903, in the aftermath of Jacob Gordin's satirical play, *The Benefactors of the East Side*. The episode allowed the public airing of eastern European resentment of German-Jewish paternalism. See 'The Benefactors of the East Side', *American Hebrew*, 72 (6 March 1903), pp. 526–7; 'Freedom on the East Side', ibid. (20 March 1903), pp. 588–9; 'The Standpoint of the German Jews', ibid. (10 April 1903), pp. 629–31.

68. 'Russia and the Jews', *Presbyterian*, 73 (27 May 1903), p. 3. 'The Kishinev Massacre: Who Is Responsible?', *Outlook*, 74 (30 May 1903), pp. 262–3; 'The Kishenev Massacre', *Outlook*, 74 (23 May 1903), pp. 203–4.

69. 'Let Christians Protest', *American Hebrew*, 73 (5 June 1903), p. 78.

70. *American Hebrew*, 78 (15 December 1905), p. 130.

71. Josephine Lazarus, 'The Duty of the Hour', *American Hebrew*, 77 (24 November 1905), pp. 806–8.

72. Benny Kraut, 'Towards the Establishment of the National Conference of Christians and Jews: The Tenuous Road to Religious Goodwill in the 1920s', *American Jewish History*, 77 (March 1988), pp. 393–5.

3

Acceptance and Assimilation: Jews in 1950s American Popular Culture

MICHELLE MART

One of the best-known examples of twentieth-century Jewish-American literature is Philip Roth's *Goodbye, Columbus* (1959).[1] Roth's collection of stories seemed to redefine the literary and popular image of American Jews, and contributed to a new narrative of assimilated, successful middle-class Jews who felt uneasy about their own social ascendancy and the parts of their culture that they were leaving behind. However, perhaps more notable than Roth's singular achievement, were the numerous novels, films and press articles that had been reshaping the image of American Jews for the decade *before* the famous collection appeared. Thus, Roth's work tapped into a cultural shift already well under way. During this period of declining anti-Semitism, the struggles of assimilation and overlapping identities were vividly played out in the popular fiction of the 1950s. The following discussion examines best-selling novels and popular Hollywood films to provide one window on changing American-Jewish identity at mid-century. The intersection of fictional and non-fictional narratives of Jewish lives are also explored.

In much of the popular fiction of the mid-1950s, Jewish characters moved beyond the stereotypical victims and symbols that had dominated the image of American Jews just a decade before. Here, they were full-fledged actors in contemporary social dramas who were distinctive from other Americans, but still shared much in values, goals and loyalties. They were accepted as full members of the national family, as long as their American identity was dominant over their Jewish identity. This fiction drew on a Cold War discourse to depict an American way of life that valued and celebrated a modified pluralism.[2] Yet, the issue of conflicting loyalties was a very real dilemma in the 1950s. Socially, the dominant culture stressed homogeneity and conformity. Politically, Americans were supposed to demonstrate unquestioned loyalty in a world of subversives and fifth columns.

The fiction about American Jews responded to these dilemmas in a number of ways. First, the central theme of this fiction was the re-enactment of the story of the American dream, from poor immigrant to successful, assimilated citizen. At the centre of this drama, Jews stood for all Americans. Second, this fiction explored the possible costs on the road to that dream – a loss of morality, roots, family values and a sense of identity – and provided solutions to avert these consequences. Third, it sanctioned small cultural differences that did not challenge the *status quo*. Fourth, in these stories, masculinity and protection of the patriarchal line were demonstrations of affinity between Americans and Jews, and were prized social values. Fifth, the fiction depicted lingering examples of anti-Semitism; but, unlike the films and books of the previous decade, Jews were not helpless victims defined by that discrimination. They were upright citizens who sometimes faced anachronistic thinking. Finally, although foreign affairs were not a primary focus in the 1950s fiction about American Jews, international events were in the background of many of the novels and films. In particular, support for the Allied effort in World War II was often linked to support for Zionism and Israel, and this dual commitment served as an affirmation of Americanness for Jews.

Importantly, Jewish writers concerned with assimilation, separatism and success in modern America penned many of the popular stories of American Jews in this period. For many Jewish writers, these cultural ideologies dominated their horizons, and they wrote about themselves fitting into the American landscape.[3] Yet, Jewish writers and artists were not just telling Jewish stories. Through their now prominent roles in American film and letters, Jewish writers and artists helped to reinvent post-war American cultural ideology, and did so in a way that shaped their own identity in the country.[4] Thus, the Jewish characters in this fiction redefined the iconographic modern American hero to include his or her particular ethnic story.

These popular works of fiction drew on a long-standing

cultural ideology that America was the promised land, ever expanding, imbued with a sense of mission and in which anyone could be the next Horatio Alger. The material and social achievements of these characters make them archetypal immigrants and exemplars of the American success story. The political resonance of this ideology increased in the early years of the Cold War. By mid-century, Jews indeed seemed to have fulfilled the mythical dream of success. The majority of American Jews – ranging from 75 per cent to 96 per cent in more than a dozen sample communities across the US – worked in non-manual professions. In contrast, just 38 per cent of the American population as a whole worked in non-manual positions. These statistics also attest to the professionalization of American Jews at rates much faster than those of non-Jews; a declining proportion of Jews had lower-level white-collar jobs, such as clerks and salesmen. Further, Jews by the mid century were better educated than their non-Jewish counterparts, with a higher percentage of Jews going to college than non-Jews. Those Jews who did go to college usually had incomes that exceeded non-college graduates, as well as non-Jewish graduates.[5]

Popular fiction of the period reflected these trends of Jewish social and economic achievement. Novels and films contained a rich collection of Jewish Horatio Algers rising from new immigrants to middle-class businessmen and professionals. The stories about the climb up the American ladder of success usually began with the poor ghetto origins of immigrant Jews. Most of the authors recreate the flavour of the old neighbourhood, usually the Lower East Side of New York, which is characterized by its religious culture, strong ethnic flavour and poverty. The Jewish authors have nostalgia for the ghetto that betrays their contradictory feelings about assimilation.[6]

In many ways, the fiction celebrates the ethnic world of the immigrants. For example, although Sholem Asch's character Isaac Grossman, in *A Passage in the Night*, grew up in a cramped tenement apartment, it was transformed on Fridays 'by the magic of his mother's Sabbath'.[7] In other novels – such as Gerald Green's *The Last Angry Man*, Jerome Weidman's *The Enemy Camp*, Saul Bellow's *The Adventures of Augie March* and Herman Wouk's *Marjorie Morningstar* – colourful ethnic characters, especially parochial, older relatives, people the 'old neighbourhood'. The young title character of Wouk's novel felt both affection for, and distance from, Old-World relatives. For Morningstar, 'Samson-Aaron had always been the soul, the visible symbol, of that group of vague people called The Family ... They had peculiar Yiddish names – Aunt Shosha, Aunt Dvosha, Uncle Shmulka, Uncle Avromka'.[8] In addition to embodying the image of an 'untouched' ethnic past, these older relatives were the ones who encouraged their grand-children, nieces and nephews to reach for their dream, to climb the American ladder to success.

While they might have depicted nostalgia for family heritage, these examples of popular fiction also presented the ghetto as a place to escape. Moreover, immigrant protagonists in Jerome Weidman's *The Enemy Camp* and Sholem Asch's *A Passage in the Night*, who were able to overcome the ghetto's disadvantages and leave its confines, seemed heroic – embodiments of the Horatio Alger story. Asch's main character moved from rags to riches, starting with just $27 which he propelled into a real-estate empire, and he firmly believed that all could achieve what he did: 'This is America. Everyone has the right to get ahead'. Critics and others endorsed these sentiments about the possibility of mobility for all in the post-war US, even as they noted the particular success of the Jews. One review, for example, called the Jewish Lower East Side, 'one of the most familiar starting points of the great American success story'. Jews, thus, embodied *the* American story.[9] (Holly-wood films such as the syrupy film biography, *The Eddie Cantor Story*, which lingers over the singing star's origins on the Lower East Side, also depicted this meteoric rise of second-generation immigrants out of the ghettos of their youth.[10]) Importantly, for the characters and the authors who created them, the story of economic climbing becomes intertwined with ethnic identity. Lower-class automatically signalled 'more' ethnic.

The most notable of these tales of intergenerational immigrant stories was *Marjorie Morningstar*, a book that symbolized the dramatic changes in the images of American Jews in the 1950s. Wouk's book was a bestseller from 18 September 1955 to 27 March 1956, and the biggest seller of all fiction books in 1955.[11] The author, and a drawing of his character Marjorie, even made it to the cover of *Time* magazine in November 1955. The popular novel was a turning point in the self-image of American Jews. Wouk's story of coming of age, ascendance to the middle class, and embracing one's heritage told young Jews that they were just like other Americans. Young Jewish and non-Jewish girls modelled them-selves on Wouk's heroine.[12] One review described the great appeal of the story to non-Jews as a 'triumph that this intensely particular background is integral to the American scene'.[13] Marjorie was hailed as 'a classic American heroine' and 'a typical American girl'.[14] Such praise underscored the novel's impact in helping to redefine Jews as typical Americans, as cultural insiders. The advertisements for the book apparently took their cue from the reviews: they highlighted the coming of age aspect of the story and the dilemmas of an American teenager: 'It's the *American* story that everyone is talking about', gushed one ad from early 1956. 'It's about people you know – There's a little of Marjorie in *every* American girl', it continued.[15] Yet, neither the reviews nor the ads omitted the Jewish content of the novel, and sometimes found a redeeming social value in the story. One pious ad quoted a *New York Daily News* editorial: 'In this city where millions of Jews and Gentiles live and work together, it seems to us that *Marjorie Morningstar* can contribute more to interracial sympathy and understanding than any number of sociological studies.'[16]

Wouk's novel resonated so powerfully with many Americans in this period of the Cold War because it celebrated the ideal of success and a certain amount of assimilation, but was also a cautionary tale against leaving behind too much of one's history and spirituality for the temptations of materialism. One of the most frequent criticisms made of the Soviets and the Communist system was their emphasis on materialism and economic determinism. Wouk showed the danger of chasing after economic success to the exclusion of other values. Marjorie wanted to assimilate and succeed in modern American society and, yet, she clung to her ethnic origins, as did many of the Jewish characters in these novels. As Richard Amsterdam observed in *Remember Me to God*, 'Richard's family, and all the Jewish families he knew, accepted as a matter of course their nearness to immigrant origin'.[17]

Some of the characters seemed to succeed in distancing themselves from their immigrant origins, but, in so doing, they paid a heavy price. For example, when Sholem Asch's Isaac Grossman was nearing death, he looked back on his life and had a spiritual crisis because he had deliberately run away from his Judaism. Moreover, he believed he had sinned further because he built his own success on money that he found in a wallet and failed to return to the owner. His efforts to make restitution to the heirs of the man from whom he took the money were met with scorn by his secular son who worried that his 'kike' father would disgrace the family. The elder Grossman, although living a non-observant life, regretted that his son left Judaism behind, and pathetically affirmed, 'he knew he would be prepared to die rather than deny his Jewishness ... And this was the sum of his Jewishness ... Outside of it he was an American'.[18] Asch's condemnation of complete assimilation and secularization could not be more pointed than when the selfish son turned aside his father's dilemmas and placed him in a mental institution for wanting to reclaim his Jewish morality. Six years later, in 'Eli, the Fanatic', Philip Roth also explored the assumption of assimilated Jews that anyone returning to a more religious life must be mentally ill.[19]

Other fathers in these novels, such as those in *Marjorie Morningstar* and *Remember Me to God*, also found themselves dismayed by their children's move away from Jewish values and customs. In part, they blamed their own ambition to assimilate and achieve financial success. Kaufmann's Adam Amsterdam, for example, was uncomfortable with his choice to leave behind Orthodoxy and become a Reform Jew. In contrast, his Harvard son who was enamoured with the lives of elite, New England Protestants described the Orthodox service as 'so vulgar and low class'. The senior Amsterdam tried to convince his son that there was value in the family heritage, an unbroken patrilinial bond spanning thousands of years: 'I say the same prayers that my father did, [and] I feel a little bit of my father's exact enjoyment living in me'.[20]

Adam Amsterdam and other Jews of popular discourse proved themselves to be insiders in American culture through their image as sage fathers. Conforming to a gendered understanding of family roles and affirming their own role as progenitors, Jewish writers depicted fathers as strong in their own right and inheritors of a patrilineal bond that they shared with the next generation. In *A Passage in the Night* and *Remember Me to God*, two male rabbis filled the role of wise counsellors to their youthful, rebellious charges. These rabbis made it clear that the young men's identity was based on the heritage that they received from their own fathers. The ideal father was not only wise, but wanted to protect his family. He demonstrated what many deemed the essential qualities of masculinity: maturity and responsibility.

While fathers such as Adam Amsterdam protected their families and preserved their religious heritage, they did 'adapt' to modern America by changing the nature of their Judaism. The

Amsterdams' change of 'denomination' was common in post-war America. Many of the wealthiest Jews were Reform, descendants of the German wave of immigrants from the mid-nineteenth century. Increasingly the children of east European immigrants from the turn of the century abandoned Orthodoxy as part of their assimilation into mainstream society. Many of the former Ortho-dox, though, were unable or unwilling to make too dramatic a break with past traditions. The greatest number of new congrega-tions in the country in the post-war period were Conservative, representing what many saw as a compromise between the 'extremes' of Reform and Orthodox. The search for a 'middle of the road' path that 'would not offend any group in the community' was especially important in new suburban com-munities that might not have had enough Jews to support multiple congregations. Certainly, the denominational changes did not mean that Jews deserted organized religion. Moreover, with the general revival of civic religion, Jews found that they had to demonstrate their religious values to gain acceptance. The mainstream press responded to the interest in religion in general, but also to Jews in particular, by printing a number of explanatory articles about Judaism and its traditions and rituals. The under-lying message of these articles was that Jews were just another group in the American family that believed in the unity of all people.[21]

Yet, even while some American Jews affirmed their civic religion and new-found Reformed values under the American umbrella, many still worried that the speed of assimilation meant Jews were in danger of losing their particular identity. This possibility loomed largest in the new middle-class enclave of Cold War America, the suburbs. Contemporary social commentators wrote about what had become the clichéd suburbanization of Jews in the 1950s. Nathan Glazer observed that 'Judaism is in large measure being re-created [in the suburbs] for the children'. Glazer, like the fictional Adam Amsterdam, worried that the assimilationist pull of middle-class communities might overwhelm particular identity: '[the suburbs] simultaneously strengthened Judaism [and] weakened Jewishness'.[22] Most of all, the suburbs posed a danger to traditional moral and spiritual values. To Glazer, and other observers, assimilation and material comforts could turn into shallowness and mere social climbing. One effort to counteract the loss of Jewishness was the formation of 'federations', established in almost every sizable Jewish community throughout the country. These organizations became the centre of Jewish life for less religious, assimilated Jews. Many suburban communities combined much of their secular and religious activities in 'synagogue-centres', religious houses attached to community centres that organized educational, social and cultural programmes. In addition to establishing a local community infrastructure, federations and synagogues contributed to increasingly organized, national political movements. A number of rabbis found themselves dismayed by a Jewish identity that seemed less and less dependent on a spiritually enriched religious life. Moreover, they distrusted the motives of some of their congregants who 'wanted an easy, relaxed kind of country club atmosphere, rather than a house of worship with a positive philosophy for Jewish life'.[23]

The dangers of assimilation, it seems, arose not only from the temptations of suburban living, but, specifically, from the desires of ambitious women. Following gendered assumptions about social roles in an era when 'Momism' was perceived as a real threat to the future of America's children, the male authors writing of Jewish-American life tended to indict their female characters for leading Jews away from their heritage. Kaufman, Wouk and Asch drew a sharp distinction between the fathers who tried to preserve a religious heritage for their children and the mothers whose vain social grasping threatened the heart of Jewish identity. In contrast to the moderate fathers who sought to blend ethnic identity and success in the American mainstream, the brash, stereotyped Jewish mothers appeared ready to throw over thousands of years of culture for quick social acceptance. Within the social prescriptions of the 1950s, it was no accident that the male heroes of these works represent stable moral values and the ideals of the American socio-economic system. A corollary assumption was that women were often ambitious, morally and physically weak and manipulative. This gendered understanding of sexual roles pervaded contemporary images of Jews, and forged an identification between American and Jewish male heroes. In addition, given the centrality of the family as a symbol of all that was good in Cold War America, it seems natural that, within these novels, the moral struggle was over the sanctity and the future of the family. Also, these struggles were, in part, efforts to restore the purity of the maternal icon as a moral ideal. The

Jewish mothers in these novels are iconographic figures turned
on their heads.

Kaufman's and Asch's Jewish mothers have unrelenting
ambition and are determined to see their children fit into the
Gentile world. They have lost any feeling for Judaism, joining
congregations for appearance's sake, although they do not
participate in services or carry on traditions at home. Yet, while
they seem to push away their religion and their ethnic identity,
they are territorial. The mother in *Remember Me to God* was
shocked to hear that her son planned to marry a Gentile. One
review of the novel likened the characters' Jewish identity to 'a
familiar garment, shabby, despised even, but dear'.[24] Wouk's
materialistic Jewish mother had much in common with the other
mothers, but she was more complex. She was determined to push
her family up the social ladder, but remained sincere in her Jewish
beliefs and practices. Moreover, although she was overbearing
and annoying to her children, her daughter admitted, with great
reluctance, that she was usually right.

The folly of Jews trying to escape completely from their
heritage was also revealed in the self-hatred of some of the young
Jews. Wouk's Marjorie, embarrassed by her parents' immigrant
background, found herself disgusted by the old neighbourhood
and its working-class life. Yet, she did not frown on all that was
foreign. She approved of French restaurants and British riding
clothes, which she deemed exotic, while she considered her
parents' working-class culture and that of the old neighbourhood
low and vulgar. Marjorie was not aware of her harsh judgements.
The aspiring actress who had chosen her own stage name was at
a loss to explain why she preferred 'Morningstar' to 'Morgenstern'.
She strenuously denied any effort to hide her Jewishness. While
most of the characters rushed headlong away from their history,
they were also aware of the selfish downside of such a quest.
Marjorie's boyfriend Noel (formerly Saul) explained his disdain
for middle-class Jewish 'Shirleys':

> The mother of the next generation, all tricked out to appear
> gay and girlish and carefree, but with a terrible threatening
> dullness jutting through … Behind her half the time, would
> loom the mother … Smug, self-righteousness, mixed with
> climbing eagerness.

Noel, thus, condemned middle-class women's desires for material
and social success. Marjorie, in turn, told him of 'Sidney' who

tried to escape his Judaism by disdaining the middle-class ethic of success: 'he wants to be a writer or a forest ranger or a composer or anything except what his father is, because he's ashamed of his father being a Jew ... and he ends up in his father's business just the same'.[25]

The life of Jerome Weidman's hero, George Hurst, was also shaped by the character's insecurity about his Jewish identity. He married a wealthy Protestant woman and felt throughout their lives that he was forever an outsider in his marriage to this woman, who had an 'indefinable air of distinction'.[26] (Other characters also felt alienated from their wives, even when they were Jewish; women, it seemed, usually trapped the men around them.) *Remember Me to God* offered the most extreme example of self-hatred. The young Richard Amsterdam came to believe that the wealthy Protestants he met at Harvard were superior in every way to Jews. He conflated class and ethnic identity, assuming that the Jewish lower-class world from which he came was completely uncivilized. He tried to emulate the manners and lifestyle of his 'betters', even writing an anti-Semitic tract, 'How to Be a Gentleman', which explained how to disguise one's Jewishness and to put on upper-class airs. He finally decided that he could not be both an American and a Jew and that what he really wanted was to be a 'plain human being', a Christian.[27]

Kaufman, Wouk, Weidman, Asch and other post-war Jews affirmed that young Jews wrestled with the feeling of what one of them termed a 'split personality', between Jewish and American identities. Instead, these authors argued, Jews should re-affirm their Jewish heritage and recommit to American society and the success ethic. In addition to fiction writers, many Jewish intellectuals probed the questions of Jewish identity, alienation and assimilation.[28] The conclusion of most writers was that American Jews should recognize that their American and Jewish identities were actually compatible, and if they were to give up religion and their Jewish heritage they would be losing something valuable for which there was no replacement. For example, when Isaac Grossman, of *A Passage in the Night*, tried to find a solution to his moral crisis and atone for his deception of years earlier, it was a compassionate and practical rabbi who used Jewish law and common-sense psychology to find a solution to the dilemma. A wise modern rabbi and a perceptive minister also helped the characters in *Remember Me to God*. Both the rabbi and minister explained to the young Richard why it was not a contradiction to be an American and a Jew, and why he could not convert to Christianity for social reasons.[29]

Marjorie Morningstar learned these lessons as she discovered that the way to be at peace with herself was to reaffirm both her Jewish and her American identities. Although sometimes bored by the religion itself, it was, nevertheless, deeply ingrained in her, and she still held a certain awe for its practices and meanings. Although Wouk ridiculed the excesses of materialistic climbing and Jewish mothers, he argued ultimately that modern Jewish-American, middle-class culture held within it a rich tradition of spirituality and affection, and that there was no better alternative for Jews. In contrast to her friends, Marjorie settled down to what appeared to be a happy life, because, we are led to believe, she followed the traditional American dream *and* held on to her Jewish identity. Many middle-class Americans shared her choices in the 1950s: she married, moved to the suburbs, stopped working outside the home, raised children, and became active in her congregation and community organizations. Wouk criticized excessive conformity and rigidity, as did other authors, but he endorsed Marjorie's choices and presented no better alternatives.

Saul Bellow's *The Adventures of Augie March* and Gerald Green's *The Last Angry Man* examined the dilemmas of assimilation and success that faced American Jews, but they differed from some other popular novels of the era, because they questioned the American success ethic.[30] Saul Bellow's *Augie March* turned the middle-class values of the post-war period upside down, as the aimless young title character grew up under the influence of the local crime boss and a money-hungry, deceitful older brother. Augie tried to fit into the mainstream, but was unable to conform to social expectations. Although Bellow's novel challenged social conventions, it, like many other popular novels about American Jews, was what one critic aptly described as a 'dialogue between alienation and accommodation'.[31] *The Last Angry Man* also challenged 1950s middle-class conventions. The title character was 68-year-old Dr Samuel Abelman who had been practising in a multi-ethnic neighbourhood of Brooklyn for 40 years. The acerbic, though dedicated practitioner, like Augie, was unable to conform to the middle-class model of the post-war period. His colleagues had all moved out to the suburbs to set up large practices, but the very 'ethnic' Abelman did not fit in the genteel world of the suburbs. An advertising producer who encountered the outspoken doctor decided to do a television series on 'real' (read ethnic, working-class) people such as Abelman. While the producer was tired of the 'lean' WASPs with 'flat voices' with whom he worked, he was dismayed to find that Abelman would not play along and romanticize his own life and immigrant roots.[32]

In part, Sam Abelman's fiery anger stemmed from the very real anti-Semitism that he experienced in Romania, as well as in the playgrounds of New York. However the reader soon learns that a more subtle form of anti-Semitism was alive in middle-class suburbs where residents recoiled at the idea that ethnic working-class people might move into their neighbourhood. As one young resident of Connecticut observes, 'I don't mind the bright creative people ... But these cloak and suiters! ... I'd dislike them even if they were Episcopalians and behaved the way they did'.[33] Characters in other novels, such as *Augie March* and *Enemy Camp*, also experienced anti-Semitism. Kaufman's novel, full of carica-tures, provided the most extreme examples of anti-Semitism, from assumptions that all Jews had long hook noses and funny black clothes to the judgement that after Jews 'denied the Saviour ... [the] religion went stale ... that's part of your punishment'.[34]

Many of the 1950s Hollywood films about American Jews also addressed the issue of anti-Semitism, but it was an isolated, lingering problem that the Jewish characters overcame when the need arose. Moreover, films before 1958 (when adaptations from Jewish novelists were put on film), minimized the ethnic identity of the few Jewish characters included. The scant attention to ethnic identity was part of a continuing pattern in Hollywood begun in the 1930s when films began to de-Judaize images of Jews.[35] Bland characterizations seemed even more prevalent in the 1950s when many filmmakers and artists did their best to avoid challenges to a homogeneous, conformist view of American life. Homogenization was apparent in the physical appearance of the film characters, the way they talked, and the near absence of any religious or ethnic rituals. Reviews of the films also reflected the inattention to Jewish themes: some of the reviews did not even mention the Jewish subjects or anti-Semitism.[36] The Jews rose above the discrimination because they were just like everyone else, and because they were brave and dignified. Importantly, their status as victims did not *define* Jews. For example, in the 1958 film *Home Before Dark*, an assistant professor at a New England liberal arts college moves to a small town where he experiences intolerance from many who are worried about 'an influx' of Jews. Although most ostracized him, a non-Jewish woman, who was also alienated from the town in part because she was an outsider, befriended him. At the end of the film, they drove off to Boston together, and the man's Jewishness became a non-issue.[37] The ubiquitous blandness of Hollywood's ethnic depictions extended to the film version of Herman Wouk's story of a Jewish-American girl coming of age.[38] The ethnic flavour of *Marjorie Morningstar* was removed to turn it into what the advertisements for the book had promised: an 'all-American' story.[39]

Many films paid lip service to a character's Jewish identity, although there was nothing distinctive that set them apart from other Americans. *Three Brave Men* told the 'basically true' story of a Jewish naval officer accused of being a security risk. As an officer in the Navy, the character was the consummate 'insider' in the Cold War tale. The film centred on the innocent, patriotic man's attempt to clear his name and the triumph of the American system despite the actual threats against the nation's security. The film was far from being a warning against the prosecutory excesses of loyalty programmes and security investigations, as Bosley Crowther wrote in the *New York Times*. The moral of the film was that one had to be patient with the security programme.[40] The image of the loyal Bernie Goldsmith in this film countered the old stereotype that Jews were more radical than other Americans, and reflected the declining association in popular belief between Jews and communism.[41] Goldsmith was not only loyal, but he endured the whole ordeal with quiet bravery. Further, the man's dignity through an experience that 'separate[d] the men from the boys' affirmed his masculinity.[42]

The protagonist of the film was also just like other Americans to the extent that he shared in the Judeo-Christian heritage. When the crisis broke, the man's rabbi was sick, so the local Presbyterian minister offered to counsel the family. Although the man's efforts to clear his name lasted many months, the rabbi never appeared, and the pastor became the Jew's greatest defender and a source of moral strength. Similarly, in a meeting to plan defense strategy, the minister led an ecumenical prayer of the assembled friends: 'We're several different faiths here, but I'm sure none of us will deny the wisdom and mercy of God'. Aside from the pastor's benign observation of difference, the only characters who mentioned the man's Jewish identity were anonymous crackpots who accused him of disloyalty, because he was Jewish. Anti-Semitism also appeared as a minority position in a film made soon after *Three*

Brave Men. I Accuse! focused on a Jew of exemplary loyalty, accused of disloyalty by his country's military establishment, who triumphed over the charges with great dignity.[43] While this re-telling of the story of Alfred Dreyfus in turn-of-the-century France lingered on the problem of anti-Semitism, it sanitized general complicity and scapegoated a few virulently anti-Semitic officers. As in the other films of the period, there was no outward manifestation that Dreyfus was Jewish, and he appeared to be like most other French officers, only more dedicated and honourable.

In 1958 Irwin Shaw's and Norman Mailer's novels about World War II, *The Young Lions* and *The Naked and the Dead*, came to the screen. They, too, looked at the difficulties faced by Jewish soldiers in a sometimes hostile military establishment.[44] Yet the Hollywood versions of these two novels were very different from the best-selling books that had appeared more than a decade before. The films played down the pervasiveness of anti-Semitism, focused on the abusive conduct of only a few characters, and paid limited attention to ethnic differences. There was little to distinguish the Jewish soldiers from the others, except when one threw out a lunch that contained pork. The film version of *The Young Lions* also reduced the problem of prejudice to one character's simple confession, 'I never knew a Jew before … Someone jolts you and you have to look inside yourself'. In keeping with the Cold War politics of the 1950s and the depiction of allies, the German soldier of Shaw's story was no longer an unfeeling automaton, but a sensitive soldier manipulated by higher officers and shocked to discover the truth of the concentration camps. In addition, in Shaw's novel, the main Jewish character was the ultimate victim, shot and killed at the end. In the film, the Jew returned home to rebuild a life with his American-Christian wife. A third film of 1958, *Me and the Colonel,* looked back on World War II and featured a prominent Jewish character. This farce, too, minimized the role of Jews as victims. The character most threatened by Nazis was not the Jewish protagonist, but a Polish officer in disguise. One Nazi even let four Jews escape, showing that he really did not believe in hurting Jews.

An essential part of the background to the fiction about American Jews in the mid-1950s was the story of World War II. The films *The Naked and the Dead, The Young Lions* and *Me and the Colonel* centred on the war and reaffirmed an active Jewish role in that war based on national identities (i.e. American and Polish) as opposed to ethnic identities. *Three Brave Men, I Accuse!* and *The Eddie Cantor Story* also aver that Jews' national loyalty was more important than their ethnicity. Yet, more complicated than the Hollywood references to identity and loyalty, were the treatments of the subject in the popular novels. World War II had an impact on almost all of the protagonists in the popular novels. The war reminded the characters that they had an ethnic identity in addition to their nationality. Some characters were more consciously affected by the war, such as those in *A Passage in the Night* and *Marjorie Morningstar*, while others, such as the protagonist in *The Enemy Camp*, merely felt the bond that the war created among all Americans.

Most of the characters also felt connected through their support for Zionism, a movement which, in these works, is tied to the mission of World War II. Zionism remained a minor theme in the fiction, forming a backdrop to the lives of American Jews, even though the ties between the characters and Israel were not always clear, and were not discussed at great length. At times, Zionist work was merely a pleasant cultural activity for Jews. In *Marjorie Morningstar*, and other books, the characters socialized through Zionist committees and parents looked for mates for their children among the volunteers. Admiration for Zionists was accepted as the norm in the world of these Jews. Nevertheless, the depiction of Israel and its relationship to Diaspora Jews remained inaccurate or sketchy, at best. For example, in the 1955 film, *Good Morning Miss Dove*, the classmates of a young Jewish war refugee who arrived in the US in the 1930s – long before the establishment of the modern State of Israel – teased him because he was different.[45] His teacher decided to educate her class about Jews, teaching a geography lesson about Palestine and arranging for the children to go to the new boy's house for a 'traditional Jewish feast'. Thus, she ignored the Arabs who comprised the majority of the population of Palestine at the time, and equated east European culture and identity with the culture of the Middle East.

The support for Zionism found in the characters of fictional works mirrored the views of many contemporary Americans, Jews in particular.[46] As Arthur Hertzberg and others have argued, the relationship between American Jews and Israel even strengthened their national identity. For example, Hertzberg writes that in the years of the Marshall Plan and the re-building of Japan, 'The creation of Israel was the equivalent task for American Jews'.[47] For many American Jews, then, supporting Israel became one way of affirming their 'Americanness'. Historian Howard Sachar writing in 1957, celebrated the importance of the 'doughty and courageous little state' to American Jews:

> [Israeli spirit] was a spirit of complete, unselfconscious, thoroughly affirmative Jewishness. Without this spirit Jewish life in America with all its wealth, security, community democracy, and pragmatic realism, would hardly signify more than the dissipation of an unprecedented opportunity for corporate self-expression. With this spirit, the American Jewish community bade fair to create a civilization of such enduring vitality as to pre-empt from medieval Spain the title of 'Golden Age'.[48]

For Sachar and other Jews, there was a symbiotic relationship between the US and Israel.[49] Given the importance of Israel for American Jews, it is interesting that the subject remained in the background in the popular fiction about the lives of American Jews. In the portraits of contemporary Jewish life, American identity was paramount and, perhaps, ties to a foreign country would have threatened that image.[50] It was apparently safer to relegate stories about Israel to the symbolic realm of distant characters grappling with larger-than-life problems and to heroic tales of Israel's 'birth'.[51]

Like historians and social observers, most American Jews agreed Jewish life in America was 'wholly unprecedented even in the millennial annals of the Jewish people'. Yet, they could not escape from the pull of Israel, the place one critic described as the 'ancestral home of the Jews'. At the same time, many Jewish writers, anxious to affirm their own national identity, put American Jews in a different category from European Jews whom they described as 'always in exile'.[52] In *Remember Me to God*, the rabbi emphatically denied that he was not at home in the US: 'in spite of this grand concept of exile from the Promised Land, the fact is that no Jew is in exile until he's exiled from the Jews ... we're aliens nowhere ... we're a worldfolk'.[53] Kaufman and many other American Jews had long before accepted Horace Kallen's early twentieth-century ideas about pluralism as an explanation for the 'multiplicity of elements' that made up America.[54]

After World War II, Jews felt, and increasingly appeared in

public culture as, part of the American pluralistic landscape. One piece of evidence of this acceptance and confidence was the widespread Jewish celebrations in 1954 of the 300th anniversary of the arrival of Jews in New Amsterdam. Prominent politicians took the occasion to affirm an identification between Jews and other Americans. For example, Adlai Stevenson, addressing one of the gala celebrations, told his audience, 'We are all descended from immigrants and from revolutionaries. And our strength is in large part due to the multiplicity of racial, religious, and cultural strands woven together into the fabric of American liberty'.[55] Other examples that Jews felt at home in America, and that non-Jewish Americans were reaching out to Jews, were numerous articles detailing Jewish rituals and foods, often with the explicit goal of 'help[ing] us to understand each other better'. Jewish leaders seemed to take it upon themselves – along with a receptive press – to educate all Americans about the tenets of Judaism. For example, the President of the Central Council of American Rabbis, Philip Bernstein, wrote an article for *Life* in 1950 called, 'What Jews Believe'. Bernstein emphasized the similarities between Jews and other Americans, noting that Liberal Jews accepted that Jesus was a 'loving teacher'. A year later, Bernstein expanded his primer into a book explaining the humanistic side of Judaism for all Americans.[56] Interestingly, as details about the beliefs of Judaism entered the public culture in the 1950s, the press could start assuming a basic knowledge on the part of many Americans. For example, a 1954 story in *Time* that mentioned Yom Kippur explained neither the name nor meaning of the holiday.[57]

In the fictional world created by American Jews, characters were increasingly at home in America, but the tension between their Jewish and American identities was a continuing theme. Unlike Sholem Asch, who professed that there was no tension, most of the authors grappled with their own questions about how these identities fit together. Even assimilated characters felt ties to Jewish culture that cast 'a spell that went back to the days of Abraham and Isaac'.[58] Moreover, the religious and cultural accommodations made on the road to assimilation were seen as problematic. For example, at the funeral of the title character of Gerald Green's *Last Angry Man*, there was tension between the religious and the non-religious; the religious asserted that they understood the man's *true* identity. Yet the author's endorsement of this view made little sense in light of the character which he had created, and implied that a man could only be an 'authentic' Jew if he was a traditional one. This view denied the value of the pluralism and modernity championed in the rest of the book. Similarly, the rise of Conservative and Reform adherents among the assimilating Jews was at once ridiculed and celebrated. Reflecting their own ambivalence about assimilation, Jewish authors implied that these denominations were less pure and, therefore, less Jewish than was Orthodoxy.[59]

Critics in the press also discussed the relationship between Jews and Christians, and among Jews, in a culture of assimilation. One liberal Congregationalist, for example, wrote in the Jewish magazine *Commentary* about the important connections between the Jewish and Christian traditions in a core of 'ethical mono-theism'. Moreover, he asserted that 'it was inconceivable that such a figure as Jesus should have appeared in any other [than the Jewish] cultural context'.[60] Such 'pro-assimilationist' views were countered by others who criticized the widespread emphasis on the 'Judeo-Christian' heritage as a threat to the unique tenets of Judaism. For example, British critic David Daiches said that American Jews were confused about whether to assimilate or cling to the fundamentals of their religion; instead, they engaged in 'a "genteel" watering-down of Judaism to conform to US cultural standards'.[61] Others concurred that any effort to sweep away all differences between Judaism and Christianity with the Judeo-Christian broom represented a wilful misunderstanding of Jewish distinctiveness.[62] Probably the most prevalent view embraced in the mainstream press was that Jews could assimilate to a certain extent, but should hold on to their Jewish identity and live 'a Jewish life' – however they might define it.[63] Moreover, many assumed that Jews had a common identity, no matter how much they seemed to have assimilated.[64] Nevertheless, the assumption in the press and public culture, just as in the popular fiction, was that Jews should be 'modern' and hold the political and cultural values of most other Americans. For example, one article in *Commentary* about the Hasidic Satmar community labelled its members 'zealots', while the community as a whole was 'character-ized by an extremist intolerance toward opponents and causes'.[65]

Early in the twentieth century, Horace Kallen had argued that modernization and assimilation would not be uncomplicated for American Jews:

> Judaism is no longer identical with Jewishness and
> Jewishness is no longer identical with Judaism. Jewishness
> … is not the Jewish way of life become necessarily secular,
> humanist, scientific, conditioned on the industrial economy,
> without having ceased to be livingly Jewish. Judaism will
> have to be integrated with this secular, cultural form of
> community which is Jewishness if Judaism is to survive.[66]

As demonstrated in popular fiction, many Jewish artists in the
1950s had not figured out how to re-integrate their Judaism and
their Jewishness. Many were ambivalent about the whole
enterprise of assimilation and the unresolved tensions between
their 'particular' (ethnic, Jewish,) and their 'universal' (national,
American, western) identities. Nevertheless, these popular works
projected a tidy co-existence for the contradictions and their
characters asserted their status as fully-fledged Americans.

Along with the celebratory images projected in popular fiction
of the decade, social and political evidence also indicated that
Jews were increasingly accepted as loyal Americans. In 1945, 67
per cent of respondents to a public opinion poll believed that Jews
held too much power. Of that percentage, 88 per cent believed
that power was disproportionately large in economic fields. By
1962, the percentage of respondents who believed that Jews held
too much power had fallen to 17 per cent (72 per cent of whom
believed that power was concentrated in economic fields). Similarly, the number of survey respondents who reported that Jews
represented a 'menace' to the US declined from 24 per cent in
1944, to 5 per cent in 1950, to 1 per cent in 1962.[67] The improved
attitudes toward Jews were so strong that they could weather the
highly publicized arrest in 1950 of Julius and Ethel Rosenberg as
Communist spies. While the Rosenbergs' trial went on for three
years (culminating in their executions), it did nothing to re-ignite
the stereotypes that Jews were more likely to be Communists or
to be disloyal.

Public opinion polls and reactions to such infamous political
events as the Rosenberg trial were clear indicators that attitudes
toward American Jews had shifted dramatically by mid-century.
However, it is valuable to put them into a broader context, to
see them not just as evidence of a changing political climate, but
also of a cultural climate in which Jewish-American identity and
image was transformed in just a decade. Popular fiction and the

mainstream press helped to create a new cultural narrative in which Jews were similar to their fellow citizens in behaviour, outlook and values. In this era of declining anti-Semitism, Jews gained full acceptance in popular culture to the extent that they became actors in central American narratives, particularly the story of the immigrants' achievement of the American dream, the strengthening of gender roles in the face of modern temptations and the struggle for justice abroad. The fiction of the decade created characters who fulfilled these roles and, thus, carved out a new understanding of Jewish-American identity.

NOTES

1. Philip Roth, *Goodbye, Columbus and Five Short Stories* (Boston, MA: Houghton Mifflin, 1959).
2. 'Discourse' is used here to denote the combination of ideas and actions that reflect socially defined truisms and the allocation of social power. Thus, 'discourse' refers to the links between institutions, power and symbolic codes in which the 'self-evident' takes on the 'privilege of unnoticed power'; see Paul Bové, 'Discourse', in Frank Lentricchia and Thomas McLaughlin (eds), *Critical Terms for Literary Study* (Chicago, IL: University of Chicago Press, 1990), p. 54. Knowledge and power, intellectual and material practices are linked and interdependent. Yet this linkage does not erase complexities or eliminate contradictions.
3. For example, a discussion on how Jewish writers fit themselves into covenantal discourse is found in Sam Girgus (ed.), *The American Self: Myth, Ideology, and Popular Culture* (Albuquerque, NM: University of New Mexico Press, 1981); esp. Girgus, 'The New Covenant: The Jews and the Myth of America' and Sacvan Bercovitch, 'The Rites of Assent: Rhetoric, Ritual, and the Ideology of American Consensus'.
4. Michael Kammen argues that after World War II there was a particularly strong motivation to construct a monolithic heritage or myth despite the increased diversity of the American population; see *Mystic Chords of Memory: The Transformation of Tradition in American Culture* (New York: Knopf, 1991), pp. 4–5, 532–3.
5. Nathan Glazer, 'The American Jew and the Attainment of Middle-Class Rank: Some Trends and Explanations', in Marshall Sklare (ed.), *The Jews: Social Patterns of an American Group* (Glencoe, IL: Free Press, 1958); esp. pp. 138–9, 140–1. Numerous histories of American Jews have described their economic and social success in the post-war years. One recent example is Edward Shapiro, *A Time for Healing: American Jewry Since World War II* (Baltimore, MD: Johns Hopkins University Press, 1992).
6. For example, one review of Sholem Aleichem's *Tevye's Daughters* observed that the Jews of the Russian Pale 'flourished before the Holocaust and … were so poor that the spoken word was their only permanent possession'. Thomas Lask, 'Humor That is Poignant', *New York Times Book Review* [hereafter, *NYTBR*], 23 January 1949, p. 12. Nostalgia seemed to hearken back to a golden past. For example, one book perennially advertised in the *NYTBR* was *A Treasury of Jewish Folklore*.

7. Sholem Asch, *A Passage in the Night* (New York: Putnam, 1953), p. 29. See also Dorothy Seidman Bilik, *Immigrant-Survivors: Post Holocaust Consciousness in Recent Jewish American Fiction* (Middletown, CT:: Wesleyan University Press, 1981).
8. Herman Wouk, *Marjorie Morningstar* (New York: Doubleday, 1955), p. 78. Gerald Green, *The Last Angry Man* (New York: Scribners, 1956), p. 119. Saul Bellow, *The Adventures of Augie March* (New York: Viking, 1953).
9. John Brooks, 'The Education of George Hurst', *NYTBR*, 15 June 1958, p. 5. Asch, pp. 87–8. Like Asch's popular biblical tales, this novel was also a bestseller from 20 December 1953 to 24 January 1954. Jerome Weidman, *The Enemy Camp* (New York: Random House, 1958). Weidman's book was a popular success, remaining a bestseller from 6 July 1958 to 7 December 1958.
10. *The Eddie Cantor Story* (Warner, 1953). Film copy from the Motion Picture Collection of the Library of Congress, Washington DC [hereafter, MPC].
11. See *NYTBR* bestseller lists, also, '60 Years of Best Sellers', *NYTBR*, 7 October 1956.
12. For comments on the impact of the book, see Shapiro, *A Time for Healing*, pp. 10, 157–8.
13. Meyer Levin, 'Central Park Revisited', *Saturday Review of Literature* [hereafter, *SRL*], 3 September 1955, pp. 9–10.
14. Ibid., and Florence Haxton Bullock, 'Herman Wouk Spins a Tale in the Great Tradition', *New York Herald Tribune Book Review* [hereafter, *NYHTBR*], 4 September 1955, p. 1.
15. *NYTBR*, 5 February, 1956, pp. 12–13 [emphasis in the original].
16. *NYTBR*, 25 March 1956.
17. Myron Kaufmann, *Remember Me to God* (Philadelphia, PA: Lipincott, 1957), p. 83.
18. Asch, *Passage in the Night*, p. 94.
19. See the collection, *Goodbye, Columbus and Five Short Stories*.
20. Kaufmann, *Remember Me to God*, pp. 257, 362.
21. For discussion of the denominational changes among American Jews in the post-war period, see Albert I. Gordon, *Jews in Suburbia* (Boston, MA: Beacon, 1959); esp. p. 97, and 'The Synagogue'. See also Shapiro, *A Time for Healing*, Sklare, *The Jews*; Charles Liebman, *The Ambivalent American Jew: Politics, Religion and Family in American Jewish Life* (Philadelphia, PA: Jewish Publication Society of America, 1973). Rabbi Philip Bernstein, 'What Jews Believe', *Life*, 11 September 1950, p. 162. For other examples, see 'Rabbis at the Bakeries', *Newsweek*, 28 March 1960, pp. 86, 88; 'Kosher Revival', *Time*, 26 February 1956, p. 54; Virginia Schroeder, 'Food Signifies Faith', *American Home*, September 1956, p. 104.
22. Quoted in Paul Ramsey, 'Approaches to a Faith', *NYTBR*, 1 September 1957, p. 7.
23. Gordon, *Jews in Suburbia*, pp. 126–7. For more on suburbanization and the reconfiguration of Jewish communal life, see E. Shapiro and J.J. Goldberg, *Jewish Power: Inside the American Jewish Establishment* (Reading, MA: Addison-Wesley, 1996).
24. Caroline Turnstall, 'Moving Saga of a Family', *NYHTBR*, 8 September 1957, p. 6. Another review dismissed the idea that the novel was about a 'Jewish problem', rather it was about dilemmas that affected all Americans. Nathan Rothman, 'Mask of Hypocrisy', *SRL*, 14 September 1957, p. 48.
25. Wouk, *Marjorie Morningstar*, pp. 172, 174. Letty Cottin Pogrebin argues that Wouk used the syllogism that Marjorie was Jewish, Marjorie is a Shirley, and, hence, Jewish girls were Shirleys. 'So goes the gospel of Jewish continuity',

she writes, 'according to Wouk, Roth, Mailer, and other literary princes who created this modern mythology to deal with their own renunciation of their pre-American past'. Letty Cottin Pogrebin, *Deborah, Golda, and Me: Being Female and Jewish in America* (New York: Crown, 1991), p. 263.

26. Weidman, *Enemy Camp*, p. 85. Reviews of the book simplified the issues of identity, even charging that the book was merely about anti-Semitism and 'anti-Gentilism'. See Brooks, 'The Education of George Hurst', *NYTBR*, and Edmund Fuller, 'Caught in Private Ghettos', *SRL*, 28 June 1958, p. 19. Also, John Chamberlain, 'Weidman Novel Shows World Within Worlds Social and Private', *NYHTBR*, 15 June 1958, p. 1.

27. Weidman, *Enemy Camp*, p. 458.

28. See, for example, the collection Harold U. Ribalow (ed.), *Mid-Century: An Anthology of Jewish Life and Culture in Our Times* (New York: Beechhurst, 1955). *Commentary* was also a forum where these issues were discussed.

29. Critics approved of the spiritual message of the novel, even if they felt that the psychiatrists were exaggerated villains. See Nathan Rothman, 'A Man's Conscience', *SRL*, 17 October 1953, p. 27, and Florence Haxton Bullock, 'A Rich, Close-Woven Novel About Man and Conscience', *NYHTBR*, 18 October 1953, p. 4. Wouk and Kaufmann also find that psychiatry is no substitute for religion, including several criticisms of the discipline in their books.

30. Both novels were very popular. *Augie March* was a bestseller from 4 October to 27 December 1953. *Last Angry Man* was one from 24 February to 22 September 1957. One critic referred to Bellow as 'the favorite novelist of the American intellectuals', and the author won the National Book Award for *Augie March* in 1953. Quoted in Sanford Pinsker, *The Schlemiel as Metaphor: Studies in the Yiddish and American Jewish Novel* (Carbondale, IL: Southern Illinois University Press, 1971), pp. 125–6.

31. Marcus Klein, *After Alienation: American Novels in Mid-Century* (Cleveland, OH: World, 1962), pp. 34, 38. Another critic commenting on Augie's inability to control his own fate called him a powerless schlemiel; see Allen Guttman in *The Jewish Writer in America: Assimilation and the Crisis of Identity* (New York: Oxford University Press, 1971). Reviews of Bellow's book avoided discussing his Jewish identity directly. See Harvey Curtis Webster, 'Quest Through the Modern World', *SRL*, 19 September 1953, pp. 13–14; Arthur Mizener, 'Portrait of an American, Chicago-Born', *NYHTBR*, 20 September 1953, p. 2; and Robert Gorham Davis, 'Augie Just Wouldn't Settle Down: Saul Bellow's New Novel is A Story of a Young Man's Fight to Be Himself', *NYTBR*, 20 September 1953, pp. 1ff.

32. Green, *Last Angry Man*, p. 27. Similarly, Kaufman uses stereotypes of cold WASPs to describe a number of characters. In his novel, WASPs are so lacking in colour and warmth that they eat colourless, non-descript food. Although Sam is not at all religious, he is unmistakably Jewish. Reviews of the book conflate all ethnicities. They do not even mention that Sam is Jewish. See James Kelly, 'The Last Angry Man', *SRL*, 2 February 1957, 12, and Fred Marsh, 'TV and M.D. in a Big Novel', *NYHTBR*, 3 February 1957, pp. 1ff.

33. Green, *Last Angry Man*, p. 56.

34. Kaufmann, *Remember Me to God*, p. 402. As father to the wayward young Jew, Adam Amsterdam argues that Jews should not melt and give up their religion and heritage, 'If the Jewish religion makes out in this country, it will prove the American idea'. The man is a dedicated patriot, telling a conscientious objector brought before him in court, 'This is the best country in the world, and you ought to be glad to defend it'. Kaufmann, pp. 36, 500.

35. See, for further discussion, Patricia Erens, *The Jew in American Cinema* (Bloomington, IN: Indiana University Press, 1984) and Lester Friedman, *Hollywood's Image of the Jew* (New York: Ungar, 1990).

36. The interviewers are uncomfortable discussing ethnic identity. In the *Variety* review of *The Young Lions*, the main Jewish character is described stiffly as 'the drafted GI of Jewish heritage', while the *NYT* review of *Three Brave Men* notes that the lead character 'happens to be a Jew'; see *Variety*, 19 March 1958, and *NYT*, 16 March 1957. For other examples, see *Variety* reviews of *Three Brave Men*, 16 January 1957; *I Accuse!*, 5 February 1958; *The Naked and the Dead*, 9 July 1958, and *NYT* reviews of *The Naked and the Dead*, 7 August 1958 and *Home Before Dark*, 7 November 1958.

37. *Home Before Dark* (Warner, 1958). Film copy from MPC. The critic for *Variety* focused on Jean Simmons' performance in the lead of this 'women's picture' and the *NYT* review did not even mention that the male lead was Jewish. *Variety*, 15 October 1958 and *NYT*, 7 November 1958.

38. *Marjorie Morningstar* (Warner/United States Pictures, 1958). Film copy from MPC. *Marjorie* was also one of the top grossing films of 1958; see Charles Aaronson (ed.), *The International Motion Picture Almanac 1960* (New York: Quigley, 1960).

39. The reviews for the film reflected that the film was a generalized American story. See, for example, *Variety*, 12 March 1958 and *NYT*, 25 April 1958.

40. *Three Brave Men* (Twentieth Century Fox, 1957). Film copy from MPC. *NYT*, 16 March 1957.

41. Charles Stember's analysis of public opinion polls demonstrates this trend. Also, he found that those respondents most likely to believe that Jews were often Communists were extreme in their anti-Communist beliefs. Charles Herbert Stember *et al.*, *Jews in the Mind of America* (New York: Basic, 1966), pp. 160–7. Anti-Communist investigations made Jews in Hollywood sensitive to charges that they were radicals and not loyal Americans. See Neal Gabler, *An Empire of Their Own: How the Jews Invented Hollywood* (New York: Anchor, 1989), and Larry Ceplair and Steven Englund, *The Inquisition in Hollywood: Politics in the Film Community, 1930–1960* (Berkeley, CA: University of California Press, 1970, 1983).

42. Most of the popular films and novels on the American-Jewish experience in the 1950s focused on male characters who resembled other Americans in most respects. Depicting their similarity to American men meant that they were masculine and could be 'tough'. One historical novel about American Jews also countered the stereotype of unmasculine Jews through the story of settlers in New York. The hero of *Blessed is the Land*, by Louis Zara, was a 'swashbuckling soldier of fortune'; see 'Ashur Levy and Co.', *NYTBR*, 12 September 1954, p. 30.

43. *I Accuse!* (MGM, 1958). Film copy from MPC.

44. *The Naked and the Dead* (RKO Teleradio, 1958) and *The Young Lions* (Twentieth Century Fox, 1958). Film copies from MPC. *The Young Lions* was one of the top grossing pictures of 1958; see Aaronson (ed.), *The International Motion Picture Almanac 1960*, p. 737.

45. *Good Morning Miss Dove* (Twentieth Century Fox, 1955). Film copy from MPC.

46. Years earlier, Horace Kallen had pointed to Zionism as the source of his own renewed Jewish identity: 'Zionism became a replacement and re-evaluation of Judaism which enabled me to respect it'. Quoted in Susanne Klingenstein, *Jews in the American Academy 1900–1940: The Dynamics of Intellectual Assimilation* (New Haven, CT: Yale University Press, 1991), p. 41. After Israel became

a political reality, views such as Kallen's were challenged by an increasingly small minority of Jews, such as Alfred Lilienthal, an anti-Zionist activist.

47. As Israel moved to the centre of Jewish community life and identity, Hertzberg concluded that 'Support for Israel, and not learning Hebrew, was the "spiritual content" of the relationship'; Arthur Hertzberg, *The Jews in America: Four Centuries of an Uneasy Encounter* (New York: Simon and Schuster, 1989), pp. 318, 342. 'Support for Israel' covered many activities as well as sentiments, and eventually helped spawn a Jewish political and philanthropic network. Jewish philanthropy focused on Israel, and the new State stood as a symbol of Jewish power within the US. For an overview of Jewish post-war political power and its relationship to Israel, see Goldberg, *Jewish Power: Inside the American Jewish Establishment*. See also Shapiro, *A Time for Healing: American Jewry Since World War II*. Jewish fundraising for Israel was sometimes a topic of press focus; see, for example, 'Dollars for Israel', *Time Magazine*, 19 November 1956, pp. 27, 68.

48. Howard M. Sachar, *A History of Israel, From Zionism to Our Time* (New York: Knopf, 1996), p. 118.

49. Further, the closeness between the two countries was symbolized by the Israeli leaders, for example, David Ben Gurion had lived in New York for a time, Golda Meir grew up in Milwaukee, and American listeners were charmed by the perfect English of Israeli diplomat Abba Eban. See Sklare, *The Jews*, and Hal Lehrman, 'The Man on the Rostrum', *NYTBR*, 5 May 1957, pp. 3ff. Importantly, American Jews were not ready to give up their nationality. From 1948 to 1967, an average of 600–1,200 American Jews moved to Israel each year, but most of them returned to the US; Sklare, *The Jews*, p. 213. American-Jewish and Israeli leaders held conflicting definitions of Zionism. The majority of the former believed that they proved their Zionism through financial and political support for the State, while many Israelis defined Zionists as those who took up residence and citizenship in the Jewish State. For a contemporary press commentary, see 'Two Kinds of Jews', *Time*, 26 August 1957, pp. 54–5, 70.

50. Stember found that most Americans did not associate American Jews with the problems between Israel and the Arab countries. In 1953, 16 per cent of respondents believed that American Jews had something to do with the trouble in the region. That figure fell to 12 per cent by November 1956, in the middle of the Suez crisis. A more significant change was in the number of people who said that American Jews did *not* have anything to do with the Israeli/Arab disputes: in 1953, 43 per cent of respondents answered in the negative, in 1956, 67 per cent of respondents did; see Stember *et al.*, *Jews in the Mind of America*, p. 189.

51. American popular fiction, in print and on the screen, which focused on Israel in the decade and a half after World War II, was most often found in heroic recreations of biblical stories and swashbuckling tales of the formation of the modern State. These themes and their impact are discussed in the manuscript in progress, Michelle Mart, *Pioneers, Prophets, and Pragmatists: American Images of Israel and Jews*.

52. Richard Sullivan, 'Always in Exile', *NYTBR*, 5 September 1954, p. 6, and Salo W. Baron, 'Three Centuries of Jewish Experience in America', *NYTBR*, 12 September 1954.

53. Kaufmann, *Remember Me to God*, p. 536.

54. Klingenstein, *Jews in the American Academy*, pp. 34–5. This pluralistic vision shaped American images of Israel as well; for example, '[American Jews'] whole *weltanschauung* posited a pluralistic society, whether in the US or in

Palestine'; see Michael J. Cohen, *Truman and Israel* (Berkeley, CA: University of California Press, 1990), p. 277.

55. Address Adlai Stevenson American Jewish Tercentenary 1 June 1955, folder 5, Series 2 Speeches, Papers of Adlai E. Stevenson, box 151, Seeley G. Mudd Library, Princeton University. There were a number of press articles about the anniversary, for example, 'Under the Fig Tree', *Time*, 20 September 1954, pp. 65ff., as well as dinners and celebrations attended by national politicians in addition to Stevenson. Official guests included President Eisenhower.

56. For examples, Virginia Schroeder, 'Food Signifies Faith', *American Home*, September 1956, p. 104; 'Food: Manischevitz Matzos', *Newsweek*, 30 April 1950, pp. 60ff.; 'Evaluation of the Jews', *Newsweek*, 6 March 1950, p. 70; 'What Jews Believe', *Life*, 11 September 1950, pp. 160ff.; 'What Jews Believe', *Time*, 19 December 1951, pp. 87–90; and 'Feast of Light', *Time*, 19 December 1955, p. 69.

57. 'Almost a Lutheran', *Time*, 5 April 1954, pp. 66, 68.

58. Weidman, *Enemy Camp*, p. 524.

59. One article about kashrut explains that the popularity of the practice was part of the general religious revival in the US. The journalist begins with a quotation from *Marjorie Morningstar* to show the value of keeping kosher. 'Kosher Revival', *Time*, 20 February 1956, p. 54; also, 'Rabbis at Bakeries', pp. 86, 88. See 'A Trumpet for Israel', *Time*, 15 October 1951, pp. 52ff., about increased religious activity among American Jews.

60. Robert Fitch, 'The Bond Between Christian and Jew', *Commentary*, May 1954, pp. 439–45 (esp. p. 444).

61. Daiches concluded that the befuddled American Jew further confused his assimilationist urge with Zionism: 'He hopes that out of Zion will come forth good Rotarian Israelites and Hebrew-speaking hot-dog sellers'; 'Common Ignorance', *Time*, 19 February 1951, pp. 59–60.

62. Jacob Taubes, 'The Issue Between Judaism and Christianity', *Commentary*, December 1953, pp. 525–33.

63. For example, 'Almost a Lutheran', *Time*, 5 April 1954, pp. 66, 68. Many disagreed about what defined a Jewish life. Stember's analysis of public opinion polls showed that many Americans in the mid-1940s and the early 1960s were confused about whether Jews were a national, religious or racial group. In 1946, Jews were named as a race 33–42 per cent of the time, as a nationality 22–26 per cent, and as a religious group 35–44 per cent. (The percentage range is due to changing answers depending on what order the categories were listed in the question.) By 1962, public thinking was still inconclusive. Jews were named as a race 21–23 per cent of the time, as a nationality 28–31 per cent, and as a religious group 38–45 per cent; see Stember *et al.*, *Jews in the Mind of America*, p. 50.

64. See, for example, Herbert Mitgang, 'A Lox is a Lox', *NYTBR*, 8 March 1953, p. 24.

65. Harry Gersh and Sam Miller, 'Satmar in Brooklyn', *Commentary*, November 1959, pp. 389, 397.

66. Quoted in Klingenstein, *Jews in the American Academy*, p. 41.

67. Stember, *Jews in the Mind of America*, pp. 121–4; also cited in Goldberg, *Jewish Power*, p. 117. In addition, those polled believed that their neighbours were also tolerant of Jews. Those who answered 'yes' to the question, 'Do you believe anti-Jewish feeling is rising?', went from 58 per cent in 1945 to 16 per cent in 1950.

4

___

Going against the Grain:
Two Jewish Memoirs of War and
Anti-War (1914–18)

MARK LEVENE

The stakes were certainly high for European Jewry during the massive and prolonged crisis of 1914–18. The Great War, a traumatic watershed for all of European society, threw into particularly stark relief the price, as well as the fragility, of Jewish emancipation, engagement with and integration into, the dominant Gentile mainstream. With the major powers of Europe locked in a life and death struggle, the loyalty and commitment of Jews to their respective citizenships (or, in the case of Russia, subjecthood) would be closely tested for their ability, willingness and, indeed, enthusiasm to make ready their young men and render them up for military service, not to say battlefield slaughter. To belong in 1914 – that is, to belong to the nation – required what the French aptly called *l'impôt du sang*, a blood tax. For Jews living in Britain, the obligation was yet more pointed. Here, in contrast to continental counterparts, there was no general mobilization or national conscription, at least not at the outset of war. The test of patriotic loyalty and proof that one merited British citizenship thus lay in *voluntary* enlistment in the new citizen army launched by Lord Kitchener. Yet how could Jews respond patriotically when some two thirds of them were recently arrived and hence unnaturalized immigrants, largely from an empire, which, even if it was Britain's ally in the war, nevertheless did not recognize their status as true citizens?

In contrast to this dilemma, the official Anglo-Jewish record is nothing less than a paean to the community's full military engagement in Britain's war effort. A thousand-page, illustrated and thoroughly monumental *Book of Honour* is its testimony, compiled and introduced by the chief Jewish chaplain to the British forces, the Revd Michael Adler.[1] Replete with endorsements and testimonials from leading British and British-Jewish military and political leaders, the *Book*'s centrepiece is a listing of the 2,400 'Glorious Dead' – in other words, Anglo-Jewry's 'ultimate sacrifice' to Allied victory.[2] Replicated in more local rolls of honour where Jews constituted a substantial element of the population,[3] a narrative of full and honourable war service was further re-inforced and perpetuated into the middle years of the century by Cecil Roth, the leading (indeed, at that stage, the only) major figure in Anglo-Jewish historiography.[4]

There is, however, another narrative of glorious war service, which, at first sight, given its lambasting of obstacles allegedly put in its path by 'assimilationist plutocrats', not to say Adler himself, seems to be diametrically opposed to that of the *Book of Honour*.[5] This is to be found in Vladimir Jabotinsky's *The Story of the Jewish Legion*, which itself draws on the writings of Lieutenant-Colonel John Patterson. Patterson was the commander of the British-created but specifically Jewish units, first in the form of the Zion Mule Corps which operated in the Dardanelles Campaign, and latterly in what eventually came to be designated the 'Judeans', a formation which saw active service in Palestine in 1918.[6] If Adler's war narrative is national in a British sense, Jabotinsky ties his to the emergence of a specifically Jewish national identity. Not only was *The Story of the Jewish Legion* intended to 'construct a vision of the new Jewish warrior' but also, in so doing, sought to legitimate the Zionist claim to Palestine.[7] Though the Judeans' role in the Palestine campaign was actually rather marginal, Jabotinsky's version of events was developed, aggrandized and ultimately mythologized so that it became a sort of Zionist revisionist wisdom.[8] This would suggest the mutual exclusivity of the Adler and Jabotinsky narratives. In fact, not so. Not only was the Judeans' service record – including a chapter from Jabotinsky himself – included in *The Book of Honour*, but in time, and with the increasingly Zionist orientation of British Jewry, the two 'stories' were allowed to fuse into a popular, if sometimes rather dubious, record of Jewish Great War service in *both* causes.[9]

Either way, these narratives have the merit of presenting Jewish communal involvement in the best possible light – and, at the time, in the most clear-cut terms. There was, on the one hand, the British 'tommy', who just happened to be Jewish, fighting alongside his Christian comrades-in-arms for King and country. On the other hand, there was the British, or possibly Russian-born, Jew who deep down knew that Zion represented both his individual and collective destiny and recognized, at this critical point, that he must shrug off centuries of unmanly lassitude in order to achieve it. The similarity, however, is also obvious. The nation in its hour of need always demands that right must enlist the support of might – and that the individual, to share in this collective belonging, must prove *himself* worthy. He must, in short, fight. However if this sounds fine in theory, how did it play itself out for 'ordinary' individuals who were actually supposed to don military uniform?

This chapter considers the question of national identity in the crucible of war with reference to two richly informative memoirs. The autobiographical accounts, however, of Henry Myer and Arnold Harris stand, to a considerable extent, in marked contrast and even give the lie to Adler's and Jabotinsky's official versions.[10] Were these two young Jewish men motivated in the face of war by ideas of nation? If so, which nation? Would the thoroughly assimilated, public school-educated Myer be oblivious, even hostile, to Jabotinsky's clarion call? Would Harris, with his strongly Zionist background and sympathies, be a natural candidate for service with the Judeans? If their minds were not already made up would their personal experience in these war years provide them with that sense of national belonging and identity? Recent historiographical scholarship suggests that the selection and categorization of Anglo-Jewry in terms of straightforward ideological cleavages is something of which we ought to be wary. Neither class nor ethnicity alone can provide entirely satisfactory explanations for what was really going on in an extraordinarily 'unstable, contested, fractured arena'.[11] Personal identities, then as now, could be multi-layered, even in some sense schizophrenic, as different perspectives and ideas fought for control in the individual psyche. Throw in an entirely unexpected contingency, such as war, and the result might be a genuine confusion. How much more, then, must this have been true for those, in their early twenties, who were on the cusp of genuine adulthood, who were yet to attain status within their communities, but not too old to have their lives terminated or crippled by the demands of war?

Neither Henry Myer nor Arnold Harris was born in London but both grew up, were schooled and moulded there, mostly within a few miles of each other. Born in 1892 and 1894, respectively, both were highly conscious of their Jewishness and both in later life became associated with communal causes, the former most particularly with Ajex (the Association of Jewish Ex-Servicemen and Women), the latter in social work, especially with the rescue and rehabilitation of young refugees from the Nazis. There the similarity ends. Myer was the quintessential product of Anglo-Jewish integration and success: the Westminster public school boy who joined his father's law firm, did soldiering in his spare time and was inducted into the horrors of the western front, in 1915, as a commissioned officer with the City of London Rifles. Harris, by contrast, was not technically British at all but a Russian subject. Born into a community that revolved around the important Slobodka *yeshiva* in Lithuania, Harris's father was a *melamed* [teacher] who had fled to Britain, possibly to avoid induction into the Russian Army, his wife and infant son joining him some time later. On account of his alien status, the younger Harris, at the outset of the 1914 conflict, was protected in his opposition to British military service. Yet if this information initially confirms what we might expect of their respective attitudes and responses to the crisis of war, the Myer and Harris memoirs throw up surprises, suggesting conclusions which would seem to go against the grain if not of our preconceptions, then certainly of crucial ideological aspects of the Adler and Jabotinsky narratives. In order to make sense of them, however, we need to sketch the broader British, as well as the more intimate Anglo-Jewish, contexts in which the specific question of military service can be understood.

In 1914 Britain had a standing army of only 244,000 men plus additional, if meagre, reserves in the form of volunteer part-time territorial battalions, in which those like Henry Myer served.[12] The original 100,000 professionals earmarked for service in support of the French alliance in the event of war were rapidly depleted in the early battles in Flanders and northern France. Though Lord Kitchener was able to raise an additional volunteer army amounting to 2.4 million men, heavy casualties throughout 1915 on the western front and at Gallipoli underscored the simple reality that if the war were to be pursued, compulsory conscription would be essential.[13] This was a major departure for the British State and for a while Lord Derby, the Director-General of Recruiting, attempted

to attenuate its coercive implications by allowing men of recruitment age, that is, between 18 and 41, to attest their willingness to
serve without actually inducting them into the colours. However,
as Jay Winter has pointed out, this simply threw up the disparity
between those willing to go and a substantial majority, not otherwise exempted through essential war work or chronic unfitness,
who were unwilling. The result was the Military Conscription Act,
which came before Parliament in January and was put into effect
in May 1916. Even this, however, did not resolve the problem of
shortfall. The crisis became acute in the autumn of 1917 as a new
Ministry of National Service attempted to reconcile the needs of
industrial manpower at home with those of the army supremos
on the western front. Further military service acts followed, in
January and March 1918. Among other things, these extended the
upper limit for conscription from 41 to 51 and tightened up
procedures that had previously enabled some men to avoid the
conscription net.[14]

In some key respects the communal Jewish picture closely
follows these national contours. Though it could boast only a few
professional soldiers, the British-born Jewish community showed
early and rapid voluntary enlistment. This was given prominence
both in the lead provided by members of the Rothschild family,
who set up a War Services Committee, and in the pages of the
Jewish Chronicle, which reported with unrestrained enthusiasm
every case of Jews 'mucking in', as well as major examples of battlefield courage.[15] Moreover, statistically the figures would at first sight
seem to bear out Michael Adler's message, namely that British Jews
were patriotic and willing to lay down their lives for King and
country. A recent analysis by the late Vivian Lipman concludes that
13.8 per cent of the Jewish population, compared with 11.5 per
cent for the country as a whole, was involved in military service
– clearly a strong record, though curiously based on an estimate
of a British-Jewish population of 300,000, which he admits to be
rather high and far beyond Adler's assumed figure of 275,000.[16]
However, Lipman's explanation for the community's apparently
strong military turn-out is less compelling. 'One can', he says:

> attribute this to the demographic structure of a largely recent
> immigrant population, with a disproportionate number of
> younger men and to the virtual absence of Jews from most
> of the occupations which provided the 2.5 million who were

exempted from military service – railways, mines, agriculture, shipbuilding, munitions.[17]

However, scrutinizing the statistics in greater detail, Lipman admits that while the number of Jewish officers killed (from both Britain and its empire), standing at 316, reflected the general national average, the number of Jews killed among other ranks was much lower: only 0.7 per cent compared with 1.7 per cent.[18] Lipman attempts to explain this discrepancy by proposing that many Jews served in war theatres such as the Middle East, or in the Royal Flying Corps, where, he suggests, casualties were lower, and to the fact that 4,900 out of a total of 41,500 Jews in the armed forces were in labour battalions, i.e. non-combat units.

However, this last piece of information puts the spotlight on the more specifically immigrant Russian-Jewish contribution to the British war effort. Of an estimated 29,000 to 30,000 Russian Jews of military age, only some 8,000 are known to have served in military units, largely in the labour battalions, or to a lesser extent, between 1,000 and 1,500, in the Jewish battalions of the Royal Fusiliers, i.e. the Judeans.[19] Putting to one side the 2,000 who returned to Russia in 1917, this would leave 20,000 men who, Lipman states in what can only be a slip of the pen, were 'exempted or not called to service'.[20] Put another way, the Jewish war record would run thus: for the 10,000 who voluntarily enlisted before the Military Service Act of 1916, there were twice as many who hid or made themselves scarce, or who were exempted mostly because they were genuinely unfit, and a further 30,000 who served because the State demanded it of them.

Using Winter's extrapolations, it is clear that such a profile of Jewish military service and non-service was not wholly peculiar to this community. One could start with a straight class analysis and note, as Winter does, that, statistically speaking, it was the better educated, professional and commercial elements in British society who volunteered, compared with the working class who had to be coerced.[21] There is also some evidence that specific areas of the country, notably the Fens and rural mid-Wales, which one might define as specific, localized, even ethnic, enclaves not particularly well integrated into the national structure, were marked by their young men's resistance to conscription. And there was, of course, one entire area of the then United Kingdom – Ireland – exempted, for entirely political reasons, from the terms of the Military Service Act.[22]

What is therefore interesting, and possibly bewildering, about the Jewish case is not so much the actual record as the version of the record which Adler (in order to massage the figures) and Jabotinsky (from a different standpoint) so vociferously touted, and the way these versions became received wisdom for later generations of British Jewry. Just as the official spokesmen of British Jewry, including historians, preferred to engage in apologetics and a celebratory mythology of communal upstandingness and rectitude with regard to the long eighteenth century – until an American historian, Todd Endelman, rounded out the picture with his portrait of crimps, pimps, fences and thieves[23] – so aspects of the Jewish response to the 1914–18 war which the community preferred not to be reminded of were duly swept under the carpet.

The coyness of British Jewry with regard to its communal history, and particularly with regard to the response of its élite to the major immigrant influx, primarily from the Russian Pale of Settlement, in the decades prior to the war, has been the subject of much recent critical scrutiny.[24] However it is the tensions centring on the so-called 'aliens question' as they built up into a series of state-communal and intra-communal crises during the war that concern us here. The official organs of the community were undoubtedly terrified, especially in the wake of 'the siege of Sidney Street' of 1911, that the reputation of the Jewish East End as a hotbed of anti-statist and more specifically anarchistic behaviour, would rebound against their carefully nurtured ideology of liberal emancipation.[25] However, it was hardly anarchists who ruptured the comfortable notion that Britishness and Jewishness were as one; rather it was the government's foreign policy orientation, launching Britain into the European conflict on the same side as an openly reactionary and anti-Semitic tsarist state. No sooner had the Russian Army run into serious military trouble than it began taking hostages amongst its Jewish borderland population, and then deporting that population *en masse*.[26] If these external circumstances suggested that official Anglo-Jewry's accommodation to the war conflicted with its *own* better instincts, the outburst of domestic chauvinism and xenophobia, whose physical manifestations were directed as much against the naturalized West End financier with the German name as against the Russian-born East End peddler, determined that there would be little or no scope for dissent.[27] Almost overnight, trumpeting one's Britishness, whilst belittling one's ethnicity or religiosity, became both for the voice of the community and for most established

British Jews as individuals, *de rigueur*. Communal duty would have to be subsumed within obligation to the Crown, achieved primarily by the enlistment of male Jewish youth at the first opportunity.

This does not, however, mean that those Jews who rushed to the colours were insincere. A diet of nation and empire for those who were educated at public school or inculcated with it in their spare-time participation in the paramilitary Jewish Lads' Brigade, ensured a steady stream of probably innocently sang-froid patriots.[28] However, as the political-military demands for general conscription intensified, and the social climate increasingly hardened against those men who were not in uniform, public and Jewish communal pressure came to bear more heavily on the immigrant masses. It was alleged that Lord Derby himself had stated that Jews were not doing their bit.[29] The columnist 'Mentor' and others in the *Jewish Chronicle* rounded on 'slackers' and 'shirkers'.[30] Those who appeared before tribunals seeking exemption on conscientious or religious grounds received similar opprobrium. An establishment Liverpool rabbi who supported some of these objectors in person was hounded out of office by his *parnassim* [synagogue wardens].[31] Paradoxically, in the pre-conscription period, recruiting officers often turned immigrant would-be volunteers away.[32] Racial and social prejudices clearly contributed to this professional military ambivalence. Just as views on colonial Blacks manifested themselves in acerbic War Office statements to the effect that it was 'against British tradition to employ aboriginal troops against a European country',[33] so too, a social Darwinian and eugenics-informed medical discourse militated against the immigrant Jew on the grounds that he was congenitally ill-equipped, both in physical and mental terms, to endure the rigours of modern warfare.[34] In addition, a wartime climate of largely undiluted anti-Semitism openly surfaced in civilian and military intelligence reports, and even War Cabinet meetings, to the effect that the Russian Jews were a dangerous and subversive element.[35]

When the government paralleled its general conscription enactment, in May 1916, with deliberations aimed at 'dealing' with immigrant military non-participation, the ensuing proposals had a curiously double-edged quality to them that appear motivated by considerations other than those of conscription pure and simple. Though not British citizens, those with Russian papers were required to enlist voluntarily in the British Army or be deported back to Russia, the latter a not very subtle way of saying good riddance. As for the immigrants themselves – caught, in effect, between the devil and the deep blue sea – radical socialist and anarchist groupings led the fight back, on grounds of the principled right to asylum, forming a Foreign Jews Protection Committee for this purpose and garnering support from dissident Liberal and Labour MPs in the process.[36]

The reaction of the Anglo-Jewish establishment, however, was – to say the least – ambivalent. It had not been consulted on the proposals, nor did it like their coercive implications. On the other hand, as popular grassroots disturbances against Jews flared in Liverpool, Manchester and elsewhere, the Jewish leadership was as keen as the government to have the immigrants *seen* in uniform. The urgency of the situation was highlighted by the fact that the Home Secretary, Herbert Samuel, on whose shoulders the issue of official judgement primarily rested, was also a prominent and active figure in Anglo-Jewry. With a potentially irreconcilable conflict of interests, Samuel attempted, belatedly, to enlist other Jewish communal establishment leaders, notably the Zionist editor of the *Jewish Chronicle*, Leopold Greenberg, and the anti-Zionist political secretary of the community's Conjoint Foreign Committee, Lucien Wolf, to devise a new volunteer scheme that would sweeten the terms of service. In mid-August, with little evidence of a positive response from the immigrants, Samuel warned a delegation of Jewish trade unionists of dire consequences to follow. Privately he expressed his exasperation even more unreservedly to Wolf: 'If the mass of Russian Jews refuse to lift a finger to help … the effect on the reputation of the Jewish name everywhere will be disastrous'.[37]

However, while ill-defined offers of naturalization for enlistees and half-hearted suggestions that they might serve in units largely comprising their own compatriots produced hardly more than a trickle of respondents,[38] the clamour from non-Jewish sources for draconian action began to take on a life of its own. East End opinion, spearheaded by the Bethnal Green Military Tribunal, local borough councillors and those also serving as members of the London County Council, organized of their own volition an East London Aliens Conference in February 1917 which called unequivocally for immigrant conscription or deportation.[39] Three months later, Sir Basil Thomson, head of Special Branch, lent support to these sentiments by conducting a highly visible and well-publicized police raid in the East End, which detained up to 4,000 suspected aliens of military age. Four were found to be eligible for service. There were more anti-Jewish disturbances in Leeds in June, and in Bethnal Green in September.[40] Clearly, these physical manifestations of pent-up anti-Jewish feeling represented more than simply resentment that 'our' boys were being killed while the 'aliens' were allegedly living off the fat of the land.[41] There was, moreover, a thin dividing line between those who were technically alien, having been born in Russia but having been brought up in Britain and those who were socially and culturally part of the immigrant milieu, yet by birth British citizens. The only difference in so far as military service was concerned was that the latter were conscriptable without qualification. It was against such a background that two partly contradictory government strategies began to emerge aimed at ironing out this anomaly.

In the first strategy, the government attempted to make it compulsory for those with Russian papers to serve in either the British or Russian Army through an arrangement with their Russian ally. Interestingly, when this idea was first mooted, in January 1917, the tsarist government was as lukewarm as the potential conscriptees themselves, on the grounds that once inducted into the Russian Army they would only cause disaffection.[42] The new post-revolutionary government, however, proved considerably more amenable and an Anglo-Russian Convention on Military Service, announced in March, was finally implemented by an Order in Council in August 1917.[43] This did not mean, however, that Russian Jews who opted to serve in Britain were to be treated on the same footing as British citizens. Though in principle no distinction was operated disabling Russian Jews from seeking exemptions before the tribunals, they were debarred from commissions. Indeed, the majority were slated for induction into the lowest form of (military) pond life, namely the labour battalions.[44] Paradoxically, this is exactly what the Anglo-Jewish establishment least desired as – true to its emancipatory principles – it wanted the Russian Jews to be treated in the same way as all other (white) Britishers.

The second strategy initially caused even more consternation and dissension within the ranks of the Anglo-Jewish establishment, even though, superficially, it looked a good deal more benevolent. This involved taking on board the proposal of an otherwise unknown Russian Jewish journalist and Zionist, Vladimir Jabotinsky, for the creation of a specifically Jewish Legion, whose remit would be to fight under British command for the 'liberation' of Palestine. An attempt to create a volunteer British-Jewish unit, along the lines of other battalions which the War Office had agreed to form from occupationally or socially cohesive 'pals', had been rejected by it and by most of the Anglo-Jewish establishment early on in the war.[45] Jabotinsky's own initial efforts, in late 1915 and 1916, to get a War Office hearing for his more politically active idea were similarly cold-shouldered.[46] Government interest only took off in the spring of 1917, as efforts to have the Russian Jews voluntarily enlist floundered. It can hardly have been coincidental, however, that the War Office announced its decision to create a Jewish regiment at the end of July 1917, both as it began its drive towards the Balfour Declaration and as General Allenby's campaign on the Palestine front moved into top gear. As I have argued elsewhere, the government's brief love affair with Zionism was largely founded on wholly misconceived notions about, among other things, the nature of a supposed collective, not to say anti-Entente, Jewry.[47] The premise that Jews who were otherwise antipathetic to the Allied cause would fight for Zion must have seemed doubly attractive at this juncture as a way of resolving immigrant Russian Jewish objections to military service. However, while Jabotinsky clearly saw the immigrants as a ready-made reservoir for his scheme, the reception he received for his recruitment efforts in the East End was anything but friendly.[48] By the same token, while some Anglo-Jewish leaders, both Zionist and assimilationist, were willing for entirely pragmatic reasons to give the scheme their support in order to raise the immigrant enlistment figures, others, *including* Zionists like Greenberg, who had initially been supportive, found themselves in opposition, perceiving the Jewish regiment as a strategy for singling out Jews.[49]

This is exactly, of course, what the government had in mind. Faced, however, with a vociferous body of Jews who petitioned against the regiment, as well as a substantial element who petitioned in its favour, the government rapidly watered down the scheme.[50] What Jabotinsky had envisaged as a mini Jewish army ended up as three active battalions of a British regiment, the Royal Fusiliers.[51] Certainly, these were identifiable as wholly Jewish units and were allowed to designate themselves as the Judeans,

particularly once mainstream Anglo-Jewish hostility had sub-
sided. Indeed, towards the end of the war the *Jewish Chronicle*
was proclaiming that the Judeans were living proof that Jews were
not cowards and shirkers, while the units' communal support
committee waxed lyrical that they had 'restored to the Jews
of England a measure of pride … of no small value in the trying
times of war weariness when the national temper was, perhaps,
excusably prone to undue irritation'.[52] Eulogies aside, the fact
remains that only some 1,000 to 1,500 immigrant British-domiciled
Jews served with the Judeans and even the majority of these,
Jabotinsky was compelled to acknowledge, were 'indifferent to
Zionism, indifferent to Palestine, angry with a world that had
disturbed their peace and dragged them across the ocean to fight
for something in which they were not interested'.[53] While the
Judeans' ranks were swelled by American, Canadian and, finally,
Palestinian-Jewish volunteers, the domestic question of immigrant military non-participation was thus, at the beginning of
1918, not substantially different from the situation 18 months
earlier. With the new Bolshevik rulers in Petrograd intent on
repudiation of the Anglo-Russian Military Convention and Lord
Derby reporting 'trouble' at the Plymouth barracks where Judeans'
enlistees were stationed, the War Cabinet, only two months after
the Balfour Declaration, secretly ordered the incarceration of
dissenting Russian Jews in concentration camps in Hull and
Aberdeen pending available ships to deport them to Russia. The
deportees would not be allowed to return.[54] Ultimately, lack of
shipping ensured that this order was not put into effect. The
government spent the rest of the war attempting to dragoon
Russian Jews into labour battalions or other units.

It is only against this background of serious state-communal
crisis, as compared with the celebratory 'all is well' versions of the
Jewish war record espoused by Adler and Jabotinsky, that the
Myer and Harris memoirs can be fully appreciated. Having said
that, there is still the question of how, or more pointedly, on what
level, we choose to read them. For instance, we might forego
attempts at any sociologically informed consideration and portray
Myer and Harris in terms of their individual responses to the
prospect of war. Myer's euphoric enlistment recalls that of Rupert
Brooke: 'Now God be thanked who has matched us with this hour,
And caught our youth and waked us from sleeping'; Harris, a later
devotee of Isaac Rosenberg's poetry was, like him, horrified at the

prospect of the long sinister night in which 'death could drop from the dark as easily as a song'.[55] A simple tale, therefore, of heroism contrasted with funk, or possibly of an individual with little or no imagination compared with another endowed with it in full measure. However, if Harris was undoubtedly the more sensitive as well as the more literate of the two, he was hardly alone in his desire to run away.[56]

If, however, the critical issue at stake in these memoirs is the contrast between the 'manly' Myer and the 'cowardly' Harris, the fact that both were Jewish also demands consideration of the dominant cultural discourse of the period in which the physical condition, not to say psychological disposition, of the Jewish male (and in different ways female) was held to be largely a matter of inherited, but almost entirely negative, racial characteristics. This made Jews *ipso facto* dubious, if not useless, war-fighting material. Indeed, questions of health and sickness are prevalent, even predominant elements in both memoirs; but in that case, how should we respond to these aspects of the narratives? Does Harris's recounting of so much of his war spent in and out of doctors' surgeries attempting to have confirmed that he was neither fit nor 'up to it' prove that Jews really were the congenitally weak-footed, diabetic, neurotic, even degenerate, 'dregs' of society of the recruiting and medical officers' stereotype?[57] Or was Harris consciously, even ingeniously, exploiting these assumptions about Jewish – certainly immigrant Jewish – weakness as a strategy for military service avoidance? By the same token, to what extent was Myer's self-portrayal as the very epitome of tough, sportsmanlike 'manliness' a conscious form of compensation for this alleged Jewish defectiveness? His repeated references to Jewish 'better types' and 'fine specimens' as compared with 'poor material' who, according to him, were unpatriotic 'shirkers' as well as 'poor', suggest that he did have an axe to grind.[58] Was Harris thus knowingly or unknowingly acting to Jewish 'type', while Myer was deliberately and energetically striving to reject it? Or are we in danger of reading too much into these 'texts'?

If textual speculation of this kind may have its strengths and weaknesses, the possible pitfalls of applying received – or even new – historical wisdom becomes more pronounced when we begin searching these memoirs for evidence of ideological predisposition as a criteria by which to understand our protagonists' actions. Harris was insistent that Herzlian Zionism gave a new meaning to his life and to others around him.[59] Myer, on the contrary, could state that Herzl 'did not find favour with me or the majority of British-born Jews'.[60] Taken at face value, and alongside what we already know about these two individuals, one might discern here motivations for particular forms of proactive martial response. Yet reading these memoirs will rapidly disabuse us of such a notion. The labels of Myer the 'assimilationist' and Harris the 'Zionist' can only take us so far in understanding their experience of war – and anti-war. Their stories tell us something that is far more nuanced, complex and multi-layered than anything which mere labels can supply. So what, then, of their stories?

Arnold Harris was born Aaron Astrinsky, though even that was not his true family name, and a considerable part of his richly illustrated personal memoir, written for his grandchildren, deals with shtetl life in Lithuania and growing up in Jewish White-chapel. If the young Harris belonged anywhere, it was to a world of Talmudic learning and *Yiddishkeit*. However, even that, as the memoir makes clear, is not quite accurate. His father had already left the family home in Yurbrik, Kovno province, when Aaron was hardly more than a baby, and it was not until 1900 when he was six years old that he accompanied his mother to 'steal' the German border and so make their way to a family reunion in England. Aaron, now Arnold, was thus like his father an alien; Myer, his younger brother, born in Whitechapel, was British. While the father attempted to eke out an existence as a *heder* teacher and the family attached themselves to the sub-culture of Machzike Hadass orthodoxy, subtle and less subtle changes began to have an impact on this traditional life rhythm.

The young Harris, clearly a bright lad but one who failed to get a scholarship to somewhere better, was educated at a local Board School where he began to evince considerably more interest in secular reading than in the Hebrew and religious schooling he was also receiving in the afternoons and evenings. By the time he was a late teenager and on a London County Council scholarship to train as a teacher, Harris had moved sufficiently far from the cloistered world of Talmudic studies to consider Blake, William Morris and Ibsen as among his pantheon of literary heroes, to have styled himself a rationalist agnostic and humanist and to have become a regular Sunday attender at the South Place Ethical Society. Unlike some of his East End contemporaries of a similar disposition, however, Harris did not reject or cut himself off from his Jewish background. On the contrary, although he had stopped laying *tefillin* [phylacteries], Harris continued to go to synagogue, to observe *kashrut*, high days and holy days, and indeed, to teach part-time Hebrew and religious classes as his father had done before him. If, in other words, Harris had moved beyond the world of traditional Jewish faith and practice, it was certainly not to take on a non-Jewish identity. Rather, Harris's Jewishness now manifested itself in classic outsider terms, as an *epikoros*, or in his own words, as a 'dilettante' or 'human bundle of contradictions'.[61]

Two other aspects of his narrative of growing up in the East End particularly stand out. First, though the family, via his mother, was as willing as the next to receive handouts from what were commonly referred to as the Philpott Street ladies – that is, rich Anglo-Jewish establishment women involved in charitable philanthropic work – this did not extend to socializing and acculturating themselves according to a preordained set of rules. Arnold's forays into the world of the establishment-run Brady Jewish Working Boys' Club proved not to be a success (ironically, given that in later life he was briefly a Brady Club warden). The efforts of his brother, Myer, to join the Jewish Lads' Brigade seem to have foundered after a couple of visits. The memoir does not offer an explanation for these particular failures. What is evident is that the establishment social scene did not suit the Harris family; even a JLB officer's effort to visit their dwelling in person in order to plead that Myer might stay in the Brigade was firmly rebuffed.

Second, and in marked contrast to their rejection of the 'assimilationist' opportunities at hand, the Harrises were, from the moment they arrived in England, clearly very enthusiastic Zionists. This again marks the family out as unusual, even perhaps rather independently minded, given that membership of an Orthodox Jewish congregation at the time was usually synonymous with indifference or even hostility to Jewish nationalism. Be that as it may, the Harrises' Zionist commitment extended considerably beyond involvement in their local Beth Zion in Commercial Road. Harris's memoirs proudly relate, for instance, the time his mother crossed London unaccompanied only a few months after having arrived in the capital, to attend the Fourth Zionist Congress at Queens Hall, while Arnold himself seems to have been dragged from pillar to post by his parents to hear speakers like Shmaryahu Levin, Israel Zangwill and a more staple, local diet of Moses Myer. If orthodoxy, assimilation, and even Tolstoyan humanism, only led to disenchantment for Arnold Harris, the Zionism definitely stuck. Indeed, Harris later averred that the Herzlian message provided the only fixed point in his often confused and contradictory musings.[62]

However, if this upbringing points towards the making of Harris as a proto-nationalist, it did not translate into enthusiasm for, or participation in, Jabotinsky's proposed national military revolution. Indeed, what is striking about the Great War section of the memoir is that there is no mention of the Jewish Regiment at all. One might speculate that the reason for this was Harris's aversion to the brand of Zionism that Jabotinsky espoused. Harris was an avid reader of the strongly Labour Zionist *Die Tsayt*, the East End Yiddish paper of which Moses Myer was long-time editor,[63] and everything that can be surmised from his memoirs, letters and conversations with his son, Ansel, suggests that this was indeed his political orientation.

Certainly, the Labour Zionist tendency would have carried with it some firm principled objections to war, particularly to what was considered an imperialist war, as well as marked sympathies for the revolutions in Russia, especially the first revolution of February 1917. Harris was an occasional visitor to the leftist, anarchist and Russian political refugee clubs in Whitechapel, and much more frequently to Golub's, a radical Hebraica and Yiddish bookseller in Osborne Street. Given these contacts, and indeed the more general ferment in the Jewish East End in the middle of the war, it is inconceivable that Harris would not have known about the organizations and groupings mustering to oppose both conscription and Jabotinsky's recruitment drive. Indeed, Dr Salkind, one of the prominent leaders of the Foreign Jews' Protection Committee, was someone whom Harris knew well. Yet what is also striking about the minutely detailed memoirs is that there is no mention of involvement in any organization of this sort, nor of having been an onlooker, let alone an objector, at any of Jabotinsky's meetings. Harris's leanings towards the left, in other words, did not translate into political action. Nor did he seek to portray himself as a pacifist or conscientious objector. Instead, 'I had made up my mind that I would not surrender to the call-up, not for ideological reasons but out of plain fear'.[64]

We might choose to treat this frank admission as a sign of personal idiosyncrasy. After all, in so doing, Harris not only steps outside an ideological categorization for his actions but also, in attempting to make himself invisible to the State, in a sense steps outside the pages of history. Harris's Great War saga is entirely one of avoidance, dissemblance and escape. Under pressure to enlist from the time of the Military Service Act by his London County Council employees, he relates how he and several other newly qualified teachers who, like himself, were 'Russians', were accompanied by an LCC official to the Russian embassy to encourage their enlistment there, only to be curtly dismissed by a monocled, tsarist gentleman who proclaimed: 'These are not Russians: they are Jews'.[65]

However, having narrowly escaped service in the Russian Army, Harris continued to fret that his 'Russian' papers and B-2 physical grading at an army medical examination would ultimately not shelter him from British military service.[66] In December 1917, with call-up papers in his pocket, Harris strove strenuously to obtain a medical certificate which would show him to be sufficiently physically unfit to entitle him to a downgraded C-3 status and hence, he hoped, full exemption from the army. He learnt, through his father, that he could have his ears punched for a fee but rejected this stratagem when he heard that the man could not guarantee that the resulting deafness would not be permanent.[67] Next, Harris took himself to Harley Street, where in return for £5 – a princely sum – he received a statement from a highly regarded surgeon that he was myopic. Armed with this document, Harris presented himself to the local Army Appeals Tribunal only to have his case for exemption rejected! 'There was', he says, 'no getting out of it this time'.[68]

However, even now, Harris strove to avoid what he must have increasingly thought was unavoidable. Again through his father, he was able to obtain false papers that identified him as an incapacitated soldier. Though being caught and found out with these would have made his position still more untenable, Harris risked going on a 'runner' with the papers to Ireland, where the Military Service Act did not apply. This proved to be a perilous form of flight and was achieved only at the second attempt. Harris's sojourn in the bosom of the small Dublin Jewish community, however, was itself short-lived. After a little less than four months there, he heard news that the representative of the Bolshevik government in London was issuing exemptions from military service following its repudiation of the Anglo-Russian Convention, and also that a challenge to its legality had been mounted in the law courts. Yet on returning to England in April or May 1918, Harris still did not feel safe. In fact the courts upheld the terms of the Convention, so Harris yet again went into hiding, living incognito in a boarding house and only resurfacing when the British government declared an amnesty at the war's end.

Throughout this whole narrative, politics is entirely extrinsic to Harris's behaviour and actions. The Balfour Declaration, for instance, receives no mention, even though he was due for call-up only weeks after it. The only guiding principle was not to be caught and not to go to the front, even though he admitted he was desperately short of money, agonizingly lonely and depressed, and recognized that the easiest thing he could have done to resolve his 'almost unbearable position' was to have given himself up.[69] Yet what is also apparent from his story, in spite of his protestations of loneliness, is how he was accompanied all the way by a panoply of friends, colleagues and acquaintances who were also absentees or deserters. Harris had friends who seem to have agonized as he did about whether to join up in Britain or to do so, under the terms of the Convention, in Russia. On arrival in Dublin he made his way to the home of a relative of one of his East End teacher colleagues, soon meeting up with many school chums who were also 'fly boys', while on his return to London he whiled away the hours with other 'comrades in distress'.[70]

The memoirs, correspondence and papers of other Jewish East Enders, both Russian and British-born, suggest that Harris's experience was far from untypical. Most of Isaac Rosenberg's immediate intellectual circle, for instance, including Sam Winsten, Joseph Leftwich, John Rodker and Lazarus Aaronson, through good fortune or more often subterfuge, avoided conscription.[71] The British-born Rosenberg, of course, despite the rabbinical Lithuanian background that he shared with Harris, did join up, doing so before conscription was enforced. Clearly, not every-body's response was the same. Yet there is not the slightest evidence to suggest that Rosenberg was motivated on ideological grounds. On the contrary, it was poverty that drove him to enlist. As he wrote in December 1915 to his one highly-placed patron, Edward Marsh, at the time Winston Churchill's secretary, 'I never joined the army from patriotic reasons. Nothing can justify war … I thought if I'd join there would be the separation allowance for my mother'.[72] Moreover, everything from the record of Rosenberg, as an army private serving in a front-line unit on the western front, suggests that he detested not only the army and all it stood for, but also the treatment he received from it, not least for being a Jew.[73] His efforts, and those of his family, from the moment of his enlistment in November 1915, were channelled into obtaining a less dangerous, preferably home-front role.[74] At the time of his death in April 1918, during the great German spring offensive, he had been petitioning the War Office to be transferred to the Judeans. However, again there is no evidence to suggest that this came from a burning commitment to the Jabotinsky ideal, so much as a rational personal strategy to attempt to stay alive.[75]

Rosenberg's army record, however, throws important light on why someone like Harris would have done all in his power to avoid service. Putting aside the fear of being killed, Rosenberg's misery had much to do with daily humiliations in camp and in training. He was particularly sensitive to foul food, bad boots that crippled his feet, and constant bullying.[76] Like Harris, he was not physically strong, which would have made enduring these conditions all the harder. Of course, one might say that this was the lot of anybody, Jewish or non-Jewish, who happened to be from a sheltered background, emotionally sensitive, or physically soft. However, there were strong social and cultural, including dietary, reasons why this should have particularly applied to recent Jewish immigrants, especially those like Harris, and to a slightly lesser extent Rosenberg, whose social existence was largely confined, if not circumscribed, by their immediate familial and communal surroundings. For those living in the Jewish ethnic enclaves, moreover, hostility and resistance to military service was deeply ingrained. Rosenberg's father had fled to England to avoid mandatory conscription in Russia in the late 1880s.[77] Harris's father had assumed a different family name as his own avoidance tactic and, one may speculate, moved to England when the authorities were close to catching up with him. When in late 1917 the younger Harris took false papers, claiming to be somebody else, he was simply following in a well-trodden family tradition. Thousands of other families also upped and left Russia as soon as their sons came close to call-up age.[78] This all happened regardless of ideology and politics – except perhaps as an anti-politics which intuitively, rather than intellectually, rejected the *maskilic* [Enlightenment] wisdom that recruitment would somehow clear the way towards emancipation.[79] And this mode of rejection carried through into the immigrant Jewish experience of the Great War.

Other examples would suggest that this is not the whole picture. A 'wilder' younger brother of Rosenberg, for instance, appears to have enlisted with enthusiasm.[80] There were also some ideologues who joined the Judeans out of conviction, as well as others who joined the ranks of the openly conscientious objectors. Rosenberg's artistic competitor, Mark Gertler, seems to have been in this category, while his better friend, Rodker, did time in the penal colony on Dartmoor for 'conchies'. However, despite Rodker's 'socialist, anti-militarist, anti-capitalist' principles, simply hiding from the authorities, if possible with his girlfriend or girlfriends, seems to have been his preferred course of action.[81] Moreover, if the cases of Rodker and Gertler demonstrate that a more brazenly seditious, consciously political dissent to the war could be a feature of the Jewish immigrant response, it should also be remembered that the 'conscientious' route was much more the hallmark of a specifically English pacifist tradition.[82] For an East End Jewish boy to respond in such terms suggests already having a foot in this camp. If, then, Gertler and Rodker remained not entirely assimilated, their education and partial Anglicization provided them with a self-confidence and familiarity with dominant modes of dissent which would not have been available to the majority of young Jewish men of immigrant background.

I would propose, therefore, that a much more typical response was that of my paternal grandfather, Lou (is) Levene. Born in the East End in 1897, though having spent some of his childhood in a distant White Russian shtetl, the 19-year-old tailor, now permanently domiciled in Whitechapel, responded to his call-up papers in 1916 with an attitude less of duty than of fatalism, because he felt he had no choice. Wounded at Cambrai in 1917, however, he took the opportunity of his first leave from the front to go on permanent absence, doubtless aided by family and friends.[83] Similarly, when Harris made his decision to abscond, he told no one but closest friends and family. For him, as for Lou Levene, these were intensely private responses to the dilemma of military service. If, then, the anti-conscription activities of Jewish socialist and anarchist groups, doubtless counting on the implicit sympathy and support of the immigrants (especially well-read, socialist-inspired ones like Harris), were loud and high-profile, the actual mechanisms and modes of resistance, for the majority, were much less the outcome of an organized and politically-based movement and much more that of families acting to protect husbands, sons and brothers. This same autonomous, family-centred behaviour had been the hallmark of the great process of migration by which they had come to Britain in the first place. With thousands of families now all autonomously resisting military service, it was inevitable that the community would find itself on a collision course with the British State, regardless of any charged ethnic dimension. Yet it was this very ethnic dimension that provided an added and highly ironic twist to the confrontation with the British government, as, in mid-1917, it abruptly appealed to the immigrant not in his capacity as would-be Briton but as patriotic Jew. Which brings us to the second of our two memoirs.

If Arnold Harris was a Jew who through migration had come to live in England, Henry Myer was an Englishman who happened to be a Jew. This is not to belittle his own sense of Jewishness. If Harris, particularly through his mother's descent from the great rabbinical scholar Isaiah Hurewitz, could claim *yichus* [prestige of family], Myer was equally proud of a family history in England dating back to the 1700s which, while successful in business and then the professions, had remained staunchly, endogamously Jewish. The first part of his memoirs, entitled 'Soldiering of Sorts', is indeed all about his family and what they did, not so much in work – though he does make special reference to a cousin who via Clifton public school went on to Sandhurst and a commission in the 10th Hussars – but rather in their spare time. Two things in particular stand out. The first is a total immersion in the volunteer units attached to the army which, after 1908, were reformed as the territorials. Being comfortable and public school-educated, all the male members of the Myer and related family who joined these did so, as one might expect, as officers. The second thing is an equally total immersion in social work activities, particularly running working boys' clubs, mostly, though not exclusively, for Jews. For Henry Myer, the two causes fuse in the person of his cousin, Ernest Alex Myer, later killed on the western front. Ernest was not only an officer in the Second City of London Volunteers, but also a founder of the Brady Street Club, as well as boy scouts and working boys' clubs for non-Jews, in his home town of Maidenhead. In spite of all these commitments, Ernest also managed to find time to be an officer in the Jewish Lads' Brigade.

It is clear from Henry Myer's memoirs that Ernest is his perfect role model. It is also evident that in imparting all this social information Myer has an agenda. For one thing, he wants his readers to know that these types of activities were the norm for his 'sort' of people: 'In fact what I have said about my wife's relations and mine and their social and quasi-military activities was typical of the upper middle class in the Jewish community in and around London'.[84] For another, speaking again of cousin Ernest, 'I mention all these aspects to show that his attitude was conditioned by a concern for the welfare of those under his command or within his sphere of influence'.[85] In other words, according to Myer's received value-system, there are patricians like himself whose role and responsibility is to lead, as distinct from plebeians who should naturally be grateful for the opportunity to be led.

Only now, having carefully crafted his terms of reference, does Henry Myer tell us something about himself, though perhaps, true to his public school education as well as his self-image, this is done without the reader getting much of a sense of the real man, and certainly not of any emotional strengths or weaknesses. The emphasis is all on the 'doing' not the 'being', except, perhaps, for a passing reference to a love of Kipling's poetry. Myer reveals his social view of the world, however, when he explains why he chose Westminster rather than the more obvious Clifton public school – well frequented by Anglo-Jewry with its own Jewish boys' house – on the grounds that the former was 'attracting some fine material ... including some of the less wealthy members of the aristocracy'.[86] What exactly Myer means by 'fine material' is never made quite clear, but throughout the narrative there is a sense – in addition to the social snobbery implicit in this particular sentence – that it involves men whose physical appearance, stature and sporting prowess make them good soldiers. Kitchener's first hundred thousand volunteers, for instance, are described as 'physically magnificent' at least compared 'with the human material the army possessed from 1917 onwards'.[87] Similarly, though Myer's own performance on the school playing fields is not reported, there is an implicit assumption that the values associated with it are directly translatable not only into the basis for decency and civilization but for its martial defense.

Myer's rendition of growing up, with all its emphasis on the School Cadet Corps, drilling, parade and camp, thus replicates the dominant class as well as social Darwinian assumptions of the

Edwardian era. And in spite of his 'Jewish' credentials, ethnicity is clearly secondary. Coming to manhood, for Myer, means being articled, in 1909 at the age of 17, to his father's City law firm, and, more importantly still, taking the exam entitling him to become a junior officer with the 6th (Territorial) battalion, the City of London Rifles. If there is any element of Jewishness here, it is only of the 'muscular' variety espoused by the founder of the Jewish Lads' Brigade, Colonel Albert Goldsmid, though also much in vogue, of course, in broader assimilationist, as well as Zionist, circles concerned to provide an antidote to the alleged problem of Jewish degeneracy.[88] But before 1914 Myer was not much interested in Zionism, or indeed in anything that equated patriotism with Jewishness. Like the many Jewish city businessmen, professionals and stockbrokers who were his officer colleagues in the City of London Rifles,[89] it was for Britannia that Myer tuned his muscles and prepared himself for war.

Most of the next section of 'Soldiering of Sorts' confronts us directly with its horror. Myer and his battalion were posted to France – and the trenches – in mid-1915. Soon he was attending the funerals, conducted mostly by the Revd Adler, of many of his Jewish officer relatives and friends. He himself was seriously wounded at the battle of Loos in September, sent home for recuperation to England, but eventually returned to France as an officer in a different regiment, this time to witness at first hand some of the worst warfare on the western front, in the late summer and autumn of 1917. In the period of his recuperation, Myer, doubtless utilizing his legal background, served at home presiding over tribunals for those seeking exemption from military service, often on conscientious grounds. He recounts that he found this task distasteful. It is perhaps at this point that his life and that of Harris came close to intersecting. Indeed, it is with the issue of the immigrant Jewish abstainers from military service that Myer's memoirs take on a remarkable and wholly unexpected turn.

As we have seen so far, Myer was a thoroughgoing product of Anglo-Jewry, certainly correctly, even proudly, carrying an outward commitment to Jewish ritual and practice into his army service but evincing no signs of a Jewish political ideology other than that of the liberal emancipatory sort. Zionism was very far from his mind when he went to war. However, the issue of immigrant non-participation clearly did touch a raw nerve. Requested by the War Office in late 1917 to consider transfer to a senior officer position with the newly formed Jewish battalions of the Royal Fusiliers, Myer, after much apparently agonized consideration, agreed. His explanation for his decision is revealing:

> I felt that every anglicized or even partly anglicized Jew would have long ago joined the armed services, for this had been my experience and that of my older cousins and friends doing social work among the Communities. I reckoned that in London, Leeds, Manchester, Glasgow, Cardiff and the like, the man who would be compulsorily recruited at this late date to the Jewish battalions of the Royal Fusiliers would be of poor material in a military sense and would need reasonably acceptable interpreters or mediators. I was not the only one similarly motivated and looking back we not only have clear consciences but feel some pride in decisions which inevitably meant a sacrifice of careers.[90]

Myer's initial rationalization for joining what became the Judeans, in other words, had nothing to do with Zionism. On the contrary, his motivation came out of a sense of belonging and duty to a wider *British* community. Though Myer clearly saw a connectedness between himself and the immigrant recruits he henceforth encountered, it was not unlike that of the colonial officer to his native *askaris*. On arrival at the Crow Hill training depot at Plymouth, where he was to serve as second in command to Colonel Fred Samuel's 40th Battalion he could, in fact, hardly disguise his contempt for the recruits: 'The 38th Battalion had already taken the cream of the rather poor milk that the British Isles had yielded from the residue of the Jewish community'. All the other 'serviceable' Jewish men had already 'enlisted, been killed or permanently disabled'. Myer was prepared to admit that there were a few young lads in the 40th who had been with the Jewish Lads' Brigade or working boys' clubs and were 'fine specimens'. This was, however, in contrast to 'types to whom soldiers and soldiering were anathema' and who queued up in droves for sick parade. Myer was relentless in harrying them:

> Few people would have understood how men who, and whose relatives, owed so much to the hospitality they had enjoyed in the United Kingdom, could have refrained from

showing gratitude in the form of sharing burdens which fell upon all Britishers.[91]

The only saving grace in all this, according to Myer, was that such men were going to be led by 'better types' of Jews who were 'physically in their prime and imbued with the ideals of leadership'.[92] The recalcitrant immigrant Jew, the individual who might have been Harris in other words, was going to be led out of his torpor, shame and effeteness by Myer, led not only into the rigours of soldiering and modern warfare but, thereby, into the light of state and societal acceptance.

Myer was never able to dispense with his negative assessment of the immigrants. However, a new and entirely more upbeat tenor to his narrative begins to emerge once his battalion had been posted to Egypt and then Palestine, in the summer of 1918. By this time the 40th had shed most of its C-3 recruits, whether 'real or imaginary', into a reserve 42nd battalion and was filling up instead with Palestinian Jews, who had been recruited either via America or *in situ*. With the battalion thus converted, bar its officer element, into a wholly Palestinian outfit, Myer starts waxing lyrical. 'Proud to be with the recruits' and of the belief 'that the battalion will be pretty satisfactory ... because Jews have plenty of imagination, guts and gumption', he is soon writing to his fiancée Louisa (Louie) Solomons:

> Aren't the Jews a marvellous race? ... some little more civilised than their ancestors 3,000 years ago while others control the destinies of great nations – almost of the world. Yet all are of the same stock, all have characteristics in common, quite apart from those of creed.[93]

If there are stirrings of a specifically Jewish national consciousness here full accolades are reserved only for the Palestinians. True, one of their number, David Ben-Gurion, Myer portrays as not only 'thrusting' but as one who had 'constituted himself prime agitator, leader, demagogue, advocate, preacher and mouthpiece for and of nationalist militarism'.[94] However, in Myer's opinion, the likes of Ben-Gurion, Ben-Zvi, Dov Hoss and Joseph L. Cohen 'are far preferable to the "Schneiderim" [tailors] of London and Leeds. They are well developed mentally and *physically and they are men*' [my emphasis].[95] What Myer means by this is that they are good military material. While Jewish Cairenes and Alexandrines are cursorily dismissed as not having 'a very high order of intelligence or physical development, the agricultural life of the Colonists' by contrast 'has made them hardy and much more amenable to discipline than other Jews with whom I have been brought into contact'. Myer concludes his panegyric with the words: 'I think they are worthy representatives of the race'.[96]

It does seem, therefore, as if several months of close contact with Zionists, and with Palestine itself, began a process through which an otherwise 100 per cent British-Jewish patriot acquired the makings of a Jewish nationalist one. Myer may have been guarded in his own self-assessment – 'I am only a sympathiser with their views and not an active Zionist' – but there is no getting away from the fact that a sympathy had been instilled.[97] Yet it is interesting to note how this shift transpired. Certainly, there is evidence to suggest that Myer's first-hand confrontation with aspects of anti-Semitism in the army may have forced a personal re-assessment. 'Whilst we were treated by the vast majority of our fellow Englishmen in similar fashion to our many Gentile friends', he wrote, 'there was a substantial number of Gentiles who either did not understand or did not want to associate with, or even disliked British Jews, no matter how assimilated they were, or appeared to be'.[98] Encountering what he believed to be indifference or even active encouragement by the British military authorities to native non-Jewish accusations and abuse against the Judeans in Palestine, Myer's sense of 'belonging' to Britain may well have been jolted, even become detached. Contact with the views of active Zionist ideologues in his battalion may also have facilitated this disenchantment. However, having belonged once, Myer had the capacity to belong again. And in the fit, muscular and martial attributes of battalion members like Hoss and Ben-Zvi he had something with which he could readily identify, applaud and embrace. The Myer version of Zionism offered a perfectly acceptable supplement to, or even replacement for, a British nationalism which, through his unexpected exposure to anti-Semitism, Myer now found to be wanting.[99] In this Myer version, Zionism simply replicated the attributes of his first patriotic love for Britain: the idea of nation linked to male prowess in war. What had enthused all those Clifton and Cheltenham public school boys and those from the Jews Free School, the Working Boys' Clubs and the Jewish Lads' Brigades[100] to offer their

lives for 'King and country' was ultimately malleable and trans-
ferable into service for Zion. In the end, the leap from Adler's
pantheon of heroes to Jabotinsky's was, for Myer, a perfectly
logical one.

However, if Myer's war service was founded on a premise of
national belonging, was it its lack that led Harris and so many
thousands of other immigrants like him to hide, abscond or
desert? On one level this was certainly the case. Britain's war,
Russia's war, was simply not their business. They had no illusions
about anti-Semitism so there was nothing much to shock when,
as in Rosenberg's wartime experience, it was encountered in all
its raw unpleasantness. Nor did the immigrants have illusions
about the nature of war itself. Rosenberg put it tersely: 'The more
men the more war'.[101] A rather more longwinded Harris agreed:
'Obviously old Woden's hunger was insatiable and he had to be
fed: he did not, now, discriminate as to the quality of the human
cannon fodder'.[102] Nor did Harris have much time or sympathy
for bodies like the Jewish Lads' Brigade who proselytized war's
cause. Hardly was it over, or he himself out of personal danger,
before he was writing to the *Jewish Chronicle* chastizing the
Brigade, which he said would do much better if it would foster
'peace ideals and the success of a League of Peoples'.[103]

Was there anything, then, that would have made immigrants
like Harris change their tune? Could an appeal to Zionism have
transcended the limitations inherent in the immigrant situation?
Could it have created a sense of belonging where there was
otherwise supposedly none? Jabotinsky, speaking of the East End
'tailors' in the Judeans, dismissed the possibility outright: 'I saw
nothing of any collective life among them. They had no common
interests, held no meetings, displayed no tendencies to any kind
of unification'.[104] However, perhaps these views tell us more about
Jabotinsky than they do about the immigrants. They did belong:
to their families, friends and community – and some like Harris
considered themselves to be Zionists – but that was no good
reason in itself to don military uniform. By the end of 1917 –
precisely the time, of course, of the Balfour Declaration and of the
Bolshevik seizure of power – the very idea of the 'nation' as
something worth fighting for was for many young men of military
age beginning to look not just jaded and outmoded, but even
ridiculous. If Jabotinsky's national military revolution was hardly
something tangible or relevant to the majority of Russian-Jewish

youth in Britain, the signposts for belonging closer to home were hardly more encouraging. At the first 'national' commemoration of British war service, held at the Cenotaph in 1919, Russian Jews alongside Indians, Africans and Afro-Caribbeans who had served with British forces were pointedly excluded from the march-past and parade.[105] Risking death for Britain did not apparently confer entitlement to civil or social acceptance.

However, a more general disenchantment amongst the great mass of combatants had already set in by the end of 1917. Few front-line soldiers on either side were still fighting or being impelled by ideals of patriotism, loyalty or the defense of civilization. The bonds which held them there were the bonds of comradeship and the knowledge of their families back home.[106] The distance between the active participant in the war and the passive desister was beginning to narrow. The rhetoric of politicians and generals was beginning to wear thin. Ideals of brotherhood and universalism were beginning to have an edge over their national competitors. Even Myer was having his doubts. He remembered the case of a Jewish would-be conscientious objector and agreed that 'there was much to be said on Rodker's behalf'.[107] His doubt turned to public remonstrance when, in early 1919, he was himself refused permission for rapid demobilization. Yet he also declined the entreaties of Dov Hoss and others that he stay in Palestine to assist the Jewish national cause. Indeed, Myer's personal agenda, by now, was clear. He had a young wife in England, and it was to her that he wished to return as speedily as possible.[108] Harris and Myer were at the war's end, perhaps, not so far apart after all. Myer ultimately had no more wish than Harris to be a warrior, a new Judas Maccabeus. If from the outset Harris had resisted the notion as having no part in his sense of Jewish, even Zionist, identity, Myer, perhaps through the sheer desire to go on living, was rapidly moving away from it too. This desire, shared by millions of Jewish and non-Jewish men alike, flew in the face of the war's essential, self-perpetuating logic. Only through a constant supply of yet more men willing to fight and die could it sustain itself. Yet this could only be achieved by imbuing them with an idea of national belonging as if it were the highest, most sacred ideal. For those who worshipped at this sacrificial altar, the libations would be duly made. For Jews living in Britain: if not a British altar, then a Zionist one. To go against the grain, to reject both, was truly to place oneself between a rock and a hard place.

NOTES

1. Revd Michael Adler, *British Jewry Book of Honour* (London: Caxton, 1922). See also a shortened version, *The Jews of the Empire and the Great War* (New York: Hodder and Stoughton, 1919).
2. These included a testimonial from Lord Northcliffe whose paper, the *Daily Mail*, had been prominent in lambasting alleged Jewish Army avoidance. See Sharman Kadish, *Bolsheviks and British Jews: The Anglo-Jewish Community, Britain and the Russian Revolution* (London: Frank Cass, 1992), p. 47.
3. See 'St George in the East and Wapping Roll of Honour', n.d., Museum of the Jewish East End (archive), Sternberg Centre, London.
4. Cecil Roth, 'Jews in the Defence of Britain', *Transactions of the Jewish Historical Society of England*, 15 (1939–45), pp. 1–29.
5. The charge made in Vladimir Jabotinsky, *The Jewish Legion* (New York: Bernard Ackerman, 1945), pp. 88, 101.
6. J.H. Patterson, *With the Zionists in Gallipoli* (New York: George Doran, 1916); *With the Judeans in the Palestine Campaign* (London: Hutchinson, 1922). Patterson himself was not Jewish, though a committed Zionist supporter.
7. Michael Berkowitz, *Western Jewry and the Zionist Project 1914–1933* (Cambridge: Cambridge University Press, 1997), pp. 7–25.
8. See the contemporary account of Redcliffe N. Salaman, *Palestine Reclaimed, Letters from a Jewish Officer in Palestine* (London: George Routledge and Sons, 1922); and latterly, Elias Gilner, *War and Hope: A History of the Jewish Legion* (New York: Herzl Press, 1969).
9. See, for example, David Kessler, 'General Knowledge', *Jewish Chronicle*, 8 December 1995, on the role of General Sir George de Symons Barrow, a Christian scion of an Anglo-Sephardi family, in the British Army breakthrough at Beersheva, November 1917.
10. Major Henry D. Myer, 'Soldiering of Sorts', ms, Imperial War Museum 79/17/1; Arnold Harris, 'Memoirs', unpaginated ms. Quoted by kind permission, Ansel Harris, London. See also Ansel Z. Harris, 'From the Memoirs of Arnold Harris', in Aubrey Newman (ed.), *The Jewish East End 1840–1939* (London: Jewish Historical Society of England, 1981), pp. 339–47.
11. David Feldman, 'Was Modernity Good for the Jews?', in Bryan Cheyette and Laura Marcus (eds), *Modernity, Culture and 'the Jew'* (Cambridge: Polity Press, 1998), pp. 171–87. See also his *Englishmen and Jews: Social Relations and Political Culture 1840–1914* (New Haven, CT and London: Yale University Press, 1994) and David Cesarani, 'Introduction', in Cesarani (ed.), *The Making of Modern Anglo-Jewry*, (Oxford: Basil Blackwell, 1990), pp. 1–11.
12. J.M. Winter, *The Great War and the British People* (Basingstoke: Macmillan, 1986), p. 28.
13. Ibid., p. 27.
14. Ibid., pp. 42–5.
15. See, for example, 'Bravery of Jewish Soldiers', *Jewish Chronicle*, 23 October 1914.
16. V.D. Lipman, *A History of the Jews in Britain since 1858* (Leicester: Leicester University Press, 1991), p. 140; Adler, *Jews of the Empire*, p. 4.
17. Lipman, *History of the Jews*, p. 141.
18. Ibid., pp. 131–2. See Adler, *Jews of the Empire*, p. 5, for a fuller casualty breakdown.
19. Jabotinsky, *Jewish Legion*, p. 160, refers rather vaguely to over 1,000.
20. See Lipman, *History of the Jews*, p. 146. Adler, *Jews of the Empire*, p. 4, is equally

opaque: 'Among the male population, a large proportion of Jews of alien birth were not available for service'.

21. Winter, *Great War*, p. 37.

22. Ibid., pp. 42–5; Linda Colley, *Britons: Forging the Nation 1707–1837* (London: Vintage, 1996), p. 254, on the Fen country; Bruce Chatwin, *On the Black Hill* (London: Picador, 1983), on mid-Wales.

23. Todd Endelman, *The Jews of Georgian England 1714–1830: Tradition and Change in a Liberal Society* (Philadelphia, PA: Jewish Publication Society of America, 1979). The 'old' historiography is examined in Cesarani, *Making of Modern Anglo-Jewry*, pp.1–11. See also Nadia Valman 'Editorial', *Jewish Culture and History*, 1, 1 (1998), pp. 1–4.

24. See Feldman, *Englishmen and Jews*, Part 3, 'The State, the Nation and the Jews 1880–1914'; Geoffrey Alderman, *Modern British Jewry* (Oxford: Clarendon Press, 1992); Eugene C. Black, *The Social Politics of Anglo-Jewry 1880–1920* (Oxford: Basil Blackwell, 1988), pp. 302–28; Tony Kushner, 'The End of the "Anglo-Jewish Progress Show": Representations of the Jewish East End, 1887–1987', in Tony Kushner (ed.), *The Jewish Heritage in British History: Englishness and Jewishness* (London: Frank Cass, 1992), pp. 78–89.

25. W.J. Fishman, *East End Jewish Radicals, 1875–1914* (London: Duckworth, 1975), Ch. 11, 'Strikes and Sidney Street'.

26. Mark Levene, *War, Jews and the New Europe: The Diplomacy of Lucien Wolf, 1914–1919* (Oxford: Littman Library of Jewish Civilisation, 1992), pp. 23–6, 48–51; 'The Frontiers of Genocide: Jews in the Eastern War Zones, 1914–20 and 1941', in Panikos Panayi (ed.), *Minorities in Wartime* (Leamington Spa: Berg, 1993), pp. 83–117.

27. See David Cesarani, 'An Embattled Minority: The Jews in Britain During the First World War', *Immigrants and Minorities*, 8.1, 2 (1989), pp.61–81; Panikos Panayi, 'The Hidden Hand: British Myths about German Control of Britain during the First World War', *Immigrants and Minorities*, 7, 3 (1988), pp. 253–72.

28. Interview with Gordon Hyams (b. 1898), formerly Jewish Lads' Brigade and Royal Flying Corps veteran, Putney, November 1990. See also Richard A. Voeltz, 'A Good Jew and a Good Englishman: The Jewish Lads' Brigade, 1894–1922', *Journal of Contemporary History*, 23, 1 (1988), pp. 119–27; Sharman Kadish, *A Good Jew and a Good Englishman : The Jewish Lads' and Girls' Brigade, 1895–1995* (London: Vallentine Mitchell, 1995), pp. 55–7, 60–1.

29. Cesarani, 'Embattled Minority'.

30. Editorial and 'Mentor', *Jewish Chronicle*, 7 January 1916.

31. Evelyn Wilcock, 'The Revd John Harris: Issues in Anglo-Jewish Pacifism 1914–18', *Jewish Historical Studies*, 30 (1987–88), pp. 163–78.

32. See Joseph Cohen, *Journey to the Trenches, The Life of Isaac Rosenberg 1890–1918* (London: Robson Books, 1975), p. 114, for the story of how the artist David Bomberg was turned away on account of his accent and beard.

33. Quoted in Peter West, 'Rank Outsiders', *The Listener*, 8 November 1990, p. 6. See also David Killingray, 'All the King's Men? Blacks in the British Army in the First World War, 1914–1918', in Rainer Lotz and Ian Pegg (eds), *Under the Imperial Carpet: Essays in Black History, 1780–1950* (Crawley: Rabbit Press, 1986), pp. 164–81.

34. See Sander Gilman, *The Jew's Body* (New York and London: Routledge, 1991); Winter, *Great War*, pp. 15–16, 62.

35. See Public Record Office HO 45/10895, Sir Basil Thomson to J.F. Henderson, 14 September 1916; CAB 23/5, WC 329, War Cabinet minutes, 23 January 1918. Also published in David Englander (ed.), *A Documentary History of Jewish Immigrants in Britain 1840–1920* (Leicester, London and New York:

Leicester University Press, 1994), pp. 325, 334–5. Such wartime prejudices need to be set against British pre-war cultural 'constructions' of Jews as devious, treacherous, filthy, amoral cowards, the ultimate expression of which was George du Maurier's Svengali. See Bryan Cheyette, *Constructions of the 'Jew' in English Literature and Society: Racial Representations 1875–1945* (Cambridge: Cambridge University Press, 1993); Daniel Pick, *War Machine: The Rationalisaiton of Slaughter in the Modern Age* (New Haven, CT and London: Yale University Press, 1993), pp. 118–19, 127–8 and Pick, *Svengali's Web: The Alien Enchanter in Modern Culture* (New Haven, CT and London: Yale University Press, 2000).

36. On the development of 'the Foreign Jews' Protection Committee against Conscription, Deportation to Russia and Compulsory Military Service' see Kadish, *Bolsheviks and British Jews*, pp. 197–206. Two thousand Polish miners in Ayrshire, who were technically Russian subjects, were also affected by the government's enlistment proposals.

37. Quoted in Lipman, *History of the Jews*, p. 143; Cesarani, 'Embattled Minority' (see note 27), p. 67, describes Samuel's predicament as 'an exquisitely agonising position'.

38. No more than 700 in total according to David Yisraeli; see his 'The Struggle for Zionist Military Involvement in the First World War, 1914–1917', in Pinhas Artzi (ed.), *Bar-Ilan Studies in History* (Ramat-Gan: Bar-Ilan University Press, 1978), pp. 209, 211.

39. See Julia Bush, *Behind the Lines, East London Labour 1914–1919* (London: Merlin, 1984), Ch. 6, 'The Jews and the War'.

40. Kadish, *Bolsheviks and British Jews*, p. 47.

41. Ibid., pp. 50–2; Cesarani, 'Embattled Minority' (see note 27), pp. 72–4. Similar accusations were made in World War II. See Tony Kushner, *The Persistence of Prejudice: Antisemitism in British Society during the Second World War* (Manchester: Manchester University Press, 1989).

42. Lipman, *History of the Jews*, p. 145.

43. Englander, *Documentary History*, pp. 328–30, for the full text of the Convention.

44. Lipman, *History of the Jews*, p. 146.

45. Winter, *Great War*, pp. 31–7, for 'Pals' and other 'fancy' units, and Cesarani, 'Embattled Minority' (see note 27), pp. 69–70, on Anglo-Jewish rejection of Captain Webber's original scheme.

46. Yisraeli, 'The Struggle' (see note 38), pp. 205–6; Jabotinsky, *The Jewish Legion*, p. 63. Jabotinsky's struggle compares and contrasts with efforts to create a Polish Legion under Allied or Central Power sponsorship. See Z.A.B. Zeman, *A Diplomatic History of the First World War* (London: Weidenfeld and Nicholson, 1971), pp. 342–7.

47. Mark Levene, 'The Balfour Declaration: A Case of Mistaken Identity', *English Historical Review*, 107 (1992), pp. 54–77.

48. David Vital, *Zionism: The Crucial Phase* (Leicester: Leicester University Press, 1994), p. 229; Shmuel Almog, 'Anti-Semitism as a Dynamic Phenomenon: "The Jewish Question" in England at the End of the First World War', *Patterns of Prejudice*, 21, 4 (1987), p. 7.

49. Levene, *War, Jews*, pp. 146–7; Cesarani, 'Embattled Minority' (see note 27), pp. 70–1. However, the strongest opposition to the Jewish Legion idea came from the Zionist executive in Copenhagen, doubtless fearing – on the record of the Turkish genocide of its Armenian population in 1915–16 – that a Jewish pro-Entente military manifestation might lead to similar retribution against the Yishuv.

50. See *Jewish Regiment Committee, August 1917 to August 1919* (London, 1920), p. 3, for the delegations and counter delegations to the War Office, 30 August and 5 September 1917.
51. The 38th, 39th and 40th Battalions. A partially constituted 42nd was kept in reserve.
52. Cesarani, 'Embattled Minority' (see note 27), p. 72; *Jewish Regiment* (see note 50), p. 4.
53. Jabotinsky, *Jewish Legion*, p. 159.
54. CAB 23/5 WC 329, minutes of War Cabinet meeting, 23 January 1918, quoted in full in Englander, *Documentary History*, pp. 354–5.
55. Poems quoted from Bernard Kops, 'Wild Honey', *Jewish Chronicle Magazine*, 30 November 1990.
56. Ansel Harris, in conversation, has described his father as a writer manqué.
57. See Winter, *Great War*, pp. 15–16. More generally Gilman, *The Jew's Body* and his *Franz Kafka: The Jewish Patient* (London: Routledge, 1995); George L. Mosse, *Nationalism and Sexuality: Respectability and Abnormal Sexuality in Modern Europe* (New York: Howard Fertig, 1985).
58. Myer (see note 10), pp. 79, 93, 95, 97–8, 106.
59. Arnold Harris, letter to Elizabeth and Ansel Harris, 16 January 1965, Arnold Harris papers.
60. Myer, 'Soldiering' (see note 10), p. 78.
61. Harris, letter to Ansel and Elizabeth.
62. Ibid.
63. Kadish, *Bolsheviks and British Jews*, pp. 185–7.
64. Harris, 'Memoirs' (see note 10).
65. Ibid.
66. Though technically only those passed as A-1 were eligible for combat units, manpower shortages and medical examination workloads often led to unfit men being passed for active service. By 1917, B-2 and C-3 grades were also being required for auxiliary roles. See Winter, *Great War*, pp. 53–61.
67. That this may have been an extensive and time-honoured practice was brought to my attention recently when an American-Jewish friend, Shifra Sharlin, told me in passing that one of her great uncles died of a punctured ear drum, attempting to avoid Russian military service.
68. Harris, 'Memoirs' (see note 10).
69. Ibid.
70. Ibid.
71. Cohen, *Journey to the Trenches*, p. 39. Also *Memoirs of Other Fronts* (London: Putnam, 1932); the 'anonymous' record by John Rodker. Of the 'Whitechapel Group' circle, Harris was friendly with Aaronson and occasionally frequented the Café Royal, their favourite meeting place.
72. Ian Parsons (ed.), *The Collected Works of Isaac Rosenberg* (London: Chatto and Windus, 1984), letter to Edward Marsh, December 1915, p. 227.
73. Ibid., letters to Sydney Schiff, Lascelles Abercrombie and Miss Seaton, December 1915, March 1916, pp. 224, 230–1.
74. Ibid., various letters mostly to Marsh, 1916–17, requesting assistance for his transfer to other non-combat units or home front work, pp. 228–9, 242, 251. See also Cohen, *Journey to the Trenches*, pp. 1–3, 136.
75. By contrast, Peter Lawson in a review of a recent Rosenberg biography – see Deborah Maccoby, *God Made Blind: Isaac Rosenberg, His Life and Poetry* (London: Symposium Press, 1999) – assumes that Rosenberg's application for transfer to the Judeans was impelled by Zionism. See Peter Lawson, 'Zionist of the trenches', *Jewish Chronicle*, 5 March 1999.

76. Take, for example, the following extract from an October 1915 letter to his sometime patron, Sydney Schiff, soon after having joined up and been posted to a depot at Bury St Edmunds, Suffolk:

> I could not get the work I thought I might so I have joined this Bantam Battalion (as I was too short for any other) which seems to be the most rascally affair in the world. I have to eat of a basin together with some horribly smelling scavenger who spits and sneezes into it, etc. It is most revolting, at least up to now – I don't mind the hard sleeping, the stiff marches, etc., but this is unbearable. Besides my being a Jew makes it bad amongst these wretches. I am looking forward to having a bad time altogether.

(Parsons, *Collected Works*, p. 219.)

77. Cohen, *Journey to the Trenches*, p. 7.
78. More work needs to be done on this aspect of the Jewish migration process. Certainly, it has remained a family article of faith that my grandmaternal Witkowsky family from Wloclawek, Russian Poland, left for England, in c.1912, when my great-grandparents' sons came of conscription age.
79. Jillian Davidson, 'Painted with a Black Brush: Recruits in Jewish History and Collective Memory', unpublished lecture, Spiro Institute, London, 8 July 1992.
80. Letter to Leftwich, 8 December 1917, Parsons, *Collected Works*, p. 266, regarding Rosenberg's brother, Dave, who enlisted in tanks and the 'wilder' Elkon, who enlisted with the South African Horse Artillery.
81. For Gertler, see Cohen, *Journey to the Trenches*, p. 131 and note 54, p. 207. For Rodker, see *Memoirs*, pp. 113, 137.
82. See John Rae, *Conscience and Politics: The British Government and the Conscientious Objector to Military Service 1916–1919* (London, New York and Toronto, OT: Oxford University Press, 1970), which, intriguingly, does not refer to Jewish COs at all.
83. Conversation with my father, Alfred Levene. My maternal grandfather, Victor Landsberger (b. 1897), a British-born East Ender of German (non-Jewish) background, also went into 'hiding' in 1916 or 1917. At least one of his brothers, fighting in the British Army, had been previously killed on the western front.
84. Myer, 'Soldiering' (see note 10), p. 2.
85. Ibid.
86. Ibid., p. 4.
87. Ibid., p. 51. See also Winter, *Great War*, pp. 15–16, for contemporary views on 'superior stocks' as opposed to 'dregs' of society.
88. See Gilman, *Jew's Body*, pp. 53–4, especially on Max Nordau's Second Zionist Congress plea for a *Muskeljudentum*. On Goldsmid see Kadish, *A Good Jew*, pp. 115–16; Black, *Social Politics of Anglo-Jewry*, pp. 141–2.
89. Adler, *Jews of the Empire*, p.1, estimates about 600 Jews in all in the British armed services, including special reserves and territorials, at the outbreak of war.
90. Myer, 'Soldiering' (see note 10), p. 79.
91. Ibid., p. 98.
92. Ibid., p. 97.
93. Ibid., letters to Louie Solomons, 3 July and 18 September 1918, pp. 106, 121.
94. Ibid., p. 101.
95. Ibid., to Louie Solomons, 24 December 1918, p. 146.
96. Ibid., to Louie Solomons, 26 September 1918, p. 125.

97. Ibid., to Louie Solomons, 16 January 1919, p. 159.

98. Ibid., p. 79.

99. See Michael Berkowitz, *Zionist Culture and West European Jewry before the First World War* (Cambridge: Cambridge University Press, 1993), for the 'supplemental nationality' argument.

100. These schools and organizations are particularly singled out and praised by Adler, *Jews of the Empire*, pp. 1–2. Jewish Lads' Brigade enlistment was particularly notable. Five hundred and thirty-five men, nearly one third of the British Jews killed, were JLB members. See Voeltz, 'Good Jew' (see note 28), p. 120.

101. Parsons, *Collected Works*, p. 219.

102. Harris, 'Memoirs' (see note 10).

103. Harris, scrapbook, November 1918.

104. Jabotinsky, *Jewish Legion*, p. 159.

105. Tony Kushner, 'Remembering to Forget: Racism and Anti-Racism in Postwar Britain', in Cheyette and Marcus (eds), *Modernity, Culture and 'the Jew'*, p. 230.

106. This sea-change is notably developed in Modris Eksteins, *Rites of Spring: The Great War and the Birth of the Modern Age* (London: Bantam Press, 1989), especially p. 246.

107. Myer, 'Soldiering' (see note 10), p. 68. This was the same Rodker who was Rosenberg's friend and author of *Memoirs of Other Fronts*.

108. Ibid., p. 159. Harris also married soon afterwards.

5

'Morally Depraved and Abnormally Criminal': Jews and Crime in London and New York, 1880–1940

SUSAN L. TANANBAUM

Jews generally have a reputation for being law-abiding. Yet, given the responses of Jews to co-religionists' skirmishes with the law, one might wonder why. Both New York and London saw large increases of Jewish immigrants after 1880.[1] In trying to understand the response of established Jews to newcomers' crimes, a number of issues and questions emerge. What do reactions, both within and beyond the Jewish community, reveal about perceptions of Jews and their self-definitions? What counted as crime and how extensive was it? Did perceptions match reality and what does that suggest about identity?

Comparison of the kinds of crimes committed and the responses they triggered in two cities with large Jewish populations reveals many similar reactions, but also striking differences. The established Anglo-Jewish community generally kept a low profile and virtually begged its immigrant community to behave in ways that would not bring dishonour to Britain's Jews. With crime, however, they often turned to visible responses that they believed would prove their commitment to British ways and distinguish them, at least in part, from their less cultured and poorer relations. In comparison to New York, the British campaign appears to have been more visible, striking in light of the generally greater level of anxiety typical of Anglo-Jewry – and its regular pattern of (over-) expressing deep gratitude to the host nation. New York's Jews, one of many immigrants groups, were arguably more secure about their place in society. They developed a number of similar programmes, but also some that were far more covert (such as the New York *Kehillah*-sponsored Bureau of Social Morals) in nature. Yet, in both countries, several key points emerge from a focus on crime: Jews were less involved in crime than their critics suggested, but not as law-abiding as defenders – Jewish and Gentile – preferred to think.[2] Extensive social service networks, patterns of communal intervention, habits of sobriety, and deep self-consciousness with regard to reputation, resulted in Jewish-sponsored programmes to combat both crime and its tarnish.

Established Jews in New York and London worked hard to eliminate crime and to rehabilitate both the fallen and the community's reputation. Such self-policing indicated a level of perceived vulnerability and an urgent need to redeem their good name. Perception, rather than reality, dictated response; yet the very over-reaction is a barometer on sense of place and level of acceptance. Reflecting Jewish anxieties, criminal activity aroused self-consciousness and, once acknowledged, led to internal communal policing, prevention and rehabilitation programmes in both cities. Established Jews undertook to reduce unlawful activity and deflect attention away from the 'Jewishness' of perpetrators and their crimes. Communal leaders regularly chastized immoral behaviour, an implicit, if uncomfortable admission of a problem of some magnitude.

It is worth a reminder that perceptions of who is a Jew matter. Because definitions of Jews varied, crime statistics are quite unreliable; undoubtedly the many negative images of Jews (Shylock, Fagin, aliens) increased the likelihood of Jews being regarded as criminally inclined. Inconsistencies abound in the language used to describe Jews: 'At various times in history, the Jews have been defined as an ethnic group, a people, a race, a nationality, a community, a linguistic group, a culture and a religion.'[3] While an old debate, it raises at least two cautions. First, perceptions of Jews have varied widely; and, second, the impreciseness of the definition means comparative studies, especially those dependent on statistics, use the same term to describe different kinds of 'samples'. Even among those who claim that Jews are not a race, some fall back on language and descriptions that reveal greater ambiguity or argue that even if Jews are no longer a race, they once were.[4] At the very least, Jews stood out;

many observers viewed them as foreign or peculiar. As David Englander noted, 'the existence of a Jewish racial type to which individuals corresponded or to which they deviated was taken for granted' by commentators, Jewish and Gentile, at the turn of the century. A variety of factors, such as concern about the financial and social impact of the newcomers, a sense of their unassimilability, questions about loyalty, and distaste for habits – real and imagined – shaped responses to Jews.

According to some scholars, this 'type' had physical, as well as mental, manifestations, some positive, some negative, and nearly always exotic.[5] Jacob Riis, writing at the end of the nineteenth century in New York, portrayed Jews as highly materialistic. In 'Jewtown' thrift was 'at once its strength and its fatal weakness'. Jews would starve themselves and work themselves 'to the point of physical exhaustion', all because 'Money is their God'.[6] Bryan Cheyette cautions us against assuming a static literary 'racial construction' of 'the Jew'. He argues that writers' images related 'to their own literary and political concerns', which led to a wide range 'of contradictory and over-determined representations of "the Jew"'. Such mutable characterizations were in themselves unsettling.[7] References to deicide, usury and clannishness have long been common in religious writings, popular culture, and literature; all play a role in creating images of Jews.[8] Established Jews internalized many of these characterizations, believing that 'the outside world is not capable of making minute discrimination between Jew and Jew, and forms its opinion of Jews in general as much, if not more, from them [immigrant Jews] than from the Anglicized portion of the community'.[9] Clearly, identity and identification are complex matters, deeply affected by internal and external perceptions.

Despite contradictory assumptions about the extent of crime, the available statistics, as faulty as they are, indicate that Jews did participate in crime, especially at the turn of the century. They were not, however, disproportionately criminal. To the extent they broke the law, Jews gravitated toward crimes against property, not persons. According to Todd Endelman, Jews in Georgian England became involved in crime as 'the outgrowth of poverty in general' and not because of 'their immediate historical experience as Jews'. Prior to the mid-eighteenth century, few Jews in England committed crimes. The numbers increased after mid-century and included 'pickpockets, housebreakers, receivers, forgers, brothel-keepers and swindlers'. Jews became especially known as receivers of stolen goods. Strikingly, complaints about criminality were rare during the controversy over the 1753 Jew Bill. Endelman concluded that while it is impossible to quantify Jewish criminality precisely, most 'were probably no more dishonest or no more virtuous than their English counterparts'. Many Christians did, however, perceive Jews in stereotypical and undifferentiated terms and assumed that they had 'deep-seated criminal instincts'.[10] Beliefs about Jewish criminal propensities derived from racialized assumption about individualism, hyper-sexuality, competitiveness (*homo economicus*), separatism and a talmudically trained intellect.[11]

Even at the peak of attention to the alien immigration at the turn of the century, police and contemporary observers tended to hold conflicting views on Jews. Either they were sober, law-abiding, and hard-working (if to a fault), or they were excessively criminal. Historian Bernard Gainer notes 'immigrants won wide acclaim for cleaning up some of the worst streets in East London'. Brothels disappeared and Jews rarely contributed to the ranks of 'habitual criminals'.[12] Isaac Hourwich made a similar claim for New York. After citing evidence from 1864 on the foul and crowded housing occupied by 'Teuton and Celtic stock', he contended that those conditions were:

> ... a thing of the past. The typical tenement house in the Jewish and Italian sections of New York to-day is a decided improvement on the dwellings of the Irish and Germans in the same section a generation or two ago.[13]

Other views though, were common. A *Daily Mail* article from 1904, for example, described by a Metropolitan Police report as 'a fair and impartial account of the state of things', characterized Britain's Jewish immigrant community as penniless 'uninvited guests' who dislodged English citizens. Competitors exported 'maimed' and 'criminal' elements to England – and left England to pay the bill.[14] Various leaders of the Jewish community, among them Stuart Samuel MP, defended Jews against such charges. He pointed out that in 1903 there were only 1,753 aliens on the rates [local poor taxes] and 652 criminals and that far larger numbers of aliens 'pay the rates'.[15] Nonetheless, several years later, in 1911, the *Standard* claimed that in Britain: 'Degenerate as the [immigrant] parents are, they are hard-working, sober and law-abiding. There is a marked change for the worse in the children, who are unsober, immoral, lazy and full of natural vices'.[16] The newspaper described Jewish immigrants as 'morally depraved and abnormally criminal', although figures compiled in 1911 by Britain's Jewish Board of Deputies (JBD) suggested that the percentage of criminals among Russians and Russian-Poles, the group typically used to estimate Britain's Jews, compared favourably with other nationalities in Britain.[17] For example, in the UK in 1909, compared to Russian women, twice as many German and French women, were recommended for deportation. While Jews in Britain could not claim a total absence of Jewish criminal activity, figures from the Visitation Committee of the United Synagogue (the Anglicized Orthodox umbrella group) indicate there were decreasing numbers of Jewish criminals between 1904 and 1910, despite increasing numbers of Jews.[18]

Most evidence suggests Jews were not delinquent out of proportion to their numbers. Lady Battersea, daughter of Louisa de Rothschild, for example, who visited Aylesbury prison for 18 years, met only five Jews.[19] As with many other issues related to alien settlement, the press focused on Jews, highlighting their deeds and misdeeds. Newspapers did not identify other criminals by religion, and the word 'Jew' caught readers' eyes. This gave rise to terms such as 'Jew crimes' that were 'used unofficially by many officials and newspaper reporters' and usually implied charges of business fraud. Jews' only vindication, claimed Basil Henriques, warden of the Bernhard Baron Settlement in East London, was that these infractions were 'were not crimes of violence'.[20]

In New York, by the closing years of the nineteenth century, the Jewish community had also begun to acknowledge some Jewish participation in crime, and their responsibility to face this unpleasant reality and to assist their co-religionists. The establishment of the Society for the Aid of Jewish Prisoners in 1893 indicated recognition of problems and a commitment to provide advice and some money to keep prisoners from recidivism.[21] As the president's report asserted:

> We feel that, when the fallen ones are of our faith, the effort to save them makes a more direct appeal to our sympathies, with a correspondingly greater desire for the best results.

And the vast number of our co-religionists who are in these straits is so appalling, that we dare not close our eyes to the facts, as we have in the past; but, knowing the existing evil, we must face it and do our best to mitigate its dire consequences.[22]

The extent of Jewish criminality garnered even more attention at the outset of the twentieth century. Whether mythic or not, many writers during the early years of Jewish immigration to London and New York had characterized Jewish parents as exemplary – as doing the best possible for the moral and physical good of the family. However, by the early years of the twentieth century, the arrival of less desirable migrants and overcrowding supposedly led to a decline in moral standards, and parental laxity – so much so, that even the workers for Hebrew charities expressed alarm.[23] Jewish and Gentile observers who believed there was extensive Jewish crime, associated it with the influx of new immigrants and the difficulties they had integrating into their new home. According to historian Moses Rischin:

> In the early years of the twentieth century the effect of such conditions upon the young deeply disturbed those anxious for the public weal. In 1909 some 3,000 Jewish children appeared before the Juvenile Court and in the next few years Jewish criminals regularly made newspaper headlines. The appearance of an ungovernable youth after the turn of the century was undeniable and excited apprehension.[24]

Several writers argued that it was not surprising that the immigrants did not adjust to new conditions. 'The result is inevitable. The child being placed in a vitiated atmosphere, imbibing the poison of that atmosphere, becoming saturated with it, crime follows as a matter of course'.[25] Crimes that were typical of immigrants differed from those of their sons. As opposed to the receiving of stolen goods, newcomers were more likely to break laws owing to 'occupational overcrowding, poverty and religious habits' and to be charged with family desertion and the breaking of commercial law.[26] Yet Dr I.L. Nasher contended that it was Americanized Jews, and not immigrants, who became involved in crime. 'It is not until they have become Americanized, have adapted themselves to the environment of the district and adopted its ways and vices', argued Dr I.L. Nasher, 'that they become full-fledged wretches'.[27]

Over time, crime among Jews – recent and established – declined. In the US, according to the Jewish Statistical Bureau (JSB), in a bulletin dated for release on (or after) 27 January 1936, Jews of New York State, home to a very large percentage of American Jewry, had a low rate of criminality. As of June 1935, among persons committed to prison, fewer than 3,000 or 5.1 per cent were Jews, who made up more than 15 per cent of the population.[28] When reviewing figures for eight states (New York, Connecticut, Maryland, Michigan, New Jersey, Ohio, Pennsylvania, Illinois) – or about 80 per cent of American Jewry – the JSB data indicate that there were proportionately fewer Jews in prison than their percentage of the population. Crime among Jewish women appeared to be even lower than among Jewish men.[29] Thus Jews seemingly were quite law-abiding – and Jewish women more so than Gentile women and Jewish men. It is possible that institutional statistics under-represented the extent of delinquency. Robert Silverman noted that studies from the 1930s claimed that 'Jews were the least likely to be labelled delinquent because they were handled outside the court system by the many Jewish self-help agencies'.[30] American and British Jews, wary of a sullied name, organized support networks both to keep Jews from engaging in crime and to re-integrate them back into society after serving time.

During the period reviewed here, observers in both Britain and America continued to disagree over the level of Jewish criminality. Their reactions highlight the level of anti-alienism, tensions between environmental and hereditary explanations of Jewish behaviour and conflicts over ethnic ties. Jewish communal workers exhibited a generosity of spirit, but also demonstrated a fear of washing dirty laundry in public. The programmes they initiated, many of them quite progressive for their time, suggest a fairly complex and sensitive perception of crime and criminals, but also the absorption of Victorian ideals of respectability. Jewish attitudes varied – from denial to self-critical, from defensive to patronizing – and translated into a range of efforts designed to underscore Jewish response and minimize negative attention. Generally, social workers and volunteers did not see transgressors as merely having weak characters, flawed morals or being irredeemably evil, but as victims of their circumstances.

Often Jews preferred to ignore those members of the community who damaged their reputation.[31] In the mid-1970s, David Singer argued that the avoidance of the subject revealed a lack of security, and noted that censorship came from within the Jewish community. Singer, in a somewhat controversial approach, suggested that Jews were very good gangsters and pioneers of industrial racketeering. Further, the incorporation of this past into the historical record would increase the range of models of normal Jewish behaviour, and offer a catharsis that would make it unnecessary for most Jews to turn to crime.[32] Jenna Joselit also concluded that American Jews generally preferred not to recognize Jewish participation in crime and pointed to two widely publicized events – the Bingham Report and the Rosenthal murder[33] – which forced New York Jewry to react to charges of extensive criminal activity.

Response to these events led to a new and unprecedented approach in New York, one that was rather different from that adopted in London: New York's Jewish leadership preferred to work behind the scenes. Also, as Lloyd Gartner noted, New York's, unlike Europe's, Jews, co-operated with police in efforts to eliminate Jewish prostitution.[34] This effort gained unified support from varied groups of Jews. Some who believed 'segregated activity' was appropriate in religious spheres alone, came to support the *Kehillah* (New York Jewry's umbrella communal organization) and its work with the police.[35] Indicative of the embarrassment over the Rosenthal murder, additional community groups chose to work with the *Kehillah*, rather than surrender control to them.[36] Much like efforts in London, nearly all of the leaders were established and acculturated Jews and involved few Jews from the Lower East Side or the East End, where large numbers of immigrants resided.

Communal policies toward children reflected many of these concerns. Only a small proportion of Jewish children had scrapes with the law, or required special schooling, but the Jewish communities of Britain and America struggled over how to deal with youth whose activity was either criminal or who lived in situations that put them at risk. Often the court placed children of this type in industrial schools, institutions designed to reform their behaviour, but not strictly speaking, a part of the penal system. In London, leaders of the Jewish community saw industrial school boys as troubled, but not really criminal. For example, in 1894 the Apprenticeship Committee, a constituent of the Jewish Board of Guardians (JBG, the umbrella social welfare organization), received a letter from Mr Ornstein, Secretary of the Visiting Committee of the United Synagogue and Superintendent of the East London Industrial School. He requested assistance in 'apprenticing and finding situations for Jewish lads leaving the School'. Some questioned whether such boys deserved the assistance of the Apprenticeship Committee. The Committee had placed one previous case, but noted that it was not to constitute a precedent. Nonetheless, the members who met decided they would help where possible, even though the apprenticeships might require special terms and cost the JBG a bit more than other placements. 'The Secretary of the Board' pointed out:

> ... that these lads have not been convicted of felony, as the School did not receive lads so convicted, but had been charged for such offences as vagrancy, loitering match-selling &c. It was for lads of such a class that the Industrial Committee was established. The Board had been instrumental in getting these lads sent to the School & after being there & receiving a good character, it would not be right for the Committee to refuse to entertain such cases & to allow the lads to again go to the bad.[37]

The Jewish communities of New York and Britain, prior to the twentieth century, faced a very limited demand for Jewish-sponsored quasi-penal institutions, such as industrial schools. As Eugene Black has noted, the numbers were too small to support an independent institution and most of the crimes were not serious enough to warrant reformatories. In Britain between 1888 and 1898 an average of only eight Jewish children per year were sent to (non-Jewish) industrial schools and probably only two of them were there because of convictions for a criminal offence.[38] There was some increase of problem children during the period of this study, but the total remained fairly small. In 1880, according to the *Jewish Chronicle* (JC), 'The number of Jewish prisoners is below the average among the general population. There are not ten boys, and not a single Jewish girl in the Industrial School and Reformatories throughout England'.[39]

Jews, however, had a complicated problem in that existing institutions often had Christian sponsorship or, at the very least,

Christian influence. Further, the Prison and Visitation Committee of United Synagogue (moderate/Anglicized Orthodox movement) noted, in a letter to Sir Richard Asheton Cross, Secretary of State for the Home Department, that the Jewish community had 'insurmountable difficulty' in inducing Industrial Schools to take Jewish boys.[40] St Paul's Industrial School accepted a few and permitted them to attend services at the East London Synagogue.[41] However, the JBD had to request that Jewish boys be discharged when St Paul's licence was withdrawn. The largest number at the school was seven and for so few truant and unmanageable boys, the Jewish community did not want to establish a school of their own, as they were convinced that such a small enterprise 'could not be of proportions to promise success'.[42] They did not, however, deny the need for access to industrial schools.

In 1888, for example, the JBD had contacted Henry Matthews, Secretary of State for the Home Department, who was about to introduce a measure into Parliament. They reminded him of his promise to consider the special privileges the Jewish community had requested.[43] In essence, they sought an arrangement that would enable Jewish boys to attend Christian denominational schools. As the JBD pointed out, Jewish boys' requirements were mostly of 'a negative character'. They requested exemptions from chapel attendance, Christian religious education and from eating pork. The deputies asked that the boys be allowed to attend Synagogue on Sabbath and Festivals (under appropriate supervision) and to receive instruction in Judaism. The Jewish community would provide a teacher who would offer lessons while Christian boys were at Chapel. Industrial schools generally refused to distinguish among boys and thus typically denied such requests. The Jewish community considered the consequences of this position to be unduly harsh. 'This practically involves the conversion of the Jewish children from their ancestral religion, a penalty which the Legislature, when the Industrial Schools Act was passed, never contemplated for such trivial delinquencies as school truancy, and small misdemeanours.' The Jewish community required a school in London or another large city, not in the suburbs, because rabbis had to be within walking distance to avoid violation of the Jewish Sabbath.[44] The JBD noted that Netherton, a Reformatory near Newcastle, received Jewish boys and worked to everyone's satisfaction.[45] Netherton accommodated

Jewish and Catholic boys and stated that the scheme caused no problems, and that they would accommodate Jewish boys even if it did. Netherton managers even thought the school was 'not without its advantages in accustoming lads of different nationalities and persuasions to live together in forbearance and harmony'.[46]

As demand in Britain grew, the community faced the reality that there was no religiously appropriate place for Jewish delinquents and neglected children. Leaders lamented that, though small in numbers, commitment to a non-Jewish School denied Jewish youth proper religious influence. New calls emerged for an industrial school to serve Jewish youth. Lady Desart described the industrial school as a place that received children whose parents were leading immoral lives. Nonetheless, such Jewish parents were upset when their daughters ended up in court and were sent to a Christian school. For example, the King Edward's School had agreed to take a few Jewish girls and to allow a Jewish teacher to come on Saturdays. However, on other days, the girls attended Christian services 'and were more or less instructed on Christian lines'. 'How', questioned Desart, 'could such an absurd system produce good moral or religious results?'[47] Efforts to rectify this began in 1898. The community purchased a site about 11 miles from London and 16 from the East End, because the Government Authority recommended that the sponsors choose a location that required parents or relatives of inmates to make a significant effort to see a child.[48] Further, sponsors wanted to separate children from bad influences, whether family members or the East End itself. The JBG was pleased with the school, and hoped it would be successful so they could be relieved of labours that resulted from the absence of such an institution.[49] The school, the Hayes Industrial School for Boys, opened in 1901.

Hayes received high marks from London County Council and soon required expansion beyond its original 60 places. Though facing financial challenges, members of the community saw it as vital. As the Chairman Mr Louis Davidson reminded readers:

> It must be borne in mind that an Industrial School was an institution not only for the reclamation and reformation of youthful delinquents, but more especially for the removal of children from surroundings in which they were likely to degenerate into a life of crime and vice.

Anglo-Jewry could ill afford to turn away those in need. 'If the class of boys which was being educated at Hayes were neglected difficulties would inevitably arise which would reflect grave discredit upon the community.' Given changes in laws and the establishment of Children's Courts, managers expected to receive additional commitments. Davidson:

> ... could not sufficiently exaggerate the importance of removing children from undesirable homes and vicious surroundings before they became irrevocably contaminated. The Jewish public had no cause for alarm at the increase in the number of Jewish boys in industrial schools, for the proportion was still below that of other denominations.[50]

In the years before World War I, the need for an industrial school for girls led to the establishment of the Montefiore House School.[51] According to Black, the girls' industrial school emerged out of anxiety over the white slave trade. The Montefiores, themselves very active in reform work, donated a house in 1905, 'to secure the welfare of children, now in danger of mental and moral ruin, often through no real fault of their own'.[52] Supported by the Jewish Association for the Protection of Girls and Women (JAPGAW), Montefiore House took girls under the age of 14 who had committed offences or could not be controlled by their parents, as well as children from parents who were neglectful or involved in criminal activity.[53] Located in Stamford Hill, it gained an excellent reputation. Poor Law Guardians committed some of the children; the cost of others had to be covered by either a guardian or voluntary contributions. Montefiore House also received grants from state and local authorities; continuation of such grants depended upon the efficient running of the school.[54] The school provided a 'refuge' to keep children from 'a life of increasing misdemeanour and further degradation'. At Montefiore, 'the best of influences surround[ed] them, and by careful, sympathetic guidance they are given every chance to grow into happy girls and women, a credit to their race, and useful citizens of the Empire'.[55]

Between 1919 and 1935, approximately 120 Jewish girls and about ten boys, convicted in Police Court, ended up at the Montefiore House School (See Appendix I). Most had been charged with 'being beyond control, stealing, larceny, or being in danger of seduction'. Among the children assigned to Montefiore House, approximately 20 per cent were illegitimate, a figure that was vastly out of proportion to the Jewish community as a whole.[56]

Industrial schools, emphasized Jewish leaders, were not reformatories and did not accept adult criminals: 'But it is the only refuge for poor children living in debased and immoral surroundings, or convicted by magistrates of minor offences.' Girls, who were 'safe from all contamination', remained until the age of 16, when the Committee placed the young women in suitable work and under the legal control of the house for two more years. In 1915 Montefiore had 65 inmates, all of whom received a 'sound education', and were 'licensed to situations' (typically domestic service).[57] The managers believed the school had economic value and was able to 'mould to good ends human material which would otherwise run to waste, but it will limit its own supply by bringing into play one of the finest characteristics of our race – the love of parents for their offspring'. Once parents learned that the State could remove their children, they would endeavour to keep them away from 'contamination and impurity'.[58] Industrial schools tried to reform their charges, but with the ultimate goals of preventing them from being treated as criminals and of re-introducing them into the larger society.

In June 1914, of 98 boys at Hayes, 61 were from London and 46 were 'aliens'. Boys learned industrial work, gardening, tailoring, metal and woodworking.[59] The school's leadership claimed great educational success; 'after-care' workers kept in touch with discharged boys and provided follow-up attention to school leavers. Staff at Hayes encouraged the boys to 'cultivate hobbies', participate in indoor and outdoor games, to join a boys' club, and to attend evening classes and scouts. The managers proudly asserted that:

> The lessons of discipline, duty and loyalty inculcated in and out of the schoolroom have not been in vain, and the promise given by every boy on leaving the school with the farewell handshake, to uphold its honour and to live up to British traditions has been well and truly redeemed. The time has long gone by when the necessity for a Jewish Industrial School could be challenged, but if justification were now needed for such an institution it is to be found in the facts here briefly set forth, where lads who might have

deteriorated into outcasts of humanity have been turned into honorable, self-respecting, and useful men.[60]

A comparable movement arose in the US. The Jewish Protectory Society emerged in 1896. In 1902 Judge Julius Mayer, having bemoaned the absence of a Jewish institution for delinquents in New York, invited Jacob Schiff to attend his court. The experience convinced Schiff to start a subscription for a reform school. The Hawthorne School for Boys opened in 1906 or 1907 in Westchester County. Hawthorne, designed more as a school than a reformatory, had a lovely country campus. Good food, exercise, academics and vocational training sought to transform Jewish juvenile delinquents into 'member[s] of New York's middle class'.[61] In 1908, the National Council of Women established the Lakeview Home for 'wayward girls', and in 1913, the Jewish Protectory and Aid Society set up the Cedar Knolls School for Girls (Bronxville) 'to care for such girls as have proved themselves unmanageable in their homes, in school, or have not responded to probationary treatment accorded them by the Children's Courts'.[62]

The New York community developed additional programmes to aid delinquent girls and women. In 1911 or 1912, perhaps at the insistence of New York's Children's Court, the Jewish Protectory formed a committee that created the Big Sisters Movement.[63] Initially, services focused on those already in the correctional system. Over time, the various organizations dealing with 'problem girls' merged with each other, and then with organizations dedicated to boys. In 1921 they took on the name Jewish Board of Guardians; their goals, structure and methods had been evolving since the last years of the nineteenth century. By 1940, the community focused its efforts on 'the prevention and treatment of delinquency and personality problems'.[64] The Jewish community was especially committed to after-care, despite its expense. This system enabled welfare workers to keep tabs on their former charges, offer advice as they entered adulthood and promote ties to the Jewish community.

While the impact of communal activism is hard to measure, it appears that Jewish crime rates in the US fell during the first third of the twentieth century. Many concluded that early immigrant misdeeds had been an aberration – one that would decline with acculturation. Between 1915 and 1931, Jewish children numbered just over 18 per cent of those brought before the New York City Children's Court. In 1917 Jewish children constituted approximately 42 per cent of children in the public schools, suggesting that Jewish children were under-represented in Children's Court. While arraignment rates of Jewish children fluctuated between 1909 and 1931, there was decline overall from 30 to 17.42 per cent. Girls accounted for a smaller percentage of arraignments than boys, among both Jews and Gentiles. Of girls arraigned, 12.8 per cent were Jewish. Among boys, Jews numbered just over 20 per cent of the arraignments. Thus the rate of arraignment of Jewish girls was about half the rate of Jewish boys. A study of the cases suggested, however, that girls' offences were of a more serious nature and 'some influences, such as the home and the organized welfare work tend to prevent the arraignment of Jewish girls for minor offences', perhaps deflating their numbers. Strikingly, Jewish girls' rates of recidivism were higher than non-Jewish girls. Yet, writing in 1931, Julius Maller concluded 'that the Jewish case brought before the court represents a less serious problem than the non-Jewish case'. Maller was uncertain if 'the character of the Jewish child and the nature of his environment' or 'the untiring efforts on the part of the numerous philanthropic agencies' explained the difference between Jewish and Gentile children.[65]

In New York, where there seems to have been a significant decline in vice, gambling, prostitution and petty theft, the community attributed this improvement to acculturation. The rhetoric for London is more complex, suggesting both a decrease in crime as well as an increase in immoral activity and theft, *also* said to be the result of acculturation and the loosening of Jewish ties. By 1930, the *Annual Report* of the JAPGAW reported that the number of new Probation Orders was 'fairly constant', but remarked that there had been a shift in the nature of the offenses from immoral offenses to stealing and receiving stolen goods.[66]

Among the crimes most associated with Jews in Britain was gambling. In one case in 1895, a boy, apprenticed through the JBG, received a three-month prison sentence for stealing a watch and chain. 'Previous to this he had been fined 10/- for gambling in the streets and had been an inmate of the East London Industrial School at Lewisham'.[67] About a decade later, the problem remained and boys' clubs responded to this communal embarrassment by creating anti-gambling leagues. In 1903, the Stepney Jewish Lads' Club magazine commended the new Anti-Gambling Association and hoped most, if not all members, would join quickly. The Stepney Managers realized that some of the boys had been engaged in gambling and betting, but not in the club, so far as they knew.

From 1885 on, leaders of the Anglo-Jewish community recognized some Jewish involvement in prostitution and the white slave trade. A mere fraction of the millions who left eastern Europe between 1880 and 1939 participated in prostitution. The most likely participants or victims were young unaccompanied women travelling to Britain: between 1890 and 1913 such travellers numbered approximately 300 to 1,100 (3 to 12 per cent of total) annually.[68] Rescue work, popular among Victorian crusaders generally, enabled Jews to prove their commitment to sexual purity and to eliminating degradation among women and children. British Jewry lacked a unified perception of their co-religionists' level of criminality, but were embarrassed over negative publicity and a sullied reputation. More than any other criminal action, Jewish leaders in Britain believed most prostitutes were more sinned against than sinning. While self-serving, in that such a view dismissed the possibility of collusion or willingness to earn one's keep on the streets, the JAPGAW felt trickery, ignorance, poverty, and abuse – as opposed to weakness of character – explained most women's involvement in prostitution.

Generally, the JAPGAW assumed that Jewish girls were victims and while many, even most, were naive, some undoubtedly saw a potential route out of poverty. The JAPGAW acknowledged that some of the girls and women were 'not unwilling to be victims, [they were] constantly devoid of moral fibre, lacking religious teaching, of low education and faulty upbringing'. Much of the effort of the JAPGAW came in the form of preventive and protective services for women and children.[69] They distributed literature warning susceptible women and unsuspecting parents of the hazards of travelling alone, of marriages that took place without proper registration, and the existence of trafficking in women.[70] Such responses provided communal assistance to young girls and women and demonstrated the commitment of the Jewish community to stamping out vice and embarrassing activity within the community.[71]

Thus, Anglicized Jews chose a very overt manner for combating vice within their own community. Such efforts were certainly typical of the charitable endeavours of the time. They sought to restore those who had slipped into immorality and to create good 'Jewesses', who were self-respecting women, capable of earning a living. Jewish rescue workers' motivations and methods did not overlap entirely with those of their Christian colleagues. Jewish tradition prided itself on commitment to sexual purity, though Jewish reformers tended to focus on the impact of prostitution on young women and on the community's reputation. Unlike the reformers Frank Prochaska studied, Jews did not emphasize that prostitution broke 'marriage and baptismal vows and poisoned family relations'. Further, unlike German-Jewish feminists, female Anglo-Jewish rescue workers rarely, if ever, entered brothels themselves.[72]

Sympathy, with an undercurrent of moral superiority, and occasional condescension, run through the JAPGAW reports. Organizers believed that the Jewish atmosphere that they could offer was an asset in setting young women on a proper moral path:

> These poor waifs and strays must learn that right conduct comes from right thinking, and wrong thoughts are out of place where heart-felt Jewish prayers are said, and sacred observances kept. We trust that the public worship in synagogue, which our girls are allowed to attend, may further a very real growth in spiritual life, and may help them in their struggle toward better things.[73]

Among American women, efforts to stem white slavery occupied the attention of the National Council of Jewish Women (NCJW). Prevention, rather than cure, guided the NCJW and the organization 'did not bombard the girls they served with religious ideology'. Anglo-Jewish reformers, often from Anglicized Orthodox families, did see a central role for religion, not so much for salvation – a concept foreign to Judaism – but to provide spiritual succour and models, perhaps idealized, of Jewish womanhood. Much like the JAPGAW, the NCJW believed that circumstances and not moral weakness accounted for Jewish female immigrants' entry into prostitution.[74]

As with other types of crime, the level of response in both countries was out of proportion to the extent of criminal or 'immoral activity'; it reflected a sense of responsibility to co-religionists and a preoccupation with stamping out Jewish delinquency. Further, vigilant response demonstrated that established Jews accepted and promoted community standards, and their involvement in rescue and reform efforts was part of their identity as Americanized and Anglicized Jews. Arguably, however, this level of self-consciousness also suggests a lack of confidence – fear of an anti-Semitic backlash, or perhaps even internalization of non-Jews' negative assessments of the Jewish character.

Several explanations recur with regard to the comparatively low crime rates of Jews and these include the strength of the Jewish family, the cohesiveness of the Jewish community, the emphasis on education, the upward mobility of most Jews and the limited use of alcohol. Heavy use of alcohol, often associated with crimes of violence, was rare in the Jewish communities in both Britain and America. Some have noted that alcohol 'is prescribed and not proscribed' and the role model for Jews is the moderate drinker.[75] As late as the 1950s, sociologists concluded that Jews drank less because, 'The Jews still see themselves as a minority group having to be reserved and controlling of its members, lest their behaviour carry negative images and reactions for the whole group by non-Jews'.[76] Extensive community-sponsored services and philanthropy provided a safety net for many Jews.

As a lens on the Jewish community, crime and reactions to it, provide insight into acculturation, internal social dynamics, and especially to the layers of Jewish identity. Often in Britain and America, Jewish responses, particularly those of the established community, indicate a strong desire to find acceptance in their 'host' societies. Equally, reactions highlight areas of anxiety, the fear of being associated with, and embarrassed by, criminal and delinquent, or even backward Jews, tension between Jewish solidarity and wider national loyalties, and point to areas of conflict and contradictory demands.

Overall, Jewish criminal activity, which was always fairly limited, seems to have declined over the first three or four decades of the twentieth century. Presumably, as the second and third generation came of age and benefited from economic mobility and social acceptance, crime no longer paid. Yet, according to the US Immigration Commission, Jews did not follow the typical pattern of movement away from crime. Joselit's work confirmed this finding. Immigrants were apparently involved in fewer property crimes than their children.[77] Behavioural problems were seemingly on the increase and these may well have been an indication that Jewish youth were coming to resemble their non-Jewish peers.

The reaction to Jewish crime and criminals speaks to Jewish concerns about their reputation, an anxiety to be perceived as patriotic and thus good Britons and Americans, as well as genuine concern for co-religionists, and thus a desire to be good Jews. Their responses – offensive and defensive – may well have been a battle against the negative stereotypes so common in the culture around them. American Jewry seemingly went about the business of eliminating crime in a very quiet and unobtrusive manner. In England, organizations such as the JAPGAW sought publicity to prove their commitment to morality and respectability. This is especially striking in light of the comfort levels of American versus British Jewry in other settings. British Jews, one of very few immigrant groups in turn-of-the-century Britain, and residents in a country that did not see itself as a land of immigration, tended to be more self-conscious – and remained so – *vis-à-vis* their relations to the host society. While there is a sense of urgency about eliminating crime among Jews, the leadership of New York's and London's Jewish communities generally accepted that their criminal element was redeemable – a rather progressive stance for the time – or perhaps wishful thinking aimed at minimizing the implications of having criminals among them.

APPENDIX I
MONTEFIORE HOUSE SCHOOL ADMISSIONS, 1919–1935

Children in danger of seduction	39
In need of care, or in moral danger	9
Residing in house used by prostitutes	5
Found wandering	24
Has parent who failed to provide efficient elementary education	4
Having unfit parent	10
Being beyond control, stealing, larceny	39

Source: University of Southampton, Montefiore House School, File 2/8/11, Montefiore House School Admissions Register, 1919–1935.

APPENDIX II
SAMPLE MONTEFIORE SCHOOL CASES:

A. 'Beyond control'

(147) – JAPGAW says she has a bad character - involved in theft.

(149) – 'Charged by father with being beyond control. Stated by father to steal and to use bad language. The father has married a Christian and there appears to be a great deal of quarrelling between the parents and grandparents, the brunt of which seems to fall on this child'.

(180) – 'Child is very untruthful – stays out late. Continually brings home articles which she has stolen. Steals from home and is under suspicion at School. Is under bad influence of sister aged 18 who is alleged to be immoral'.

B. 'Risk of seduction'

(148) – Father weak, mother immoral. 'Parents do not occupy same room. For some time past mother has been bringing home men. Children left to themselves, dirty and neglected'.

C. 'Residing in house used by prostitutes for prostitution'.

(152) – Very neglected. Father's whereabouts unknown, said to have been deported. 'Bad case of immorality. Child and brother (now at Hayes) found in a disorderly house. Mother of children resides with parents who were convicted and sentenced to three months' imprisonment for living on the proceeds of daughters [*sic*] immorality. She was discovered with a man in their room'.

(156) – Grandmother in prison, mother in Canada – 'Child has had to be excluded from school on account of her verminous condition. Has been outraged. Man committed to prison for six months'. 'Home surroundings dirty and unsatisfactory in every way'.

D. 'Found wandering'

(153) – Neglected, Father's address unknown. 'Found in Wentworth St., Spitalfields, apparently placed there by mother to beg. No home – parents apart, five other children illegitimate. Mother immoral and neglectful'.

(173) – 'Child has been neglected, badly fed and lodged. Had to sleep on chairs for two years past. Told to go away by Aunt as she could not afford to keep her'.

NOTES

The author also presented a version of this paper at the Race and Europe Study Group, Center for European Studies, Harvard University, April 1999. The author is thankful for helpful suggestions from Michael Berkowitz, Peter Laipson, Daniel Levine and Susan Pennybacker and gratefully acknowledges research support from Bowdoin College (Faculty Development Summer Research and Travel Grants), Brandeis University (Sachar Fellowship), the Indiana Center on Philanthropy, the Lucius Littauer Foundation, the Hartley Institute (University of Southampton) and the Oxford Centre for Hebrew and Jewish Studies.

1. In London, Jews were the second largest ethnic minority. Irish immigrants made up the largest and were more dispersed than Jews. See David

Englander, 'Booth's Jews: The Presentation of Jews and Judaism in Life and Labour of the People in London', *Victorian Studies*, 32 (1989), p. 551. By 1914, some 1.4 million Jews (approximately 28 per cent) made New York their home. See Moses Rischin, *The Promised City: New York's Jews, 1870–1914* (London and Cambridge, MA: Harvard University Press, 1977), p. 94.

2. Jenna Joselit, *Our Gang: Jewish Crime and the New York Jewish Community, 1900–1940* (Bloomington, IN: Indiana University Press, 1983), p. 29.

3. Robert Silverman, 'Criminality Among Jews: An Overview', *Issues in Criminology*, 6, 2 (Summer 1971), p. 2. Silverman notes that C. Snyder and M. Herskovits explore definitions of Jewishness. See C. Snyder, *Alcohol and the Jews* (Glencoe, IL: Free Press, 1958), p. 15, and M. Herskovits, 'Who Are the Jews?', L. Finkelstein (ed.), in *The Jews, Their History, Culture and Religion* (Philadelphia, PA: Jewish Publication Society of America, 1949), p. 1156.

4. Robert Silverman, for example, noted that 'the Jews are not a race', but then added (drawing on work from 1949), that the Jews' 'original ancestors were a Mediterranean sub-race of the Caucasoid but they are now so mixed they are not racially distinguishable'. Krogman, as quoted in M. Hershkovits, 'Who Are the Jews?', p. 1158, and cited by Silverman, 'Criminality Among Jews', p. 2.

5. Consider the 'Jewess' Mirah, in George Eliot's *Daniel Deronda*. D. Englander, 'Booth's Jews', pp. 552, 555–6.

6. Jacob A Riis, *How the Other Half Lives* (New York: Dover, 1971 [1890]), p. 86.

7. Bryan Cheyette, *Constructions of 'the Jew' in English Literature and Society: Racial Representations, 1875–1945* (Cambridge: Cambridge University Press, 1993), pp. 10–11, 268–9.

8. See Anne Aresty Nathan, 'The Jew and His Image', *The Jew in the Victorian Novel: Some Relationships Between Prejudice and Art* (New York: AMS Press, 1980), pp. 31–56.

9. *Jewish Chronicle* (JC), 12 August 1881.

10. Todd Endelman, *The Jews of Georgian England*, 2nd edn (Philadelphia, PA: Jewish Publication Society of America, 1979, Ann Arbor, MI: University of Michigan Press, 1999), pp. 192–5, 212–13, 225–6.

11. See, for example, David Feldman, *Englishmen and Jews* (esp. 'Dimensions of Difference'); Cheyette, *Constructions of 'the Jew' in English Literature*; Sander Gilman, *The Jew's Body* (New York: Routledge, 1991); Montagu Modder, *The Jew in the Literature of England* (Cleveland, OH and New York, 1960).

12. Bernard Gainer, *The Alien Invasion* (London: Heinemann, 1972), p. 52.

13. See Isaac A. Hourwich, *Immigration and Labor: The Economic Aspects of European Immigration to the United States* (New York: G.P. Putnam's Sons, 1912), p. 66, who refers to Kate Claghorn on this issue, p. 234.

14. 'Influx of Aliens', PRO, MEPOL 2/260/97779, 6 December 1904; extract from 'The Outlook – The Growing Influx of Aliens', *Daily Mail*, 1 December 1904.

15. 'Notes of Deputation from the Jewish Board of Deputies (hereafter, JBD) on the Aliens Bill', 19 May 1904, PRO, HO 45, 10303-117267.

16. The *Standard*, 30 January 1911 as quoted by JBD, 'Alien Statistics prepared by the Jewish Board of Deputies in February 1911 in reply to published and misleading statement', JBD, Aliens: Criminal Immigration, File B2/1/9.

17. Immigration officials lacked a specific category to enumerate Jews. English- and American-Jewish scholars utilize data for those emigrating from Russia and Russian Poland and estimate the Jewish component to be least 80 per cent. Jewish immigrants settled almost exclusively in urban areas increasing the likelihood that Russians and Russian-Poles in London, Manchester, Liverpool and Leeds, or New York City, were indeed Jewish. 'European

Immigration into the United States, Its Nature and Effects', PP 1893–4, LXXI, C. 7113, 229. Irving Howe, *The World of Our Fathers: The Journey of the East European Jews to America and the Life they Found and Made* (New York: Harcourt Brace Jovanovich, 1976), p. 80. See also Lloyd Gartner, 'Notes on the Statistics of Jewish Immigration to England, 1870–1914', *JSS*, 22, 2 (1960), pp. 97–102. S. Rosenbaum, 'A Contribution to the Study of the Vital and Other Statistics of the Jews in the United Kingdom', *Journal of the Royal Statistical Society*, 68 (1905), pp. 526–62. Russians and Russian-Poles accounted for 28 per cent of all aliens who settled in England between 1881 and 1911, and were about one third of the immigrants to Britain in 1901 and 1911. Compiled from the Census of England and Wales, 1901, 1911.

18. Of all foreigners sentenced in the UK in 1909, fewer 'than 20 per cent were Russians and Poles (517 out of 2,617)'. That same year, when Britain extradited thirteen Germans, seven French, five Austrians and ten other foreigners, no Russian was extradited as a criminal refugee. JBD, 'Alien Statistics', JBD, Aliens: Criminal Immigration, File B2/1/9. On 28 March 1906, 257 Jews were incarcerated, in England, Wales and Scotland, compared with 16,089 Anglicans, 4,397 Catholics and 352 Wesleyans. 'Jews in Prison', *Jewish Chronicle* (hereafter JC), 11 May 1906.

19. *Daily Graphic*, 24 (?) March 1914.

20. University of Southampton, AJ 195/3/25, Typescript of Basil Henriques's Life by Rose Henriques, 1934.

21. By 1897, 200 of 912 inmates in the New York Juvenile Asylum were Jewish. *Annual Report of the Society for the Aid of Jewish Prisoners*, April 1897, p. 8.

22. *Annual Report of the Society for the Aid of Jewish Prisoners*, April 1896, p. 5.

23. Ernest Coulter, 'Alien Colonies and the Children's Court', *North American Review*, CLXXIX (1904), pp. 732–4.

24. Rischin, *The Promised City*, pp. 89–91.

25. *Annual Report of the Society for the Aid of Jewish Prisoners*, April 1897, p. 37.

26. Rischin, *The Promised City*, pp. 89–91.

27. I.L. Nascher, *The Wretches of Povertyville* (Chicago, IL: J.J. Lanzit, 1909), pp. 10–12, 40; as cited by Rischin, *The Promised City*, p. 90.

28. Of 2,045 individuals responsible for 'grave' crimes, Jews numbered 197 or 9.6 per cent. They constituted 8.1 per cent of people in reformatories and '2.5 per cent of those sent to the institutions for defective delinquents'. For 'light offences', Jews constituted 5.4 per cent of those sent to jails and 0.7 per cent of those sent to penitentiaries. New York City had similar statistics. Thirty per cent of the population was Jewish and made up 19.4 per cent of those committed to New York City prisons (17,302 of 89,075). JBD, File E1/59, US: Jewish Statistical Bureau, for release 27 January 1936 or later.

29. Of 741 committed for grave offences for the year ending 30 June 1935, 4.3 per cent were Jewish women. The courts sent four women to state prison, 26 to the reformatory, and two to the institution for defective delinquents. Jewish men equalled about 8.8 per cent of the total number of male prisoners committed for grave offences. For light offences, 3.7 per cent of those committed to penitentiaries and county jails were Jewish women as compared to 4.9 per cent Jews among the 175,024 male prisoners. In New York City, Jewish women made up 10.1 per cent of female prisoners and Jewish men, 20.5 per cent of male prisoners. JBD, (Britain), File E1/59, US: Jewish Statistical Bureau, for release 27 January 1936 or later.

30. Sophia Robison, *Can Delinquency be Measured* (New York: published for the Welfare Council of New York City by Columbia University Press, 1936), p. 67; as cited by Silverman, 'Criminality among Jews', p. 6.

31. As Lara Marks notes, 'Very little is known about Jewish prostitution and many in the Jewish community deny its existence'. She argues that, 'Economic and social dislocation in the ghettoes of Eastern Europe meant that even the Jewish community had experiences of widespread prostitution'. See Lara Marks, 'Jewish women and Jewish prostitution in the East End of London', *The Jewish Quarterly*, 34 (1987), p. 6. The extent of Jewish participation remains debatable. Gartner concluded that prostitution had a long history among English Jews, but its extent 'was negligible when compared with the extent of prostitution in England at large'. Most Jewish prostitutes remained in Europe, but the most 'conspicuous' and 'undoubtedly the most profitable' branch was in overseas procurement and many such girls and women passed through London. Gartner, 'Anglo-Jewry', pp. 146–7.
32. David Singer, 'The Jewish Gangster: Crime as "Unzer Shtik"', *Judaism* (1974), pp. 71–4. Rich Cohen who also notes that Jews 'have suppressed the memory of Jewish gangsters' suggests that he finds some appeal in the image of Jews as bullies, that he wants 'the freedom to be a bully'. His decision then not to be a bully has more meaning. See Rich Cohen, *Tough Jews* (New York: Simon and Schuster, 1998), pp. 130–1.
33. Jenna Joselit, *Our Gang: Jewish Crime and the New York Jewish Community, 1900–1940* (Bloomington, IN: Indiana University Press, 1983), pp. 23–5, 75–7, 84. In 1908, New York Police Commissioner Theodore Bingham reported that 85 per cent of New York's population was either foreign-born or had foreign-born parents (many of whom were Jewish) and that it was 'only a logical condition that something like eighty-five out of one hundred of our criminals should be found to be of exotic origin'. Jews, claimed Bingham, were responsible for 50 per cent of New York City's crime, while making up only 25 per cent of the population. Thomas Bingham, 'Foreign Criminals in New York', *North American Review* (1908), pp. 383, 384. In 1912 a group of young Jews from the Lower East Side murdered Herman Rosenthal, a well-known gambler. Suffering the effects of a police crackdown on his business, Rosenthal had decided to testify before a grand jury on ties between the police and the underworld. His murder involved members of the labour movement and led to an embarrassing trial, despite the fact that the jury acquitted the accused. Ernest Coulter, 'The Jews War on Crime', *Outlook and Independent*, 158 (1931), p. 463.
34. Gartner, 'Anglo-Jewry', p. 139.
35. The *kehillah* was the traditional form of Jewish communal government in Eastern Europe.
36. Arthur Goren, *New York Jews and the Quest for Community: The Kehillah Experiment, 1908–1922* (New York: Columbia University Press, 1970), pp. 159, 162–3, 165.
37. University of Southampton, Letter, Mr Ornstein, Secretary of the Visiting Committee of the United Synagogue, MS 173, Jewish Care Archives, 1/6/1, Minute Book, Industrial Committee, 1894–1963, 31 October 1894.
38. Visitation Committee Meeting, United Synagogue, 5 July 1898 and JC, 6 May 1898 as cited by Black, *The Social Politics of Anglo-Jewry*, p. 239. For a general discussion see pp. 236–42.
39. JC, 24 September 1880.
40. PRO, HO45 9673, Letter, Louis Davidson, United Synagogue, to Sir Richard Asheton Cross, MP, HM Secretary of State for the Home Department, 12 January 1886.
41. JC, 24 September 1880.

42. PRO, HO45 9673, Letter, Louis Davidson to Sir Richard Asheton Cross, 12 January 1886.
43. PRO, HO45 9673, Letter, Arthur Cohen, President, London Committee of Deputies of the British Jews, to The Honourable Henry Matthews, QC, MP, Secretary of State for the Home Department, 6 July 1888.
44. PRO, HO45 9673, Letter, Louis Davidson to Sir Richard Asheton Cross, 12 January 1886.
45. PRO, HO45 9673, Letter, Arthur Cohen to Henry Matthews, 6 July 1888.
46. PRO, HO45 9673, Letter, R.R. Redmayne, Secretary of Reformatory, Infirmary, Newcastle on Tyne, to Reverend S. Friedberg, 5 June 1888.
47. JC, 7 April 1905.
48. AJ 243/1, Hayes Industrial School, Minute Books, Meeting, 16 November 1898.
49. AJ 243/1, Hayes Industrial School, Minute Books, Letter from JBG, 13 December 1898.
50. AJ 243/1, Hayes Industrial School, Minute Books, Article on prize distribution, appeared with Managers' Meeting Minutes, 28 May 1908, probably JC.
51. JC, 7 April 1905.
52. JC, 21 July 1905 as cited by Black, *The Social Politics of Anglo-Jewry*, pp. 238–41.
53. Placement in an industrial school did not necessarily indicate delinquency on the part of the child. Courts committed children whose parents had involvement in prostitution and petty crime.
54. JAPGAW, *Annual Report*, 1919, pp. 13–14.
55. *Jewish Graphic*, 18 May 1928.
56. University of Southampton, Montefiore House School, File 2/8/11, Montefiore House School Admissions Register, 1919–1935.
57. JC, 8 January 1915.
58. JC, 21 July 1905.
59. JC, 5 June 1914.
60. JC, 21 May 1915
61. Joselit, *Our Gang*, pp. 14, 20–1.
62. Goren, *New York Jews*, p. 134. Alexander H. Kaminsky (ed.), 'The Problem of Delinquency in the Jewish Community', *Jewish Communal Register of New York City, 1917–1918* (New York: Kehillah (Jewish Community) of New York City, 1918), p. 1141.
63. Kaminsky, 'The Problem of Delinquency', pp. 1135, 1141. Ernest Coulter, 'The Jews War on Crime', p. 464.
64. J. E. Caldwell (?) 'A History of the Jewish Board of Guardians', pp. 3, 4, 5, 1.
65. Julius B. Maller, 'Juvenile Delinquency among the Jews in New York', *Social Forces*, 10 (1931–32), pp. 542, 543, 544, 548.
66. JAPGAW, *Annual Report*, 1930, p. 47.
67. University of Southampton, MS 173, Jewish Care Archives, 1/6/1, Minute Book, Industrial Committee, 1894–1963, 25 July 1895, [PL, case 1537]. The JBG clerk received instructions to cancel PL's indentures on the best terms possible.
68. Lloyd Gartner, 'Anglo-Jewry and the Jewish International Traffic in Prostitution, 1885–1914', *AJS Review*, 7–8 (1982–83), p. 155.
69. Rescue work attracted a number of women who sought to purify public and private spheres. They tried to close brothels and promote restrictive legislation – a controversial approach for feminists. Some acted out of religious ideology. See L. Bland, '"Purifying" the Public World: Feminist Vigilantes in Late Victorian England', *Women's History Review*, 1, 3 (1992), pp. 397–412.
70. Phyllis Gerson, *Social Service in the Jewish Community* (London, 1974), p. 8.
71. JAPGAW, *Annual Report*, 1904, pp. 8, 13.

72. F.K. Prochaska notes that rescue was tied to the social purity movement: 'The moral reform societies of the late nineteenth century wanted nothing less than the regeneration of English family life through the transformation of the relations between the sexes'. F.K. Prochaska, 'In Streets and Dens of Vice', in *Women and Philanthropy in Nineteenth-Century England* (Oxford: Clarendon Press, 1980), pp. 182–221. Certainly some Jewish feminists shared such goals, but these issues seem to be of only limited concern in the sources.

73. JAPGAW, *Annual Report*, 1898, p. 36.

74. Faith Rogow, *Gone to Another Meeting: The National Council of Jewish Women, 1893–1993* (Tuscaloosa, AL: University of Alabama Press, 1993), pp. 130, 131, 136–8.

75. Silverman, 'Criminality among Jews', p. 26. Silverman draws on Miruchi and Perruci, 'Norm Qualities and Differential Effect of Deviant Behavior', *American Sociological Review*, 27 (1962), pp. 391–406; Robert F. Bales, 'Cultural Differences in Rates of Alcoholism', *Quarterly Journal of Studies on Alcohol*, 6 (1946), pp. 480–99; and Jerome H. Skolnick, 'Religious Affiliation and Drinking Behavior', *Quarterly Journal of Studies on Alcohol*, 19 (1958), p. 456. As Silverman notes, studies on Jewish criminality often tend to focus on middle-class Jews and no one has focused on the drinking habits of poor Jews, and so to assume a 'firm connection' among Jews, limited alcohol and low rates of crimes of violence is problematic. Silverman, 'Criminality among Jews', pp. 26–7.

76. Nathan Glazer, 'Why Jews Stay Sober', *Commentary*, 13 (1952), p. 181; as cited by Silverman, 'Criminality among Jews', p. 26.

77. United States Senate Documents, Reports of the Immigration Commission. 'Immigrants and Crime', 26 (Washington, 1911), pp. 14, 69; as cited by Jenna Joselit, 'An Answer to Commissioner Bingham: A Case Study of New York Jews and Crime, 1907', *YIVO Annual of Jewish Social Science*, 18 (1983), fn. 34, p. 140.

6

Marcel Proust and the Comedy of Assimilation

SAM W. BLOOM

[Proust's] style is comedy, not humour; his laughter does not toss the world up but flings it down – at the risk that it will be smashed to pieces, which will then make him burst into tears.

Walter Benjamin[1]

An old Jew appears as a witness before the magistrate. The judge asks him the following:

– Your name?
– Moishe Feinberg.
– Place of birth?
– Odessa.
– Occupation?
– Rag seller.
– Religion?
– I have told, you, your honour, sir, that my name is Moishe Feinberg, that I was born in Odessa, and that I sell rags. Do you think I'm a Muslim?[2]

This anecdote comes from one of two volumes of Raymond Geiger's collection of *histoires juives or* Jewish Jokes from the mid-1920s.[3] That the above joke's comic potency has endured was proven when I told it in front of a sleepy but responsive audience at nine o'clock in the morning in Utrecht in 1996. The comic effect, in part, results from the self-awareness of the rag seller set against the bureaucratic impassability of a representative of the law. The rag merchant's sarcastic reply, while, albeit superfluously, affirming his own Jewish identity, illustrates a lack of deference for authority that can only be classified as *chutzpah*. The Jew paradoxically uses his inferior social status to gain the rhetorical advantage. When stripped of every other arm of self-defence, one can see self-deprecating discourse as a victory in one-upmanship: 'I can insult myself better than you, my enemy, can'.[4] More frequently, though, Geiger favours the inclusion of variations of the converse situation whereby the overly signified Jew lacks this self-awareness. The latter character thus finds himself at a loss for words when someone identifies him as Jewish:

> On his return from a trip, Moishela, whose nose, eyes, hair, voice, manner designate him as son of Shem from a mile away, recounts to his wife how his fellow travellers persisted in making horrible anti-Semitic remarks.
> – And you weren't frightened, my poor dear Moishela?
> – See here, Rebecca, I wasn't so stupid as to tell them who or what I am [*qui je suis*].[5]

Especially when the Jew's interlocutor is an avowed anti-Semite, it is difficult to overlook the less than benign potential of such a 'comic' exchange, especially in the post-Shoah context. In his *Réflexions sur la question juive*, published in the aftermath of the Nazi persecutions, Jean-Paul Sartre relates a similar anecdote for the more didactic purpose of distinguishing between his concepts of 'authentic' and 'inauthentic' Jews:

> I knew a Jewish lady whose son was obliged to travel to Germany for business reasons around 1934. Her son reflected the typical [physical] characteristics of the French Israelite: hooked nose, spread-out ears, etc., but, on one of his business trips when we showed our concern, his mother replied, 'Oh, I'm not the least bit concerned; he doesn't look at all Jewish'.[6]

For Sartre, his example illustrates that when Jews are exclusively among themselves, as when families are closed off to the outside world, they lose sight, however temporarily, of what distinguishes them from Gentiles. Sartre opposes this situation of the Jews' 'natural habitat', in which he refers to 'biological' and 'hereditary' differences, to that of situations when Jews find themselves in the mixed company of other Jews and Gentiles. For Sartre, it is in such social settings that the Jew's attempt to assimilate results in the figure of the 'inauthentic' Jew. Sartre's description of this phenomenon is quite reminiscent of Proust's *Sodome et Gomorrhe I*. Using descriptions similar to Proust's, Sartre disserts on how the inauthentic or assimilating Jew will even go so far as to shun a fellow Jew in mixed social situations in order to deny his own Jewish identity (III, 8).[7] As the title of this particular section of *A la recherche du temps perdu* does more than suggest, Proust's principal interest is how the same dynamic applies to his homosexual characters.[8]

Accordingly, the current study examines the relationship between Jewish jokes in this second category, found in the Geiger collection and several episodes from Proust's epic novel, *A la recherche du temps perdu*, known to readers in English as *Remembrance of Things Past*. I will show that such comic instances underlie an ideology that rejects the possibility of complete assimilation on the grounds that Jewishness, like Proust's conception of homosexuality, is an inherent trait bordering on the pathological. Two other Proust scholars who have already made a foray into jokes and their relation to the *Recherche* deserve mention. In the *Proustian Community*, Seth Wolitz, one of the first in a long line of critics writing on the Jewish question in Proust, makes the connection between Proust's buffoonish character of Albert Bloch and Geiger's jokes. Wolitz remarks, for instance, that Geiger uses the name Bloch some 40 out of 200 times for the name of his joke protagonists in the 1923 volume.[9] In fact, the similarities between some of Geiger's characters and Proust's Bloch go beyond a shared surname.

The French novelist and critic, Henri Raczymow, goes further in his examination of some of these same Jewish jokes, and, in an entirely different context, he also touches upon the subject of Jewish humour in Proust.[10] For Raczymow, Geiger's *histoires juives* only disparages unassimilated eastern Jews.[11] Raczymow has similar criticisms of Freud's illustrative *witz* (joke) in *Jokes and their Relation to the Unconscious*. For Raczymow, Freud's jokes do not represent Jewish humour *per se*, as they do not necessarily come from Jewish sources and in some instances could even originate from anti-Semitic ones. Raczymow contrasts Freud's 'Jewish jokes' with those from the ghetto or shtetl where 'Yid' essentially refers to another man.[12] Raczymow's jokes are specific to an ethnic community as opposed to other Jewish jokes in which the Jew lives in a religiously diverse community and is portrayed by his

stereotypical negative qualities (parsimony, uncleanness, etc.).
Proving the self-evidence of his assertion, Raczymow asks what
the tales of Shalom Aleichem have in common with either the
jokes of Sigmund Freud or the narrative of Marcel Proust –
nothing.[13] In fact, Raczymow's abstraction of the 'Yid', arguably
most closely resembles that of Sartre's authentic Jew.

Unquestionably, some of Raymond Geiger's *histoires juives*
would be patently offensive if articulated by a non-Jew. On this
account, Raczymow's assertions are not without merit. What
then is their meaning if a Jew recounts them? Is this an instance
of 'inauthenticity', a tactic to distance oneself from one's own
people, or an instance of Jewish self-hatred? In the preface to the
second volume, Geiger, who uses his own surname and Jewish
identity to authenticate his authority, counters criticism that his
jokes only add fuel to anti-Semitic fires. Like Freud, Geiger argues
that they are illustrative of a penchant for self-criticism and hence
a conscious effort to correct 'Jewish' faults. Similarly, Freud finds
this very same quality in his examples of what he terms
'tendentious jokes':

> A particularly favourable occasion for tendentious jokes is
> presented when the intended rebellious criticism is directed
> against the subject himself, or, to put it more cautiously,
> against someone in whom the subject has a share – a collec-
> tive person, that is (the subject's own nation, for instance).
> The occurrence of self-criticism as a determinant may explain
> how it is that a number of the most apt jokes (of which we
> have given plenty of instances) have grown up on the soil of
> Jewish popular life. They are stories created by Jews and
> directed against Jewish characteristics. The jokes made about
> Jews by foreigners are for the most part brutal comic stories
> in which a joke is made unnecessary by the fact that Jews are
> regarded by foreigners as comic figures. The Jewish jokes
> that originate from Jews admit this too; but they know
> their real faults as well as the connection between them and
> their good qualities, and the share which the subject has
> in the person found fault with creates the subjective deter-
> minant (usually so hard to arrive at) of the joke work.
> Incidentally, I do not know whether there are many other
> instances of a people making fun to such a degree of its own
> character.[14]

Somewhat akin to Raczymow, Eliot Oring makes the case that
Freud's reliance on Jewish jokes in his essay on the comic reveals
his own ambivalence towards Jewish identity. According to one
of Oring's sources, Freud modified his given name 'Sigismund' to
'Sigmund' because the former name appeared quite frequently
in anti-Semitic Viennese jokes.[15] In an analysis of Freud through
his jokes, Oring argues that a variety of jokes illustrates Freud's
apprehension that his Ostjuden roots will be discovered through
an inadvertent return to innate 'Jewish' behaviour. Oring analyses
an anecdote that Freud classes as an instance of 'unmasking', a
sub-category of the comic:

> The doctor, who had been asked to look after the Baroness
> at her confinement, pronounced that the moment had not
> come, and suggested to the Baron that in the meantime they
> should have a game of cards in the next room. After a while
> a cry of pain from the Baroness struck the ears of the two
> men: *'Ah, mon Dieu, que je souffre!'* Her husband sprang up,
> but the doctor signed to him to sit down: 'It's nothing. Let's
> go on with the game!' A little later there were again sounds
> from the pregnant woman: *'Mein Gott, mein Gott, was für
> Schmerzen!'* – 'Aren't you going in, Professor?' asked the
> Baron. – 'No, no. It's not time yet.' – At last there came from
> next door an unmistakable cry of *'Ai, waih, waih!'* The doctor
> threw down his cards and exclaimed: *'Now* it's time.'

According to Oring, ' … in certain circumstances, particularly
those of physical or emotional crisis, the true identity will emerge.
Despite wealth, social status, and education, the Jew will [come]
out'.[16] Applying the most negative of interpretations, the anecdote
depicts a process of linguistic degeneration from 'high-culture'
French to 'low-culture' Yiddish.[17]

Yet, even without superimposing this last linguistic and
cultural value judgement, jokes like these may simply satirize the
pretensions of the Jewish upstart. At the same time, they convey
a cautionary message relayed in aphoristic form: the Jew must
remain constantly on guard in a potentially hostile environment.
In this same spirit, other jokes, that unmask Jews of more modest
social status, reflect the Jewish psyche as it survives in a culturally
diverse environment. In more than a few of these jokes, the focus
of the current study, the punchline equals the recognition or

discovery of one of the joke's characters as Jewish. As in the anecdote that Sartre relates, the humour revolves around the dramatic irony of one character's complete obliviousness to how identifiably Jewish he or a family member looks. There often is paradoxically no need for unmasking. A typical joke of this type reads as follows: a passenger on a train confronted with an uncommunicative fellow traveller in his compartment makes several overtures to engage in conversation. Finally, reasoning that the man will not talk to him because he has not introduced himself, Otto Bloch decides to introduce himself offering his name to which the other replies, 'And me, I am an anti-Semite.'[18]

Proust relates his own character Bloch's experience *mutatis mutandis* in an episode touching upon the Dreyfus Affair. In *Le côté de Guermantes*, Albert Bloch makes a rather awkward entry in the salon of Mme de Villeparisis. Interjecting his unsolicited opinions, opening windows, even breaking a vase, Bloch goes a few steps farther in demonstrating what Sartre mentions as the distinguishing *manque de tacte israélite*.[19] He is a Dreyfusard surrounded on all sides by overtly hostile anti-Dreyfusards – with the exception of the Narrator, who has the poise to keep his opinions to himself. In an effort to sound out the diplomat, M. de Norpois, on his conviction of Dreyfus's guilt or innocence, Bloch engages the former in a conversation. In typical fashion, he stonewalls Bloch with a rambling and convoluted account of the Affair. While de Norpois will not give a precise answer, the reader has little difficulty determining where his loyalties lie. The duc d'Argencourt whom Bloch automatically assumes an ally because he is a foreigner will ironically reply to the latter's plea that it is an affair that only concerns the French. At the same moment, the duchesse de Guermantes whispers 'malevolently' a reference to Bloch's religion into d'Argencourt's ear. Bloch's name, then, does not go unnoticed by the duke. When Bloch appeals to this potential ally, Proust weaves in the familiar preamble of a Jewish joke: 'You, Sir', said Bloch, turning to M. d'Argencourt to whom he had been introduced [*by name*] with the rest of the party on that gentleman's arrival, 'You are a Dreyfusard, of course. Everyone is, abroad' (II, 543).[20]

The tension finally comes to a head when Bloch turns to the duc de Châtellerault of whose Dreyfusism he has heard from the Narrator's aristocratic friend Saint-Loup. Rather than offer a helping hand, the duc de Châtellerault conforms to salon politics:

But the young Duke, who felt that everyone was turning against Bloch, and was a coward as people often are in society, employing a mordant and precious form of wit which he seemed, by a sort of collateral atavism, to have inherited from M. de Charlus, replied: 'Forgive me, Monsieur, if I don't discuss the Dreyfus case with you; it is a subject which, on principle, I never mention except among Japhetics'. Everyone smiled, except Bloch, not that he was not himself in the habit of making sarcastic references to his Jewish origin, to that side of his ancestry which came from somewhere near the Sinai. But instead of one of these remarks (doubtless because he did not have one ready) the trigger of his inner mechanism brought to Bloch's lips something quite different. And all one heard was: 'But how on earth did you know? Who told you?', as though he had been the son of a convict. Whereas, given his name, which had not exactly a Christian sound, and his face, his surprise argued a certain naiveté. (III, 544)[21]

The paucity of the Narrator's own commentary on Bloch's reaction to this instance of anti-Semitism leaves ample room for the reader's speculation. Prior to this episode, the Narrator quite clearly explains the psychology underlying an instance of Bloch's own anti-Semitism. In *A l'ombre des jeunes filles en fleur*, coming out of his changing tent (a significant image when associated with a Jew!) Bloch complains of what he sees as the overabundance of Jewish vacationers in the Norman resort town of Balbec. Bloch makes his remarks in a Germanic accent adhering to the same phonetic conventions as those Balzac used for his Jewish Banker Nucingen (II, 97). For Henri Raczymow, Bloch's almost speechless reaction to the duc de Châtellerault's affront simply represents the true side of Bloch's anti-Semitism, that is self-loathing.[22] The question nevertheless remains if Proust's lengthy staging of a joke at his character's expense does not point to the author's own underlying ideology regarding assimilation.

In *Sodome et Gomorrhe I*, the Narrator's discovery of Charlus's homosexuality serves as a pretext for Proust's long comparison between homosexuals and Jews. In this context, Proust glosses over Jews who socialize exclusively among themselves. He mentions the almost 'religious' witticisms and jokes that they normally have at the ready to tell one another: '... les mots rituels et les plaisanteries consacrées' (III,18). This scant reference to Jewish humour will apply to the character of Charles Swann in *Sodome et Gomorrhe II*. An unwelcome guest at the prince de Guermantes's soirée because of his Dreyfusism, Swann makes an attempt at Jewish humour. While Swann's witticism falls flat, the episode itself is structured on the matrices of two types of *histoires juives*.

The first involves jokes told among Jews in unwelcome or hostile circumstances. In such instances, the joke offers something of an oasis of comfort and reassurance. In an isolated conversation with the narrator and Saint-Loup, Swann quips, 'Heavens! all three of us together – people will think it's a meeting of the Syndicate. In another minute they'll be looking for the money-box!' (III, 96).[23] The Narrator observes that Swann, more accustomed to the pleasantries of high society, is ill-equipped at *la gaîté juive*.[24] Despite this putative refinement, Swann, displaying his own Jewish 'lack of tact', makes this remark within earshot of one of the more prominent members of the French military: 'He [Swann] had not observed that M. de Beauserfeuil was just behind and could hear what he said. The General could not help wincing'.[25] At bottom, Swann appears torn between the innate behaviour of his Jewish biology and his acculturation in French high society. Swann's effort then in articulating some form of Jewish humour to show solidarity with Dreyfus and the Jewish community might be dampened by his assimilation, but this does not preclude at least a partial integration into the community that he formerly ignored.

Proust compares Swann to the archetypal prophet who returns to his people in times of trouble (III, 89, 103). In this case, the trouble takes the form of increasing French anti-Semitism and its culmination in the Dreyfus Affair at the end of the nineteenth century. In this context, Swann's identification with other Jews relies on a personal conception of Jewish humour. As an assimilated Jew, the product of a mixed lineage, he lacks the religious elements that could also foster ties to this community. In Arnold Mandel's autobiographical *Nous Autres Juifs*, for instance, the author asserts that Hebrew is the glue that holds the collective Jewish identity together. Mandel illustrates this point with an anecdote supposedly dating from World War I. At the very moment a German is about to thrust his bayonet into his French adversary, the latter intones 'Shema Israel'. The German soldier lowers his weapon and says, 'Shema Israel, Prisoner'.[26]

However, Mandel also uses a burlesque variation of this same story structure to illustrate that nothing in Judaism is so sacred or solemn that it cannot be used to illustrate or teach. It involves a poor Jew who finds work dressing up as a lion for a carnival. The first day on the job, he is put into an arena with a tiger named Sultan. Shuddering with fear, the lion also desperately begins 'Shema Israel'. The tiger continues, 'adonai elohanu …'[27] Mandel's two accounts of Jews in danger, one quite dramatic, the other quite farcical, relate inversely to the circumstances that Swann or Bloch find themselves in. Swann and Bloch appeal to those within their immediate surroundings and yet are not greeted with a comforting, reassuring or pleasant response.

The second group of jokes of this episode in the *Recherche* opposes the superficial or cosmetic trappings of assimilation to what is true, biological identity. Proust causes this Jewish identity to manifest itself in Swann's physical appearance. Due to his terminal and hereditary illness, Swann undergoes the transformation whereby his weight loss makes his large 'Jewish' nose more noticeable. Even at Bloch's insistence, Swann refuses to sign a petition for Dreyfus because he fears that his name might sound too 'Hebraic' and, hence, too partial. Henri Raczymow interprets Swann's quizzical reaction as Proust's own Freudian slip. For the name Swann sounds English and gives an indication to what extent the snob appeal of Victorian English styles had for Parisians.[28] According to Raczymow, Proust would have made the slip while thinking of the Jewish-Germanic name of Charles Haas, the historical figure who informed Proust's literary one.[29]

I would contend, however, that at issue is a process of forgetting that underlies the conception of imperfect assimilation. In his chapter on Israel Zangwill in *Quelques Juifs*, André Spire recounts a chance meeting with his childhood friend Gustave Martin. Spire lists the evolution of the latter's surnames in ascending order: '… Martin, autrefois Sittenème-Martin, Sittenème, Sittenheim'. Having withdrawn from politics, Gustave Martin has time to write at leisure. Martin tells Spire of his trip to Syracuse where he visits the Capuchin catacombs. His first impressions are those of awe at the age-old tradition of leaving the deceased monks to decompose in their own little enclaves. Hanging around their necks is a modest sign that states, 'Remember my poverty'. The following day, Martin is disillusioned by his 'monastic' tour guide, a friar whose mores might have even made Rabelais blush.

Because of such things, Martin tells Spire, he has never written a book on Italy. Martin explains: 'If I were to let go and write on Catholicism, I would not be able to remain sincere for long. And could I possibly knock it with my name?'[30] André Spire reminds his friend that his name is presently Gustave Martin. The latter admits that he has forgotten.[31]

As a strategy in assimilating, conversion often accompanies onomastics and similarly displays the same quality of instability. In Proust's successive drafts of the *Recherche*, Swann becomes progressively less Jewish in his genealogy.[32] In the final version, some of it reconstituted posthumously by Proust's brother, other characters and the reader are left to speculate upon Swann's degree of Jewishness. One character, Mme Gallardon, for example, believes that Swann has converted from Judaism to Catholicism. For her, conversion represents nothing other than a tenacious loyalty to his former religion (I, 329). There is very little that is comic in Mme Gallardon's anti-Semitic or anti-Judaic reflection. It is only when Swann begins to view himself as Jewish that his status as a character becomes more comic. When this same perception of Jewish self is added to the preoccupation of how others perceive us, the substance of a joke lies nearby. In the following joke from Geiger's collection, the protagonist is outrageously conscious of how others might view him:

Weill runs into Wolff.
– Say, Wolff, Is it true what Blum has just told me?
– What's that, Weill?
– He told me that you had converted to Catholicism.
– It's true.
– But you had already converted to Protestantism, what does this all mean?
– I'll explain it to you, Weill. When I turned Protestant and someone would ask me what I was before, it bothered me to say I was Jewish before. Whereas, now, I can say without it bothering me, that before becoming Catholic, I was Protestant.[33]

Proust's description of Bloch's assimilation and acceptance into French high society presents an equally farcical picture:

I had difficulty in recognizing my friend Bloch, who was now in fact no longer Bloch since he had adopted, not merely as a pseudonym but as a name, the style of Jacques du Rozier ... Indeed an English *chic* had completely transformed his appearance and smoothed away, as with a plane, everything in it that was susceptible of such treatment. The once curly hair, now brushed flat, with a parting in the middle, glistened with brilliantine. His nose remained large and red, but seemed now to owe its tumescence to a sort of permanent cold which served also to explain the nasal intonation with which he languidly delivered his studied sentences, for just as he had found a way of doing his hair which suited his complexion, so he had found a voice which suited his pronunciation and which gave to his old nasal twang the air of a disdainful refusal to articulate that was in keeping with his inflamed nostrils. And, thanks to the way in which he brushed his hair, to the suppression of his moustache, to the elegance of his whole figure – thanks, that is to say, to his determination – his Jewish nose was now scarcely more visible than is the deformity of a hunch-backed woman who skilfully arranges her appearance. (IV, 530–1)[34]

As Jeffrey Mehlman,[35] Seth Wolitz, and Henri Raczymow[36] have pointed out, the irony in Bloch's choice of new name is apparent. Anyone familiar with the topography of Paris immediately thinks of the homonymous rue des Rosiers in the predominantly Jewish Marais. As Wolitz notes, Charlus, whose anti-Semitism can only be characterized as burlesque, has difficulty recalling the name of this *Judengasse* that runs through the Marais but says that it is where Bloch ought to live.[37] The Narrator informs us that it would take his grandfather's special gift, described in the beginning of the *Recherche*, to identify Bloch as Jewish, for the latter succeeds in hiding his Jewish traits. Proust's description of Bloch is troubling because it adheres to an anti-Semitic comic image of the Jew.[38] Despite Bloch's new appearance and acceptance into *le grand monde*, his behaviour continues to give him away. He steps on the feet of other visitors and interrupts a salon performance by Rachel, another Jewish character.

That Bloch's efforts to hide his Jewish nose are compared to those of a hunchback woman who camouflages her hump makes the synecdochic connection between Jewishness and deformity. As Sander Gilman has shown, anti-Semitic discourse often associates Jewishness with illness and deformity.[39] Swann's terminal illness coincides with his so-called 'return to the flock' as well as with his pronounced Jewish traits, particularly his nose. The hunched back when associated with the Jew is hardly without its own significance *sui generis*.[40] In Anatole France's *L'Anneau d'améthyste*, for instance, this same trait gives away the blond duc de Bonmont whose mother, née Wallstein, had converted and married a nobleman.[41] As evidenced in the following joke from Geiger's collection, the same spinal irregularity is as intrinsic and noticeable as Jewishness:

– My dear Durand, here we've been working together for the last 20 years. I need to confide in you something that maybe I should have earlier.
– What might that be, my dear Abraham.
– Well, you see, I'm Jewish.
– Well, my dear Abraham, one confidence for another: I'm going to tell you a secret: I'm a hunchback.[42]

In terms of the ideological underpinnings, we would be correct to say Bloch's metamorphosis and Swann's so-called return to the flock refute the possibility of total assimilation. By the end of the *Recherche*, the comedy of Bloch resides in the latter's painful efforts to assimilate juxtaposed with those treacherous qualities that continue to give him away.

NOTES

1. Walter Benjamin, 'The Image of Proust', *Illuminations*, trans. Harry Zohn (New York: Shocken, 1969), p. 207.
2. Un vieux Juif est entendu comme témoin. Le président l'interroge:

   – Votre nom?
   – Mosché Feinberg.
   – Ou êtes-vous né?
   – A Odessa
   – Votre métier?
   – Marchand de chiffons.
   – Votre religion?
   – Je vous ai dit, monsieur le président, que je m'appelle Mosché Feinberg, que je suis né à Odessa, que je suis marchand de chiffons: croyez-vous que je suis mahométan?

   Raymond Geiger, *Nouvelles Histoires juives* (Paris: NRF, 1926), pp. 244–5. Unless otherwise stated, all translations are my own.
3. Raymond Geiger, *Histoires juives* (Paris: NRF, 1923) and *Nouvelles Histoires*

juives were both published by the NRF. A study remains to be done on
Geiger's critical study of the illustrator and caricaturist Hermann Paul (Paris,
1923). While Hermann Paul remained dedicated to the Dreyfusard cause,
he nevertheless indulged in anti-Semitic caricatures.

4. Martin Grotjahn, *Beyond Laughter: Humor and the Subconscious* (New York:
McGraw-Hill, 1966), pp. 92–3.

5. Moschelé, que son nez, ses yeux, ses cheveux, sa voix, son allure, désignent
à un kilomètre comme un fils de Sem, raconte à sa femme, au retour d'un
voyage, que pendant tout le temps du trajet, ses compagnons n'ont cessé de
faire d'atroces déclarations antisémitiques.
   – Et tu n'as pas eu peur, mon pauvre Moschelé chéri?
   – Voyons, Rebecca, je ne suis pas assez bête pour leur avoir dit qui je suis.
   Geiger, *Histoires juives*, pp. 202–3.

6. Je connaissais une dame juive, dont le fils, vers 1934, était contraint par sa
situation de faire certains voyages d'affaires en Allemagne nazie. Ce fils
présentait les caractères typiques de l'Israélite français: nez recourbé,
écartement des oreilles, etc., mais comme on s'inquiétait de son sort,
pendant une de ses absences, sa mère répondit: 'Oh, je suis bien tranquille,
il n'a absolument pas l'air juif'. Jean-Paul Sartre, *Réflexions sur la question juive*
(Paris: Galimard, 1954), pp. 123–4.

7. This, and all subsequent citations in French of *A la recherche du temps perdu*,
refer to the four-volume edition under the supervision of Jean-Yves Tadié
(Paris: Gallimard, 1987–1989); see Sartre, *Réflexions sur la question juive*.

8. Or, as Jeanne Bem contends, Proust only uses Jewish identity as a metaphor
to explain the less familiar theme of homosexuality to his readers. Jeanne
Bem, 'Le Juif et l'homosexuel dans *A la recherche du temps perdu*', *Littérature*,
37 (February 1980), pp. 100–12.

9. Seth Wolitz, *The Proustian Community* (New York: New York University Press,
1971), p. 187.

10. Henri Raczymow, *Le Cygne de Proust* (Paris: Gallimard, 1989).

11. Henri Raczymow, '"Du Shlemil au shnorrer": A propos des histoires juives',
in Luc Rosenzweig (ed.), *Catalogues pour des juifs de maintenant* (Paris:
Recherches, 1979).

12. Depending on the speaker, 'Yid' may have either positive or negative
connotations. In the shtetl, 'Yid' might just mean another person. In the
culturally diverse world, if uttered by a Jew it might have the positive value
of brethren; and if uttered by an anti-Semite, it would mean something more
akin to 'Kike'.

13. Henri Raczymow, '"Du Shlemil au shnorrer"', and a conversation I had with
Raczymow on the eve of Yom Kippur, 1996.

14. Sigmund Freud, *The Standard Edition of the Complete Psychological Works of
Sigmund Freud*, Vol. 8, trans. James Strachey, pp. 111–12, *Jokes and their
Relation to the Unconscious* (London: Hogarth, 1960).

15. Friedrich Heer, 'Freud, the Viennese Jew', trans. W.A. Littlewood, in
Jonathan Miller (ed.), *Freud: The Man, His World, His Influence* (Boston, MA:
Little, Brown & Co., 1972).

16. Eliot Oring, *The Jokes of Sigmund Freud: A Study in Humor and Jewish Identity*
(Philadelphia, PA: University of Pennsylvania Press, 1984), p. 49. The
situation can be found in Strachey's translation of Freud's collected works,
Vol. 8, p. 18.

17. For the many implications of Yiddish and what he terms the 'hidden'
languages of Jews, see Sander Gilman, *Jewish Self-Hatred: The Jew's Body*
(Baltimore, MD: Johns Hopkins University Press, 1986); and *The Jew's Body*

(New York and London: Routledge, 1991).

18. Dans un train en Allemagne, Otto Bloch voyage en face d'un Ober-
lieutenant. Il tente d'engager la conversation. L'officier répond à peine. Otto
Bloch réfléchit:
  – Je vois pourquoi il ne veut pas causer avec moi. Il ne me connaît pas.
  Il se lève et se présente:
  – Otto Bloch.
  L'officier répond.
  – Et moi: Antisémite

  (Geiger, *Nouvelles Histoires juives*, pp. 128–9.)

19. This Sartre himself awkwardly explains and defends. His defense rests in
the Jew's disdain for the irrational, the intuitive. By being rational, the Jew
can break out of the particularistic mould of 'Jew' and become the universal
'man'. Analytical and rational, the Jew lacks tact. Curiously, Sartre lists
Proust as a typically Jewish author. Cf. Raczymow, 'Proust et la Judéité',
Pardès ('Littérature et judéité dans les langues européennes', 21, 1995).

20. Translation from C.K. Scott Moncrieff and Terence Kilmartin, Vol. 3,
pp. 281–3; revised by D.J. Enright, *In Search of Lost Time, Guremantes' Way II*
(London: Chatto & Windus, 1992):
  'Vous, monsieur', dit Bloch, en se tournant vers M. d'Argencourt, *à qui on
l'avait nommé en même temps que les autres personnes*, 'vous êtes certainement
dreyfusard: à l'étranger tout le monde l'est' [my emphasis].

21. Ibid., Vol. 3, pp. 282–3:

  Pour se rattraper Bloch se tourna vers le duc de Châtellerault: 'Vous,
  Monsieur, qui êtes français, vous savez ce qui se passe à l'étranger. Du
  reste je sais qu'on peut causer avec vous, Saint-Loup me l'a dit.' Mais
  le jeune duc, qui sentait que tout le monde se mettait contre Bloch et
  qui était lâche comme on l'est souvent dans le monde, usant d'ailleurs
  d'un esprit précieux et mordant que, par atavisme, il semblait tenir de
  M. de Charlus: 'Excusez-moi, Monsieur, de ne pas discuter de Dreyfus
  avec vous, mais c'est une affaire dont j'ai pour principe de ne parler
  qu'entre Japhétiques.' Tout le monde sourit, excepté Bloch, non qu'il
  n'eût pas l'habitude de prononcer des phrases ironiques sur ses
  origines juives, sur son côté qui tenait un peu au Sinaï. Mais au lieu
  d'une de ces phrases, lesquelles sans doute n'étaient pas prêtes, le
  déclic de la machine intérieure en fit monter une autre à la bouche de
  Bloch. Et on ne put recueillir que ceci: 'Mais comment avez-vous pu
  savoir? qui vous a dit?', comme s'il avait été le fils d'un forçat. D'autre
  part, étant donné son nom, qui ne passe pas précisément pour
  chrétien, et son visage, son étonnement montrait quelque naïveté.

22. Raczymow, 'Proust et la Judéité', p. 219 (see note 19).

23. Moncrieff and Kilmartin, Vol. 4, p. 113: '… tous trois ensemble, on va croire
à une réunion du Syndicat. Pour un peu on va chercher où est la caisse!' The
anti-Semitic press, particularly Edouard Drumont's *La Libre Parole*, imagined
a conspiracy of Jewish interests allied together to liberate Dreyfus. It was
metaphorically referred to as the 'Syndicate'.

24. In the same fashion as one might assert in the case of using Yiddish,
Raczymow contends that such humour then is necessarily considered lowly
by Proust (see *Le Cygne de Proust*, pp. 18–19).

25. Moncrieff and Kilmartin, Vol. 4, p. 113: 'Il ne s'était pas apperçu que M. de
Beauserfeuil était dans son dos et l'entendait. Le général fronça
involontairement les sourcils'.

26. Arnold Mandel, *Nous Autres Juifs* (Paris: Hachette, 1978), p. 185.

27. Ibid., p. 213.

28. 'The great Victorian era in England left its marks on all aspects of [Parisian] life, including architecture and house decoration. Odette de Crécy [whom Swann will marry] represents those Frenchmen who became enamoured of things English,' Maxine Arnold Vogely, *A Proust Dictionary* (Troy, NY: Whitson Publishing Co., 1981), p. 26.

29. Raczymow, *Le Cygne de Proust*, p. 122. In a reply to a curious correspondent by the name of Harry Swann, Proust explains his choice of Swann, in part, as based on its 'Anglo-Saxon' ring, Philippe Kolb (ed.), *Correspondence* (Paris: Plon, 1970–90), Vol. 19, p. 661.

30. 'Si je m'abandonne au catholicisme, je ne reste pas longtemps sincère. Et le railler, le puis-je avec mon nom?'

31. André Spire, *Quelques Juifs et demi-Juifs* (Paris: Grasset, 1928), pp. 109–11.

32. In one of the first drafts, Swann's mother was Jewish, Bernard Brun 'Brouillons et Brouillage: Proust et l'antisémitisme', *Littérature*, 70 (May 1988), pp. 110–28.

33. Weill rencontre Wolff:
    – Dis donc, Wolff, est-ce vrai ce que Blum vient de me raconter?
    – Quoi donc, Weill?
    – Il m'a dit que tu t'étais converti au catholicisme.
    – C'est vrai.
    – Mais tu t'étais déjà converti au protestantisme, qu'est-ce que cela signifie?
    – Je vais t'expliquer, Weill. Quand je suis devenu protestant et qu'on me demandait ce que j'étais avant ma conversion, ça me gênait de dire que j'étais juif. Tandis que, maintenant, je puis dire, sans que ça me gêne, qu'avant de devenir catholique, j'étais protestant.
        (Geiger, *Nouvelles Histoires juives*, p. 127.)

34. Moncrieff and Kilmartin, Vol. 6, pp. 326–7:

    J'eus de la peine à reconnaître mon camarade Bloch, lequel d'ailleurs maintenant avait pris non seulement le pseudonyme, mais le nom de Jacques du Rozier, sous lequel il eût fallu le flair de mon grand-père pour reconnaître la 'douce vallée' de l'Hébron et les 'chaînes d'Israël' que mon ami semblait avoir définitivement rompues. Un chic anglais avait en effet complètement transformé sa figure et passé au rabot tout ce qui se pouvait effacer. Les cheveux, jadis bouclés, coiffés à plat avec une raie au milieu, brillaient de cosmétique. Son nez restait fort et rouge, mais semblait plutôt tuméfié par une sorte de rhume permanent qui pouvait expliquer l'accent nasal dont il débitait paresseusement ses phrases, car il avait trouvé, de même qu'une coiffure appropriée à son teint, une voix à sa prononciation, où le nasonnement d'autrefois prenait un air de dédain d'articuler qui allait avec les ailes enflammées de son nez. Et grâce à la coiffure, à la suppression des moustaches, à l'élégance du type, à la volonté, ce nez juif disparaissait comme semble presque droite une bossue bien arrangée.

35. Jeffrey Mehlman, 'Literature and collaboration: Benoist-Méchin's return to Proust', *Genealogies of the Text* (London: Cambridge University Press, 1995), p. 53. Mehlman also relates another joke that we may add to our anthology: a German Jew, upon immigrating to France, wishes to Gallicize his name, Katzmann, and literally translates it to Chat-L'homme.

36. Raczymow, *Le Cygne de Proust*, pp. 39–40.

37. Wolitz, *The Proustian Community*, p. 205.

38. See Freud's *Jokes*, pp. 111–12.
39. Sander Gilman, *Franz Kafka, the Jewish Patient* (New York: Routledge, 1995); and *Jewish Self-Hatred*. Naomi Diamant also makes the connection in her article on Proust where both homosexuality and Jewishness are linked with illness, 'Judaism and other Sign Systems in *A la recherche du temps perdu*', *Romanic Review*, 82, 2 (March 1991), pp. 179–92.
40. In Freud's *Jokes and their Relation to the Unconscious*, hunchback jokes, for example, occur in the context of the *Schadchen* jokes. Though Freud contends that these jokes criticize the institution of marriage, one suspects that they also insinuate an association between Jewishness and defect.

> The *Schadchen* was defending the girl he had proposed against the young man's protests. 'I don't care for the mother-in-law', said the latter. 'She's a disagreeable, stupid person'. – 'But after all you're not marrying the mother-in-law. What you want is her daughter'. – 'Yes, but she's not young any longer, and she's not exactly a beauty'. – 'No matter. If she's neither young nor beautiful she'll be all the more faithful to you'. – 'And she hasn't much money'. – 'Who's talking about money? Are you marrying money then? After all it's a wife that you want'. – 'But she's got a hunchback too'. – 'Well, what do you want? Isn't she to have a single fault?'

> A *Schadchen* had brought an assistant with him to the discussion about the proposed bride, to bear out what he had to say.
> – 'She is straight as a pine tree', said the *Schadchen*. – 'As a pine tree', repeated the echo. – 'And she has eyes that ought to be seen!' – 'What eyes she has!', confirmed the echo. – 'And she is better educated than anyone!' – 'What an education!' – 'It is true there's one thing', admitted the broker, 'she has a small hump.'
> – 'And what a hump!', the echo confirmed once more.

> (*Jokes*, 61, 64)

41. Anatole France, *L'Anneau d'améthyste*, Vol. 3, ed. Marie-Claire Bancquart (Paris: Gallimard, 1991), p. 111.
42. A la fin d'un bon dîner, Abraham dit à son vieil ami Durand qui est bossu:

> – Mon cher Durand, voilà vingt ans que nous travaillons ensemble. Il faut que je vous fisse une confidence que j'aurais peut-être dû vous faire plus tôt.
> – Quoi donc, mon cher Abraham?
> – Eh bien, Durand, je suis Juif.
> – Eh bien, mon cher Abraham, confidence pour confidence: je vais vous dire un secret: je suis bossu.

> (Geiger, *Histoires juives*, pp. 202–3.)

7

Mikhail Zhvanetskii: The Last Russian-Jewish Joker

ALICE NAKHIMOVSKY

> You know what, Pani Sholem Aleichem? Let's talk about something more cheerful. Have you heard any news about the cholera in Odessa?
>
> *Tevye the Dairyman*

Russian-Jewish ethnicity, with the peculiar modern mix of talent and anxiety, pride and envy that has characterized it for over a century of Russian, and then Soviet, rule may have reached a historical end. The pressures that produced and reproduced it have diminished. Jews have emigrated or freely disaffiliated; and while those who remain can pursue Jewish activities unimaginable to their parents and grandparents, the new synagogues, summer camps, even klezmer festivals have non-Russian models and represent a sharp break in continuity.[1] As the civic and psychological vulnerability of the Jew retreats into the past, along with it goes an important source of Jewish ironic humour. Mikhail Zhvanetskii, one of the great exponents of that humour, may be the last of his line.

By origin and loyalty, Zhvanetskii belongs to Odessa, where he was born in 1934. Educated as an engineer, he found a more congenial spiritual home in that city's satirical clubs and theatres, which operated on the borderline of the permissible. He wrote sketches for the Odessa branch of the KVN ('club of the cheerful and resourceful') – a nationwide group of competing comedy teams that valued wit, improvisation and youthful impertinence[2]; later, he wrote for Odessa's Theatre of Miniatures. The fame of the Odessans spread until, on one legendary evening, they put on a special performance for the legendary comedian, Arkadii Raikin. Raikin (also a Jew, but, in keeping with his celebrated status, not prone to publicize that fact) hired Zhvanetskii and two of his compatriots as writers.

Zhvanetskii remained with Raikin, in Leningrad, from 1965 to 1969. A comic actor of immense gifts, Raikin was nonetheless a one-man show, and eventually Zhvanetskii and his Odessa colleagues, Kartsev and Il'chenko, went to Moscow, with Zhvanetskii again the writer. In 1972, he began performing his own material, and has continued to do so ever since.

In 1991, when political circumstances finally permitted the publication of a serious Zhvanetskii anthology (several small books had come out previously[3]) novelist Andrei Bitov wrote about his 'boundless' popularity.[4] Everybody knew Zhvanetskii. Confined, because of censorship, to secondary venues, he was at the same time appreciated by an increasingly cynical political elite. The ephemerality of what seemed to be an 'oral' genre (his solo performances) saved him, as it did the 'bards' – urban folksingers – of the Brezhnev years. Like all liberals, Zhvanetskii rode the crest of glasnost, with high expectations of democracy and capitalism. When these failed to materialize, he satirized the results. He moved back to Odessa – now, of course, in a different country – from where he travels regularly to perform in Russia, Israel and the US.

Though Zhvanetskii is in some ways comparable to an American (or American-Jewish) standup comic, he differs significantly in what might be called his 'literariness'. The Israeli scholar, Rita Genzeleva, has called attention to Zhvanetskii's stage role, with its emphasis on a 'stable literary text'.[5] Indeed, Zhvanetskii's performances begin with his walking out on stage with a battered briefcase, from which he retrieves, and proceeds to read, typewritten sheets. It is unclear that he is really reading – his delivery is that of an actor – but the persona is significant: the comic as Russian intellectual.

To consider Zhvanetskii as a Jew requires some explanation. For most of his audience, and certainly for his Russian audience, Zhvanetskii is a Russian joker, the satiric synthesizer of the Soviet, and now the post-Soviet, experience. Before Russian audiences, and throughout the Soviet period, his approach to Jewish matters was discreet; while he allowed himself an occasional sharp one-liner, most of his references were oblique. If we consider these references now, along with some of his characteristically Jewish patterns of language and imagery, we will find a more Jewish Zhvanetskii than has been presumed.

In taking up the Jewish aspects of Zhvanetskii's satire and persona, we are treading on the edge of Jewish marginality. Zhvanetskii's affiliation as a Jew is limited. Like many of his compatriots, he was baptized as an adult. Russian Jews who take this step tend not to see it as a repudiation of Jewishness, which, following Soviet practice, they regard first and foremost as an ethnicity. In the excerpt below, from an uncharacteristically serious poem of 1995, Zhvanetskii stands out from his generation by viewing his own baptism as a repudiation with ambiguous consequences:

> неясное какое-то еврейство.
> молитва разномастая.
> Сплевывает, крестится.
> И свечи ставит.
> Запутал Господа.
> И получил очередное наказанье.
> (удивление; published online 1995[6])

> A vague Jewishness
> Multicoloured prayer.
> He spits it out, gets baptized.
> And lights [church] candles.
> He mixed God up.
> And got the expected punishment.

In this poem, Zhvanetskii presents himself as a man adrift, without – at that time – children, and without a solid written legacy.[7] His abandoned Jewishness forms part of a pattern of insubstantiality that he finds painful. However, the estrangement is far from all-encompassing. Counterbalancing it is his loyalty to Odessa, that eccentric but symbolically and culturally Jewish outpost of the Diaspora. While Odessa Jews may have lost their religion – to the extent that they ever had one – they retained what we might call a Jewish way of looking at the world. The same birthright that gave the not very affiliated Isaac Babel a sense of how Jewish Jews got through life filled the same function, half a century later, for Mikhail Zhvanetskii. The combination 'Odessa' and 'Jew' is so tight that in some ways 'Odessan' can be a sub-category of 'Jew', rather than the other way around. As the poet Igor Guberman put it,

можно выставить еврея из Одессы
но не вытравишь Одессу из еврея[8]

You can take the Jew out of Odessa
But you can't scrub Odessa out of the Jew.

Before turning in detail to the Jewish Zhvanetskii, it is worth taking a brief look at Russian-Jewish jokes, considering their perspective on the Russian-Jewish dilemma and their sense of what constitutes a Jew. Below I single out six categories. The first four involve issues of identity and vulnerability that the Soviet-era Zhvanetskii utilized with caution. The final two are about a specifically Jewish use of language and the Jewish notion of family: these categories Zhvanetskii appropriated wholesale, though with a particular twist.

First, *Jewishness is indelible*. This category has to do with the persistence of Jewishness: to be a Jew is to bear a mark that you cannot shake off. You can change your nationality, you can change your name, but the underlying Jewishness will resurface. This category is well-represented in Yiddish and American-Jewish jokes, but with a significant difference. In non-Russian contexts, Jewishness is an inner state of mind: a Jew can assimilate to the point of conversion, but his specifically Jewish mentality remains in force.[9] In Russian jokes, and in Zhvanetskii as well, the designation is less psychologically complex, functioning more like a bureaucratic or physical black mark.

Second, *Jewishness is not always visible*. This reflects a paradox: while the mark of Jewishness is indelible, it is not always visible. Potentially anyone can turn out to be a Jew, with all the resulting symbolic baggage. The identification does not need to be accurate, and in jokes, as in life, it often is not. A pair of jokes that illustrate this point start from the familiar situation of Jews seeking other Jews in a non-Jewish context. The context is the opera *Eugene Onegin*, and the Jews are in the audience. Watching this most Russian of operas, one of the Jews assumes that Pushkin or Tschaikovsky must have written in at least one Jewish character and he nudges his companion repeatedly to find out just who that is. 'All right', says his exasperated friend, 'the nurse is a Jew'. 'Bravo, nurse', says our fellow, ever ready to declare solidarity. The other version is more maudlin: this time the annoyed companion declares that the tragic youth, Lenskii, is a Jew. 'He's the one who'll get killed', predicts the Jew, quite accurately, though for the wrong reasons.[10]

Third, *Jews are illogically vulnerable.* The underlying assumption of the *Onegin* joke leads us to the third category: if you are a Jew, you are in trouble. This trouble has no logical cause and cannot be combated through argument. At the same time, the consequences can be catastrophic:

– Арон, куда ты бежишь?
– Ты слышал? Верблюдов кастрируют.
– Ну, а ты-то что бежишь?
– Иди докажи, что ты не верблюд.[11]

– Aaron, where are you running?
– Did you hear? They're castrating camels.
– But what are you running for?
– Go prove you're not a camel.

Fourth, and paradoxically, *Jews are illogically powerful.* A joke set in World War II is a good example: a nearsighted, physically inept Jew is ordered to go behind enemy lines and hand out propaganda leaflets. Three days later he's back: 'Mission accomplished', he says, 'what do I do with the money?' Zhvanetskii, not surprisingly, doesn't touch this usage.

Standing behind all these jokes is the crucial fifth category: a large number of Russian-Jewish jokes show *a Jew using language to outwit or irrevocably disparage a powerful opponent.* This may indeed be the thrust of the camel joke just cited, in which the joker, for all his vulnerability, nevertheless exposes the illogical approach of his persecutors. A number of Russian-Jewish jokes appear to take on the Deity – though the ambiguous 'they' of the pair below could also suggest a secular power whose dominion is satirically exaggerated:

– Рабинович, посмотрите, какое красивое небо!
– Да, это они умеют

– Какая мерзкая погода
– Что и хотят, то и творят[12]

– Rabinowitz, look what a beautiful sky!
– Yeah, that they can do.

– What rotten weather.
– What they want, that's what they do.

More often, Jews in Soviet-era Russian jokes manipulate language to assert their superiority over customs officials, anti-Semites and even other Jews. This use of language as a weapon can be further categorized in terms of the type of weapon. In the world of Jewish jokes, Jews answer questions with questions:

– Почему ты всегда на вопрос отвечаешь вопросом?
– Почему бы и нет?[13]

– Why do you always answer a question with a question?
– Why not?

or reinterpret the question to give the answer they prefer:

– Рабинович, говорят, что вы большой ннтриган.
– Да, а кто это теперь ценит?[14]

– Rabinowitz, they say you're a big schemer.
– Yes, but who values that nowadays?

or transform meaning through intonation:

20-е годы: Как вы живете?
Начало 30-х. Как вы? Живете?
1937: Как: вы живете?[15]

The 1920s: How are you living?
The start of the 30s. How are you? Living?
1937: Well? [*Russian: How?*] Are you living?

All these devices appear in Zhvanetskii's satire, in addition to two other language-related characteristics which both Zhvanetskii and the anonymous joke-tellers use as ethnic markers. First is Jewish verbosity:

в трамвае.
– Мадам, вы выходите на следующей?
– Выхожу.
– А впереди вас выходят?
– Да.
– А вы у них спрашивали?
– Спросила, спросила.
– А что они сказали?[16]

In a streetcar:
– Madame, are you getting out at the next stop?
– I am.
– And are the people in front of you getting out?
– Yes.
– But did you ask them?
– I did, I did.
– And what did they say?

As if the verbosity is not enough, Jews talk with their hands:

Рабинович увидел изображение многорукого индийского бога Шивы.
– Вот кто был разговорчивым![17]

Rabinowitz saw an image of the many-handed Indian god Shiva.
– Now there was someone who liked to talk!

Sixth, *Jewish family ties are like no other.* In Jewish jokes, the terms 'Jew' and 'family' are often ironically linked:

Кто с кем приходит в гости? Француз – с новой любовницей, англичанин, с новым анекдотом, русский – с бутылкой водки, а еврей – с двоюродным братом.

А кто с кем уходит из гостей? Француз – с новой любовницей, англичанин – с новым анекдотом, русский, с синяком под глазом, а еврей – с кусочком торта для тёти Песи.[18]

Whom do you bring to a party? The Frenchman brings his new mistress. The Englishman brings a new joke. The Russian brings a bottle of vodka, and the Jew brings his cousin.

And whom do you leave with? The Frenchman leaves with a new mistress. The Englishman leaves with a new joke. The Russian leaves with a black eye, and the Jew leaves with a piece of cake for Aunt Pesya.

Even the Russian in this joke starts out in pursuit of pleasure – but the family-burdened Jew does not even have a chance of living it up.

For most of his public life (pre-1991), Zhvanetskii limited the overt use of the word 'Jew' to the category I have called 'Jewishness is indelible', in the specific sense of a permanent disabling classification. A striking example is embedded in a sketch called 'What? They haven't said anything to you?' (1982). The premise of this absurdist dialogue is that in the Soviet world your identity – like everything else – can be administratively re-assigned. The speaker is the object of this existential reassignment, a middle-aged man; he is on the telephone with an obviously bored female clerk, Number 15. Everything has been switched around for this man – except for one detail; and he takes it all in without protest – except for one detail:

> он: Простите, милая пятнадцатая, как меня теперь зовут?
> она: Это Крысюк?
> он: Д – да
> она: Сейчас, сейчас. Семен Эммануилович.
> он: Так я уже не
> она: Нет-нет. Это все осталось, Год рождения – 1926
> он: Мне же сорок два
> она: Это по-старому. Вам теперь пятьдесят шесть, еврей!
> он: Опять?![19]

> He: Excuse me, dear Number 15, what's my name now?
> She: Is this Krysiuk?
> He: mmm. ... yes.
> She: One moment. Semyon Emmanuelovich.
> He: Then I've stopped being ...
> She: No, no. All that stays. Year of birth: 1926.
> He: But I'm 44.
> She: You used to be. Now you're 56, a Jew!
> He: Again?!

Everything is malleable, except for the designation Jew.

As in the world of Jewish jokes, while the Jewish mark may be indelible, it is never completely clear who bears it. What happens when an unsuspecting Soviet citizen turns out to be a Jew is the subject of a pair of sketches called 'Comrade Grebenko' and 'Answer'. When Comrade Grigorii Ivanovich Grebenko (the last name and patronymic are markedly un-Jewish) makes this unwelcome discovery, his co-workers send him a letter which begins as follows:

Дорогой товарищ Гребенко. Мы, группа сотрудников, совершенно недавно и совершенно слуайно узнали, что вы еврей, и решили этим письмом как-то поддержать вас в настигшем горе. Извините, что 'вас' с маленькой буквой, но уж так получилось. (p. 132)

Dear Comrade Grebenko. We, your colleagues, quite recently and quite by chance found out that you are a Jew, and decided by means of this letter to somehow support you in your moment of need. Excuse us for writing 'you' with a small letter, but that's how it came out.

Further on, the letter writers express their hopes that the discovery will not harm their own careers. As the implications continue to dawn on them, they slide from polite 'you' to insolent 'thou' and cease using the polite but by now inappropriately Russian patronymic.

Comrade Grebenko's 'Answer' constitutes the second sketch in the pair. The unfortunate Grebenko shares both the perspective and the language of his co-workers:

Товарищи! Мое горе не разделить ни с кем! Спасибо за поддержку! Здесь, в больнице, неплохой коллектив больных и даже двое из тех, что уже прошли через это. (...) Вы говорите, что я знал давно. Как у вас рука подымается такое сказать. Да вы бы это почувствовали: и походка была б неуверенной, и голос подернутый, и, что главное, я б их всех выгнал, чтобы скрыть. (...) Что ж я, теперь, картавить буду, перхоть по углам собирать виноватым перед всеми ходить? ...[20]

Comrades! No one can share my sorrow! Thank you for your support! Here, in the hospital, there's a decent patient collective, and even one or two who have already gone through this (...) You say that I always knew. How can you even express such a thought? You would have known it too: my stride would have been uncertain, and my voice would have been *shrouded*, and, most important, I would have fired all of them [other Jews – AN], in order to hide it (...) What's going to become of me, am I going to start talking like one, sweeping up dandruff out of the corners, acting guilty in front of everyone?

To refer so openly to Jewish stereotypes was audacious in a Soviet context. However, even more surprising, was Zhvanetskii's parody of the self-hating Jew.

If Jewishness in Zhvanetskii were no more than a disabling bureaucratic classification, there would not be much to discuss. There is, however, one area of his work which mirrors the features of Jewish jokes and Jewish self-description, though the Jews in it are not always named as such. I have in mind the stories that are set in Odessa. I have argued elsewhere that the Odessa stories are very different from Zhvanetskii's works that are – or, we can say now, 'were' – set in some kind of abstract 'Soviet space'.[21] The individual in the Soviet stories is often trapped in some kind of absurdist – though not unrecognizable – hierarchy from which escape, if it occurs, is a matter of luck; in the Odessa sketches the individual can escape from hierarchy through the adroit use of language. The Soviet sketches are about an unwanted austerity; the Odessa sketches are about abundance. The Soviet sketches are about institutional life; and the Odessa sketches – written, I should say, at a time when capitalism presented itself as an ideal – are about life on the street, including trade.

Writing about his Odessa, Zhvanetskii mutes its overt Jewishness. As I noted previously, the stories do not use the word 'Jew' and – unlike Russian-Jewish jokes – are not populated by characters named Avram and Izia. On the contrary, Zhvanetskii emphasizes the inclusivity of Odessa ethnicity:

Рты прекрасные: смесь украинской, русской, греческой и еврейской породы.[22]

The mouths are beautiful: a blend of Ukrainian, Russian, Greek and Jewish stock.

Zhvanetskii's approach bears some resemblance to the famous pronouncement of the American-Jewish comedian Lenny Bruce ('To me, if you live in New York, you're Jewish. Even if you're Catholic. If you live in Butte, Montana, you're goyish even if you're Jewish'.[23]) Zhvanetskii's Odessa is a lot like Bruce's New York – in fact, we might note, a large portion of it simply relocated there.

It is not difficult to see why Zhvanetskii understated the Jewish element of this ethnic amalgam, but certainly his own mixed loyalties come into play here, as well as the obvious impediments of the Soviet context in which he wrote and performed. To his knowing audiences, the word 'Odessa' has a Jewish subtext. At a performance in New York, in 1999, Zhvanetskii told a story about finding himself at a reception standing next to Gorbachev. Does the famous comedian talk to the famous ex-leader? Not according to Zhvanetskii: 'He's the General Secretary, and I'm … from Odessa'.[24] Behind this self-declared unfitness to hobnob even with the out-of-work ruling elite is at least a whiff of the word 'Jew'.

Given these qualifications, Zhvanetskii's Odessa remains a recognizably Jewish place. A case in point is a sketch called, 'How do you get to Deribassovskaia Street?' The sketch, unusually for Zhvanetskii, belongs to that genre of jokes in which a series of national types reveal their inner selves. Zhvanetskii pictures himself in a number of Soviet cities asking for directions. The Latvian in Riga is tall, handsome, and refuses to speak Russian. The Georgian in Tbilisi makes an instantaneous move from enemy to dearest friend. Moscovites are too busy to answer. As for the Odessan, like the Jews of Jewish jokes, he answers a question with a question:

> – Скажите, пожалуйста, как пройти на Дерибасовскую?
> – А вы сами откуда будете?
> – Я из Москвы.
> – Ну, а что там слышно?
> – Ну, а что там слышно?
> – Ничего, а что Вас интересует?
> – Меня лично что интересует?
> – … Меня лично?
> – Меня интереует … что меня может интересовать?
> – У вас Москва, у них Воронеж, у нас Одесса, чтобы мы все были здоровы. Вы работаете?[25]

> – Could you tell me how to get to Deribassovskaia Street?
> – And where might you be from?
> – Moscow.
> – So, tell me what's new there?
> – Nothing – what interests you?
> – What interests me? Me in particular? My interests are … well, what can interest me? You have Moscow, they have Voronezh, we have Odessa, may we all live and be well. Do you have a job?

In the next sentence, without giving his interlocutor a clue about the location of Odessa's biggest street, he invites him to the cemetery.

As slight as it is, the Deribassovskaia sketch includes a number of themes that mark a Jewish Odessan. Prominent among them are specifically Jewish patterns of speech. The Odessan is not interested in imparting a simple piece of information. He is interested in speech for the sake of speech, or speech as a means of emotional contact.

Zhvanetskii, in general, is drawn to language that misses its target, to empty and misdirected communications, but only in the Odessa stories is speech so full of emotion and empty of content. A good example is a story called, 'On the porch'.[26] It is set at Zhvanetskii's own dacha, and records a conversation between Zhvanetskii, his mother and a neighbour. The neighbour is trying to marry off her slightly over-aged daughter. Zhvanetskii's mother patiently considers the situation; Zhvanetskii, his irony almost suspended, gives helpful advice. Each character has a theme and when the time comes to speak, repeats that theme with small variations: the relationship to what the other speakers have said is not very close. This is a comedy of empty communication, as well as a comedy of Jewish family life: the telling of it presupposes a knowing irony, but also a large measure of emotional warmth.

The same mix of elements – contentless speech, plus the Narrator's ironic indulgence – can appear in Odessa sketches that are not about Jews. Such is the case in 'My courtyard', a sketch whose sole premise is the fact that earlier that day, an actress came to see Zhvanetskii. Half a dozen speakers approach him with their own version of this information, which by the second, and certainly the third, time around is not new information: these Odessans are talking to talk, to establish an emotional connection.

Returning to 'How do you get to Deribassovskaia Street?', we can note that the most defining single feature of the Odessan is his insistence on answering a question with a question, or redefining the question so it better suits the answer he wants to give: both well-known Jewish devices, brought together by Irving Kristol under the term 'rebellious rationalism'.[27]

A good example of the rebellious rationalist is an Odessa sketch called 'At the port'. The hero, Kol'tsov, bears a Russian name – either because of the ethnic syncretism discussed earlier, or because Zhvanetskii consciously avoided making his work-shirking, quick-thinking hero an obvious Jew. The story follows a pattern that Zhvanetskii was drawn to in the late 1970s and 1980s.

The idea is that two speakers are involved in a hierarchical relationship. One is the boss, or the clerk; the other has no power at all. The conversation between them moves quickly into the realms of the absurd, with comic-frightening overtones. Sometimes the tables turn – but not because of quick thinking on the part of the victim. In 'At the port', we have the beginnings of the same situation with the added twist that the powerless Kol'tsov is actually guilty of something. He has skipped work to go to the beach, and while he was gone, a crane at his worksite fell down. Will Kol'tsov get out of it? Yes, because he uses language as a weapon. In the excerpt below, the boss is trying to get a response to the straightforward question: were you at work or not?

> начальник: Я вас спрашиваю!
> – Что вы спрашиваете?
> – Я говорю, вы, конечно, были на работе? Да?
> – Ага? значит, вы были на работе?!
> – А уто, кто-нибудь сомневался? я не сомневаюсь.
> – Вот тут я не пойму, если вы спрашиваете, я буду отвечать. Если вы отвечаете, я буду спрашвать.
> – Пока я начальник, я спрашиваю!
> – Почему пока? Вас могут снять? Вы так хорошо работаете, мы так к вам привыкли все. Почему 'пока', почему 'пока', почему 'пока'?!
> – Тише! Короче, были на работе или нет?
> – Попробовал бы я не быть! Что это, частная лавочка, что ли?[28]

(Boss): I'm asking you!
– What are you asking?
– I'm saying, you, of course, were at work, right?
– What, did somebody doubt that? I have no doubts.
– Aha! So you were at work?!
– I can't understand this. If you're asking, I'll answer. If you answer, then I'll ask.
– As long as I'm the boss, I'm doing the asking.
– Why do you say 'as long as?' Is your job in danger? You do such a fine job, we've gotten so used to you. Why 'as long as?' Why 'as long as?' Why 'as long as'?
– Quiet. In short, were you at work or not?
– I should try not being there! What is this, a private business or something?

So overwhelming is the verbiage that when it transpires that Kol'tsov has a towel wrapped around his neck, that rather incriminating evidence has no force at all.

Like the Jews of Jewish jokes, Zhvanetskii's Odessans are resolutely family-centred. This was true even of the Odessan in 'How do you get to Deribassovskaia Street?', for whom family, characteristically, includes not only the living:

> – Вы понимаете, что мне нужна Дерибасовская?
> – Понимаю, конечно понимаю. Так и я – все нет времени съездить на кладбище, а если ваши дети не приедут к вам на могилу, они тоже будут правы, потому, что они скажут: наш папа не ходил ...[29]

> – You understand that I need Deribassovskaia Street?
> – I understand, of course I understand. It's the same way with me: I never have any time to get to the cemetery, and if your children won't visit your grave, they will also be right, because they will say: 'Our Papa didn't go either'.

Family in Odessa is the immediate family, of course, but it also includes the street: the Odessa courtyard is family writ large. Everybody knows everybody's business, and everybody is connected. The sketch 'Cholera', addressed to Odessans, begins with the words

> родственники, знакомые, знакомые наших знакомых[30]

> Relatives, acquaintances, acquaintances of our acquaintances ...

In Zhvanetskii's world, this sense of connection is peculiar to Odessa; outside of Zhvanetskii, it is a feature of Jewish self-irony going back at least to Sholem Aleichem.[31]

Zhvanetskii's extended Odessa family is preoccupied, on the one hand, with eating, buying on the black market, and making connections; on the other, it focuses on matchmaking and children. Matchmaking reveals its Jewish origins through its concern not only with the young, but also with the middle-aged and even the elderly. Zhvanetskii, often the protagonist of these stories, is himself the matchmakers' favourite target: the fact that he was unmarried for so long (though a self-described womanizer) marked his status as both inside and outside this community. As for children, anxiety about children, and a fixation on their success, is described in the story, 'Origin', as an Odessa trait: 'From the time of Babel and up to now people put all their hopes in their children'.[32] That the fixation is not Odessan so much as Odessa-Jewish is hinted at through the reference to Babel; the connection is even stronger in the story, 'Give me your hand, grandson'; a monologue whose speech patterns and names point to its Jewish origin. The story is about grandparents who have given everything to their intellectually achieving children; like many Jewish stories, it combines success with sadness.

The epitome of this category is the story, 'A wedding for 170 guests.' This Soviet wedding – the characters' names makes it an explicitly Jewish one – is marked by excess. There is an excess of food, an excess of guests, and an excess of verbiage. More important with respect to issues of identity, is Zhvanetskii's self-presentation in this explicitly Jewish context. In stark contrast to stories not set in Odessa, Zhvanetskii in this company is *svoi*, an untranslatable word meaning 'one's own'. He is 'thou'. He is the object of matchmaking and the subject of their critique: whether or not they liked his latest work, they are sure to let him know.

The behaviour of the wedding guests is also worthy of note. When not eating or reading sentimental telegrams, they are busy making contacts with anyone who might be of use to them. This particular activity has nothing Odessan about it – everybody in Zhvanetskii's Soviet-era work engages in it. What is Jewish is the type of connections these guests are seeking:

> – Шура, кто этот толстый?
> – Он печально известен.
> – Чем?
> – Он директор еврейского кладбища.
> – У тебя есть к нему ход?
> – Через Зюню. А что тебе нужно? Сколько мест?
> – Пока сделай два.[33]

> – Shura, who's that fat guy?
> – A man of sad repute.
> – How so?
> – He manages the Jewish cemetery.
> – You have access to him?
> – Through Ziunia. What do you need? How many plots?
> – Make it two, for now.

We know, of course, that the linkage of death and weddings is a commonplace of folklore and lyric poetry. However, that is not the source of tension here: what is animating Zhvanetskii is the Jewish triad – wedding, cemetery and a business deal. We saw a similar combination earlier: the Odessan who fails to give Zhvanetskii directions does invite him to the family plot. For the Jew, as we have seen in the Jewish jokes, the expectation of trouble is part of the fabric of everyday life.[34] Look at it from the outside, and the inappropriateness makes great comedy.

No discussion of Zhvanetskii's Odessa would be possible without some mention of Odessa language. Consider the following excerpts:

> I write strangely. I hear myself when I write. A book for me is like a jar holding vegetables that once were fresh. Forgive me. I suffer from the loss myself, though there are people who can read these things from the printed page. They feel the intonation and can hold a pause.[35]

> Our [jargon] has more scope for satire … with a small shrug, a sentence turns satirical.[36]

The first one is Zhvanetskii; the second, Sholem Aleichem, comparing Yiddish, most likely, to the Russian that he spoke and wrote fluently. Sholem Aleichem is referring to the properties of Yiddish in general; Zhvanetskii to his particular Russian. Is there a common lineage?

It is well known – though nowhere, to the best of my knowledge, documented – that Odessa language, particularly its syntax and turns of phrase, is influenced by Yiddish.[37] In Zhvanetskii, Yiddishisms include sarcastic rejoinders, emphasized by intonation:

> откуда я знаю (…) Что, я всех должен помнить?[38]

> How should I know? (…) I should remember everybody?

Equally typical are tag phrases, some of which negate what might appear to be a curse:

> малолентого бандита, чтоб он был здоров[39]

> That juvenile delinquent, he should live and be well …

Others deflect the curse elsewhere, as in this grandfather's reminiscences about his children:

> Потом вы устраиваете нам поступление в институт – мы
> ночи не спим. Потом вы женитесь – с нами такое
> творится, моим врагам.[40]

> Then you give us *getting into college*: we don't sleep nights.
> Then you get married: and what we go through, my enemies
> should only know it.

The last two examples, both taken from 'Give me your hand,
grandson', may simply be a way of characterizing the speaker as
a Jew. A similar effect, with different syntactic means, results from
the following exchange, this from 'Wedding for 170 guests':

> – Рая, останови его, в него больше не входит, ты будешь
>   иметь ту ночь.
> – я имела уже прошлую ночь[41]

> – Raia, leave him alone, no more [drink] will go into him,
>   you're going to *have* it tonight.
> – I already *had* it last night.

This use of 'have' is inadmissible in standard Russian: it is a
borrowing from another language, almost certainly Yiddish.

If in some contexts, Jewish-influenced language is used by a
character who is obviously Jewish, in other instances it indicates
a more inclusive Odessa identity. The direction, however, is one-
way: a spill-over from Jewish to Odessan. Thus, in Jewish jokes,
Jews talk with their hands; in Zhvanetskii, all Odessans do. In
Jewish jokes and, sometimes, anti-Jewish ones, Jews talk in
incorrect Russian; in Zhvanetskii's world, all Odessans can do
this, to similar effect.

In the bilingual world in which Yiddish has always operated,
that language has often been used to deflate the higher-status
language with which it is paired. It had that function with respect
to Hebrew; remnants of Yiddish in American speech serve the
same role with respect to standard English. Zhvanetskii in his
Soviet period used Odessan language to deflate official speech of
any kind. Note the following announcement made through a
loudspeaker on an Odessan, or rather, Zhvanetskian, beach:

Потерялся мальчик пяти-шести лет, зовут Славик. Мальчик находится в радиоузле. Ненормальную мамашу просят подойти откуда угодно.

A five- or six-year-old boy has been lost, his name is Slavik. The boy is now at the communications centre. His crazy mother is asked to come from wherever she might have gotten herself.

Odessan language has domesticated, lowered, official speech: there is just too much emotion, too much irony and private detail for a public announcement.

The impropriety of Soviet-era Odessan speech combined non-standard grammar with politically unacceptable contents. Consider the following line, which Zhvanetskii claims to have heard:

Что вы несете, Гриша, в одеяле с женой?[42]

What are you carrying there, Grisha, in the blanket with your wife?

Moving the phrase 'your wife' to the end of the sentence allies two equally improper subtexts: illicit trade and some elusive kind of sex. The instinct for trade (in jokes, an attribute of Jews; in Soviet-era Zhvanetskii, an attribute of Odessa) combines with Odessan language in numerous examples. A short and particularly rich example is the following two-liner, which Zhvanetskii once again claims to have overheard:

– Скажите, в честь чего сегодня помидоры не рубль, а полтора? В честь чего?
– В честь нашей встречи, мадам[43]

– Tell me, in whose honour are your tomatoes not one rouble, but a rouble and a half? In whose honour?
– In honour of our meeting, Madame.

The comedy in the exchange results from the fusion of two contexts, the market place and the drawing room, that clash both with each other and with Soviet norms of behaviour and forms of address. That the two speakers are Jews, or at least Jewish-influenced, comes through in their spontaneous command of ironic one-upmanship. Both parties to what should have been a simple exchange at a farmer's market ('How much are the tomatoes?' 'Two roubles') are using language as a weapon, and appear as interested in their linguistic transaction as in the commercial one.

Not all examples of Odessa speech have roots in Yiddish. Some examples merely reflect the linguistic internalization of the black market:

> Надежда Тимофеевна, что у вас в руках такое круглое? – Это левая краска, занесли в двор. – Какая эта краска? – Я вам говорю, левая. – Я понимаю, левая, но она имеет цвет. – левая бордо.[44]

> 'Nadezhda Timofeevna, what is that round thing you're carrying?' 'Black market paint, just got delivered'. 'What kind of paint?' 'I'm telling you, black market'. 'I understand, black market, but it has a colour'. 'Black market bordeau.'

'Black market' is used here as a commonplace adjective, on the level of colour. However, what seems to draw Zhvanetskii to this particular interchange, is more than linguistic. Because Odessa language, like Odessa commerce, broke rules, it represented an act of freedom. In the introduction to his collection of stories on Odessa themes, Zhvanetskii is quite open about this connection, speaking not only of the enchantment of Odessa's 'enchanting ungrammatical language',[45] but specifically categorizing it as forbidden and the object of repression:

> Нам запрещали говорить одесским языком, нам запрещали одесские песни и танцевать под них.[46]

> We were forbidden to use our Odessa language, we were forbidden to play Odessa songs and dance to them.

The combination of many of these elements – Odessa Jews, mild criminality, Yiddish words and Yiddish irony – is particularly striking in a story called (in a nod to Babel) 'How they played jokes in Odessa'. The story is about a gang of musicians who appear at somebody's door insisting they've been summoned to play a funeral march. The fact that nobody has died is immaterial. Zhvanetskii's musicians combine their extortionary intentions with language that is Babellian in its out-of-place formality and also in its ultimate harmlessness:

Константин, застегнитесь, спряуьте вашу нахальную татуировку с этими безграмотными выражениями.[47]

Konstantin, button yourself up, hide your audacious tattoos with their ungrammatical expressions.

These are not serious criminals, and in fact, the story ends with the would-be victim winning the day by having the musicians play their dirge in the name of his annoying (and also, obviously, Jewish) neighbours: Играйте, только пойте: в память Сигизмунда Лазаревича и сестры его из Кишинева.[48] (Play, only sing this: in memory of Sigismund Lazarevich and his sister from Kishinev.)

With so much of Zhvanetskii's Soviet-era work dependent on the contrast between 'Jewish' and 'Soviet', it is interesting to consider the effects of a radically altered political and social context. What happened to Zhvanetskii when the rules got thrown out, so that, for example, to mention the word 'Jew' was not itself a bold act, and the anti-Soviet implications of Jewish Odessa were no longer relevant? What happened when the Jews themselves emigrated?

In practical terms, Zhvanetskii's audience has split into three parts. To Russian audiences he remains a commentator on what is happening now. To his Jewish audiences in Israel and America he has the same function, but, as he might put it, there is a nuance. One qualification is that to emigré audiences, he presents himself, at least on occasion, as a Jew among Jews. At a performance in New York in 1999, he told a joke about then prime minister Primakov, who is of Jewish origin. At the end of the joke he looked at his audience and said: 'A Russian wouldn't speak to you like this' (Россиянин так бы с вамн не говорил). This was an off-the-cuff remark for Jews, emphasizing his affiliation with them; it was not on the tape of the performance, produced in Russia.

Among emigrés in the post-Soviet world, his role has switched to that of courier, the deliverer of real news from *over there*. Listening to Zhvanetskii, Russian-Americans and Russian-Israelis can feel eminently satisfied about their decision to go, a point of view codified in one of his recent pieces, called, 'Who was right – those who left or those who stayed?' The conclusion is that, for the time being, the emigrés were right – but the categories could switch. And how does one know? Simple, says Zhvanetskii, look where the Jew is facing:

это будет зависеть от того, куда еврея поставишь лицом.[49]

It will depend on where you point the Jew.

Unlike the Primakov joke, this sketch, in its entirety, was on the tape. Remarks of this kind would have been impossible in the Soviet era *in public*. As the old distinction between public and private ceases to hold, so, to a large extent, does the ban on talk about Jews. In Zhvanetskii's usage, Jews become an indicator of the peculiar changes in the Russian condition. This is equally true for the Jew who stays put:

> Живу с Изей 30 лет, не знала, что он новый русский.[50]

> I've been living with Izia for 30 years, and I never knew he was a New Russian.

In the space of a single sentence, Zhvanetskii has denigrated the novelty of the common term 'New Russian' (Russian business-man) by confounding it with its diametrical opposite, 'old Jew'. While in terms of status, the two could not be more different, they are united by a real occupational link.

One final point remains to be considered: what has become of Zhvanetskii's Odessa? In Zhvanetskii's Soviet-era prose, Odessa was a special city in which the unspoken term 'Jew' expanded to include the entire rebellious population. Now, when Moscow is no longer Soviet and Jerusalem is a plane ride away, Odessa remains special:

> Пусть люди хвастают просторами и полями, у нас единственная родина – Одесса и единственная партия – одесситов.[51]

> Let people sing the praises of their open spaces and their fields. Our only homeland is Odessa and our only party is the party of Odessans.

Distinct from Russia (the source of the fields and open spaces), it is in its idiosyncratic way a substitute for Jerusalem, a homeland with its own diaspora:

> Из Одессы можно выежать, можно уехать навсегда, но сюда нельзя не вернуться.[52]

> You can leave Odessa, you can leave it forever, but you can't not return.

This Sacralized Odessa has its own spiritual face, and even its own prayer:

> О боже, сохрани этот город, соедини расбросанных, тех, кто в других местах не может избавиться от своего таланта и своеобразия.[53]

> O Lord, preserve this city, unite those who have been scattered, those who in other places cannot escape their talent and their uniqueness.

This essay began with a selection from Zhvanetskii's introspective poem, 'Surprise', in which he underscored his distance from a Jewish identity and his lack of a significant written legacy. At the end of that poem, he makes his peace with both of these facts, uniting his own 'light' genre with the 'lightness' of migrating Jews and ultimately with Odessa as his own Jewish homeland:

> А ну давай энциклопедию по легче.
> Для легких жанров.
> Для своих.
> … Для легких жанрах коротко живущих.
> Энциклопедию Одессы по всей земли.
> И всей Земли в Одессе.
> И всех евреев.
> Пере … недо … некочевавших …[54]

> Let's have a lighter encyclopaedia
> For lighter genres.
> For ourselves.
> (…) For light genres with short lifespans.
> An encyclopaedia of Odessa in all the world
> And of all the world in Odessa.
> And of all the Jews
> Who have over, under, or never roamed.

One of Russia's last Jewish jokers, Zhvanetskii is likely its greatest. Heir to the Jewish ironic disposition, he knows the vulnerabilities of Russian Jews and also their strengths. His Soviet-era sketches treated Jewish anxieties in an oblique way. Now, in the post-Soviet world, his Jewish references have become freer but never quite standard. Idiosyncratic as ever, Zhvanetskii has created his own Odessan ethnicity, an amalgam of Jew and non-Jew with the same loquaciousness and sceptical turn of mind.

NOTES

1. None of these activities took place under Soviet rule. The revival of Jewish life in the 1970s – the era of refusniks – was self-directed. More recently, the broader revival of Jewish cultural and religious life has used western models, aided by western teachers, western rabbis, and of course western funding. Given 70 years of Soviet rule, it could hardly be otherwise. Soviet Russia had no klezmer festivals or Jewish summer camps.
2. The 'Club of the Cheerful and Resourceful' (*klub veselykh i nakhodchivykh*) began in the mid-1960s in Moscow, quickly branching out to Odessa and other cities. It is still very much in existence, and, as a consequence of the largely Jewish emigration of the past decades, has become global. A 1999 competition, broadcast on Israeli TV, had a team from Israel competing against a team from Russia. The previously taboo issue of Jewish identity and Jewish emigration was given a thorough airing. Some information in English on KVN can be found in Maurice Friedberg, *How Things Were Done in Odessa* (Boulder, CO, San Francisco, CA, Oxford: Westview Press, 1991), pp. 47–8.
3. Mikhail Zhvanetskii, *Vremia bol'shikh peremeshchenii* (Moscow: Iskusstvo, 1977); *Vstrechi na ulitsakh* (Moscow: Nauka, 1980).
4. Andrei Bitov, 'Pod kupolom glasnosti', in Mikhail Zhvanetskii (ed.), *God za dva* (Leningrad: Ekslibris, 1991), p. 4.
5. Rita Genzeleva, 'Smekh Mikhaila Zhvanetskogo: problema natsional "nogo svoeobraziia"', forthcoming. My thanks to the author for sharing this essay and much else.
6. Mikhail Zhvanetskii, 'Udivlenie' (http:///win.www.online.ru/sp/magazine/mag-17/zwanec.xhtml).
7. In Russian terms, a solid written legacy would imply a 'Collected Works' (which, as of 2000, was in preparation).
8. Quoted in Leonid Stolovich, *Evrei shutiat* (Tartu/St Petersburg, 1996), p. 132.
9. An example of a persisting Jewish mentality – quoted from Joseph Telushkin, *Jewish Humor* (New York: William Morrow, 1992), p. 136 – is the following: A Jew converts to Christianity. The next morning, his wife sees him in the living room wearing his *tefillin* (phylacteries) and praying in Hebrew. 'I thought you were a Christian now', she tells him. 'Oy', he says, smacking his head. 'Goyishe kop'.
10. The two Onegin jokes can be found in Leonid Stolovich, *Evrei shutiat* (Tartu/St Petersburg, 1996), pp. 48–9, 74–5.
11. Ibid., p. 117.
12. Ibid., p. 116.
13. Ibid., p. 117.
14. Ibid., p. 42.
15. Ibid., p. 36.
16. Ibid., p. 45.
17. Ibid., p. 33.
18. Ibid., p. 134.
19. Mikhail Zhvanetskii, *God za dva* (Leningrad: Ekslibris, 1991) p. 347.
20. Mikhail Zhvanetskii, *Moia Odessa* (Moscow: Olimp/PPP, 1993) pp. 132–5. Russian culture associates dandruff with Jews.
21. Alice Nakhimovsky, 'Public and Private in the Satires of Mikhail Zhvanetskii', paper read at the conference, 'Three Centuries of Russian Humour and Satire', University of Nottingham, UK, 20–23 July 2000.
22. Zhvanetskii, *Moia Odessa*, p. 7
23. John Cohen (ed.), *The Essential Lenny Bruce* (New York: Ballantine, 1967), pp. 41–2.

24. 'он генеральный секретарь, а я … из Одессы'. This is on the tape of the performance 'Kriticheskie dni' (1999).
25. Mikhail Zhvanetskii, *Vremia bol'shikh peremeshchenii* (Moscow: Iskusstvo: 1977), p. 46.
26. In Zhvanetskii, *Moia Odessa*, pp. 94–6.
27. Irving Kristol, 'Is Jewish Humor Dead?', in Harold Ribalow (ed.), *Mid-Century: An Anthology of Jewish Life and Culture in our times* (New York: The Beechhurst Press, 1955), p. 432.
28. Zhvanetskii, *Moia Odessa*, pp. 77–8.
29. Zhvanetskii, *Vremia bol'shikh peremeshchenii*, p. 46.
30. Zhvanetskii, *Moia Odessa*, p. 28.
31. Both the citation from *Tevye the Dairyman* (see epigraph) and Zhvanetskii's title go back to the saying, 'Cheerful as the cholera in Odessa'. Zhvanetskii's sketch refers additionally to a genuine outbreak of cholera.
32. Zhvanetskii, *Moia Odessa*, p. 9.
33. Ibid., pp. 162–3.
34. Robert Alter has put it this way: 'Jewish humor typically drains the charge of cosmic significance from suffering by grounding it in a world of … practical realities'; see also 'Jewish humor and the domestication of myth', in Sarah Blacher Cohen (ed.), *Jewish Wry* (Bloomington and Indianapolis, IN: Indiana University Press, 1987), p. 26.
35. Zhvanetskii, *Moia Odessa*, p 3.
36. Meyer Wiener, 'On Sholem Aleichem's Humor', in Cohen, *Jewish Wry*, pp. 45–6.
37. A discussion of Odessa vocabulary, including multiple borrowings from Yiddish and Hebrew, is in Aleksei Stetsiuchenko and Aleksandr Ostashko, 'Gorobtsy khekaiut i zontik ne raschepirivaetsia: slovar' poluzhivogo odesskogo iazyka', *Novoe vremia*, 2–3, 5, 9, 32, 39, 43–4 (1998).
38. Zhvanetskii, *Moia Odessa*, p. 13. Rita Genzeleva gives more examples in 'Smekh Mikhaila Zhvanetskogo: natsional'nogo svoeobraziia' (see note 5).
39. Zhvanetskii, *Moia Odessa*, p. 14.
40. Ibid., p. 26.
41. Ibid., p. 160.
42. Ibid., p. 29.
43. Ibid., p. 59.
44. Ibid., p. 29.
45. Ibid., p. 4.
46. Ibid., p. 137.
47. Ibid., p. 14.
48. Ibid.
49. 'Kriticheskie dni' (audiotape, 1999)
50. Ibid.
51. Zhvanetskii, *Moia Odessa*, p. 147.
52. Ibid., p. 30.
53. Ibid., p. 61.
54. Zhvanetskii, 'Udivlenie'.

8

Between Two Worlds: The Dual Identity of Russian-Jewish Artists in the Late Nineteenth Century

MUSYA GLANTS

What may be termed the 'dual identity' of the world-famous Jewish artists who first appeared on the Russian art scene in the late nineteenth century has received limited attention. Regarding the sculptors Mark Antokolskii (1843–1902), Ilya Gintsburg (1860–1939) and Naum Aronson (1875–1943); and painters Isaak Asknazii (1856–1902), Isaak Levitan (1860–1900), Moiseii Maimon (1860–1924), Leonid Pasternak (1862–1945), Lev Bakst (1866–1924), Boris Cramer (1861–1945) and Peter Geller (1862–1924), we may ask: what is the significance of their Jewish origin to both Russian and Jewish culture? The answer depends as much on the human and artistic fate of the individual artists as on the social and political context and circumstances in Russia. The experience of duality, though, became the dominating factor of their lives, affecting both their personal and artistic destinies.

The appearance of these masters became possible both as a result of the policies of Alexander II and the Jewish struggle for emancipation that lessened Jews' resistance to secular education in general, and Fine Arts in particular. Despite the many changes in Jewish life during the late nineteenth century, anti-Semitism, though fluctuating, was always present.[1] As part of the Russian intelligentsia, these artists shared, to a certain degree, a common fate in Russian society, but as a small and recognized ethnic/religious group, they had distinctive qualities. Despite differences in age, background and artistic style, a common designation as 'Jewish' artists united them.

These artists were doubly unique because they were a part of both the first and the last generation of Jewish intellectuals who belonged equally to Russian and Jewish culture. Like the Russian intelligentsia, they loved Russia and its people, while maintaining fidelity to their own Jewish 'nation'. From the Pale of Settlement, those areas of the Russian Empire where most Jews were obliged to live, they carried memories of Sabbath prayer and freshly baked *chala*, even as they rose to the heights of Moscow and St Petersburg intellectual society. There was always, however, a struggle between the two elements of their identity, no matter how famous they became. The symbolism of the two words, *Bread and Matzoth*, which the Jewish-Russian poet and writer Sofia Dubnova-Erlikh chose as a title for her autobiography, mirrored the spiritual condition of those artists, the twin foundations of their identity, which were often at odds[2]:

> A Russian Jew … A Jew, a Russian … How much blood and tears were shed around these words which, for a Jew, meant both unity and separation. How much suffering has collected around them … 'Who are they?', the Russians asked. 'Who are we, Russians or Jews?', the Jews asked themselves then and later. Two loves, two passions and two struggles at once. Isn't it too much for one soul? 'Yes, it is'.[3]

It was precisely this feeling of tragic destiny that became the dominant factor in their personal and artistic lives. Like all Jews in the Pale, they experienced inequality and limited rights. They witnessed and endured cycles of torment both from the government and from the people. Every artist had his or her own indelible memories. Mark Antokolskii could never forget the inhuman recruitment of Jewish children into the military, which he himself escaped by mere chance in the early 1850s. One sees vestiges of this experience; Antokolskii was obsessed with expressing it in his sculpture. In 1873, in a letter to Vladimir Stasov, he wrote:

> I want to work on sketches for the subject I have had in my mind for more than six years. In my imagination grows a new project, which I consider as one of the most serious and fundamental. This work will be based on a dramatic historical fact. It is an episode from my childhood. Would you like to hear about it?[4]

Although a great deal has been written about the cantonists, Antokolskii's emotional intensity is exceptional.[5] His 1890s letter to Baron Horace Ginzburg also strikingly documents the Jewish condition. He recalled his youth during the 1850s, when a scarecrow resembling a typical Jew, a 'kike', was displayed and ceremonially whipped in the Vilna churches. Jews on the streets at such times could be beaten and even killed. Antokolskii bitterly remembered how a certain Count T., in order to entertain his guests, would buy a barrel of tar from one Jew and a feather mattress from another. He would use a third Jew on whom to employ these materials.[6] In his book of memoirs *Iz moiei zhizni* (*From my Life*), the sculptor Ilya Gintsburg, Antokolskii's pupil, recalled the authorities' cruelty and the humiliation he and others experienced. For example, the geography teacher in his St Petersburg's school ordered him to the front of the class where a map hung. To the amusement of the other students, the teacher laughed and said: 'Now show us on the map where is your "kike" country. Is there such a country?'[7]

The 1850s and 1860s, however, witnessed important changes in Jewish life. A great many Jewish youths in the Pale, touched by the Haskalah, the Jewish version of the pan-European Enlightenment movement, resolved to serve faithfully the country which they considered their homeland. They devoured Russian and European literature, philosophy, history and science:

> It should, of course, be borne in mind that this phenomenal progress in Jewish responsiveness to propaganda for education was primarily due to the confidence inspired by the reforms of Alexander II. It was this encouragement from the government, combined with the exhortations of the Jewish press, that produced a new generation of Jews who regarded themselves no longer merely as subjects of the Russian government but as part and parcel of Russian culture and the Russian people.[8]

Those who dreamed about the arts were already fascinated with Christian images; like Antokolskii, who was bewitched by the beauty of the statues in Saint Anne's Cathedral in Vilna. In fact, he began to carve his first figures there. Such young Jews realized that there was not much of an artistic future for them in the Pale. They yearned to join the free world and become part of Russian and European culture. 'Russification became the war cry of these Jewish circles, as it had long been the watchword of the government. The one side was anxious to Russify, the other was equally anxious to be Russified', as the Russian-Jewish historian Shimon Dubnov defined the situation.[9]

The emerging Jewish presence in the Russian art world was, however, hardly appreciated by Russians or Jews. To Russians, these artists were intruders, and to Jews, apostates who betrayed their own people. Whereas youth saw salvation in the outside world, the lack of intergenerational understanding was one of the most serious problems in the Jewish community. Although Jews could attend schools for a short time in the 1850s, the majority of their elders, alarmed by the prospect of assimilation, tended to resist Russian education in general, and anything related to art in particular. It was not enough for a young Jew to have the talent and skills to become an artist. He had to defy conventional notions of a 'good future'. To achieve his goal, he endured hardships associated with poverty: squatting in poorly heated apartments, hunger and illness which sometimes led to an early death, as in the case of Levitan. Outside the Pale, many young Jews had to live under false documents and study in hidden attics, lofts and basements. Gittelson, the Rabbi of Vitebsk, remembered that in the spring of 1858, when he was a student at the rabbinical school in Vilna, he tutored 15-year-old Mark Antokolskii, whose studies included German and French, world history – including Jewish history – and German and Russian classical literature. The boy paid for the lessons himself by working as an apprentice for a woodcarver because his father had long disapproved of his dream of attending the Academy of Arts in St Petersburg.[10]

The restricted exposure of Jews to fine arts and the limited opportunity to appreciate them was one more reason for artists to leave the Pale. This negative attitude towards the arts was especially acute because of religious prohibitions.[11] Eventually, though, families acquiesced. Even Antokolskii's father, who struck his son more than once for his carvings and drawings, finally allowed him to leave Vilna for the Academy. Isaak Levitan's father personally brought him to the Art School in Moscow, where his brother was already a student. The grandfather of Ilya Gintsburg calmed the protests of relatives and encouraged his grandson to become an artist. On the day when Naum Aronson, the future sculptor, left for Paris, relatives and friends cheerfully accompanied him to the

outskirts of his hometown, Kreslavka (now in Latvia). Leonid
Pasternak's parents sent him to Moscow. Even the religious Isaak
Asknazii came to the Academy with the endorsement of his
family. Resistance to the arts as a calling diminished somewhat
among Jews over the decades, but not enough to lead to widespread understanding and support. Art was largely a 'good-for-
nothing' occupation for a Jew.

Additionally, wealthy Jews scorned the works of Jewish artists
because these magnates thought that acquiring Russian art by
non-Jewish artists would more readily facilitate their social acceptance. In the writings of many artists one finds complaints that
non-Jewish art collectors such as Koz'ma Soldatenkov or Pavel
Tretiakov bought their work, but not rich Jews.[12] The impressionist
painter Leonid Pasternak noted that in order to please important
Russian guests, Jewish tycoons showed works of the Russian
painter Ivan Aivazovskii. After the funeral of Isaak Asknazii,
Pasternak complained in a letter to Baron David Guenzburg, and
later in a letter to the poet C.N. Bialik, that Asknazii died virtually
penniless.[13] Pasternak returned to this subject in his *Autobiography*
and added that not a single affluent Jew supported the landscape
painter Isaak Levitan during his impoverished student years.
He also remarked that at the beginning of his career in Odessa,
generals from the local garrison, but not Jewish financiers, eagerly
bought his depictions of Jewish life. One such painting, *Before
Passover* (1887), showed a Jew walking in the rain through the
dirty streets of a shtetl holding a goose for the holidays.[14] One
finds similar bitterly expressed statements and complaints in
Moiseii Mimon's unfinished article, *Kto vinovat* ('Who is to
Blame?').[15]

To be sure, this group was duly lauded in their own time. 'Long
ago Antokolskii was recognized in all the cultural centres of
Europe as one of the greatest and most original artists of the nineteenth century', concluded Vladimir Stasov in the sculptor's
obituary.[16] Many reviewers concurred. According to the London
magazine, *The Studio*, 'In Mark Antokolskii we have one of the
many proofs of the force of genius, the force that cannot be
repressed, that finds its level above all difficulties'.[17] More than
once the German and French press emphasized Antokolskii's
greatness as a sculptor. Critics recognized that a struggle for ideals
and nobility marked his works.[18] Isaak Levitan had enormous
influence on Russian art, to which he introduced a new type of

landscape painting, in which serenity and natural beauty evoked a widespread emotional response. His landscapes were often compared with Anton Chekhov's writings: 'Chekhov expressed in words what Levitan inspires with colours: the poetic sadness of things and their spiritual concealment behind the visibility of the tangible world'.[19] Leonid Pasternak became valued as one of the best Russian impressionists. Naum Aronson had attained success far beyond Russia and France for his busts of Pasteur at the Pasteur Institute in Paris and Beethoven in Bonn. Both Russian and western audiences were astonished at Lev Bakst's exceptional stage designs: their richness of fantasy, delicate style and refinement of colour. Because of their artistic originality, the works of these distinctive artists, along with those of Isaak Asknazii, Moiseii Maimon, Boris Cramer, Piotr Geller and others, are in numerous museums and collections around the world.

However, in this new and unfamiliar world, every step was full of surprise and confusion. Sometimes this led to humour, but also pain and humiliation. Ilya Gintsburg richly described his feelings of awkwardness and embarrassment. As a youngster who had never seen a concert hall or heard classical music, he remembered the first time he attended a performance of the pianist Anton Rubinstein: 'I saw the huge and brightly illuminated hall full of people. I was struck by the enormous white columns. The storm of the applause frightened me, while the classical music itself left me quite unmoved'.[20] Especially mortifying for young Jews was the fear that their command of Russian and high culture might be imperfect. In the story, *Obed* ('The Dinner') Gintsburg wrote:

> It was an official dinner. People approached the table in couples. I was seated between an English lady and a man who spoke French. The number of goblets and the table setting confused me enormously. I could sense that people here were dining in a special way and that I must learn by observing them. Carefully, I spread a thick napkin and began to cut the egg in my soup as my neighbour was doing. The egg refused to obey me; when I pushed harder, the soup splashed out of the plate onto the wonderfully white tablecloth … I become very disconcerted. Looking around and seeing that nobody was paying attention, I carefully moved a piece of bread to cover the stain … I promised myself not to eat anything further.[21]

To fit into new surroundings it was not enough to adopt a different lifestyle by changing clothes, food and other habits. Something more fundamental was required: the artists were tempted to understand and in many cases, follow, their new friends in their beliefs and ideas. They had to learn to appreciate people who earlier had seemed alien to them and rid themselves of prejudices against the goyim, or non-Jews. Earlier, Christianity had seemed to them a strange religion. Now they knew it as the faith of the majority and especially their friends. Often it became something worth comprehending and regarding differently, with interest and respect. Nonetheless, contact with Christians and Christianity evoked mixed feelings. On the one hand, the fact that Christ himself was a Jew could provoke the artist's interest in Christianity. On the other hand, Christianity's obvious role in anti-Semitism made them hesitant to embrace it fully.

The confusion created by these conflicting moments led the artists to try to bring Judaism and Christianity together in their works, as, for example, Antokolskii did in his many Christian images, especially in *Christ Before the People* (1876) and the *Christian Martyr* (1884). Christ was for him, as for other artists, an embodiment of their dual intellectual and emotional experiences. Most often the artists interpreted Christ not so much as the Son of God, but as the rebelling, thinking and caring human being. In Christ's Jewish origin, they especially emphasized the ethics that Christianity shared with Judaism: the eternal struggle between Good and Evil; and the absolute necessity of moral and religious criteria in human deeds. Antokolskii's interpretation of Christ showed that he was familiar with the biblical criticism of the time, which suggested that Christ, being born a Jew and remaining a Jew, must be studied in Jewish as well as Christian contexts. Such a view incorporated the justification for remaining Jewish and called on Christians to tolerate Jews without trying to convert them. There were other reasons for the sculptor to stress these ideas: to defend his Jewishness with dignity as well as to oppose anti-Semitism.

The interest of different artists in Christianity assumed various forms. For instance, the setting of Orthodox churches in nature, attracted Levitan. He especially experienced this during his trips on the Volga River, when he could explore the numerous picturesque churches, monasteries and cemeteries, sometimes neglected and concealed deep in the woods. In his paintings they became metaphors for emotions. To a great extent Levitan was influenced by his fellow artist Mikhail Nesterov, a deeply religious man who understood nature as a place of divine retreat, a place to remove oneself from the world and its evil. This attitude coincided with Levitan's search for spiritual peace. Nature was an escape from his troubles and suffering, wherein he found happiness. Although Levitan's views were more philosophical than religious, Nesterov's approach was congenial to him. This mood was strongly manifested in his works of the 1890s, such as *Silent Monastery* (1890), *The Evening Bells* (1892) and, finally, in his masterpiece, *Above the Eternal Peace* (1894).

Such notions expressed by other sculptors and painters through their art were stated explicitly by Pasternak in his writing, such as his essay 'Rembrandt and the Jews'. Here he discussed the images in Rembrandt's *The Return of the Prodigal Son* (c. 1668–69).[22] Pasternak's interpretation referred to the renowned Rabbi Hillel. Many consider Hillel as having reformulated the basis of the teachings of Christ: 'What is hateful to thee, do not unto thy fellow man: this is the whole Law; the rest is mere commentary'. The struggle of the artists to bring together two different religious principles was a search for common grounds.

Each artist had to decide whether, and how, to reconcile the world from which he came with his new life. He had also to decide the extent to which he would assimilate. Needless to say, assimilation was extremely tempting. Its ultimate stage – conversion – promised freedom, a better future and hope for equality, as well as the liberation from what Vladimir Korolenko called in his novel, *Bratia Mendel* ('The Mendel Brothers'), 'the constant condition of national disability'.[23] However, unlike the numerous Jews in other professions, there were only a few in the arts and often they experienced isolation from each other – but most of the artists chose not to abandon their heritage, either in life or art.

Despite the diversity of their personalities and social position, even those who were personally estranged from religious observance retained respect for Judaism. Asknazii grew up in a family that was religious and affluent, which he left after he had already formed his religious views. From the time he attended the Moscow Art School, Levitan lived and worked for many years practically in a pure Russian milieu. According to his confidante Sophia Kuvshinnikova, although Levitan considered the Orthodox rites mysteriously beautiful, they remained alien to him.[24] For some, the yearning to gain acceptance within their Russian surroundings made assimilation more acceptable. This was so for Pasternak, although it caused him much distress and regret in later years and led him to write his *Autobiography* and *Rembrandt and the Jews* (1918–20), as well as to participate in a number of Jewish activities. Even before the revolution Pasternak developed a close relationship with Zionist leaders such as C.N. Bialik and David Shor.[25] In 1917 the newspaper, *Russkie Vedomosti* ('Russian Gazette'), published both a programme to defend Jews during revolutionary times and a list of candidates for the Moscow Jewish Community Council that included Pasternak.[26] The artist himself made a trip to Palestine in 1924 and renewed his interest in Jewish topics for his art.

Others shared such Jewish concerns. Antokolskii wrote to Stasov in 1874 about his criticism of the artist's depiction of Christ, particularly his overly prominent forehead:

> I have not looked for an ideal image of Christ among other people. I was only depicting what I had seen and felt among the Jews in their real life. Who had not seen and does not know the masses of the poor, ragged and starved Jews who are spending days and nights in the synagogues where they sleep on bare wooden boards, sometimes 40, 50 people in one room?; who has not seen their ecstatic faces when they are studying their complicated and intricate but beloved Talmud? – he can not even imagine the surrounding where Jesus came from. These poor and ragged men were always, and are now, the Jewish intelligentsia. They are all ardent people who love to think passionately over the Talmudic ideas. This is the surrounding where Christ and Spinoza came from. The Jew's forehead develops this way and is a reflection of how his memory is trained since childhood. Eight- to ten-year-old boys have already finished the Bible and now learn weekly up to 20 pages of this intricate Talmud with all the commentaries. And all this, they learn by heart.[27]

Despite persistent oppression and humiliation, none of these men fully embraced Christianity. When Lev Bakst converted in 1902, to be able to marry Pavel Tretiakov's daughter, he felt uncomfortable and returned to Judaism immediately after their divorce. Bakst's friend, the artist and art historian, Alexander

Benois, remembered that he was always faithful to Judaism and spoke about it with reverence and almost in a tone of 'patriotism'.[28] Remaining a Jew was a way to assert one's dignity, despite the likelihood of advancing one's career through baptism. They considered apostasy as betrayal. When Antokolskii found out that one of his nephews was willing to convert, he wrote to Stasov: 'My nephew upsets me very much. His stupid and trivial act (if he is already baptized) does not touch me by itself. As you correctly remarked, the hell with him, but I feel sorry for his parents'.[29]

The painter, Boris Cramer (18??–1945), newly graduated from the Academia in the 1880s, was offered a commission to decorate two churches in St Petersburg, but only on the condition that he be baptized. Cramer, an avowed atheist, refused and emigrated to America instead.[30] In the 1880s, Levitan and Pasternak received invitations to teach at the Moscow School of Painting and Sculpture. The latter immediately indicated to the Director, Prince A.E. Lvov, that it would be impossible because Grand Duke Sergeii Aleksandrovich, trustee of the School, would not authorize a Jew. Pasternak declared that he was unwilling to be baptized for the sake of professional advancements. Both artists were finally accepted without baptism, but only as adjunct professors without most of the regular benefits.[31]

However, most believed that, even if converted, as Jewish artists they could not expect full recognition or acceptance from the Russians, even the progressive sort. Anton Chekhov explored this in his story, 'Perekati-pole'. As historian, Michael Stanislawski, remarked, a persistent paradox defined Russification; even the most Russified Jews understood that they were not Russians, nor could they ever become Russians. They could adopt Russian as their mother tongue, abandon traditional Jewish practices, replace the Bible, Talmud and Jewish folk culture with Pushkin, Gogol and Turgenev and the talk of the street, become bearers and creators of Russian culture, and even proud and loyal citizens of Russia – but not Russians, that is, Russians by nationality.[32]

It is crucial to recall that for Russian society it was a new experience to see Jews in so many spheres of Russian life and culture. Understandably, their attitude towards the newcomers was covertly and, often, overtly wary. The Jewish intelligentsia and the artists in particular had numerous entrenched stereotypes to overcome. 'To the inhabitants of the two Russian capitals and of the interior of the Empire', noted Shimon Dubnov, 'the Pale of Settlement seemed as distant as China'.[33] These alien 'oriental'-looking people with their guttural language, strange habits and dress code, had been a target of cruelty and mockery for generations. The memoirs of Princess Lidia Vasil'chikova, a daughter of Prince Leonid Viazemskii, illustrate how wicked many, even well-educated and noble, Russians considered them:

> The Jews of Urburg (Lithuania) treat their animals terribly. They load their horses excessively, whip them without mercy and don't feed them. Besides, they kill the animals according to their rituals, which stipulate that it be done in a way that causes the greatest possible suffering to the animals.[34]

Although anti-Semitism was omnipresent, its intensity varied. Antokolskii and Gintsburg were fortunate enough to become part of the liberal and democratic milieu of the 1860s, when many aspired to positive changes. According to Gintsburg: 'This was a time of spiritual enthusiasm for the intellectual part of society. Everybody was friendly, and everything bright and good was immediately taken up and exalted. A Jew, a Ukrainian and a Pole – all were equal'. He described the amiable atmosphere at frequent gatherings where fellow artists were united by true friendship; the question of nationality never even arose.[35] At that time, it was shameful to be an anti-Semite. Antokolskii could never forget the kindness of such Russians as the governor of Vilna, Vladimir Ivanovich Nazimov, and his wife, who exerted great effort to help him get to St Petersburg.[36] He also recalled that Tsar Alexander II came to his loft-studio at the Academy to see his sculpture, *Ivan the Terrible* (1871), and commissioned a copy for himself. Alexander II was the first and only Russian tsar to attend a service in a Jewish synagogue during his visit to Vilna. One particular detail suggests the flavour of the period. When in 1858 the magazine, *Illustratsia* ('Illustration'), of St Petersburg published an anti-Semitic article and was abusive to Jewish authors, it aroused a storm of indignation in the literary circles of both capitals. One hundred and forty writers signed a public protest that condemned the article as insulting to all Russian literature.[37]

Unfortunately, this brief period of toleration did not last. Signs of a new wave of reaction appeared in the early 1870s and clearly intensified in the 1880s and 1890s. After the assassination of Alexander II in 1881, both official and unofficial anti-Semitism became especially open and strong and continued until the Revolution. As is well known, anti-Jewish pogroms became a common part of Russian life. One of the first occurred in Odessa in 1871. Later years witnessed accusations of ritual murder. During the reign of Alexander III, Jews, among them the artists, were victimized in many different ways. Antokolskii was repeatedly defamed by the reactionary Russian press, in particular by Alekseii Suvorin and his friends from the newspaper, *Novoe vremia* ('New Times').[38] The sculptor, who was then in Italy to improve his health, had all the more reason not to return to Russia, and he settled first in Rome (1871) and later in Paris (1877).

Levitan, too, was singled out for persecution. In September 1892, he was exiled from Moscow for not having permission to live outside the Pale, despite the fact that he was a widely recognized artist whose works had been purchased by notables such as the governor of Moscow, Grand Duke Sergeii Aleksandrovich.[39] After many interventions by influential people, he was allowed to return, temporarily, in December. Levitan's painting, *Above the Eternal Peace*, reflected his emotional state. Finally, in 1894 he received permission to reside where he desired. In Spring 1912, Lev Bakst, the world-famous stage designer, the so-called 'King of Paris', travelled to Russia for a short visit. Within 24 hours he was deported. After this experience he resolved never to return to his homeland.[40] Naum Aronson, a widely recognized sculptor, was commissioned shortly before World War I to come to Russia from Paris to work on two monuments. His friends inadvertently neglected to obtain permission for him to stay in the capitals. In St Petersburg, he was forced to live in the Academy, since, as the Vice-President Count Ivan Tolstoi told him, 'Nobody will come to look for you here'. The situation was even worse in Moscow. Not being able to settle anywhere officially, one night Aronson wandered around the city, drinking tea in every restaurant on his way. 'That night', he recalled in his reminiscences, 'I had more tea than I usually drink in a month ... I walked the streets of Moscow, a beautiful city, where there was no place for a Jew even for one night'.[41] Ilya Ginzburg articulated similar sentiments:

> I found out that from the State's point of view I am nothing. I am a Jew, but the State is Russian. They are the masters of the country, while I am only an alien. Although I am a Russian subject, I have a different religion, which means that

my brothers and sisters are not allowed to live in Petersburg and to see me.[42]

Especially painful were the anti-Semitic remarks of fellow artists or supposed friends, such as Antokolskii's former friends, the painters Ivan Kramskoi, who criticized his *Christ* for looking too Jewish, and Nikolaii Bogoliubov, who wrote an essay calling him and his wife 'kikes' [*Zhidy*].[43] Such instances hurt all the more because they made one ashamed of the Russian people who degraded themselves either by revealing their own anti-Semitism or tolerating that of others. Antokolskii wrote that:

> I know many households where they [anti-Semites] are hated as much as one can hate an abscess in a most sensitive place. But even so, the newspaper *Novoie vriemia* is on their tables. Some of them do it out of cowardliness, others because of stupidity, and the rest simply because of their meanness, saying that 'I am yours, I am a true patriot'.[44]

During the darkest years, when even such leading figures as Ivan Turgenev and Leo Tolstoi failed to raise their voices against the mistreatment of Jews, the bond of Jewish artists to their roots was no longer a question of pure religious or social preference. It had become an expression of principle and courage, a form of self-assertion and protest.[45] The artists believed that the betrayal of their origin and faith would make them look exactly as the anti-Semites wanted to see them – weak and cowardly. The leitmotiv of the aforementioned letter from Antokolskii to Baron Horace Ginzburg was that the Jews should forget their eternal fear and forego their struggle to please their enemies by endlessly 'improving themselves'. Instead they should show their resistance, for nobody in the world would save them but themselves.[46]

What can one say, however, about the Jewish 'content' of their art? When these artists introduced images of Jews it was for various reasons. Often, it was at the early stages of their careers, when they were still close to their origins and knew their own people best. Even Levitan, who was not particularly attracted to the topic, painted a portrait of an identifiable 'Jewish' girl. A second reason was the general liberalization of the 1860s. The resulting democratic trends in art led to a new interest in daily life of common people of different nationalities within the Russian

Empire. This was demonstrated, for example, in the works of the *Peredvizhniki* ('Wanderers').[47] Antokolskii began the trend toward a new portrayal of Jews. He was the first to depict his people as the antithesis of anti-Jewish stereotypes. His sculptural works, *The Tailor* (1864) and *The Miser* (1865), recalled the Russian *prostoi chelovek* ('simple man') as exemplified by Kramskoi's *Mina Moiseiev* (1882). Antokolskii's bas-relief, *Inquisition* (1868), and such figures as *Nathan the Wise* (1868), showed people of dignity from a rich and ancient culture. This devotion to heroic Jewish themes continued into the 1880s and beyond, when it took on added significance. Previously, one motive was Jewish self-improvement, in order to compel the Russians to accept the Jews as equals. Now self-improvement gave way to a sense of opposition or resistance. Characters ready to fight and die for their beliefs became the heroes of works by Moiseii Maimon, in the *Marranos and the Spanish Inquisition* (1893), Isaak Asknazii, in *The Drowning of the Jews in the River Polotsk by Order of Ivan the Terrible in 1563* (1893), and Lev Bakst, in the portrait of *Uriel Akosta* (1892). Antokolskii returned to his *Inquisition* (1896–1902) and also worked on the images of *Moses* and *Deborah*. Along with the heroic past, the artists created scenes of pogroms and their victims, often in the same epic style.

With similar inspiration, genre art was especially popular among the Jewish artists at the end of the century as a symbol of self-expression and self-respect. Realistic depictions of tailors and shoemakers, bakers and horsemen, blacksmiths and *balagulas* ('coachmen'), milkmen and traders, scenes of holidays, days of celebration and days of mourning, were purposely meant to oppose the images of 'betrayers', 'parasites' and 'crooks' fabricated by the anti-Semites. Unpretentious people, who were forced to fight poverty and persecution, were now glorified not only in literature and music but also in fine arts. They appear in Isaak Asknazii's paintings, *Bad News* (1890s) and *The Jewish Wedding* (1893), Moiseii Maimon's, *After Work* and *Street in the Town of Vilna* (1890s), Leonid Pasternak's, *Musicians* (1890s) and Yeguda Pen's, *The Old Tailor* (1903). Along with the former depiction of mostly elderly people, praying and studying, the artists now rendered young men, women and children at different moments in their lives. It would be misleading to call this 'national Jewish art'. It would perhaps be more appropriate to describe this movement as art of the Jewish people asserting their rights and equality. The motive was probably more socio-political than artistic, a form of national defence. Although these art works, created by talented and well-trained professionals, were innovative in subject, stylistically they followed the way of their non-Jewish colleagues. This step, however, taken by the artists of the first generation, was brave and inventive, considering the circumstances.

These distinguished Russian-Jewish artists of the late nineteenth century become world-known celebrities. Yet each of them, in his own way, experienced an unrequited love for his country. As Antolkolskii asked:

> What have I done to Russia which is so bad? I am devoted to it fully, with all my heart and soul. Its life and history have become dear to me, even dearer than my own. I have devoted my life and my talent to it. If I receive glory and honour in Europe, I receive it not as a Jew, but as a Russian. Now I ask – why am I so painfully beaten and antagonized precisely by those whom I trusted the most?[48]

The sense of dual identity was inescapable. This contributed to victories and defeats, spiritual struggles and broken dreams. Nevertheless, their devotion to Russia was boundless. 'I still have not stopped believing in the strength of the Russian soul; all my works, feelings and thought, all my joy and grief, which are feeding my spirit – all this is from Russia and for Russia', wrote Antokolskii. Travelling abroad, Levitan always felt nostalgic for the Russian countryside, for him the most beautiful in the world. Aronson's wish, according to his widow, was to leave his works to the museums in Russia. We are left, then, with a paradox: these artists saw their work as part of, and belonging to the glory of Russia, despite their problematic place in its life and history.

NOTES

1. S.M. Dubnov, *History of the Jews in Russia and Poland*, Vol. 2 (Philadelphia, PA: Jewish Publication Society of America, 1918), pp. 154–83.
2. Sophia Dubnova-Erlikh, *Khleb i matsa* ('Bread and Matzoth') (St Petersburg: Maksima, 1994).
3. St. Ivanovich (S.O. Portugeis), *Semen Yushkevich i evreii* ('Semen Yushkevich and the Jews') (Paris, 1927); cited in Eduard Kapitaikin (ed.), *Dve liubvi, dve strasti, dva borenia* ('Two loves, two patiences and two struggles'); and in Mikhail Parkhomovskii (ed.), *Evrei v kul'ture Russkogo zarubezhia, I* (Jerusalem, 1992), pp. 26, 27.

4. M.M. Antokol'skii, 'Edin, "Pis'mo k V.V. Stasovu" ('Letter to V.V. Stasov'), no. 85, Rome, 4(16) December 1873', in V.V. Stasov (ed.), *Mark Matveevich Antokol'skii. Ego zhizn', tvorenia, pis'ma i stat'I* (Moscow: Izdanie T-va M.O. Vol'f, 1905), p. 103.

5. Nicholas I began the conscription of Jews into the Russian Army in 1827, allowing under-age recruits (Cantonists) to be given in lieu of adults. This reform was intended, at least in part, to 'reform', and assimilate them, and was often accompanied by semi-forced conversion. See Michael Stanislawsky, *Tsar Nicholas I and the Jews* (Philadelphia, PA: Jewish Publication Society of America, 1983), p. 115.

6. M.M. Antokolskii, 'Pis'mo k Baronu Horatsiu Ginzburgu' ('Letter to Baron Harace Ginzburg'), 1890s. Russian National Library. Manuscript Department, F.183. The Baron Ginzburg's Family Archive: Antokol'ski's Letters to the Ginzburg Family.

7. I.Y. Gintsburg, *Kak ia sdelalsia skulptorom* ('How I became a sculptor'), in *Iz moei zhizni* (St Petersburg, 1908), p. 37.

8. Louis Greenberg, *The Jews in Russia: The Struggle for Emancipation*, Vol. 1 (New York: Schocken, 1976), p. 118. Yulii Gessen, *Istoria evreiskogo naroda* ('History of the Jewish People') (Moscow and Jerusalem, 1993), pp. 171–4; Stanislawsky, *Tsar Nicholas I*, p. 115; Eliakum Zunser, *A Jewish Bard* (New York: Zunser Jubilee Committee, 1905), p. 28.

9. Dubnov, *History of the Jews*, Vol. II, pp. 210–21.

10. V.V. Stasov, 'Mark Matveevich Antokolskii. Biograficheskii ocherk', in Stasov, *Mark Matveevich Antokol'skii*, p. vii.

11. This has been increasingly called into question since the appearance of Cecil Roth's edited volume, *Jewish Art: An Illustrated History* (London: W.H. Allen, 1961). All kinds of evidence prove that since antiquity Jews have produced visual images, using mosaics and paintings in synagogue decoration and book illustration. An especially rich source is the numerous issues of the Haggadah. See R. Keller (ed.), *The Jews: A Treasury of Art and Literature* (New York: Beaux Arts Edition, 1992); Irene Korn, *A Celebration of Judaism in Art* (New York: Smithmark Publishers, 1996); *Jewish Art from the Skirball Cultural Center and Museum, Los Angeles* (Hong Kong: Hugh Lauter Levin Associates, Inc., 1996); Marc Michael Epstein, *Dreams of Subversion in Medieval Jewish Art and Literature* (University Park, Pennsylvania, PA: Penn State University Press, 1997).

12. Koz'ma Soldatenkov (1818–1901), a financier and businessman, as well as a famous Moscow collector, patron of Russian arts and publisher. He bequeathed his collection to the former Rumiantsevskii Museum, which later became a part of the State Tretiakov Gallery. Pavel Tretiakov (1832–98), a Moscow merchant and a famous collector and patron of Russian art; the founder of an art gallery which he donated, together with the collection of western art of his deceased brother Sergeii, to the city of Moscow in 1892. After 1918 the gallery was known as the State Tretiakov Gallery.

13. V. Kelner (ed.), 'Leonid Pasternak, "Venok na mogilu khudozhniku". Pis'mo Baronu D.D. Ginzburgu' ('Leonid Pasternak, "A wreath for the artist". A letter to Baron D.D. Ginzburg'), *Vestnik evreiskogo universiteta v Moskve*, 1, 5 (1994), p. 233; Zh.L. Pasternak and L.L. Pasternak-Sleiter (eds), 'Pis'mo L.O. Pasretnaka k Kh.N. Bialiku' ('Letter of L.O. Pasternak to Kh. N. Bialik'), *Slavica Hierosolymitana: Slavic Studies of the Hebrew University*, 1 (1977), pp. 306–7.

14. Leonid Pasternak, *Fragmenty avtobiografii* ('Autobiographical Fragments'), unpublished typescript, 1943, p. 48; private collection. They were not included in *Zapiski raznykh let* (Moscow: Sovetskii khudozhnik, 1975). I

would like to thank John Bowlt for allowing me to read and to quote from his copy of this typescript.

15. Grigorii Kazovskii (ed.), 'Evreiskii khudozhnik v Rossii na rubezhe vekov: statia M.L. Mimona "Kto vinovat?"' ('The Jewish Artists in Russia at the turn of the century': M.L. Maimon's article "Who is to blame?"'), *Vestnik evreiskogo universiteta v Moskve*, 2 (1993), pp. 127–9.

16. V.V. Stasov, 'M.M. Antokol'skii', *Novosti i birzhevaya gazeta*, 175 (1908). Quotation from E.V. Kuznetsova, *M.M. Antokolskii, Zhizn' i tvorchestvo* ('Life and Work') (Moscow: Iskusstvo, 1989), p. 280.

17. Frances Keyzer, 'Mark Antokolsky', *The Studio*, 11 (London, 1897), p. 125.

18. See, for example, 'M.M. Antokolskii', in *Allgemeine Zeitung: Morgenblatt*, Munich, 28 June 1892, pp. 1–2; *Münchener Internationale Ausstellung von 1892: Die Kunst für alle*, Vol. 2, p. 20.

19. S. Laffitte, 'Deux amis: Chechov et Levitan', *Revue des etudes slaves*, 41, 1–4 (1962).

20. Anton Rubinstein (1829–94), Russian composer, pianist and conductor, founder of the St Petersburg Conservatory in 1862, the first in Russia. A Jew by origin, Rubinstein was baptized, as was his brother Nikolai, also a noted pianist and the founder of the Moscow Conservatory in 1866.

21. Gintsburg, 'Kontsert. Obed' ('Concert; The Dinner'), in Gintsburg, *Kak ia sdelalsia skulptorom*, pp. 94, 98.

22. L. Pasternak, *Rembrandt i evreistvo* ('Rembrandt and the Jews') (Berlin: Saltzman, 1923).

23. V.G. Korolenko, *Bratia Mendel* ('The Mendel Brothers'), *Sobranie Sochinenii*, Vol. 2 (Moskva: Gosudarstvennoe izdatel'stvo khudozhestvennoii literatury, 1954), pp. 399–462.

24. Fiodorov-Davydov (ed.), *Isaak Iliich Levitan: Dokumenty, materialy, bibliographia*, Vol. 2 ('Isaak Ilych Levitan: Documents, Materials, Bibliography') (Moscow: Izdatel'stvo 'Iskusstvo', 1966), p. 147.

25. David Shor, a famous pianist and Zionist in Russia. He later immigrated to Palestine.

26. *Russkie vedomosti* (27 September/7 October); see 'Sumerki svobody: o nekotorykh temakh russkoi ezhednevnoi pechati, 1917–1918 gg.', *Minuvshee*, 3 (1987), pp. 192–3.

27. M.M. Antokolskii – V.V. Stasovu, Rome, Letter no. 134, 27 September (4 October) 1874; in Stasov, *Mark Matveevich Antokol'skii*,' pp. 183–4.

28. Aleksandr Benua, *Moi vospominaniia* ('My Reminiscences'), 3 Vols (Moscow: Izdatel'stvo 'Nauka', 1980), p. 610. The fact that Aleksandr Benois put the word 'patriotism' in quotation marks may be interpreted as his irritation with Bakst's devotion to his people.

29. M.M. Antokolskii – V.V. Stasovu, Letter no. 472, Paris, 1888; in Stasov, *Mark Matveevich Antokol'skii*, p. 620.

30. From the 'Reminiscences' of Boris Cramer's daughter, Valentina Cramer, written in Boston, MA, in 1989, and given to the author.

31. Pasternak, *Fragmenty avtobiografiia*, p. 50.

32. Michael Stanislawsky, 'The Jews and Russian Culture and Politics', in S. Tumarkin-Goodman (ed.), *Russian Jewish Artists in a Century of Change, 1890–1990* (Munich and New York: Prestel, 1995), p. 16.

33. Dubnov, *History of the Jews in Russia and Poland*, Vol. 2, p. 138.

34. Kniaginia Lidia Vasil'chikova, *Ischeznuvshaia Rossiia Vospominaniia, 1886–1919* ('The Extinct Russia: Reminiscences of Princess Lidia Leonidovna Vasil'chikova, 1886–1919') (St Peterburg: Peterburgskie sezony, 1995), p. 186.

35. Gintsburg, *Kak ia sdelalsia skulptorom*, p. 18.

36. Vladimir Ivanovich Nazimov (1802–74), general, member of the State Council, general-governor of Vilna.

37. Dubnov, *History of the Jews in Russia and Poland*, Vol. 2, pp. 184–205; see also John Klier, *Imperial Russia's Jewish Question, 1855–1881* (Cambridge: Cambridge University Press, 1995), pp. 57–65.

38. Alekseii Suvorin (1834–1912), journalist, critic and publisher. His famous newspaper *Novoe vremia* ('New Times'), published since 1876, was known for its extreme anti-Semitic orientation.

39. Fiodorov-Davydov (ed.), *Isaak Iliich Levitan: Dokumenty, materialy, bibliographiia* ('Isaak Ilych Levitan: Documents, Materials, Bibliography'), pp. 46–8.

40. Benua, *Moi vospominaniia*, p. 627.

41. Naum Aronson, *V tsarskoi Rossii* ('In Tsarist Russia'), *Novoselie*, 1943, pp. 33–8. [Russian-language monthly journal, published in New York.]

42. I.Y. Gintsburg, *Kak i chemu menia uchili* ('How and what I thought'), in *Iz moei zhizni*, p. 88.

43. N. Bogoliubov, 'Mark Matveevich Antokolskii', Essay, Paris, 1894, Russian National Library, Manuscript Department, F. 82, ed. kh. 7, Antokol'skii's Archive.

44. Antokol'skii, 'Pis'mo k V.V. Stasovu', no. 483, Biarritz, received 24 August 1888, in Stasov, *Mark Matveevich Antokol'skii*, p. 640.

45. Antokol'skii, 'Pis'mo k I. S. Turgenevu', no. 314a, Paris, 4 July 1881; no. 316a, Paris, Fall 1881, pp. 1005–12; 'Pis'mo k I.Y. Gintsburgu', no. 739, Paris, December 1899, p. 860; in Stasov, *Mark Matveevich Antokol'skii*.

46. Antokolskii, 'Pis'mo k Baronu Goratsiu Ginzburgu'.

47. *Peredvizhniki* ('The Wanderers'), were a group of artists who appeared in the 1860s and were united by 'realism, populism and national character'. They were termed 'Wanderers' because they took exhibitions to various cities and towns of the country in order to introduce art to the masses. They believed that art could be a powerful tool in the struggle for social reforms. The leading figures among them were such artists as G.G. Miasoiedov, I.N. Kramskoi, V.G. Perov and N.N. Ge. See Dmitri V. Sarabianov, *Russian Art* (New York: Abrams, 1990), pp. 111–33.

48. Antokolskii, 'Pis'mo k V.V. Stasovu', no. 481, Biarritz, received August 10, 1888; in Stasov, *Mark Matveevich Antokol'skii*, p. 636.

9

Between Identities:
The German-Jewish Youth Movement Blau-Weiss, 1912–26

GLENN R. SHARFMAN

> German Zionism had a strong power of attraction on young
> people for whom the fact that they became Zionists meant
> the return to Judaism. German Zionism was and remains a
> youth movement (*Jugendbewegung*).[1]

The Blau-Weiss was the most popular and influential of the German
Zionist youth groups, yet it also emerged as the most controversial
of the myriad of Jewish groups in early twentieth-century
Germany. George Mosse described it as a *völkisch* movement that
did not substantially differ from its German counterparts. 'The
Blau-Weiss', he wrote, 'was an offshoot of the German youth
movement and shared its ideology as well as its action ... the
emphasis on nature rambling, on learning to live in nature and to
"view it with one's soul"'.[2] Another historian goes even further,
asserting that the Wanderbund Blau-Weiss was largely indistin-
guishable from the German Wandervogel of which it was the
Zionist counterpart, and shared its programme of outdoor
rambling, glorification of nature and rejection of urban culture
and bourgeois adult values.[3] A former member of an Orthodox
youth group interpreted the *völkisch* ideology of the Blau-Weiss as
a surrogate for Jewish reality.[4] Yet, perhaps the most acerbic
criticism of the Blau-Weiss, came from Gershom Scholem, the
eminent Jewish scholar and expert on Jewish mysticism. Scholem
castigated the Blau-Weiss for purely imitating the German youth

movement. He believed it was devoid of any Jewish content, and that it was delusional to think a nature hike nurtured one's Jewishness. Its emphasis on empty romanticism, Scholem intimated, led the Blau-Weiss in 'fascist' directions during the 1920s.[5]

While the Blau-Weiss patterned itself after the Wandervogel, and the members exhibited great pride in their German heritage, the Blau-Weiss did contain a certain degree of Jewish content – and more than its critics were willing to admit. Clearly, Judaism received less emphasis than in the more religious groups, but one must realize that most of the Blau-Weiss members came from assimilated homes where the traditional practices of Judaism played little or no role.[6] Critics of the Blau-Weiss often do not take into account the changes within the movement itself. In the early years the youths in Blau-Weiss consumed themselves with hiking and singing German folk-songs; but, by the 1920s, the group had constructed elaborate plans on two occasions to immigrate to Palestine. Their settlement ended in failure but it was not from lack of effort on the part of the youngsters or their commitment to practical Zionism – preparing one's life for *aliyah* rather than just a passing political or economic interest in Zionist matters. The Blau-Weiss had a dual agenda. On the one hand, its members fought against the liberal and utilitarian world of middle-class Germany, much like its non-Jewish counterpart. Yet, on the other hand, the movement sought a new set of spiritual and cultural values rooted both in its Jewishness and Germanness. Thus, members cultivated their religion within the framework of the Wandervogel.[7] Their goal of escaping the bourgeois German-Jewish milieu and the group's fascination with nature no doubt later played a part in the Blau-Weiss's plans to immigrate to a new frontier, but their commitment to Zionism was genuine.

In fighting for these two objectives the Blau-Weiss rescued many young Jews from a life of confused identity and spiritual emptiness. On the fiftieth anniversary of the Blau-Weiss's founding, in 1962, Pinchas Rosenblüth recalled that those who joined the Breslau chapter – the oldest and one of the strongest – were able to break away from the repressive 'Victorianism' present at home and in school. Rosenblüth characterized the Jewish community this way:

> In a milieu of materialist things and a growing importance
> of business, in the environment that was sceptical, ironic,

unhappy and where people were removed from nature, in the atmosphere where Jewish jokes and self-mockery were on the rise, our young boys and girls were a generation whose general conception of life in our parents' house was corrupted.[8]

The Blau-Weiss's basic aim was to bring pride back to Judaism. Fearful of becoming a people who perceived their religion as an albatross, the Blau-Weiss instilled hope that they could be Jewish without diminishing their love for their German Fatherland.

One contemporary suggested that the Blau-Weiss's motto of complete rejection of the *status quo* accounted for the group's expansion.[9] The Jewish youth movement aimed not to assimilate passively or melt into the German people but to rekindle a spirit of Judaism that had long since passed. Critical of their parents, both for 'abandoning' Judaism in the haste to acclimate to German culture, and for personifying materialist bourgeois lifestyles, Blau-Weiss members sought to be better Germans by being better Jews. The movement tried to change the basic stereotype of the German Jew by focusing on nature, physical fitness, romanticism and religion; a strategy they borrowed from the earlier sports groups and fraternities. For many of the young Blau-Weissers, Judaism meant something more than just a *Glaubensgemeinschaft*, or a community of faith; rather, Jews constituted a *Volksgemeinschaft*, or people's community, bonded not only by religion but also by common heritage.

The Blau-Weiss's determination to redefine what it meant to be a Jew in Germany brought out its critics. Ludwig Mayer, writing in the *Kartel-Convent* [K-C] *Blätter*, advocated that Jewish youths join the Wandervogel rather than a distinctly Jewish group. He conceded that some degree of anti-Semitism tainted certain factions of the Wandervogel, but he implored Jews to join the religiously neutral groups since the Jews had to show the Germans that they too were part of the German *Volk*.[10] Like most assimilated Jews of the day, Mayer believed that a separate Jewish group would spur anti-Semitism. This theory stemmed from an interpretation of anti-Semitism that posited that Germans mistrusted Jews because they were different, and that the situation could be rectified only if Jews abandoned their unsavoury characteristics such as clumsiness, over-intellectualism, individualism and ostentatiousness.[11]

The second reason for the criticism levelled against the Blau-Weiss was that, despite the Blau-Weiss's proclamation that it was politically and religiously neutral, Mayer contended that the Blau-Weiss was *kryptozionistisch*, or secretly Zionist.[12] To Mayer, the Blau-Weiss was political and thus embodied the very antithesis of the apolitical nature of youth movements. Mayer labelled the Blau-Weiss's claim of neutrality as pathetic, believing that elder Zionists controlled it. Mayer called on other Jews to combat it. 'Neutrality was nothing more than a shield behind which Zionists are attracting youths', Mayer complained. As proof that Blau-Weiss was really a Zionist organization, he noted that some chapters participated in Zionist meetings. The Blau-Weiss song book, he further claimed, was littered with 'Jewish songs'.[13] 'Can one still wonder then when anti-Semitism denies us the right to consider ourselves as German and Germany as our Fatherland?' Mayer asked. He considered all songs that were not written and sung in German as unpatriotic and especially objected to songs in Yiddish, which he called 'Jargon' and a bastardization of German, and added that Jewish songs lacked melody and rhythm.[14] At the heart of this apologetic and self-defacing attitude was the discomfort with reasserting the belief in a Jewish people because it was anachronistic and would impede the progress of German Jews towards full and equal participation in German society. Many *K-C* members operated under the assumption that the Blau-Weiss was nothing more than a harbinger for Jewish nationalism.[15] The philosophy of the *K-C* can be summed up this way: 'We want our youths to be good Jews, but they must also be educated as good Germans, and will only look to Germany as their Fatherland'.[16] This critique is especially intriguing when juxtaposed with Gershom Scholem's who viewed the Blau-Weiss as a mere copy of the German Wandervogel.

The Central Union of German Citizens of Jewish Faith, or CV, was also adamant about keeping youths away from the Blau-Weiss. Jehuda Reinharz uncovered a secret CV memorandum that warned all members to protect their children from joining the 'Zionist Wandervogel', which it referred to as chauvinistic. The communiqué cautioned parents that it was 'of the utmost importance to counteract the attempts of the Blau-Weiss'. 'It is necessary to inform parents about the Zionist orientation of the Blau-Weiss', continued the note. 'We recommend that Jewish teachers discourage their students from joining'.[17] Again, in 1916, the CV distributed a circular which condemned the Blau-Weiss's Zionist programme.[18] Originally, the official policy of the CV was to ignore Zionism, reasoning that any attention paid to Zionism, even critical press, would serve to popularize it. In 1912, however, the CV abandoned this policy and denounced Zionism publicly because of its ever increasing influence on youths. The CV acted out of the same concern as the K-C. Its members feared that the Zionists were targeting their propaganda and recruiting at youths.[19]

One of the early members of the Blau-Weiss, Georg Todtmann, in the first issue of the *Blau-Weiss Blätter*, summarized the movement's aims: to enable all Jewish youth, especially *Schuljugend*, to wander.[20] Not only would roaming through the woods show that Jews had a deep affinity with nature, and build up their bodies, but wandering was an escape – both real and symbolic – from the rigidity and imprisonment felt by big-city youth who were facing ever greater responsibility and expectations. One can also imagine wandering in the Zionist context as searching for wisdom and a lost community. After all, the image of the 'wandering Jew' was legendary. Communing with nature proved to be a central motive for joining the Blau-Weiss. One leader wrote that, 'one need not be in Palestine to imbibe a new, happy, natural and honest view of life measured by what is beautiful and good, not by the standards of expediency and advantage'.[21]

The Blau-Weiss also strove to strengthen youths' bodies, mind and spirit with an introduction to Jewish education. They pledged to arrange a hike every Sunday, rain or shine – to escape the city's decadence. This would facilitate the aim of 'returning to everything that is natural, to all simplicity which best suits youth'.[22] These values essential to this life with and within nature were honour, courage and camaraderie. Todtmann's final point for the Blau-Weiss concerned Judaism: 'But our movement wants more. The basis of our Bund', he wrote, 'is a deep and strong love for Judaism'.[23] Hiking was prohibited on Saturdays and members had to follow a kosher diet on trips. Instead of the normal Wandervogel greeting of 'Heil', the Blau-Weiss substituted 'Shalom'. Members were encouraged to learn Hebrew and celebrate the Jewish holidays. Hanukkah was especially singled out, and the flames of the menorah were compared to the flames of the campfires which took on mystical qualities. The Festival of Lights also signified Jews fighting metaphorically and physically, against all odds, for respect and recognition; this seemed particularly pertinent to the Blau-Weiss.[24] Todtmann strongly urged Blau-Weiss to fight for Jewry: 'For no one of us should ignore or accept it as an insult. We fight for our Jewish honour.'[25] Implicit here was the belief that by courageously asserting their Judaism within Germany, the Blau-Weissers could live more contentedly.

The excursions into nature every Sunday were quite similar to the hikes of the Wandervogel. The groups wore identical clothing – usually brown shorts and ankle-length boots – and underscored discipline.[26] The Blau-Weiss also prohibited alcohol and tobacco, and discouraged premarital sex. One of the founders, Joseph Marcus, used the term *Wanderdiszplin* to indicate that members needed to stop their 'degeneration'.[27] Discipline included the principles of order, unity and strength. Marcus emphasized that wandering was not just an idle walk in the woods, but instead embodied an educational experience. Connected with the idea of discipline was the focus on a strong leader. Usually in their late teens and early twenties, leaders were often members of the Zionist fraternities who commanded a great deal of respect from their underlings. Marcus pictured the ideal leader as pure, intelligent and courageous, but above all devoted to wandering: 'A leader is never unsure, as he must obtain the trust of the pack', said Marcus, 'He can never lose sight of the whole.'[28] On the more mundane level, a leader was presumed to educate his troop on hygiene (especially foot care), to inform the group about proper eating habits, and to be able to navigate the German landscape in all conditions. Girls were, in theory, to be treated equally and not separated from boys, though in practice the Blau-Weiss, like most German youth movements, was male dominated.[29]

Singing played a large part on hikes.[30] The Blau-Weiss sang and marched both to traditional German folk-songs and some Jewish songs like *Ha-Tikva* ('The Hope'). Many considered singing, marching and revelling in the German countryside the most important ingredients to young Jews to live a more 'normal' life. Moses Calvary, for example, commented on the Blau-Weiss in 1916: 'In wandering and through wandering one's Judaism will become conscious, that means a deepening of community life which has already today manufactured the wishes of the wandering youth to take hold and seize Judaism'.[31] Calvary, unlike Scholem, did not see any contradictions between hiking and Judaism. Through nature, according to Calvary, one could come closer to becoming a 'total person' and nearer one's Jewish existence.[32] Masked in this thought was the latent acceptance of many anti-Semitic characterizations of Jews as alien to nature.

Though the Blau-Weiss did not yet identify as a Zionist group, certain Zionist thinkers had great influence. That is not to say that the authors who were popular with the non-Jewish Wandervogel, such as Fichte, Nietzsche, Kipling, Dostoyevsky and Karl May, were not read, but the Blau-Weiss had an added dimension. Theodor Herzl, the founder of political Zionism, received some attention, but his theory that Zionism was a political movement and should only proceed within the parameters of international agreements held little attraction for youth.[33] Yet his metamorphosis from an assimilated Jew to a nationalist Jew served as an inspiration for many 'post-assimilatory' Zionists.[34] His utopian novel *Alt-Neuland*, in which he envisioned a future Jewish society living in harmony, appealed to the youth, as Herzl's idyllic society was similar to their idea of a *Gemeinschaft*.[35]

Much more influential for the Blau-Weiss, and on the Jewish youth movement in general, was Martin Buber.[36] Buber's impact was probably greater in the late 1920s and 1930s than earlier, but there is no doubt that the Blau-Weiss absorbed his views. Buber became a Zionist in 1898 and was a spiritual and intellectual leader for decades. For Buber, Zionism meant a return to one's Jewish roots. Zionism was not a party but a *Weltanschauung*. Buber appealed to youths because he perceived the western (emancipated) Jew as wanting in spirituality. When Buber spoke to the Bar Kochba youth group in 1903, his theme was how youth were to return to Judaism.[37] He criticized modern Jews for lacking the vital, elemental experience of God and the dedication to His mission. Buber assailed contemporary Jewish practices as formal and lacking spirit. He also eschewed any form of Jewish nationalism as he looked on the whole concept of nation-states as a foreign invention. Nationalism, for Buber, was as empty as modern Judaism. To Buber, and many second-generation Zionists, Zionism ceased to be just a political solution and instead became a necessity to answer the questions of personal identity.

Buber's mystical conception of Judaism (as opposed to the purely rational view of their parents) swayed young Jews. He perceived youth as the eternal chance of hope, and commitment to Palestine as the only way to achieve true happiness within Judaism.[38] Whereas the first generation of Zionism looked to men like Herzl and his brand of Zionism, the young were more captivated by Buber and his exhilarating, romantic view of Zionism. Part of this attraction to Buber's Zionism sprang from the idea of the vitality of Judaism. Buber's ideas were a more positive catalyst and effective propaganda for the Zionist cause than Herzl's Zionism, which was a response to anti-Semitism or negative stimulus. To some of Buber's followers, most notably Gershom Scholem, the Blau-Weiss did not live up to Buber's expectations as its devotion to religion was wanting. According to Scholem, the Blau-Weiss lacked 'wholeness, spirituality and greatness'.[39] Scholem believed the Blau-Weiss was more dedicated to wandering than Judaism. Nevertheless, while the Blau-Weiss may not have epitomized a Buberian view of Zionism, Buber certainly influenced it in regard to Judaism, Palestine and Zionism. Before 1914, the Blau-Weiss seemed to alienate all adult constituencies: to religious Jews the Blau-Weiss lacked devotion; to the non-Zionists the Blau-Weiss was too Zionist; and to the Zionists the Blau-Weiss was not political enough.

The Blau-Weiss emerged from the war stronger than it had been in 1914. Chronic anti-Semitism, the Balfour Declaration and the influx of the Ostjuden had sharpened the image of Zionism to the Blau-Weiss's profit. The war experience proved pivotal for the Zionist youth groups. In the early stages of the war, the Blau-Weiss was torn by its double loyalty, not knowing to whom it belonged. One young Zionist, Walter Preuss, expressed his sentiments in 1914:

> We are going into battle with the feeling that if only we were already happily back home – a feeling not shared by anyone who is either one hundred per cent German or one hundred per cent Jewish. We are only half of each.[40]

The war reinforced the Blau-Weiss's love for Germany, while simultaneously augmenting their Jewish feeling. Thus, despite the protestations of some Blau-Weiss members that they came together solely because of their positive Jewish outlook, even their own *Blätter* admitted that the movement kept to itself 'not because we want to but because we have to'.[41]

Surprisingly, the war years transformed Zionism from a defensive movement whose cohesion was maintained by outside hostility toward Jewish youths to a movement which positively affirmed the identity of the Jewish *Volk* and its unlimited possibilities in Palestine. If the emphasis of the Blau-Weiss before the war focused more on the Wandervogel aspects than on Judaism and Palestine, after the war the priorities were reversed. The metamorphosis of the Blau-Weiss was, however, more gradual than commonly assumed. During the war the original leaders, like Moses Calvary and Joseph Marcus, who had their roots firmly planted in Germany and who held fast to the principles of the Wandervogel, left the movement. The new contingent of leaders were more committed to Zionism as a reality rather than just as a dream. Among the most influential figures in the post-war era were Ferdinand Ostertag, the new editor of the *Blätter*, Georg Strauss, Martin Bandmann and Walter Moses. The ascendancy of the charismatic personality, Walter Moses, and his radical blend of *bündisch* ideology and a staunch myopic goal of settling in Palestine in his own way, completed the transition. Ultimately, Moses's dream ended in ruin, when the Blau-Weiss dissolved in 1926 after the attempt to settle in Palestine failed and most of the members returned home.

The Blau-Weiss numbered 1,800 youths in the middle of 1918 and grew when the war concluded.[42] Disagreement continued, over the group's ideology. The leadership had to decide whether it was to be Zionist in the political sense or more religious, or was simply to concentrate on the outdoors.[43] Already, in 1917, Ferdinand Ostertag wrote: 'At the same time we know and recognize that only Zion will lead to the completion of our actions, and that only Zion is our guarantee for the eternal duration of true humanity'.[44] Ostertag's use of the term 'Zion' is ambiguous for it could be taken to mean a physical sanctuary in Palestine itself or it could connote a more amorphous meaning of Jewish revival in the Diaspora. These two conflicting approaches – of Zionism as a charitable organization, or as a movement with personal commitment – plagued German Zionism throughout the 1920s. Yet from the beginning there was no doubt that Walter Moses wanted to direct the Blau-Weiss to Palestine.[45] Moses made a splash at the national Jewish youth festival in October 1918 in Berlin, but did not gain control over the group until 1922. His enthusiasm was contagious and his wish to create a Blau-Weiss community in Palestine appealed to youths who were discovering numerous social and economic hardships in Germany. Impressed by the rising desire to settle in the Holy Land, one Zionist commentator exclaimed that the new generation was no longer asking whether to go, but how.[46]

The Blau-Weiss's increasing radicalism heightened the tensions with the *Zionistische Vereinigung für Deutschland* (ZVfD) soon after the war ended.[47] The Blau-Weiss participated in a three-day festival in

Berlin for national Jewish youth (*Nationaljüdischer Jugendtag*) in October 1918. Ignoring the chaos that no doubt surrounded them, thousands of youths turned out to listen to speeches, sing songs, observe the Sabbath and compete in sports; all with the purpose of uniting Zionist youths. The list of speakers read like a Who's Who in German Zionism: Kurt Blumenfeld, Walter Moses, Moses Calvary, Ferdinand Ostertag, Victor Arlosoroff and, at the centre of attention, Martin Buber.[48] Buber spoke of the need for religion in a Jewish youth movement and warned against turning Zionism into a cheap imitation of colonial nationalism. The spiritual aspects of Judaism were much more valued than the political ones. The ideal of Zionism was to form a better community which could be best served by youths.[49] Even former leader Moses Calvary exhorted national Jewish youths to take seriously their commitment to Zion and not to allow their movement to become stifled, though he stressed nature rather than religious thought.[50] Again, for Calvary, Zion was not a specific physical concept, but vaguely referred to an inner strengthening of the individual which enabled one to have a positive self-image. Most Zionists anticipated that great vitality and unity would emanate from the festival. The lone pessimistic analysis belonged to Gershom Scholem who voiced suspicion of a united Zionist youth movement, as he considered the nationalist Jewish youths to be spiritually empty. To him, rather than pursuing a strict programme emphasizing Hebrew and the Torah, the German youngsters merely sought a Bund where they could be secure and insulated from the outside world.[51]

The meeting commenced optimistically as Blau-Weiss leader Karl Glaser declared that the national Jewish youth movement had grown to approximately 7,000 members.[52] The goal now was to organize these youths into a solid band of young Zionists. 'Our strength does not lie in our numbers', Glaser proclaimed, 'but in our vitality, in the moral pathos and in the earnestness of Judaism in our youths'.[53] Glaser was disturbed by the group's 'un-Jewish' and anti-intellectual quality, and he sniped that one could not concoct a Jewish youth movement merely by substituting 'Shalom' for 'Heil'. He viewed the Blau-Weiss as a revolutionary group but cautioned about the perils of a revolution in Judaism without Jewish fundamentals. His criticism was not entirely justified as many of the individual groups were led by religious youths.[54] If, however, the goal of the meeting was unity, the festival was a disappointment. Divisiveness emerged after Walter Moses's speech in which he criticized the present state of Zionism. He wanted to liberate Zionism from unnecessary constrictions, grounded in its history, that had rendered the movement stale. He asserted that only youth had the will and the ability to lead Zionism as the elders had been remiss in their efforts to motivate Jewish youths to concrete goals. No doubt Moses was frustrated by the dichotomy between the rhetoric of Zionism and its deeds.

Kurt Blumenfeld, the leader of German Zionism and for so long the idol of Jewish youths, sharply chastized Moses. Blumenfeld defended the value of Jewish history in Zionism; for Zionism was an organic movement with 2,000-year-old roots and one simply could not sever them without damaging the movement's essence. Moreover, Blumenfeld chided him for trying to foster an esoteric movement of youths who would promote and precipitate generational conflicts. According to Blumenfeld, this separatism, both from the Zionist community and the older generation in general, was anathema to the national Jewish youth who should be striving for unity with each other and the adult Zionists. Blumenfeld offered his thoughts on what the goal of a Zionist youth movement should be:

> Zionism does not signify a stand against non-Jews which would limit the movement. Our youth movement is not, as the German's is, a rebellion against the older generation. The goals of our youth movement are not the youth but the adult.[55]

Youth just for the sake of youth – a familiar theme in Wandervogel lore – proved too limiting for Blumenfeld's conception of Zionism. For him, Zionism meant a rejuvenation of Judaism, a renewed interest in Jewish culture, a more positive self-esteem for all assimilated Jews, and an effort gradually to build up Palestine as a home for Jews who have nowhere else to go and for all those who want to experience the joys of dwelling in a Jewish state. While he theoretically embraced the concepts expressed in the Posen Resolution about each Zionist making a pledge to go to Palestine, Blumenfeld realistically knew that the process had to be measured for two reasons. The first was that Palestine was simply not equipped to handle a massive influx of settlers. The second problem was that assimilated Jews were not physically or emotionally ready to uproot their lives. He promoted the idea that all Jews should begin to distance themselves from German culture and society before leaving, something the Blau-Weiss did not think necessary.[56]

In a scathing review of Moses's performance, Hans Goslar attacked him for destroying the felicity of the occasion with such confrontational language. He was astonished that Moses quoted from Tolstoy, Socrates and other non-Jewish writers, but did not mention any Jewish authors. He was also concerned that Moses was riling the youth with negative slogans about German Zionism rather than extolling its positive virtues. Goslar, like many of the older Zionists, thought Moses was alienating young Zionists with his elitist, dogmatic and essentially un-Jewish beliefs. Zionists like Goslar and Blumenfeld who had once been considered so radical in their opposition to the political Zionism of the first generation, now appeared mainstream. They were reluctant for youths to stray too far out of the sphere of the *ZVfD*.[57]

Blau-Weiss leader, Ferdinand Ostertag, claimed that, unlike adult groups, the task of the Blau-Weiss was to organize a tightly knit Bund. Compared with the Blau-Weiss before the war, which was more carefree and interested in individual development and confidence, the characteristics of the group after the war took on a more *bündisch* appearance which encouraged a closed circle of youths who felt a tremendous sense of togetherness and a feeling of belonging. It was controlled by older adolescents or young adults who assumed the role of *Führer* with all its authoritative connotations. As discipline increased, the emphasis shifted to one's duty to the group, not to oneself. All the Blau-Weiss members dressed identically. On hikes, participants shared food and everything else equally and the activities stressed group rather than individual achievement. They expended less effort on intellectual exercises, as the Blau-Weiss eschewed ideology. Martin Bandmann illustrated the changes in the Bund this way:

> Our Bund is based on a philosophy of vitality and presents itself as a revolt against the dominance of ideology. Its ideal is the real person as opposed to the ideological person. Our motto is *Primum vivere deinde philosophari* – first to live, then to philosophize. Real people want life, ideological people want life only with conditions.[58]

Ostertag reminded the members that individuals must never forget that they were part of a Bund and individual chapters must not lose sight that they were part of something greater.[59] That something greater did not explicitly refer to Zionism – at least the kind of intellectual Zionism practised by the ZVfD – it referred specifically to the Blau-Weiss and the commitment to a life-changing experience. As early as 1918, Hans Oppenheim concluded that one of the major evils that the Blau-Weiss hoped to overcome was personal vanity, which he associated not only with assimilation, but also with lack of courage and will to sacrifice for one's people. He admonished the ZVfD for being nothing more than a charitable organization which compromised its principles. Insisting that the Blau-Weiss was a movement and not a club, Oppenheim asserted the essential righteousness of the Blau-Weiss because it was concerned with people, not individuals.[60] Since the Blau-Weiss believed the return to Eretz Israel must always be at the centre of Jewish thought, and because it had lost all confidence in the elder Zionists to lead them to the promised land, the Blau-Weiss moved increasingly away from the elder Zionists.[61] These facets of a more isolated, communal-oriented Bund paralleled the non-Jewish German youth movement, which also voiced criticism of adult organizations and strove to accentuate the nurturing of close-knit, independent groups of youths.

The Blau-Weiss's shift toward a more confrontational stance was due not so much to a change in ideology by individual members but to the fact that the Bund went through a comprehensive turnover in membership.[62] Older members drifted away from the movement and younger Jews who had been too young to fight in the war entered the Blau-Weiss.[63] Throughout 1920, the Blau-Weiss developed its own training centres to prepare young Jews for occupational skills which would be needed in Palestine. These *Practikantschaft* focused mostly on crafts and agriculture, and trained youths – who had been geared for mostly business and academic positions – to survive in a land that needed farmers more than lawyers. These centres, coupled with the exalted position of the leader in the Blau-Weiss, made it increasingly distinct from other Zionist groups.[64] Commenting on the Blau-Weiss's Bundestag in Mühlberg in 1920, which attracted over 1,000 youths, the *Jüdische Rundschau* condemned the group's exclusiveness and feared that the Blau-Weiss would precipitate conflicts within Zionist families. Nonetheless, the reporter did not conceal his respect for the group's discipline, indefatigable enthusiasm and intense commitment to Palestine.[65]

Joining the Blau-Weiss often carried a stigma. One former

member recalled that the parents of some of his classmates would not allow their children to have any contact with him simply because he was part of the Blau-Weiss.[66] The *ZVfD* no doubt feared the political orientation of the Blau-Weiss because Zionist youth groups had always provided a source for members, and the parent organization worried what would happen when the rank and file of the Blau-Weiss became adults. In 1921, the Blau-Weiss continued its move toward separatism when Martin Bandmann became the editor of the leaders' journal. Bandmann believed that the Blau-Weiss had surpassed the German Wandervogel in both ethics and vision because the German youth had abandoned their mission to change the world while the Blau-Weiss was more resolved than ever to doing so from their homeland in Palestine. He insinuated that its movement had also become superior to German Zionism, which showed little commitment to Palestine. Bandmann thus believed the Blau-Weiss should encourage all Zionists to unite behind its programme.[67]

The formal break from German Zionism came in the small South German town of Prunn in August of 1922. There, the Blau-Weiss issued a declaration that surpassed any previous proclamation in asserting the group's independence and militancy. Authored by Walter Moses, the manifesto reviewed the evolution of the Blau-Weiss from its genesis before the war, when, like the Wandervogel, its emphasis was the return to nature, to its embrace of Zionism during the war, and on to the post-war period with its army of young Zionists marching to Palestine.[68] The sentimental idea of everlasting youth had been replaced by one of solid deeds. No longer would the Blau-Weiss be dictated by self-enjoyment but would instead become a Bund of action. Part of the Prunn declaration stated:

> The Blau-Weiss has put the difficult crisis of transition behind it. It has decided on its own, in view of the catastrophic Zionist position, that it knows whoever waits today for help from a saviour from the outside gives up on oneself and the task.[69]

This manifesto opposed the oscillating position taken by the *ZVfD* with regard to actual emigration. Moses perceptively realized that it would take something out of the ordinary to convince and motivate German Jews to surrender their careers and relinquish their comfortable life in Germany to trek to Palestine which – compared to Germany – was an economic and cultural wasteland. This something special, for Moses, took the shape of an army. His imagery was reminiscent of war and battle, which no doubt made a profound impression on youths who had been too young to fight for their country:

> Powerful tasks require leaders and armies. Leaders in order to command and armies in order to serve ... The epoch of everyone only enjoying one's life for oneself is over. The consciousness of the Blau-Weiss now becomes a unity of everlasting duty. Freedom and obedience are connected and will lead to a new attitude. The hope of the fulfilment of life through the triumph of freedom will be broken by resolute faith in the victory of strength ... He who serves the flag of the proudest Bund, whether he serves it as a leader or a soldier, is deeply shielded and advances to life, whoever rebels from it will be an enemy and loses the protection.[70]

Although the Blau-Weiss gradually progressed toward this kind of disciplined Bund, the Prunner ordinances made explicit what had been only suspected. The whole concept of Judaism and Zionism now took a back seat to the physical task of preparing for actual immigration to Palestine. The movement's anti-intellectualism and increasing radicalism again heightened the tensions between the *ZVfD* and the Blau-Weiss. Many Zionists feared that the Blau-Weiss was a real cause for concern not only because of its corruption of Zionist youths, but also because of its constant criticism of Zionism in general. It replaced traditional Jewish notions of liberalism and individualism with obedience and conformity. One's allegiance was no longer principally directed to Judaism but to the Bund. 'The Bund is not only [the Blau-Weiss's] task, his daily deed; the Bund itself is it'.[71] The Prunner laws left no doubt that the individual was subservient to the whims of the leaders and the totality of the cause. The idea of a strong, all-powerful leader was not unique to the German youth movement as many of the German *Bünde* tried to adhere to the philosophies of Möller van den Bruck and Stefan George.[72] The omniscience of the leader was however a radical departure from the traditions of the Jewish youth movement.

With the Prunner laws the Blau-Weiss became more exclusive and exclusionary. One law commanded that 'the membership of a Blau-Weisser to a club, party or any other organization in all cases requires the approval of the Bund's leaders'. Moreover, the

Blau-Weiss reserved the right to expel any member who dis-
obeyed any of the regulations. This declaration separated it from
almost all other branches of Zionism, which encouraged membership in several Zionist organizations. Many of the Blau-Weiss's
features would resurface later in the revisionist Zionist youth
group Betar.[73] Moses made it clear that all this discipline and order
would serve a purpose:

> We are the Jewish youths of Germany who want to go to
> Palestine; we are a part of a whole *Volk*, but within it a special
> feature. Not from vanity, not from narcissism, not from
> special wishes, but from origin and being.[74]

The *ZVfD* was profoundly disturbed about the Prunner laws,
their influence on youth and on Zionism in general and
confronted the Blau-Weiss, on 2 September 1922, at a meeting in
Kassel. The fury began when Martin Bandmann immediately
berated the *ZVfD* for being little more than a conglomeration of
intellectuals. He proclaimed that Zionism, for the Blau-Weiss,
signified an emigration movement.[75] Bandmann also stated that
Jews should not go to Palestine as individuals, or even as families,
because they would merely be duplicating their mundane lives in
a new setting. 'Those who go to Palestine as individuals, go lost',
said Bandmann.[76] Rather, one must emigrate in a Bund because
that was the only form to guarantee true happiness, strength
and security. Otherwise, they would be simply transplanting
their unhealthy and unnatural life styles to a new environment.
Bandmann admonished the *ZVfD* for trying to create a Jewish
culture in Germany first instead of developing one in Palestine
free of foreign interference. Arguably, the *ZVfD* was more
interested in developing Jewish culture in Germany so one could
live more freely there, while the Blau-Weiss was more bent on
perpetuating German culture – as it was defined by some German
youth – in Palestine. Bandmann also condemned the constant
petty ideological debates that permeated the adult Zionists. He
reasoned that for the members of the Blau-Weiss it would be more
difficult to remain in Germany than to leave.

Kurt Blumenfeld tried to be more conciliatory than confrontational to the youths. He opposed the immediate departure for
Palestine on the grounds the Blau-Weiss was not yet ready and
that to do so and then fail could badly damage Zionism. He
directed his criticism of the Blau-Weiss at its lack of Judaism:

'Jewish content is foreign to you. You are oriented to the culture of the Galuth. I know for example that you are more familiar with German peasant songs than with Hebrew melodies'.[77] Blumenfeld attempted to convince the Blau-Weiss that it was not professionally equipped, nor had its members sufficient knowledge, to survive in Palestine.

At a meeting in Berlichingen, in 1922, spokesmen of the Blau-Weiss engaged in a stormy discussion about religion with the anti-religious forces prevailing. The Blau-Weiss even published a resolution that proclaimed: 'Judaism is a matter which inwardly does not concern us, which is unimportant for the education of our members, and is without significance for the future'.[78] One member, Stephan Cohn, went so far as to assert: 'The Bible is worthless for the Blau-Weiss … The break with Jewish tradition is the destiny about which we must be completely clear before we approach the holy scriptures of our fathers'. It may not have been so much a rejection of Judaism by the Blau-Weiss as a generational break. Cohn wanted to make certain that the Blau-Weiss rejected the Jewish traditions of its fathers, as well as those of the Ostjuden. Members of the Blau-Weiss wanted to escape from tradition in all areas of life and begin something new and vibrant, and in many ways religion provided an attractive target.[79]

Three factors became clearer about the Blau-Weiss and Zionism after Prunn. One was that Blumenfeld, who had spent his youth fighting against the conservative 'Herzlites' trying to direct Zionism into more than just a political movement, was now more or less defending the *status quo*, whereas young Bund leaders were trying to transform Zionism from a *Lebensauffassung* to an emigration movement.[80] The second was the feeling of superiority expressed by the Blau-Weiss. Enthusiasm, discipline and youthfulness supplied energy and resolve that the *ZVfD* lacked. Finally, the *ZVfD* detested the Prunner laws not only because of the separatism it promoted but also because some of the charges levelled at it had some validity. No doubt, part of the animosity and attention directed at the Blau-Weiss reflected a crisis of conscience within the *ZVfD*. It was easy to be a fervent Zionist in one's youth, but once a youth came of an age where career and family decisions had to be made, few Zionists were willing to leave what was most likely a profitable and comfortable existence in Germany. Thus, the leaders of the Blau-Weiss knew that the most opportune time to emigrate was before the responsibilities of adulthood had set in.

The rank and file of the German Zionists bitterly objected to the youth's independence. Blau-Weiss member, Benno Cohen, denounced the criticism as sour grapes, and argued that many of the Zionist critics were only frightened of the detrimental effect that the Blau-Weiss would have on the Zionist fraternities.[81] He replied to the charge that the Blau-Weiss wanted to erect a cultural enclave in Palestine by arguing that the Blau-Weiss was more realistic in perceiving that culture could not be fabricated just because of geography. In other words, moving to Palestine would not eradicate the fact the Blau-Weiss was a German Bund, and it was a delusion to think that one was going to feel at home immersed in a Jewish culture, which was foreign to most German Jews, solely because one resided in Palestine. The Blau-Weiss was proud of its German roots and could do nothing other than love German culture. Cohn mocked Scholem's charge that the Blau-Weiss was an army by retorting that the army was only a symbolic term that connoted action, and he used the term *Arbeitsarmee* ('workers' army') to denote the type of movement that promoted work rather than talk.[82]

Writing after the final break-up with the mainstream Zionist groups, the *Kartell Jüdischer Verbindungen* (*KJV*) and the *ZVfD*, Moritz Bileski placed the blame squarely on the shoulders of Blau-Weiss.[83] He believed the Blau-Weiss had over-estimated its importance within Zionism and thus had developed an uncompromising attitude. Bileski stated that 'the Blau-Weiss lacked all feeling for moral responsibility toward Zionism'. He suspected the Blau-Weiss was deceiving itself into thinking that it had discovered the solution to the Jewish problem. For Bileski, the Jewish question was more complex than the Blau-Weiss imagined:

> But all Zionists know – only the Blau-Weiss does not know – that there is nothing unproblematic in Judaism, that everything is questionable. If one abandons the 'organic development' [of Judaism] the result would be the destruction of Jewry [*der Untergang des Judentums*].[84]

It seemed that both the *KJV* and the Blau-Weiss had an agenda separate from merely a Jewish renaissance. Whether it admitted it or not, the *KJV* members were entrenched in German university life and already preparing themselves for lives in Germany. Their fraternity system was infused with its own honour and traditions that the Blau-Weiss rejected. For the Blau-Weiss, Zionism was not a movement that united all Jews regardless of age or country, but an opportunity to combine some of the traditions and mores of the German youth movement with the excitement of resettling in a distant, enchanted land. One Blau-Weisser compared moving to Palestine to the kind of adventure one reads about in the 'westerns' of Karl May. Thus, even in a minority group (the Blau-Weiss) that existed within a minority of German Jews (Zionism), there was a cacophony of charges and counter-charges.[85]

After 1923, the *Jüdische Rundschau* more or less gave up on the Blau-Weiss. When the journal reprinted the statutes of Prunn. in February of 1923, a scathing editorial concluded: '[the Blau-Weiss] is the spirit of fascist *Machtbündelei* which celebrates its resurrection. In the realm of the Jewish people these things are generally foreign'.[86] From the *ZVfD*'s point of view, the Blau-Weiss was not really a Zionist organization, but rather a group bent on self-destruction. The *ZVfD* still adhered to Herzl's principle of Zionism as returning to Judaism before returning to a Jewish land. Martin Bandmann offered an interesting analysis of the differences between the youth movement and the fraternities. He understood the conflict as a generational one.[87] He believed that the Zionists in their late thirties who felt threatened by the actions of the younger Blau-Weiss controlled the fraternities. *KJV* members had already passed through the threshold of adulthood and could no longer break away from the path that destined them for a life in the Diaspora. The generation of the Blau-Weiss, on the other hand, 'is ready to go to Palestine. They have for five years initiated an occupational transformation on the land and in the work colonies'.[88] He concluded by prophesizing that the son cannot travel the same path as his elder brother and that the success of the endeavour will depend on the wisdom of the father as to whether family relationships will be shattered when the Blau-Weiss emigrates.

Ironically, the fracas between the Blau-Weiss and German Zionism strengthened the youth group. Youths who were not certain of the Blau-Weiss's programme left the group and the ones who stayed were unyielding in their determination.[89] More of the youths participated in the training centres scattered around Germany, which sought to prepare youth for a life of farming and craftsmanship.[90] The Blau-Weiss set up a model settlement in Karlsruhe, in 1921, that was meant to approximate the colony envisaged for Palestine. The brochure on the settlement was largely written to show that the Blau-Weiss had carefully thought out its expedition.[91] It emphasized that the Palestine settlement would not work unless the youths were willing and competent. Throughout 1923, the Blau-Weiss became even more single-minded about its goal. All meetings and hikes concentrated on skills and knowledge that the Blau-Weiss thought would be necessary for emigration. One of the main problems was securing enough funds for the adventure, because after the split with the *KJV*, the *ZVfD* had abandoned the Blau-Weiss. Therefore, its efforts turned to raising private funds.[92]

As early as 1921, some of the older Blau-Weiss leaders had visited Palestine to scout out locations and conditions.[93] By the end of 1923, 89 Blau-Weissers had settled in Palestine, most near the port city of Haifa, choosing to remain isolated from the rest of the Palestinian-Jewish community.[94] In February 1924, a Blau-Weiss chapter in Tel Aviv was formed.[95] Moses's dream to transplant the *bündisch* idea to Palestine seemed real. The goal was to go to Palestine as a group, not just to spread out all over the Holy Land.[96] For Moses, this would combine the best of both worlds. It would allow the Blau-Weiss to adhere to its German heritage in a land that would be free of anti-Semitism.[97] Moses expressed little sympathy for the majority of eastern European settlers who had come to Palestine in the preceding two decades. Cultural differences, as well as the Ostjuden's inclination toward socialism, prevented Moses and the Blau-Weiss from forming close ties to the settlers.[98] In fact, for all of his tirades against Herzl's brand of Zionism, Moses seemed to cling to the old Zionist's idea of an aristocratic leadership in Palestine and envisaged the Blau-Weiss as perfect for the role. Moses decidedly rejected the idea of class and class conflict and instead chose to see nationalism as a stronger and more valid classification in society.[99] He also thought that socialist dogma was ruining Palestine's development. Gladly separating the Blau-Weiss from the eastern European Jews and the labour movement, Moses asserted that the Blau-Weiss did not look on Palestine as merely a place where refugees could congregate but as an opportunity to build the highest form of society. The Blau-Weiss members saw themselves as heirs to Herzl and as the only group equipped to govern Palestine because they were 'children from the best circles'.[100]

By 1924, the Blau-Weiss realized the time had come for decisive action and channelled all its efforts towards colonization. Each member was to give the project complete dedication or else leave the movement.[101] The hopes of the settlement rested on the success of Hans Simon's company that he had formed in Tel-Aviv – with Moses's approval – which specialized in electrical engineering. In the beginning, the company performed fairly well, receiving contracts on jobs in both Jerusalem and Tel Aviv. It ran into problems, however, with the Histadrut, the general federation of Jewish labour in Palestine. Although some individual Blau-Weissers joined the Histadrut, neither Hans Simon nor his company associated with the union. The friction between the young Germans and the eastern European-run federation occurred after the British commissioned the Blau-Weiss to install electricity in St George's Cathedral in Jerusalem. Because this was the Blau-Weiss's largest job, it needed to hire outside labourers in order to finish the project on time. The Blau-Weiss soon encountered difficulties with two of its hired help and fired them for laziness and incompetence. The workers subsequently lodged a complaint with the Histadrut which ruled that the Blau-Weiss was guilty of unfair labour practices.[102] The Histadrut set strict hours for workers, and in its haste to finish the job on schedule the Blau-Weiss exceeded the prescribed number of hours per day, even making workers toil on holidays – on the Jewish Sabbath, as well as on Yom Kippur. Simon defended the company's practices by arguing that since it was working on a church it could not very well work on Sundays, and thus, to complete the task, required extra work on Saturdays.

The Blau-Weiss complained of Histadrut intrusion into what it believed was purely a private matter, but the union was not sympathetic. When the story circulated around Jerusalem, a strike was proclaimed against the Blau-Weiss's project. The Blau-Weiss then exacerbated the situation by attempting to bring in Arab workers to finish the job.[103] The incident ended when a compromise was reached, but the Blau-Weiss felt cheated, and its reputation was irreparably tarnished.

Hans Simon blamed the dispute on the Histadrut, with its overbearing style and countless regulations that made it difficult for any entrepreneurial enterprise to succeed. The problem, however, went deeper. Writing back to the Blau-Weiss in Berlin, Felix Rosenblüth, a *KJV* member living in Palestine, admitted that the Histadrut over-reacted to the firing of workers who were justifiably dismissed for laziness and incompetence. However, the

Blau-Weiss needed to make more of an effort to integrate into the community and must join the union and abide by its rules.[104] Simon agreed with Rosenblüth but insisted that the practices of the union were detrimental to the development of Palestine.[105] The Blau-Weiss in Germany issued a circular to its members siding with its brethren in Palestine.[106] Further, it defended the Blau-Weiss's adherence to 'western culture'. Agreeing that Palestine must develop into a combination of eastern and western ways did not mean subordinating German practices to those of the Ostjuden.[107] The Blau-Weiss's difficulties in Palestine were discussed at the twentieth congress of the *ZVfD* in December 1924, and many of the speakers condemned the Blau-Weiss for its aloof nature.[108] The Blau-Weiss, on the other hand, chided the *ZVfD* for its lack of financial and moral support.[109]

The character of the future Jewish State was a constant source of debate in late 1924 as the Blau-Weiss knew it had to blend in with the more numerous eastern European settlers, but the group did not want to lose its German heritage. This perhaps has parallels to non-Zionists trying to blend into German culture without losing their Judaism. Georg Strauss preached that the Bund had to realize that the Ostjuden had a more revolutionary make-up owing to their past oppression. The Blau-Weiss should not oppose 'constructive socialism', but had to make clear that it was free to offer new approaches to Palestine's development. Strauss compared the importance of socialism to the eastern European Jews, with the primacy of the idea of the Bund to the Blau-Weiss.[110] However, for many of the few hundred Blau-Weiss settlers in Palestine, the security and intimacy of the Bund disappeared amidst the stark reality of Palestine.

While members paid lip service to learning Hebrew, the Blau-Weiss never saw it as a pressing need. It intended to bring with it its German culture, with the implicit idea that it would spread because of German superiority.[111] The settlement aborted within a year for numerous reasons. Walter Gross offered this analysis of why the group failed:

> The first establishments were the so-called Blau-Weiss artisans and an agricultural settlement. Unfortunately, the newcomers were inadequate in their command of the Hebrew language; and while revolutionary in their attitude *vis-à-vis* the older generation of German Zionists, they were

not socialists and were averse to becoming merged into the sector of organised labour. To the Histadruth and the official Zionist leadership in Palestine, they appeared as separatists. They were accused of forming a *Landsmannschaft* – regarded as a sin against nationalism in those days.[112]

Labour problems occurred not just with Jewish immigrants – the Blau-Weiss settlers also had difficulty getting along with their Arab neighbours.[113] An outbreak of malaria afflicted the settlement, and a lack of funds from official channels exacerbated their problems.[114] Their enthusiasm was no match for the many difficulties of life in Palestine.[115] Their lack of language skills and their inclination for aloofness made surviving in Palestine impossible. They disliked the Zionist organization, distrusted the Ostjuden and had nothing in common with the non-Jewish population. Most of Moses's army beat a hasty retreat back to Germany in 1925 and the débâcle was such that the Blau-Weiss could never regroup. The older members joined the *KJV* while the younger ones either joined the Kadimah or the more socialist-oriented *Bünde*.

The Blau-Weiss did not collapse immediately as is commonly assumed. Martin Bandmann vigorously tried to rejuvenate the Bund from Berlin. He urged members to begin more intense and diversified training.[116] By the end of 1925, however, a faction within the Blau-Weiss led by Hans Kaufmann gained control of the Bund and repudiated the Prunner laws and political Zionism and began the Bund anew. In essence, this ended one tradition of the Blau-Weiss based on strong leaders and a dedication to develop Palestine immediately. However, Kaufmann was able to carry the original message of wandering, nature and Jewish education through to the new scouting group, Kadimah.[117]

Moses grew bitter because of the failure and left no doubt that he blamed the socialists for destroying their experiment. Unlike most Zionist youth groups who disdained the influence of the British in the Holy Land, the Blau-Weiss believed that Palestine could never be settled without the aid of western capital. According to Moses: 'Capital is the means of our national idea, an extraordinary valuable means that leads modern armies like generals with economics'.[118] He criticized both the *ZVfD* and the World Zionist Organization for being manipulated by eastern Europeans, whom Moses considered Bolsheviks. Since German Jews epitomized the middle class, Moses logically concluded that they could only set up a state that reflected their background. Moses's views on the Ostjuden tended to alternate between patronizing and contemptuous. He left Palestine convinced that the confusion within Zionism and Palestine would never be successfully settled.[119]

The option most of the young Blau-Weiss members chose after their group dissolved was to join the Kadimah. This group resembled the early Kameraden and Blau-Weiss in many ways with its emphasis on wandering.[120] 'Wandering is the form and basis of our life', proclaimed one member.[121] By scouting, the Kadimah aimed to make young Jews into better adults and leaders of their *Volk*. It inherited the romantic nature of the Blau-Weiss but was not at first as fervently Zionist nor as independent. It focused on members becoming better Jews in Germany before they uprooted themselves and went to Palestine. To the Kadimah, politics had deterred the Blau-Weiss and it had lost its way to its true goal. The leader of the Kadimah, Walter Mecklenburg, saw the task of the Kadimah to work for all Jews, not just the elite, and to try to lead Jews out of their abnormal existence in society.[122] No concrete plan was ever offered; only a vague ideal that educating youths to be scouts and to learn the true teachings of the Bible which would enable Jews to live a healthy life. Gradually, however, the Kadimah began to turn more towards Zionism and Palestine. By 1931, it had joined with Hashomer Hazair as the new Kadimah leadership did not want to repeat the mistake of the Blau-Weiss by remaining isolated from other youth movements and, in 1933, the Kadimah merged with Brith Haolim.[123] The shift in the Kadimah, however, came more from the imminent dangers in society than from an independent desire to emigrate like the Blau-Weiss.

Still, some of the ideas of the Blau-Weiss resurfaced in the scouts, as Walter Mecklenburg wrote: 'The Bund must be the true community; it must not yield in the demands of the Hebrew-ization or Judaization and in the struggle against all conventionality and apathy'.[124] He added Hebrew to his programme, but the rest of the precepts remained similar to the Blau-Weiss. Therefore, although the Blau-Weiss had dissolved, its ideas penetrated other Zionist groups as well as the *ZVfD* which learned from its mistakes. Its commitment to Palestine made an impression on the community and the legacy of the Blau-Weiss would not soon be forgotten. As one former member recalled: 'For us, for a whole generation of Jewish youths from Germany, the Blau-

Weiss was the great awakener, the great educator, and as such it fulfilled its historical mission'.[125]

NOTES

1. Kurt Blumenfeld, 'Ursprünge und Art einer zionistischer Bewegung', *Bulletin des Leo Baeck Instituts*, 4 (1958), p. 137.
2. George Mosse, *Germans and Jews: The Right, the Left and the Search for a Third Force in Pre-Nazi Germany* (New York: Grosset and Dunlap, 1970), pp. 94–5.
3. Stephen Poppel, *Zionism in Germany 1897–1933* (Philadelphia, PA: Jewish Publication Society of America, 1977), p. 134.
4. Harry Abt, *Die jüdische Jugendbewegung* (Berlin, n.d. c. 1933).
5. Gershom Scholem, *On Jews and Judaism in Crisis: Selected Essays* (New York: Schocken, 1976), pp. 11–12; also see his autobiography *Von Berlin nach Jerusalem* (Frankfurt-am-Main: Suhrkamp, 1977). Scholem was not the only one who saw fascist tendencies in the Blau-Weiss. The Zionist paper also noticed the similarities in Moritz Bilwiski, 'Aufhebung der Fusion zwischen KJV und Blau-Weiss', *Jüdische Rundschau*, 16 February 1923; also Hermann Meier-Cronemeyer, 'Jüdische Jugend-bewegung', *Germania Judaica*, 8 (1969), p. 64.
6. See the unpublished memoirs of an ex-member Herbert Nussbaum, 'Weg und Schicksal eines deutschen Juden', Memoir collection at the Leo Baeck Institute in New York. Many German Jews were derogatorily referred to as *dreitage* Juden because they only attended synagogue on the three High Holidays. Although there was evidence of religious revival among some German Jews, apostasy and mixed marriages were greater signs of religious decline. Donald Niewyk estimates the average synagogue attendance on High Holidays during the late 1920s to be 50 per cent. Donald Niewyk, *The Jews in Weimar Germany* (Baton Rouge, LO: Louisiana State University Press, 1980), p. 102. See also Gustav Loeffler, 'Religiöse Not', *Der Morgen*, 2 (1926), pp. 259–71; and Friedrich Rölf, 'Untergang der deutschen Juden?', *Israelitisches Familienblatt*, 7 September 1922. When one young Jew attending a Berlin Gymnasium was asked what the difference between him and his non-Jewish colleagues was, the youngster retorted, 'They don't go to church and I don't go to synagogue'. Quoted in Peter Gay, 'In Deutschland zu Hause', in *Die Juden in Nationalsozialistischen Deutschland* (Tübingen: Mohr, 1986), p. 35.
7. Peter Stachura, *The German Youth Movement: A Documentary and Interpretive History* (New York: Macmillan, 1981), p. 87.
8. Pinchas Rosenblüth, *Das Jubiläums Treffen des Blau-Weiss* (Naharia, Israel, 1962), p. 7.
9. Ernst Holzer, 'Jüdische Jugend-bewegung', *Der Morgen* 3 (1928), p. 281; also 'Das Ziele des Blau-Weiss', in *Leitfaden für die Gründung eines Jüdischen Wanderbundes Blau-Weiss: Streng Vertaulich*: 'The Blau-Weiss educates its children in opposition to the *Lebensauffassung* of the elder generation, not in opposition to their Jewish view'. Quoted in Jehuda Reinharz (ed.), *Dokumente zur Geschichte des deutschen Zionismus* (Tübingen: Mohr, 1982), p. 116.
10. Ludwig Mayer, 'Der jüdische Wanderbund Blau-Weiss', *K-C Blätter*, August 1914, pp. 248–52. This journal was the organ of the group of non-Zionist fraternities at German universities.
11. Mayer, 'Der jüdische Wanderbund', p. 239. For the quintessential example of this, see Walter Rathenau, 'Hore Israel', *Die Zukunft*, 1898. Zionism saw

these traits as a result of rootlessness which it meant to correct. Moses Calvary, 'Die erzieherrische Aufgabe des deutschen Zionismus', *Die Welt*, 6 January 1911, pp. 5–8.

12. Karl Glaser, 'Aus der Bewegung', *Blau-Weiss Blätter: Eine Flugschrift des Blau-Weiss* (Berlin, nd.), p. 31.

13. Mayer, 'Der jüdische Wanderbund', p. 240. Hans Tramer points out that only 27 of the 117 songs were Jewish. Tramer, 'Jüdischer Wanderbund Blau-Weiss', *Bulletin des Leo Baeck Instituts*, 17 (1962), pp. 23–43; esp. p. 28.

14. Mayer, p. 241: 'Unsere deutsch-jüdische Jugend kann jüdische Volkslieder *nur* gebrauchen, wenn sie nach Text, Melodie und Rhythmus sich mit *deutsche* Empfinden vereinen lassen!'

15. The *K-C*, or *Kartell-Convent*, was an umbrella group of German-Jewish fraternities that espoused the idea that German Jews were Germans of Jewish faith and not a part of a separate Jewish *Volk*. Norbert Kampe, *Studenten und 'Judenfrage' im Deutschen Kaiserreich* (Göttingen: Vandenhoeck & Ruprecht, 1988).

16. Mayer, 'Der jüdische Wanderbund', p. 244.

17. Jehuda Reinharz, *Fatherland or Promised Land: The Dilemma of the German Jew, 1893–1914* (Ann Arbor, MI: University of Michigan Press, 1975), p. 202; see also the article in *Im Deutschen Reich*, July/August 1912, pp. 373–4.

18. Felix Rosenblüth, 'Judischer Wanderbund Blau-Weiss', *Blau-Weiss-Führer*, 1917, p. 28; Tramer, 'Jüdischer Wanderbund Blau-Weiss', p. 25.

19. For the emphasis of the Posen meeting, see the *Jüdische Rundschau*, 13 May 1912, p. 199.

20. The youth who were not attending secondary school were more apt to join the Zionist group, the Herzl-Bund, which began December 1912. See *Herzl-Bund Blätter*, 1 (February 1913).

21. Quoted in Michael Berkowitz, *Western Jewry and the Zionist Project, 1914–1933* (Cambridge: Cambridge University Press, 1996), p. 152.

22. Georg Todtmann, 'Was wir Wollen!', *Blau-Weiss Blätter*, May 1913, pp. 2–4; Jospeh Marcus, 'Wanderpflichten', ibid., September 1913, p. 5.

23. Todtmann, 'Was wir Wollen!', p. 2.

24. 'Wie wir Chanukah feiern', *Blau-Weiss Blätter* (December 1913). Even Martin Buber proposed, in 1899, that Hanukkah be turned into a Zionist festival.

25. Todtmann, 'Was wir Wollen!', p. 3: 'We are not Zionists as we are labelled. We have nothing to do with parties and party politics'.

26. The idea behind all the members wearing similar clothing was to mask the differences in wealth among the group.

27. Joseph Marcus, 'Wanderpflichten', *Blau-Weiss Blätter*, September 1913, p. 6.

28. Joseph Marcus, 'Der Führer', *Blau-Weiss Blätter*, May 1914, n.p. Kurt Blumenfeld recalled that the Blau-Weiss differed from the student fraternities. The students fostered an atmosphere of brotherhood while the Blau-Weiss was based on the principle of the leader. See his contribution, 'Verein jüdischer Studenten Königsbert: Aus Erinnerungen, die mit dem Sommer-semester 1906 beginnen', in, *Rückblick und Besinnung: Aufsätze Gesammelt aus Anlass des 50. Jahrestages der Gründung der VJS im KJV* (Tel Aviv, 1954), pp. 4–13; esp. p. 12.

29. Helene Hanna Cohn, 'Die Frau in der nationaljüdischen Jugendbewegung', *Jüdische Rundschau*, 27 September 1918, p. 303; Berkowitz, *Western Jewry*, p. 153.

30. Karl Glaser, Introduction, in *Blau-Weiss Liederbuch* (Berlin, 1914); Berkowitz, *Western Jewry*, p. 151.

31. Moses Calvary, 'Blau-Weiss: Anmerkungen zum jüdischen Jugend wanderer', *Der Jude*, October 1916, p. 451.

32. Calvary, 'Blau-Weiss Anmerkungen', p. 456.

33. 'Unser Herzeltag', *Blau-Weiss Blätter*, September 1913, p. 3; Theodor Herzl, *Der Judenstaat* (Vienna: Breitenstein, 1896).
34. On this term, see Blumenfeld, 'Ursprünge und Art einer zionistischer Bewegung', pp. 133–5.
35. Theodor Herzl, *Altneuland* (Leipzig: Hermann Seemann Nachfolger, 1902).
36. Chaim Schatzker, 'Martin Buber's Influence on the Jewish Youth Movement', *Leo Baeck Institute Yearbook*, 24 (1979); Jehuda Reinharz, 'Martin Buber's Impact on German Zionism before World War I', *Studies in Zionism*, 6 (1982), pp. 171–85.
37. Buber's writings had great appeal for the young. Hans Kohn, 'Rückblick auf eine gemeinsame Jugend', in Hans Tramer (ed.), *Robert Weltsch zum 70. Geburtstag* (Tel Aviv, 1961), p. 115.
38. Reinharz, 'Martin Buber's Impact', pp. 178–9; Buber's three speeches on Judaism are reprinted in Martin Buber, *On Judaism*, Nahum Glatzer (ed.) (New York: Schocken, 1967), pp. 149–77. Martin Buber, *Drei Reden Über Judentum* (Frankfurt: Jüdischer Verlag, 1920).
39. Gershom Scholem, 'Jüdische Jugendbewegung', *Der Jude*, 12 (1917), pp. 822–5.
40. Walter Preuss, *Ein Ring schliesst sich* (Tel Aviv, 1950), p. 82.
41. Quoted in the *Blau-Weiss Blätter*, 1 May 1914, p. 3; Chaim Rinott, 'Major Trends in the Jewish Youth Movement in Germany', *Leo Baeck Institute Yearbook*, 19 (1974), p. 81; also 'Über einige Fragen jüdischer und "Menschlichkeit" zusammenhänge im Blau-Weiss', *Führerzeitung*, October 1917, pp. 52–5.
42. Tramer, 'Jüdischer Wanderbund Blau-Weiss', p. 30. Martin Bandmann put the number at 3,000 in 1917, though that may be overly optimistic. Oral History of Martin Bandmann Jerusalem, 1981, Central Zionist Archives (CZA), A365/60. Three thousand was probably the peak membership of the Blau-Weiss in 1923. Memo from Walter Moses to members and parents, 2 January 1924, CZA, A365/34.
43. On the relationship of the Blau-Weiss to religion, see Mosche Unna, 'Die Anfänge der Religiösen Kibbuzbewegung in Deutschland', *Bulletin des Leo Baeck Instituts*, 78 (1987), pp. 72–114.
44. Ferdinand Ostertag, 'Von der Aufgabe', *Führerzeitung*, August 1917, p. 24.
45. Walter Moses, 'Die Übersiedlung nach Palästina', *Führerzeitung*, March 1918, pp. 63–8.
46. Fritz Löwenstein, 'National-jüdischer Jugendtag', *Jüdische Rundschau*, 5 July 1918, p. 285. He credited the war with Zionism's new strength and vitality.
47. ZVfD was the central organization for German Zionism.
48. A pamphlet was published commemorating the event: *Zur National-jüdischen Jugendtag* (Berlin 1918); see also 'Die national-jüdische Jugend-bewegung in Deutschland', *Jüdische Rundschau*, 18 October 1918, p. 302.
49. Martin Buber, 'Wandlung', *Jüdische Rundschau*, 18 October 1918, p. 302; Buber, 'Zion und die Jugend', *Der Jude*, 3 (1918/19), p. 102; On the Austrian branch of the Blau-Weiss, see Gerhard Seewann, *Österreichische Jugend-bewegung 1900–1938*, Vol. 1 (Frankfurt: Dipa-Verlag, 1971), pp. 121–35; also 'Bericht über die Gründung des Blau-Weiss in Österreich', CZA, A66/22.
50. Moses Calvary, 'Gleitwort', *Der Jüdische Wille*, 4/5 (September/October 1918), pp. 213–16; reproduced in Reinharz, *Dokumente*, pp. 228–32.
51. Gershom Scholem, 'Al Chet…', *Jüdische Rundschau*, 27 September 1918, pp. 303–4. For the positive expectations, see Karl Glaser, 'Der Nationaljüdische Jugendtag', ibid., 20 September 1918, pp. 297–9; Max Mayer, 'Zum Jugendtag', ibid., pp. 301–2; and Israel Richert, 'Die erlösende Tat', ibid., p. 304.
52. This figure also included the gymnastic clubs and the fraternities.
53. Karl Glaser, 'Die national-jüdische Jugendbewegung in Deutschland',

Jüdische Rundschau, 4 October 1918, pp. 309–10.

54. Blau-Weiss clubs from Munich, Mannheim, Fulda, Breslau, and Frankfurt-am-Main were led by Orthodox leaders. Mosche Unna, 'Die Anfänge der Religiösen Kibbuzbewegung in Deutschland', *Bulletin des Leo Baeck Instituts*, 78 (1987), p. 79. Unna and his sister were members of the Mannheim group. Like Benno Cohen, he too later served in the Knesset.

55. Glaser, 'Der nationaljüdische Jugendtag', p. 317.

56. Arnold Zweig, 'Der Jude in der deutschen Gegenwart', *Der Jude*, 14 (1925/26), pp. 1–8.

57. Hans Goslar, 'Jugendtag-Referate: Ein offener Brief an Walter Moses', *Jüdische Rundschau*, 11 October 1918, pp. 318–20. Goslar's remarks were supported by Alfred Kupferberg, 'Das Wert des Historizismus', ibid., 18 October 1918, p. 326.

58. Martin Bandmann, 'Unsere Erziehungsbild', *Blätter*, January 1923, p. 25.

59. Ferdinand Ostertag, 'Blau-Weiss Blätter', *Blätter*, November 1918, n.p. Martin Bandmann recalled that Ostertag's speech had a great influence on the movement. 'Oral History of Martin Bandmann', CZA, A365/60.

60. Hans Oppenheim, 'Kritik', *Führerzeitung*, August 1918, pp. 96–7.

61. 'Erziehungsreferat gehalten auf dem Jugendtag', *Führerzeitung*, January 1919, pp. 103–18.

62. Hans Tramer sets the date for the Blau-Weiss's transformation at their Bundestag in Sachenheim as August of 1919, though I would date it a bit earlier. The change in membership can be gauged by scanning the leadership lists in the *Blätter*.

63. Perhaps the excitement of going to Palestine could compensate for the feelings of inadequacies of not being able to participate in the war effort.

64. Martin Bandmann, 'Leben und Aufgaben eines Blau-Weiss Bundes', *Führerzeitung*, December 1920, pp. 57–63; and Martin Bandmann, 'Typus und Individum', ibid., May 1920, p. 4. The largest centres were set up at: Messingwerk, 1920; Halbe, 1921; Hausen, 1923; Ludwighorst, 1923; and Hohenberg, 1923. 'Interne Informationen über die Arbeit der Bundesführung in Monat Januar', 1 February 1925, CZA, A66/11.

65. C.Z. Klötzkel, 'Der Blau-Weiss', *Jüdische Rundschau*, 10 August 1920, pp. 427–8. Klötzkel noted how physically fit both the boys and girls appeared.

66. Dolf Michales, 'Mein Blau-Weiss Erlebnis', *Bulletin des Leo Baeck Institut*, 17 (1962), pp. 44–67.

67. No doubt this kind of confidence was gained by listening to Buber and others who had so much faith in the youth and their ability to change the world. Martin Bandmann, *Blätter*, August/September 1921, p. 216 ; Tramer, 'Jüdischer Wanderbund Blau-Weiss', p. 35. One of the leaders, Georg Strauss, wrote that 1921 was a difficult year for the Blau-Weiss as many of the local leaders had left the movement under pressures of exams but inner strength would pull it through. Georg Strauss to Martin Bandmann, 21 September 1921, CZA, A365/32.

68. Walter Moses, 'Das Bundesgesetz von Prunn', *Führerzeitung zweites Heft*, 1922, pp. 17–26; the laws are reproduced in Reinharz, *Dokumente*, pp. 312–14 and in 'Das Gesetz des Blau-Weiss', *Jüdische Rundschau*, 16 February 1923, pp. 77–80.

69. Moses, 'Das Bundesgesetz von Prunn', p. 26.

70. Ibid. This was, no doubt, a condemnation of the Jews' attachment to liberalism.

71. Ibid., p. 21.

72. On the nature of the German Bund, see Felix Raabe, *Die bündische Zeit* (Stuttgart: Diedrichs, 1961); and Matthias von Hellfeld, *Bündische Jugend und Hitlerjugend: Zur Geschichte von Anpassung und Widerstand, 1930–1939*

(Cologne: Verlag Wissenschaft und Politik, 1987), pp. 9–33.
73. On Revisionist Zionism, see Joseph B. Schechtman *et al.*, *The History of the Revisionist Movement, 1925–1930* (Tel Aviv: Hadar, 1970); Joseph B. Schechtman, *The Life and Times of Vladimir Jabotinsky* (Silver Spring, MD: Eschel, 1986); and Francis Nicosia, 'Revisionist Zionism in Germany I', *Leo Baeck Institute Yearbook*, 31 (1986), pp. 209–40.
74. Moses, 'Das Bundesgesetz von Prunn', p. 19.
75. Martin Bandmann, 'Vorkonferenz über die Jugendbewegung in Kassel', *Jüdische Rundschau*, 29 September 1922, pp. 517–18; also cited in Reinharz, *Dokumente*, pp. 315–18.
76. Bandmann, 'Vorkonferenz', p. 517.
77. Ibid.
78. Point four, in the *Rundschreiben des Jüdischen Wanderbundes Blau-Weiss* (Frankfurt, 1922); cited in Unna, 'Die Anfänge der Religiösen Kibbuz-bewegung', pp. 81ff.
79. Unna, 'Die Anfänge der Religiösen Kibbuzbewegung', p. 81. Unna deplored these 'destructive tendencies'. In general, though, hostility toward Judaism did not seem to be widespread in the Blau-Weiss.
80. At the Prunn declaration, Bandmann was 22 and Strauss 25, while Blumenfeld was 39 years old. A fourth stage in German Zionism would later develop when emigration became assumed and socialism was added.
81. Benno Cohn, 'Die Gefahr', *Jüdische Rundschau*, 19 December 1922, p. 657.
82. Ibid.
83. Moritz Bileski, 'Aufhebung der Fusion zwischen KJF und Blau-Weiss: Post Festum', *Jüdische Rundschau*, 6 February 1923, p. 60; also, 'Post Festum', *Sonderabruck aus Der Jüdische Student 20. Jahrgang*, pp. 17–20. The Blau-Weiss defended itself in 'Erklärung', *Jüdische Rundschau*, 16 February 1923, p. 78. In a circular to its members, the Blau-Weiss left no doubt that the *KJV* was at fault: *4. Rundschreiben*, 15 June 1923, CZA, A365/33; and Georg Strauss and Martin Bandmann, 'Memorandum: An die Mitglieder des Präsidiums des KJB-Blau-Weiss', *Sonderabruck*, pp. 8–13.
84. 'Erklärung', p. 78.
85. The Blau-Weiss blamed the *KJV* at their meeting in February; this was reproduced in 'Ein Entschliessung der Blau-Weiss Führerschaft', *Jüdische Rundschau*, 2 March 1923, p. 103. For the *KJV* side, see 'Kartelltag des *KJV*', ibid.
86. 'Das Bundesgesetz Prunn', *Jüdische Rundschau*, 16 February 1923, pp. 77–81.
87. Martin Bandmann, 'Die Generation', *Jüdische Rundschau*, 13 March 1923, p. 129; and Michaelis, 'Mein Blau-Weiss Erlebnis', p. 64.
88. Bandmann, 'Die Generation', p. 129.
89. In the autumn of 1923, the Blau-Weiss had over 3,000 members.
90. These centres included training for women as well. 'Handfertigkeits-nachmittage für Mädchen', *Blätter*, 2 (1923), p. 4; also 'Kolonie', ibid., p. 9; and 'Unsere Werkstätte', p. 5.
91. The brochure was entitled, *Die Karlsruher Siedlung: Plan einer Blau-Weiss Werkstätte in Palästina* (Munich, 1923). A copy of this can be found in the Leo Baeck Institute Library. See also Hans Simon, 'Bericht über die inneren Vorgänge der Karlsruher Siedlung', 5 July 1923, CZA, A365/33.
92. Erich Cahn, 'Leipzig', *Blätter*, February/March 1924, pp. 47–63. Memo from Erich Cahn to the Bundesleitung, 28 March 1923, CZA, A365/33; and Walter Moses memo to members and parents, 2 January 1924, CZA, A365/34.
93. The Blau-Weiss's first attempt at a settlement was on Kibbutz Zwi, which failed by the end of 1922. Letter from Benno Cohn to Martin Bandmann, 17 March 1923, CZA, A365/33. This failure, however, did not seem to

discourage other efforts at emigration, though it did strengthen the resolve that a settlement based completely on farming was impractical for western Jews.

94. The name of the settlement was Kwuzah Zwi. Schlomo Ettinger, 'Die Kwuzah Zwi', in Rosenblüth, *Das Jubiläums Treffen des Blau-Weiss*; and Benno Cohn, 'Schlussrede', in ibid. Both members recall major problems in the settlement like lack of money, little support from parents and a clash of personalities.
95. On the meeting, see *24. Rundschreiben*, 1924. The Blau-Weiss then consisted of a Wanderbund for teenagers, an Älterbund for those in their early twenties, and a Palästinabund for those who had settled in Palestine.
96. *Rundschreiben an die Nadelträger*, 22 May 1925, CZA, A365/36.
97. Walter Moses, 'Bundesidee und Zionismus', *Blätter*, September 1925, pp. 1–8.
98. Moses believed that the capitalist form of production was the most productive and the best inducement to attract youths. In this he differed from mainstream German Zionism which, led by Robert Weltsch, was left-leaning. Moses's preference for capitalism also set him at odds with other non-Zionist Jewish groups which saw in capitalism the source of society's misfortune, as well as anti-Semitism.
99. Walter Moses, 'Zur nationalen Kolonisation', *Blätter*, September 1925, pp. 15–20.
100. Moses, 'Bundesidee und Zionismus'; and 'Was hat der Bund Blau-Weiss gewollt?' ibid., p. 10. It is interesting that the left-wing Zionist groups – while paying lip-service to Herzl – generally saw him as a bourgeois who represented a generation from which they wanted to distance themselves. The Blau-Weiss though saw Herzl as the patron saint of Zionism.
101. *Rundschreiben*, 2 December 1924, CZA, A365/35.
102. Hans Simon, 'Bericht über den Konflikt der Blau-Weiss Werkstätten mit der Histadruth in den Novembertagen des Jahres 1924' (very secret), CZA, A365/35.
103. A meeting with Arsloroff and other leaders of the Histadruth was unsuccessful and the Blau-Weiss complained that the union was taking on governmental functions; Simon, 'Bericht über den Konflikt'. While there was no evidence the Histadrut called the strike, the union did not at first discourage it.
104. Letter from Felix Rosenblüth to the Bundesleitung in Berlin, 3 December 1924, CZA, A365/35. He urged the Blau-Weiss not to treat workers according to German standards. Rosenblüth believed the Blau-Weiss demanded too much discipline of the workers, and by all means must respect Jewish holidays.
105. Hans Simon to the Bundesleitung in Berlin, 30 December 1923, CZA, A365/35.
106. *Rundschreiben*, 13 December 1924, CZA, A365/35.
107. 'Erwiderung von Hans Kaufmann auf das Diskussionsrundschreiben von Richard Markel zum Theme landsmannschaftliche und bündische Siedlungen', n.d., CZA, A365/35.
108. See the comments of Fridl Rosenblatt, Georg Landauer and Fritz Löwenstein, in 'Der XX. Delegiertentag', *Jüdische Rundschau*, 2 January 1925, pp. 4–5.
109. Georg Strauss, 'Memorandum über den Blau-Weiss an Walter Moses', 31 December 1924; and a letter from Werner Bloch to Martin Bandmann, 25 March 1925, CZA, A365/35.
110. 'Palästina und der Blau-Weiss: Referat gehalten auf der Wintertagung in Erfurt von Georg Strauss', December 1924, CZA, A365/35.

228 *Forging Modern Jewish Identities*

111. Georg Strauss, 'Palästina und der Blau-Weiss', *Blätter*, September 1925, pp. 22–33.
112. Walter Gross, 'The Zionist Students' Movement', *Leo Baeck Institute Yearbook*, 4 (1959), p. 158.
113. At one of its training centres in Hilsbach, the members of the Blau-Weiss were regaled with adventures of Jews and Arabs reminiscent of Cowboys and Indians: see *Blätter*, 1 (1925), p. 15; cited in Niewyk, *The Jews in Weimar*, p. 135.
114. Michaelis, 'Mein Blau-Weiss Erlebnis', p. 67; where Michaelis mentions the malaria. Meier-Cronemeyer includes a helpful discussion of the group's problems interacting with labour, see 'Jüdische Jugend-bewegung', pp. 68–9. In another article on the effect of the youth movement on Palestine, Meier-Cronemeyer all but ignores the Blau-Weiss, believing that only the left-leaning groups had a measurable impact. Meier-Cronemeyer, 'Wirkungen der Jugendbewegung im Staatsaufbau Israels', *Jahrbuch des Archivs der deutschen Jugendbewegung* (Burg Ludwigstein: Archiv der Deutschen Jugendbewegung, 1974), pp. 38–57.
115. Margarete Buber-Neumann was impressed with the pride and diligence of the Blau-Weiss: see *Von Potsdam nach Moskau* (Stuttgart: Deutsche Verlags-Anstalt, 1957), p. 56.
116. See the series of letters by and to Bandmann, in CZA, A365/36, and A365/37.
117. Hans Kaufmann, 'Bericht über den Verlauf und das Ergebnis der Dresdener Tagung', 25–27 December 1925, CZA A365/38; for the protocol of the meeting, see CZA, A66/13/1.
118. Walter Moses, 'Was hat der Bund Blau-Weiss gewollt?' *Blätter*, September 1925, p. 12. Moses later became a successful businessman in Palestine. Ironically, he became one of the richest men in Israel by owning a cigarette factory. This was ironic because of the Blau-Weiss's adherence to the belief that tobacco was a great evil of bourgeois society.
119. Ibid., p. 14; also, 'Wirtschaftsbund des Blau-Weiss', 1925, pp. 1–17, CZA, A365/37. Moses seemed to relish challenging the dominant trends in Zionism whether it be the ZVfD in Germany or the Histadrut in Palestine. He wrote: 'Since the beginning, the Blau-Weiss has led the conscious stage of an incessant passionate fight against the prevailing ideas in Zionism'. For a rather patronizing portrayal of the Ostjuden, see Georg Strauss, 'Palästina und der Blau-Weiss', *Blätter*, September 1925, pp. 22–33.
120. The Kadimah began in Berlin and published its own journal entitled, *Der Jüdische Pfadfinder: Eine Zeitschrift für die Mittleren und Jüngeren*. The group had 1,500 members by the end of 1926 as they had attracted some of the 'Ring' group within the Kameraden. Its complete title was: Kadimah, Ring jüdischer Wander- und Pfadfinderbünde.
121. Walter Levy, 'Ziel und Weg', *Der Jüdische Pfadfinder*, October 1926, p. 8.
122. Walter Mecklenburg, 'Weg und Ziel', *Der Jüdische Pfadfinder*, October 1927, pp. 2–3; Mecklenburg, 'Deutschjüdische Jugend und Zionismus', *Jüdische Rundschau*, 4 March 1930, p. 121. Mecklenburg believed the first task of western Jewish youths lay in the Galuth and he rejected all political means either Zionist or socialist, Walter Mecklenburg, 'Der Bund', *Älterensblatt*, December 1929, CZA, A/66/7.
123. Reinharz, 'Hashomer Hazair in Germany I', *Leo Baeck Institute Yearbook*, 31 (1986), pp. 187–92. Reinharz details how Mecklenberg was forced out of the Kadimah by the Zionist and socialist members.
124. Walter Mecklenburg, 'Ein Ältererblatt', *Der Jüdische Pfadfinder*, December 1929; reproduced in Werner Kindt, *Die deutsche Jugendbewegung 1920 bis 1933: Die bündische Zeit. Quellenschriften* (Düsseldorf: Diedrichs, 1974), p. 788.
125. Michaelis, 'Mein Blau-Weiss Erlebnis', p. 67.

10

Assimilation and Return in Two Generations of Czech-Jewish Women: Berta Fanta and Else Fanta Bergmann

MIRIAM DEAN-OTTING

Beginning with the Haskalah, the question of how to live in the modern world as a Jew was one that men and women of the Jewish communities of Europe confronted in different ways. Many assume that it was predominantly men who had to grapple with assimilation while women preserved the tradition for future generations. A prominent example of this gender divide is that of Sigmund Freud and his wife, Martha Bernays Freud, whose husband coldly dismissed her wish to kindle Sabbath candles.[1] While men such as Samuel Holdheim, Zecharias Frankel, Samson Raphael Hirsch, Leopold Zunz and Abraham Geiger made their mark in the public sphere and became the well-known articulators of Jewish thought, it would be an oversight to assume that Jewish women were not pondering the impact of modernity on their private lives. Paula Hyman has cautioned historians that to understand fully the effects of modernity on Jewry we must carefully examine the experiences of both the general population (that is, not the intellectuals and leadership) and women.[2] Marion Kaplan has pointed out in her study of Jewish women in Imperial Germany that, 'memoirs, although limited mainly to middle-class women, come closest to presenting women as whole persons engaged in the public and private spheres'.[3] Journals and family histories, then, rather than theologies or *wissenschaftliche* treatises, were significant means by which Jewish women addressed the

pressing challenge of modernity. Two turn-of-the-century Czech-
Jewish women from one family, Berta Fanta and her daughter,
Else Fanta Bergmann, were extraordinary informants in this
regard. Berta Fanta kept an extensive journal that reveals in subtle,
and not so subtle, ways a frank disaffection from Judaism. Else
Bergmann's family history, on the other hand, appears to reclaim
in some manner the Jewish roots of the Fanta family.

With disaffection and reclamation taking place from one
generation to the next in the Fanta family, the use of the term
'assimilation' is problematic. Hyman's reflection on the complexities inherent in the term, and what she describes as the
'paradoxes of assimilation', are useful to this study:

> A number of historians have suggested that the blunt term
> 'assimilation' obscures the varieties of behavior and the
> nuances of identity that characterize modern Jewry. The
> term 'assimilation' often does not convey the multiple influ-
> ences that together forge individual as well as collective
> identity, the different social contexts in which various aspects
> of identity are expressed, or the coexistence of the desire for
> full civic integration with the retention of what we might
> today call ethnic particularism.[4]

Hyman dismisses a characterization of the 'processes of assimilation of modern Jews as rapid and disruptive – causing a
traumatic break with the past',[5] because investigation of women's
experience offers a different picture. Furthermore, she carefully
delineates the differences between two aspects of assimilation, *the
sociological process* and *assimilation as a project*[6]:

> As a *sociological process*, assimilation consists of several differ-
> ent stages. The first steps, often called acculturation, include
> the acquisition of the basic markers of the larger society, such
> as language, dress and the more amorphous category of
> 'values'. The integration of minority-group members into
> majority institutions follow, along with the attendant weak-
> ening of minority institutions.[7]

Both Fanta and Bergmann, as will be demonstrated in this essay,
participated in the sociological process of assimilation and were,
inevitably, influenced by assimilation as a project, which Hyman

defines as 'the official response of Jewish communal leaders ... to emancipation'.[8] This of itself is hardly remarkable since, as Hyman has demonstrated in her study, the large majority of nineteenth-century Jews of central Europe and the US participated in, and were influenced by, both aspects of assimilation. What is note-worthy is the response of Bergmann to this assimilation and her yearning, despite her mother's disaffection, to recover her Jewish past.

While Bergmann herself inherited her mother's disaffection from Judaism, her attempt to reconnect with the family's Jewish past is reminiscent of Glueckel of Hameln's memoir.[9] In Glueckel's writings we find one of the earliest examples of a Jewish woman's voice self-consciously articulating the role of religion in her and the family's life. Writing as a means of alleviating her grief upon her husband's death, Glueckel set as her main purpose the goal of describing for her children the family's history. Glueckel sought to create a document that would guide her children to lead Jewish lives even as they interacted with the larger culture in their commercial dealings:

> Moreover, put aside a fixed time for the study of the Torah as best you know how. Then diligently go about your business, for providing your wife and children a decent livelihood is likewise a *mitzvah* – the command of God and the duty of man.[10]

It is particularly striking that Glueckel aimed to instil Jewish family values (to use a contemporary turn of phrase) in her children, even though she was not confronted by the challenges of modernity which would divide Jews about a century later. Her work is an important 'ancestor' for the family history of Else Bergmann, even though Bergmann's intent does not seem to have been the same as Glueckel's. Unlike Glueckel, Bergmann did not write in order to solidify an already strong Jewish religious identity. However, she did, as we shall see, have an interest in preserving the Jewish roots of her family.

A closer 'relative' to Bergmann's writings is perhaps Pauline Wengeroff's *Memoiren Einer Grossmutter*.[11] Wengeroff, who was born in Bobruysk in 1833 and died in Minsk in 1916,[12] was con-scious not only of the question of modernity versus tradition, but also openly lamented the transformation of her community. She quoted her mother as having said:

> Two things I know for certain. I and my generation will surely
> live and die as Jews. Our grandchildren will surely not live
> and die as Jews. But what our children will be I cannot
> foresee.[13]

Wengeroff watched her children leave Judaism through baptism
and recognized that loss not solely as a personal one but also
described it as, 'the character of a national misfortune'.[14] Bergmann
may have begun to think about her family's disaffection from
Judaism as unfortunate as well and thus felt compelled to create
a memoir which rooted the family in its Jewish past.

While Glueckel was a seventeenth-century German Jew and
Wengeroff's experience was that of nineteenth-century Russia,
the case before us, that of the Fanta family, was perhaps somewhat
typical for urban Czech Jewry of the nineteenth and twentieth
centuries. Students of Czech Jewry are familiar with Franz Kafka's
remarks concerning Judaism that he made in his 'Letter to his
Father', a lengthy accusation that was never actually mailed to
Hermann Kafka. Among other criticisms, Kafka points to his
father's hypocritical participation in Jewish rituals:

> I found equally little means of escape from you in Judaism.
> Here some escape would, in principle, have been thinkable,
> but more than that, it would have been thinkable that we
> might both have found each other in Judaism or even that
> we might have begun from there in harmony. But what sort
> of Judaism was it I got from you?[15]

Having pointed out his father's failings with regard to religion,
Kafka sought an explanation for his father's estrangement from
Judaism in what he deemed typical of Jews of the time:

> You had really brought some traces of Judaism with you from
> that ghetto-like little village community; it was not much and
> it dwindled a little more in town and while you were doing
> your military service, but still, the impressions and memories
> of your youth did just about suffice to make some sort of
> Jewish life ... The whole thing is, of course, not an isolated
> phenomenon. It was much the same with a large section of
> this transitional generation of Jews, which had migrated
> from the comparatively devout countryside to the towns.[16]

Hermann Kafka's 'immigration'[17] to Prague from the country-side was part of a large movement in late nineteenth-century Bohemia and Moravia. This came about largely because of two specific forces. First, the industrial revolution precipitated movement among both non-Jews and Jews. A second catalyst specifically affected the Jews: a change in their legal status through the *Freizügigkeit*, an edict promulgated after the 1848 revolution, that gave Jews the right to live in areas from which they had largely been banned since the Middle Ages. Sooner or later for many Jews this migration resulted in anything from a modest association with Judaism in the context of assimilation (Herman Kafka, case in point) to outright disaffection from Judaism (Berta Fanta). Her daughter, Else Bergmann, a younger contemporary of Franz Kafka, voiced dismay at her family's distance from Judaism. Her disenchantment is reminiscent of Kafka's lament that his father did not have much of Judaism to pass on. Some time in the 1930s she wrote that, 'We children received a so-called liberal upbringing, which later hurt us much, for we were insecure. In my family the Jewish tradition had already disappeared in the time of my great-grandfather'.[18] And yet, had Judaism and Jewish identity vanished in either the Kafka or the Fanta family?

The example of Franz Kafka is well known and his relationship to Judaism much discussed. I am concerned here with less famous people, two women whose names – if they are recognized at all – are familiar because their lives intertwined briefly with Kafka: Berta Sohr Fanta (1866–1918), who sat at the centre of a turn-of-the century intellectual circle in Prague, and her daughter Else Fanta Bergmann (1887–1969), the wife of the philosopher Schmuel Hugo Bergmann. Both women wrote – although not great literature (like Franz Kafka), nor philosophy (like Hugo Bergmann) – and most likely not even for others to read; but perhaps we can learn more about the complex issues of Jewish identity in modern Bohemia by examining the unpolished documents of these women. Berta Fanta kept a journal detailing the most intimate details of both her daily life and her intellectual endeavours. Else Fanta Bergmann composed a family history and wrote poetry. These works serve as the main sources for this study.

Berta Fanta was an intriguing woman and several of her contemporaries (Max Brod, Felix Weltsch, Gerhard Kowalewski, to name a few) noted her philosophical proclivities. Her daughter described her as having, 'a deep reverence for Wagner [which] awakened in her mystical and religious experiences', and as 'a fanatic follower of Nietzsche'.[19] Passion for Nietzsche led her to private philosophy lessons with a student of Anton Marty, Alfred Kastil. She then sat for examinations in philosophy at the German University in Prague in order to gain permission to study in Marty's seminars. While her husband, Max, also participated in the philosophical meetings, it is through Berta that the Fanta name became significantly associated with two intellectual circles in *fin-de-siècle* Prague.

The two parallel groups, with some members in common and driven by a passion for the philosophy of Franz Brentano, met to discuss philosophy and attend lectures by invited guests. One group was called the *Louvrezirkel* because members gathered every two weeks in the Café Louvre. The other group, equally passionate about Brentano's philosophy, had broader philosophic interests. It came to be called the *Fanta Kreis,* or Fanta circle, because the Fantas hosted the alternative intellectual salon at the family home attached to Max Fanta's pharmacy, Zum Einhorn.[20] Those who attended included, among others, Albert Einstein, and his successor at the German University, Philipp Frank, as well as Hugo Bergmann, Felix Weltsch, Max Brod, and, occasionally, Franz Kafka.[21] The mathematician, Gerhard Kowalewski, also a member of the *Fanta Kreis*, described Berta Fanta and the nature of her salon with particular fondness in his autobiography:

> In Prague there was a highly spiritual woman, Frau Berta Fanta, who, similarly to Madame de Staël in her time, gathered a circle of intellectuals around her. One read either Hegel or Fichte, and the philosopher Dr Hugo Bergmann, the son-in-law of Fanta, functioned as an interpreter … We were astonished during the Fanta evenings at the high spiritual level of this woman.[22]

In the Fanta circle there were lively discussions of a wide range of subjects, such as psychoanalysis, Einstein's theories and other ideas in the field of physics, and Kantian philosophy. According to Max Brod, both Kant's *Prolegomena* and his *Critique of Pure Reason* were read aloud 'page for page' and reading did not proceed until every question was discussed. Reading Kant took a full two years of Tuesday evenings; thereafter they spent a year

on Johann Gottlieb Fichte and then a year on Hegel. Brod enthusi-
astically reported: 'I have never in my life studied so thoroughly
and with such joy as in the Fanta house'.[23] Study in the Fanta circle
appears to have been as rigourous as that of a *yeshivah*, but the
texts were secular, not sacred, and the convener was a woman.

Fanta kept a journal that is revealing about her relationship to
Judaism, for the most part because of its near silence about the
subject. There are a few brief anecdotes, yet the tone displays
neither familiarity nor affection. In an entry where one might
expect some semblance of family pride, there is none. For 13 April
1902, Fanta described a gathering at the Weinberger Temple when
a memorial plaque and a picture of her grandfather, Simon Engel,
were unveiled. Engel had been a key fundraiser for the building
of the Temple. Berta's remarks convey a lack of enthusiasm for the
memorial and the participants, most of whom she characterizes
as 'humble and serious'.[24]

One draws from the journal a picture of a woman who was a
romantic intellectual with a deep love of nature and a curiosity
about all kinds of philosophical inquiry. She explicitly described
'her religion' in five points with no obvious reference to Judaism:

1. Worship the creator not as a human, for you would diminish
   him. He is unimaginable in his unending goodness.
2. Create for yourself your own world according to his example,
   in which the laws of your existence rule.
3. Handle your body and your spirit with reason, that you may
   live healthfully on earth.
4. Try to find beauty and art everywhere, if you seek with all
   intelligence, then you are already driven into a state of beauty.
5. Give of your wealth to the poor and not merely from your
   generous intellect; seek the rich in spirit, whatever they give
   you of their [spiritual] wealth.[25]

She proclaims a creator God who has no human form, which is
certainly a fundamental Jewish teaching; at the same time she
takes an anthropocentric stance which runs contrary to Judaism
when she writes: 'Create for yourself your own world according
to his [God's] example in which *the laws of your existence rule*'.
While this may be an unintentional rather than deliberate rejection of *halakhah*, it illustrates Fanta's Nietzschean bent. A brief
reference to charity at the end of her entry may be rooted in the

Jewish emphasis on *tzedaqah* or it could simply be an indication of the social status of the family which saw an important role in taking care of those less well-off.[26]

In her family history, Bergmann devoted much space to a description of her mother's deep interest in both theosophy and anthroposophy. Rudolf Steiner even visited the Fanta Salon and founded there a 'lodge' devoted to his teachings.[27] It was probably through this fascination with theosophy and anthroposophy that Fanta was drawn to study some of the Hindu classical literature.[28] One can conclude from this that Fanta's failure to express any affection for Judaism was not for lack of interest in religion. Rather, she specifically rejected Judaism.

Even while Fanta rejected Judaism, it is hardly surprising that she and her family were exposed to Zionism, as Prague was notable as a Zionist enclave. Bergmann notes in the family history that Theodor Herzl spoke at the German Kasino frequented by the Fantas and that he 'kindled great astonishment'.[29] Surely Fanta had heard much about Palestine and Zionism from her son-in-law Hugo Bergmann, for he had been deeply involved in cultural Zionism even before he married Else in 1908. Unfortunately, she does not comment on her attitudes towards the movement. After World War I, when Else and Hugo Bergmann were making plans to immigrate to Palestine, Berta Fanta seems to have suddenly developed an interest in Jewish matters, specifically Zionism. At this time, she wrote to Hugo Bergmann expressing a wish to change herself radically in order to prepare for the rigours of life in Palestine. Fanta had enjoyed the comforts of the upper middle-class urban elite all her life and her preparation for life in Palestine would have taken into consideration the primitive conditions she would be encountering. Given the obstacles, it is remarkable that she even contemplated the move. It is difficult to know how much of her decision had to do with a need to be close to her daughter and son-in-law, although it is likely that that was the primary motivation. Nevertheless, she does express an interest in learning Hebrew and she laments the current situation in Europe, a clear reference to the growing discomfort of Jews who were ever more caught in the conflict of nationalities in the newly formed Czech Republic.[30] She wrote:

> If only I had the head to learn Hebrew. I can hardly say to you how unspeakably repugnant to me is our society. To me

it is as if I am stepping over a quagmire in which I believe I am about to sink. Could there be deliverance there? If I could live as one free among free people, then nothing would keep me in Europe. I think that the renunciation of the enjoyment of higher culture would be for me very easy. So I have a hope before me.[31]

With these words Fanta articulated a deep disappointment at her inability to live fully in the social context she had struggled to join all her life. Ironically, she describes that social context as a 'higher culture' in spite of its rejection of her. Her desire to be part of it was increasingly compromised by the strictures that culture placed upon her. The stage of assimilation described by Hyman,[32] in which integration comes about through changed attitudes of both the minority and the majority, never happened for the Fanta family, nor for most of European Jewry. Fanta, however, was not given an opportunity to start over in Palestine for she died suddenly in 1918 at the age of 52, having just begun to train as a cook in preparation for the move to Palestine.

The eulogies given for Berta Fanta celebrate her influence. Felix Weltsch spoke and significantly gave her what *he* called a 'Jewish eulogy':

> We can, therefore, give this woman the highest eulogy which I can think of, a truly Jewish eulogy, in which we bring together the memory of this life in words. Frau Berta Fanta strove her whole life long without easing to find the spirit and to realize it on earth.[33]

Gerhard Kowalewski later reminisced: 'Her memorial [service] in the old Jewish Town Hall, the large hall of which was full, remains unforgettable to me'.[34] It is clear that, whatever Berta Fanta's relationship to Judaism in life might have been, upon her death she was mourned as a Jew.

The first piece of writing in the family that conveys any direct interest in Jewish identity came from Fanta's daughter, Else Fanta Bergmann. Her family history and her poetry, both unpublished, reveal nostalgia for the family's buried Jewish past. The family history is undated, but Else probably began it in the late 1930s and reworked it over the course of her lifetime, until her death in January 1969. Bergmann's son, Dr Martin S. Bergmann, and daughter, Dr Eva Short, have speculated that their mother began writing the family history at a time when she felt most acutely her separation from her birthplace.[35] She had immigrated to Palestine with her husband, Schmuel Hugo Bergmann, in 1920. Nearly 20 years in her new home had not resulted in her feeling fully a part of it.[36] According to her children, even in Palestine, Bergmann's identity remained wrapped up in that of her German-cultured, Prague-centred family. In Palestine, she surrounded herself with others who shared her cultural background and never made much of an effort to learn Hebrew. Until World War II, Else continued to make frequent visits to her family and friends in Prague. A letter from Hugo to Else, in August 1923, is illustrative of the difference between them; while Else was back *home* in Prague, Hugo wrote of his exploration of Palestine, and his enchantment with the land is evident:

> I have used the presence of Hans Kohn in Palestine ... to make the most of two and a half free days to travel by car around Nablus ... to Bet Alpha ... after Caesarea ... in glorious landscape, well irrigated, near Bedouin tents. Caesarea in the setting sun a fairytale.[37]

Both the family history and the poetry support the children's speculation, for they reveal Bergmann's melancholy. In a vignette about her great-grandmother Charlotte Engel's habit of quoting 'charming old Prague proverbs', Bergmann cites one that points to life's unpredictability: 'Do you know what life will bring you? A little glass box, a little bit of time'.[38]

Bergmann comments on her great-grandmother's sagacity, pointing out Charlotte Engel's capacity to see into the future and predict Bergmann's own disappointments in life:

> ... for life gave me much, took it away suddenly, and left me (apart from these three things) that which I myself have earned with difficulty, and also this is yet uncertain.[39]

These words particularly convey the wistful despair that is typical of the memoir. It opens with two of Bergmann's poems that capture the same mood. Bergmann conveys distinct aspects of her Jewish identity in the opening poetry as well. The first poem, 'If we knew whence we came ...', captures something of Else's sense of responsibility as she approaches the task she has set for herself, to record a nearly lost family history:

> In remembering, all is clarified
> And yet so unworldly and foreign
> And so am I myself also – and timid
> If I think of my loved ones
> Those removed, I hope to earn their
> forgiveness.[40]

She reiterated this idea in her prose when she described how she relied on a kind of 'blood memory', and not documents such as letters and journals, to reconstruct the life of her predecessors.[41]

It is apparent that Bergmann approached the task with trepidation. She perceived that her history was not only an exploration of her own identity. She was acutely aware of the role she played in assuming to convey the identity of those whose lives were distinct from her own, even as they were part of a shared family line. Two other themes emerged in the second poem. They are poignant because they illustrate both Bergmann's nostalgia for her home city of Prague and the family's ambivalent relationship to Judaism. The poem, *Lost, found city*, prefaced with, 'From Petrin, 7:00 in the evening, a view of the synagogue[42] in Weinberg', opens with these lines:

> And so have I found you again
> Lost, forgotten but ever loved city
> Difficult was it to find you,
> For hidden deep lay your image.[43]

In her imagination the author returned to her girlhood and the view of Prague that she had from her home. She vigorously bound her affection for her home city of Prague to a vivid memory of the two-towered synagogue, the erection of which, her great-grandfather, Simon Engel, partially funded:

> You are mine, city – my forgotten home!
> My claim on you
> No one can dispute
> For the hundred-steepled picture
> Would not be complete,

If two towers were lacking in it
Which, wide on the horizon, as already in a veil of mist,
I greet.
These the great-grandfather set there, the believing
unbeliever,
A house of God he built with his friends
For his people, for the thousand-year-old custom.
With this seal on your countenance you are mine!

In this poem she alluded to the family's distance from Judaism by calling her great-grandfather an 'unbelieving believer'. Here she elevated both the synagogue and the great-grandfather to almost heroic stature in the imagination of the poet. One cannot help but contrast this to Fanta's indifferent description of the memorial given for the same man. In a later portion of the family history, Bergmann described how her great-grandfather told her of his role in the building of that synagogue and once again we hear something of the nostalgia associated with the synagogue's role in the Prague landscape:

> When he gathered money for the synagogue he travelled around all of Austria and Germany. He showed me once with great pride the little travelling bag which he had with him then, which was canvas embroidered by great-grandmother with large flowers, saying, 'Once the Vinohrady Temple was in this!'
>
> As a child I looked with pride from Petrin at these two gold, shining towers on the horizon.[44]

Particularly worth noting are the final words of the poem: 'With this seal on your countenance you are mine!' Perhaps Bergmann was alluding to verses from Song of Songs 8:6, 'Let me be a seal upon your heart, like the seal upon your arm', thereby announcing in the same breath both her great love for Prague and her tremendous pride in her family's history in that city. The designation of Simon Engel as an 'unbelieving believer' is more enigmatic.[45] Elsewhere it is reported that Simon Engel had held services in a rented hall in that same section of Prague before the synagogue was built and thus the phrase 'unbelieving believer' is open for interpretation.[46] Perhaps this is a projection on the part of Bergmann whose own distance from Judaism made it difficult for her to envision the role religion might have played in the life of her great-grandfather.

Bergmann makes very few direct references to Jewish religious expression in the family history. The history contains absolutely no mention of Sabbath rituals or High Holy Days, not even a Passover *seder,* yet she describes family outings to cafés, concerts in the park and other leisure activities, such as bicycling trips and card parties at the home of grandparents, in great detail. The family's emphasis on science and culture led Bergmann to assert that a belief 'in science and the high development of humanity ... took the place of the religious, that is the Jewish faith'.[47] Despite this obvious rejection of *religious* Jewish identity it is very clear that, in contradistinction to her mother, Bergmann wished to convey something of the family's strong Jewish *heritage*. Significantly she remarked on the closeness of the family as being a particularly Jewish phenomenon: 'I do not believe that other families stayed together as well as mine. Or might it have been that well-known old Jewish family feeling which held us together up to the present day?'[48]

Bergmann begins the history by establishing the family's Jewish roots in several ways. First, she points out that family names are still visible in the cemeteries of the three towns of Raudnitz, Libochowitz and Budin (the first two of which had significant Jewish populations): 'One finds there the names of our family in all the cemeteries, which still possess impressive gravestones, all of which are shaped like the Mosaic tablets of the law'.[49] She proposes a connection to the medieval commentator Rashi: 'One branch of the family is said to have emigrated with Rashi from Germany to Prague in the year 1055'.[50] This assertion, while hardly historically accurate, fits with a common Jewish practice of seeking some familial tie to the famous medieval scholar.

Bergmann reveals her attachment to the Jewish culture of old Bohemia and a pride in three specific aspects of Bohemian Jewish culture: its uniqueness, its ability to meld itself to the surrounding non-Jewish environment and its renown. Significantly she points to religious leaders, specifically rabbis, as the crown of that now fading culture. More telling (and also significant for the sake of a possible dating of Bergmann's writing), she indicates that the gravestones that evoked so much for her are the last vestige of Bohemian Jewry: 'For the final remains of a tragic epoch are perishing with these simple stones'.[51] The words seem to indicate that she wrote this portion after the *Shoah*.

While her nostalgia for Jewish roots is manifest in such ruminations on cemeteries and ancestors, there is clear evidence of the family's early interest in the Haskalah both in a preserved family anecdote and in external evidence. Bergmann conveys a story about the earliest member of the family recorded in family memory, Lazar Taussig of Budin, who owned a leather factory and dabbled in philosophy. He was visited by the poet Johann Gottfried Seume (1763–1810). Seume recorded this visit in his *Spaziergang nach Syracus im Jahre 1802* and remarked that, despite the poverty of the community, Taussig had a number of good books and that he 'borrowed from him for the night, Kant's *Beweisgrund zur einzig möglichen Demonstration über das Dasein Gottes* since he had loaned Lessing's *Nathan* to a friend'.[52] An early edition of Moses Mendelssohn's *Biur* has the Fanta name on the subscription list, clear evidence both of someone's desire to own a Jewish Bible translation and an interest in enlightenment ideas.[53]

How long the family maintained an interest in Jewish subjects is difficult to assess. Jewish schooling was a matter of course for Bergmann's grandparents, boys and girls alike; the family history describes the rather brutal treatment of children by the *Gabbe* (warden).[54] Bergmann's great-grandfather, Jacob Sohr, still pursued talmudic study. His wife, Katherine, who peddled goods by foot, supported him. Bergmann recorded that she travelled as far as Prague, 'a march of at least ten hours'.[55] Bergmann also wrote that Jacob and Katherine's son, Albert Sohr (Berta's father), was said to have frequently served as *Gemeindevorstand* (leader of the community) in Libochowitz.[56] The break with Jewish education seems to have occurred in the generation of Berta and her sister Ida. This came about in conjunction with the move away from small towns and towards Prague, a move that the family was beginning to make in the last quarter of the century. Both girls received an education typical of upper-class daughters, with an emphasis on German culture, art and music. A story recorded by Bergmann sharply illustrates Fanta's place in the family's transition to secular culture. Fanta, it appears, had developed a close relationship with her German composition teacher, until one day when she used the Yiddish word *nebbich* in an essay she was reading aloud in class:

> The teacher stopped immediately and said to her that this
> was no German word. My mother became dark red with
> shame and said to the teacher that it was not possible, for her
> mother used this word frequently. The teacher became even
> more firm about this, that this word no longer ought to be
> used, since it was *Jewish* [Yiddish]. My mother burst into tears
> and thereafter this affection came to an end.[57]

This kind of incident was undoubtedly common, but for Fanta it
appears to have been devastating. While others resolved to hold
on to their Jewish identities in spite of this kind of verbal abuse
and marginalization,[58] Fanta responded differently. Her upper-
class education, coupled with such clear signals from the Christian
culture with which she was beginning to mix socially, seems to
have resulted in complete alienation from Judaism for Fanta, and
thus also for Bergmann. Fanta spent the whole of her life seeking
to belong to the tiny German-oriented upper class of Prague. Like
many of this generation, she found her social niche in the German
Kasino, pursued a love of Wagner by frequenting the theatre,
organized masked balls that revolved around themes from the
writings of Goethe, and involved herself in charities that addressed the needs of indigents, regardless of their religion. There is no
doubt that there was compromise at work at all times in the Fanta
family's social life. For instance, Bergmann referred to the quotas
placed on the number of Jews permitted on the guest lists of
charity balls organized by Berta and her sister:

> It was a well-kept secret that the number of participants was
> carefully counted. Only a third of participants could be Jews
> and even these had to be invited by the Christian partici-
> pants, in [Karl] Lueger's words, '*Wer ein Jud ist, das bestimme
> ich*'.[59]

It seems inevitable that the blood libel would surface as a question
posed casually by someone described as one of Fanta's best
friends: 'Berta, we are such good friends, say to me candidly and
in trust, do Jews use Christian blood at Passover?'[60] All of these
experiences seem to have deeply discomforted Fanta.

Both mother and daughter lived in a state of compromise as
they made their fragile home in Prague. Yet it is also clear that both
slowly awakened to the reality of their marginality in European
society. Fanta began to lament her plight at the end of her life, as

the letter to Hugo Bergman cited above demonstrates. Given more time, and the hindsight of the destruction of European Jewry which she witnessed from the distance of her residence (if not truly *home*) in Palestine, Bergmann came to express emotions more complex than those of her mother. Her appreciation of her family's Jewish roots, emphasized in the family history, is manifest in a distinctly different tone in a poem dated to Yom Kippur, 1947.[61] It begins with Bergmann looking out on the Mediterranean Sea; she imagines the ships bearing refugees that were due to appear on the horizon. Their arrival would culminate in the assembling of the remnant of European Jewry in their new land. The scene then switches to the lamentations of observant Jews at prayer on the most solemn day of the Jewish year:

> From the early morning Jews cry and rage
> And they will yet watch through the night.
> They assail their God and his gates
> They can no more wait, no longer suffer
> They assail God finally to be God
> They recite to him his conduct, how he promised to be.
> They assail humans finally to be humane
> And not the destroying, burning wild animal.

Yet those who appealed to God would not be victorious over the oppressors, but rather power was now to be manifest in the hands of youth:

> But the youth look defiantly at each other, eye to eye
> Conscious of the new time and their new power
> They feel strong, this time God must be willing;
> This time it succeeds – all or nothing.

In these words I detect two changes in Else Fanta Bergmann's perspective. First, she seems to have begun to turn away from yearning and alienation towards a new vision of Jewish destiny, one which would no longer allow for the marginalization experienced by both mother and daughter for most of their lives. Second, and certainly less subtle, is another aspect of the closing words of this poem: the transformation of *hibbat zion* (love of Zion) into political Zionism. Whether Bergmann personally subscribed to political Zionism is difficult to determine, but with some certainty I can assert that she seems to have rejected the kind of resignation articulated by Pauline Wengeroff at the opening of this study. One cannot help but notice the stark differences between the Bergmann and Wengeroff perspectives. It is quite clear that the reality of the destruction of European Jewry moved Bergmann to embrace an emotional intensity that is certainly Zionist.

Significantly, and even surprisingly, considering Bergmann's own disaffection from Judaism, one can even discern in that fervency a subtle messianic tone. We are left with a complex portrait of a woman whose own assimilation was the source of her fascination with Jewish life. Her compositions were the offspring of that assimilation and thus it is all the more intriguing that they had Jewish life at their centre. Treated separately, the memoir examines Jewish life as if it were something obsolete. The poem adds another dimension: Jewish life now has a future and a destiny.

In this study of a mother and a daughter we find, just as Hyman asserted in her *Gender and Assimilation in Modern Jewish History*, that assimilation among Jews was rarely a 'traumatic break with the past'.[62] It is significant that both women seem to be exceptional in their rejection of Judaism when compared with women in Imperial Germany in the same period and circumstances: 'And there were some women who for social reasons assumed that a denial of their Jewish identity, religious or otherwise, would improve their position in Gentile society. Yet these were the minority'.[63] Berta Fanta struggled to escape the limitations that society imposed on her because she was a Jew. Perhaps only at the end of her life did she recognize the futility of her expectations for full integration into the dominant society and she began to make plans to emigrate to Palestine. One can speculate that it was, at least in part, the reality of life in Palestine, increasingly removed from the exclusive society of German-speaking Czech Jews, that prompted in Else Fanta Bergmann a nostalgic reconnection with her family's Jewish past. Together, they represent a small but significant window on the complexities of assimilation experienced by European Jews before the Holocaust.

NOTES

1. Marion Kaplan, *The Making of the Jewish Middle Class: Women, Family and Identity in Imperial Germany* (New York: Oxford University Press, 1991), p. 79.
2. Paula Hyman, *Gender and Assimilation in Modern Jewish History: The Roles and*

Representation of Women (Seattle, WA: University of Washington Press, 1995), p. 4.

3. Marion Kaplan, 'Tradition and Transition: Jewish Women in Imperial Germany', in Judith Baskin (ed.), *Jewish Women in Historical Perspective* (Detroit, MI: Wayne State University Press, 1991), p. 203.

4. Hyman, *Gender and Assimilation*, p. 11.

5. Ibid., p. 12.

6. Ibid., pp. 13ff.

7. Ibid., p. 13.

8. Ibid., p. 14.

9. *The Memoirs of Glueckel of Hameln*, trans. Marvin Lowenthal (New York: Schocken, 1977).

10. *The Memoirs of Glueckel of Hameln*, p. 2.

11. The full title of this two-volume memoir is, *Memoiren einer Grossmutter: Bilder aus der Kulturgeschichte der Juden Russlands im 19. Jahrhundert*. An excerpt is found in Lucy Dawidowicz, *The Golden Tradition* (New York: Schocken, 1984), pp. 160–8.

12. Dawidowicz, *The Golden Tradition*, p. 160.

13. Ibid., p. 163.

14. Ibid., p. 168.

15. Franz Kafka, 'Letter to his Father', in Ernst Kaiser and Eithne Wilkens (eds), *Dearest Father, Stories, and Other Writings* (New York: Schocken, 1954), p. 171.

16. Kafka, *Dearest Father*, p. 173.

17. Called by Ruth Kestenberg-Gladstein, 'internal immigration'; see her article 'The Jews between Czechs and Germans in the Historic Lands, 1848–1913', in *The Jews of Czechoslovakia*, Vol. I (Philadelphia, PA: The Jewish Publication Society of America, 1968), pp. 21–71.

18. Else Fanta Bergmann, 'Familiengeschichte', unpublished ms, Leo Baeck Institute, New York City. All quotations from this are taken from my unpublished translation of this document which is designated hereafter by the initials 'FG'. Page numbers refer to those in the German original.

19. 'FG', p. 31. Bergmann uses the German word *Nietzcheanerin* and elaborates stating, 'Daily speech was dominated with the sayings of Nietzsche and Wagner'.

20. The pharmaceutical career of Berta's husband Max was largely orchestrated by his mother-in-law, Emilie Engel Sohr, who initially purchased a pharmacy in Libochowitz with the intention that Max Fanta would take it over. Else reports about the eventual move to Prague: 'She [later] bought for my father the house on Altstaedter Ring with the pharmacy Zum Einhorn, because Mama by no means wished to live in the country'. 'FG', p. 23.

21. Max Brod explained that Kafka had not much interest in systematic philosophy. In a letter of 6 February 1914, Kafka had written: 'Morgen zu Kafka komme ich kaum, ich gehe nicht gerne hin'. [I'll probably not go to the Fantas tomorrow; I don't like to go there.] Max Brod, *Streitbares Leben* (Munich: Kinder Verlag, 1960), p. 250.

22. Gerhard Kowalewski, *Bestand und Wandel, Meine Lebenserinnerungen zugleich ein Beitrag zur Neueren Geschichte der Mathematik* (Munich: Verlag von R. Oldenbourg, 1950), p. 249.

23. Brod, *Streitbares Leben*, pp. 253–4.

24. Berta Fanta, 'Tagebuch', unpublished ms, Leo Baeck Institute, New York City, p. 58. All quotations are my own translation. Hereafter this document is designated as 'TB'. It is unclear what Fanta meant by this description but it is possible that she thought those attending the temple were Orthodox. If

that is the case, then it is an indication of her ignorance as to the difference between an Orthodox community, which would attend a synagogue, not a temple, and a Reform community.

25. 'TB', pp. 10–11.
26. Bergmann describes in great detail the various charitable acts of Berta and her sister, Ida Freund. These included soup kitchens, providing for unwed mothers and patronage of artists.
27. 'FG', p. 44.
28. 'I am reading now the *Bhagavad Gita*', 'TB', p. 90.
29. 'FG', p. 27. Else's remark concerning her astonishment possibly reveals something of the attitude of the Fanta family, that is that Herzl's ideas were intriguing but not to be taken seriously.
30. See Hillel Kieval's *The Making of Czech Jewry: National Conflict and Jewish Society in Bohemia, 1870–1918* (New York: Oxford University Press, 1988).
31. 'FG', p. 48.
32. Hyman, *Gender and Assimilation*, pp. 13–14.
33. Eulogy given by Felix Weltsch, unpublished ms in the Leo Baeck Institute, New York.
34. Kowalewski, *Bestand und Wandel*, p. 253.
35. These observations came forth in interviews which the author had with Dr Bergmann and Dr Short, on 8 and 10 March 1996.
36. Divorce from Hugo Bergman and his subsequent marriage to Else Escha Scholem, in 1936, surely deepened Else Fanta Bergmann's feelings of dislocation and yearning for happier times of her past. One can speculate that if the war had not intervened and the Holocaust had not happened, Else Fanta Bergmann would have returned to Prague.
37. Schmuel Hugo Bergman, *Tagebuecher und Briefe*, Vol. 1 (Koenigstein/Ts.: Juedischer Verlag bei Athenaeum, 1985), p. 182.
38. 'FG', p. 12. '*Ein gläsernes Buchsel, ein silbernes Nixel, ein goldenes Wart' eine Weil*'. *Nixel* can be translated literally as 'elf' but it is really a play on words and means, rather, 'nothing', as in *Nichtsel* – 'a little nothing'.
39. 'FG', p. 12.
40. 'FG', p. 1.
41. 'I have unfortunately no reports, letters are practically non-existent. So must I write that which this blood sings to me in dark nights, on lonely evenings, in memory-saturated days'. 'FG', pp. 3–4. Contrary to these protestations, I have discerned that Bergmann does draw on her mother's journal for some of the family history and thus she is informed by conversations with members of the previous generation that Berta Fanta had recorded in writing.
42. Bergmann's confusion about the difference between a synagogue and a temple is evident in her consistently using the word synagogue for Vinohrady Temple that her great-grandfather built. She does not seem to be aware of the differences between Orthodox and Liberal Judaism.
43. 'FG', pp. 2–3.
44. 'FG', p. 10.
45. A few verses earlier in the history, Bergmann writes that her great-grandfather raised the money for the Temple, 'not out of piety, but only to secure a post for his best friend, Rabbi Stark'. Rabbi M. Stark was a teacher of Talmud in the Jewish secondary schools in Prague and became rabbi of Vinohrady in 1884. He raised some of the funds for the building of a temple, probably, as Bergmann reports, due to the efforts of Simon Engel, although money had to be borrowed as well. See *The Jewish Encyclopedia* (New York:

Funk and Wagnalls, 1904), s.v. 'Koeniglicher Weinberge'.

46. Simon Engel held the first services in Vinohrady, a southeastern suburb of Prague where Jewish farmers had vineyards (hence it was also called Weinbergen) in a hall which he rented. See *The Jewish Encyclopedia*, s.v. 'Koeniglicher Weinberge'.

47. 'FG', p. 50.

48. 'FG', p. 10.

49. 'FG', pp. 4–5.

50. 'FG', p. 5. Bergmann is misinformed here, for it is not possible that the family came with Rashi, who lived most of his life in northern France. This is a common legend told by Jewish families who understandably wished to trace their roots back to the renowned teacher. Even so, it is possible that the Fanta family came in a later emigration in the wake of the Second Crusade (1146–47), and the name Fanta is possibly to be traced back to the French word *enfant*.

51. 'FG', p. 5.

52. 'FG', p. 6.

53. The edition was published in 1795 and the subscriber is Wulff Fanta. His name does not appear in the family history.

54. 'FG', p. 17.

55. 'FG', p. 16.

56. 'FG', p. 22.

57. 'FG', pp. 29–30

58. Hannah Senesh is a case in point. She wrote at the age of 16, in 1937: 'Only now am I beginning to see what it really means to be a Jew in a Christian society. But I don't mind at all. It is because we have to struggle, because it is more difficult for us to reach our goal, that we develop outstanding qualities'. *Her Life and Diary* (New York: Schocken, 1973), p. 32.

59. 'FG', p. 30.

60. 'FG', pp. 29–30.

61. Else Fanta Bergmann, unpublished poetry, Leo Baeck Institute, New York.

62. Hyman, *Gender and Assimilation*, p. 12.

63. Kaplan, 'Jewish Women in Imperial Germany', p. 208.

11

Epiphanies: Hungarian-Jewish Experiences and the Shoah

PÉTER VÁRDY

The distinguished Dutch essayist, Rudy Kousbroek, refers in his 'Museum of Dreams' to the loss of individual memories with the passage of time: 'The great decay already starts during our own life, and with each heart stopping a unique collection of memories disappears forever, never to be reconstructed'.[1] Indeed, memories of individuals, and with them tastes, colours, shades and emotions, usually fade over time. It is nonetheless significant that individuals' poignant memories play a part in the making of enduring, collective group memory and identity.

The aim of this investigation is, first, to save from oblivion a set of unique personal recollections, and second, through these stories to shed some light on, and to gain an impression of, the changing atmosphere of everyday life in World War II Hungary and its implications for Hungarian Jewry. Its focus is on relations between Jews and non-Jews. I am mainly concerned with individual acts of civilians during anti-Semitic persecutions, underscoring the bewilderment, for Jews, wrought by conflicting standards of private versus public morals. However, instead of a clear-cut picture, what results is more a foggy landscape, every now and then enlightened by a few sudden flashes.

This project is based on World War II-era recollections of both Hungarian Jews and non-Jews. My investigation relies mainly on oral history, especially interviews.[2] This material touches on some of the essential questions of my own generation: how to react to insult and injustice; how to survive as an 'outlaw'; how to re-integrate as a survivor into a partly indifferent, partly suspect society; how to go on living with continuing and untold mourning, guilt, suspicion, anger and fear. Furthermore, questions arise such as: why and when do victims, persecutors, and bystanders act as they do; why and when are they passive, vicious, indifferent or compassionate?

Among the interviewees who volunteered for this study, the eldest was born not long after the beginning of the century, and the youngest was three years old in 1944. Methodologically speaking, the wealth of problems one encounters with respect to the reliability of spoken evidence is immense, albeit not necessarily greater than with written sources. Yet, surely, special care must be taken so as not to lose one's way in the jungle of subjective memories.[3] Each interview, however, shares a common reference: the basic facts of Jewish life in Hungary in the 1930s and 1940s – discrimination, persecution, and attempts to elude state-sponsored torture and mass murder – dominate the recollections.

The interviews excerpted here are from a collection of around 140, of which I conducted 60, and focus on everyday relations between Jews and their non-Jewish neighbours, schoolmates and colleagues; initial juvenile experiences of discrimination; humiliations and sympathy faced during the persecutions; responses to those returning from the camps; imbroglios around claims concerning property; expressions of gratitude and revenge. In the themes that emerge, we may recognize distinct patterns. This yields revelations not readily available from secondary literature and other sources.[4]

My interpretation centres on recollections that reflect clashes between conflicting moral values and visions. As opposed to Hungarian Jewry's experience in concentration camps,[5] we know much less about everyday relations between Jews and their social surroundings. Similarly, we know little about how these relations changed during the persecutions, at the end of the war, and in the post-war period. Nor do we know much about the ways discrimination, persecution, expulsions and looting of the Jewish population influenced civil society and everyday life.[6]

Owing to the lack of data concerning post-war Jews in Hungary, the selection of interviewees was not representative. Most candidates were located through acquaintances and by invitation to name further possible candidates. The interviews usually took place at the home of the interviewee, and were recorded on tape. Sessions started with my explanation of the aim of the project. Generally, these led the interviewee to ask a question intended to reveal my own involvement in the subject. My response, 'In 1944 I was eight years old and one of the persecuted', helped in establishing confidence. Frequently, interviewees spoke of exceptionally painful wartime memories for the first time. Even in less extreme cases, various topics touched traumatic complexes, intimate subjects and probing of one's own personal identity. The interviews tended to be something like a confession, and often had cathartic effects.[7]

I organized the interviews around a set of common 'epiphanies', and use the term 'epiphany' to mean 'appearance' in the sense of 'manifestation', a sudden insight brought about by a word, a gesture, hint or story. An epiphany sheds light on an unsuspected side of history. The term is James Joyce's, who used it for revealing moments in *Dubliners*.[8] The peculiar – perhaps uncanny – atmosphere of those days seems to be the most important trigger of the recollections.

Before explicating the interviews, a brief discussion of the historical background is necessary. The modern history of Jews in Hungary dates from 1686, after the Jews living on Hungarian territory had been killed, sold or chased away by the soldiers of Eugene of Savoy at the end of the period of Turkish domination. During the eighteenth century and the first half of the nineteenth century, increased opportunities encouraged a significant influx of Jews from Moravia and Austria. Hungarian liberalism, the dominant political stream from the 1830s to World War I, fostered additional migration, mainly from the Habsburg crown dominions in southern Poland. Economic transformations, as well as the growth of the Jewish population and its prosperity and the readiness to assimilate, meant Jews made rapid progress in Hungary in the last third of the nineteenth century. Up to 1918, Jewish–Hungarian co-existence, founded upon mutual interests of the ruling liberal nobility and the Jewish minority, was an extraordinary success in terms of demographics, civil rights, mutual economic advantages, social progress and Jewish assimilation. The decline of this co-existence began at the end of World War I, with the end of Hungarian liberalism. It reached its nadir with a series of discriminatory laws from 1938 onwards, up to the deportation, from the Hungarian-ruled countryside, of a total of some 437,000 Jews (plus the Jewish population of the Bácska and Bánát regions) between 15 May and 8 July 1944. An estimated 55 per cent of the 825,000 citizens falling under the rule of anti-Jewish measures lost their lives through persecutions.[9] The present-day number of Jews in Hungary, while unknown, is estimated at between 56,000 and 100,000 persons,[10] not more than 10 per cent of whom are religiously observant.

Between 1938 and 1945, a series of legal measures and criminal acts destroyed around 50 per cent of the Jewish minority in Hungary and had a devastating effect upon mutual respect. Personal recollections provide vivid impressions of how this worked, for instance, concerning the rush at Jewish assets in the aftermath of the deportations. At the same time, however, we find remarkable cases of individual humanity. Occasionally compassion proved to be stronger than the prevailing greed and violence. On the other hand, some institutions, such as the Red Cross and the Community Councils, instead of being safeguards of humanitarianism, lent the appearance of legitimacy to prejudice or even criminal behaviour like looting. From 1938 on, legalized discrimination, and the eventual deportation of the total Jewish population from the Hungarian provinces in 1944, exacerbated a previously extant and palpable social distance between Jews and non-Jews. The looting of the Jewish houses by a part of the surrounding population, apathy of the majority of citizens, mutual mistrust, suppressed feelings of guilt on the side of both the victims and those unable or unwilling to render assistance, and finally incidental guilt on the Jewish side,[11] even deepened this gap in the aftermath of the persecutions.

The following texts represent different times and aspects of the persecutions.[12] We begin with a recollection concerning the forced labour battalions in 1942/3, followed by examples of a clash between traditional social codes and legalized barbarism. Next, a case of human decency in a military hospital shows that peristent medical ethics could be stronger than prejudice. Finally, a number of recollections shed an ambiguous light on the attitudes of non-Jewish bystanders when Jews were moved *en masse* as a part of anti-Semitic policy.

Labour battalions ('Auxiliary Defence Labour Service Companies') were conscripted from 1940 onwards as part of anti-Semitic policy. These were units for forced labour, manned by the so-called 'politically unreliable', i.e. left-wing civilians, Jewish men, preferably intellectuals, who had to serve regardless of any infirmity or disease. These battalions suffered their worst losses during 1942/3 in the Ukraine, and at the end of the war, in 1944/5, through famine, murder and diseases. On the other hand, forced conscriptions did, in the spring of 1944, rescue a huge number of Jewish men from deportation to Auschwitz.[13] In 1942, between 10,000 and 50,000 mainly Jewish men were conscripted into the labour battalions of the Second Hungarian Army in the Ukraine. Both before and after the Russian breakthrough at the Don, in January 1943, criminal acts of commanders and guards intensified their suffering.

Our first witness, VL, a barrister, was conscripted in the summer of 1942. VL represented an (incidentally non-Jewish) client in a claim against the opposite party of a (Jewish) debtor, who, in turn, had a (non-Jewish) barrister. Finally, VL invoked the help of a bailiff, which led the non-Jewish barrister to summon VL to abandon the writ immediately. If he refused, the barrister would see to it that VL was conscripted. Prevailing standards of the time made it unthinkable for VL to submit to this blackmail to the detriment of his client. Indeed, shortly afterwards, he was conscripted, with nearly fatal consequences. VL's labour battalion was sent by train to Gomel. On arrival, the military gendarmes searched the men, robbed them of their possessions, and marched them off with full packs to the front on the river Don. No one was permitted to travel on a cart. At best one might put his backpack on a cart if he produced a voucher.[14] When horses became stuck in the mud, men replaced them. One conscript on the march, a pharmacist, had severe coronary disease. As a special favour, the military commander gave the pharmacist permission to start marching before the others in order to gain some time. One day he was so utterly exhausted that, in the words of VL, 'he walked on into eternity'.

Upon the Russian breakthrough in January 1943, the labour battalions fled in disarray with other remnants of the Second Hungarian Army, while fighting for self-preservation against war, hunger, lice and the outrages committed by the gendarmes. Eventually, the Jewish survivors were nearing their homeland with the retreating army by the end of October:

> At Lavocne station we were received by representatives of the Hungarian Red Cross, nurses in white coats. Everyone was given a 'cloakroom-ticket'. I have kept mine, number 125, lest I ever forget the 'humanitarianism' of this international organization. We were told that on producing this ticket everybody would get a Red Cross parcel. The

soldiers and staff were given their parcels but when we joined the queue, they told us that Jews were excluded. This didn't even come as a surprise for us as we had got used to discrimination long before.[15]

These recollections give an impression of how integral to life discrimination had become. Blackmail on the part of professional colleagues had already corrupted public life. In the case of VL, it is little wonder that a lawyer could actually carry out his threat, but more remarkable that he could utter it without any fear of retaliation. This is all the more striking in that, in contrast to the medical profession, the legal profession seemed to have been more successful, up to that point, in thwarting discrimination.[16]

Corruption of public institutions occurred to an even greater extent on the battlefield, where men doing forced labour were at the mercy of commanders and their staff. However, a number of officers did their best to save people, while others ordered killings of Jewish subordinates and prided themselves on their cruelty. There were official measures to restrict such arbitrariness, to be sure, but they had a limited effect since a legalized spirit of anti-Semitism had penetrated the army.

In fact, anti-Semitism had pervaded the army more than perhaps any other institution. Mrs PB-F, the daughter of a former member of the Hungarian House of Lords, related that:

> In 1944, during the bombings of Budapest, a retired colonel settled in the cellar of our house together with his Alsatian dog. On one occasion I was hiding at home when there was an air raid. The colonel sent up his servant-girl with the request to 'the lady of the house' to refrain from coming down to the cellar, the reason being that, as she was Jewish, he could not kiss her hand, so it would have been very embarrassing to him.[17]

This is a grotesque example of a clash between two social codes. Good manners required that a gentleman give due respect to a woman associated with Hungarian nobility; on the other hand, legal discrimination did not permit him to offer such respect if she was Jewish.

Occasionally, traditional institutions, moral codes and social conventions played a part in resistance to extreme forms of persecution. The Christian Churches, the Regent Admiral Horthy and the army had been founts of racial prejudice. Conversely, from time to time, they functioned as an effective antidote to anti-Semitism and genocide, as guardians of traditional morality and decency. For instance, the Churches undeniably contributed through their protest, during June–July 1944, to the halting of the deportations (as did the Pope and the Swedish king, both of whom had previously shown signs of pro-German sympathy and kept a conspicuous silence on the matter of the persecution of Jews). Finally, the explicit order of Admiral Horthy, on 7 July, stopped deportations.[18] With this, the Regent significantly contributed to the survival of the majority of Budapest's Jews. Owing to his halting the deportations (and to the 15 October armistice), the Allied Powers refrained from charging Horthy at the Nuremberg tribunal.

Traditional religious precepts and the Hippocratic Oath also prompted acts of resistance. One witness remembers a rumour greatly horrifying the inhabitants of Budapest in the winter, probably December 1944. Armed members of the Arrowcross were driving a column of Jews, probably towards the ghetto, when an old woman fell to the ground. Two Christian girls from the public came running to help her and were shot on the spot, together with the old woman. The bodies were left untouched all day as a deterrence.

Other testimonies show further examples of moral courage. Around April/May 1944, in the capital of Transylvania, Kolozsvár (Cluj):[19]

> The Headmaster of the Calvinist Grammar-school, a certain Császár, whose Christian name I forget, had only one message for his students on graduation day: 'If only you have learned one thing: to accommodate the persecuted, then you will really have learned something!' Such individual attitudes did exist.[20]

Transylvania had a reputation for religious tolerance and even civil radicalism.

Another Transylvanian ghetto, that of Nagyvárad, was the centre of the deportations of the Jews of Bihar County. It was here that a demonstration of workers apparently took place against the deportations.[21] Áron Márton, the Roman Catholic Bishop of

Gyulafehérvár (Alba Julia), likewise protested (the only Transylvanian churchman to do so) in a vehement sermon.[22] The farewell
speech of the Protestant headmaster equally revealed the
existence of a spirit of civil disobedience in Transylvania.

The following excerpt from another interview shows the
complexity and tangle of the connections between persecutors
and persecuted. The witness TI came from a pious Jewish family
in Szatmár in Northern Transylvania. As a young man, TI had
been active in a communist youth movement; he was arrested and
spent the remainder of the war in a prison in Nagyvárad. This
turned out to be his salvation, as the Hungarian administration
did not deport the sentenced Jewish prisoners along with the rest
in May–June 1944. Finally, however, the Nazis discovered that a
bunch of Jewish prisoners had eluded the deportation, and so
their turn came on 6 June. The Jewish prisoners had already
boarded the carriages but, owing probably to the invasion of
Normandy that day, a Hungarian officer ordered their return.
Then TI had an accident:

– Laci Deutsch, a Jewish boy, threw a block of concrete at me,
nasty scum!
– Why did he do that?
– He must have been told to. I was on very bad terms with
the jailers. They always picked on me to do the nasty jobs.
This was the first day the chief-warden told me: 'Come on,
today I'll give you something easy!' And this was the result!
– Was your life endangered?
– I had a fractured hip.
– Did you have an operation?
– Not until after the war! I was in a military hospital and they
did not do any operations. I had my accident on 6 July, a
month after we had been dragged from the carriages. They
put me in the ward of the seriously injured. They treated me
very well, they were curious, they observed me. Thanks to
the nurses I was given the same food as officers who were
gravely injured at the front. Then the ward-matron found
out and put an end to it. So, I was rather well treated. The
superintendent of the hospital, a Major Ábrahám, was generally known as an Arrowcross and a Nazi. When he made his
rounds he wore white gloves and had a solemn air. As the
senior medical officer he asked me, of course, how I was, but

just walked on without waiting for an answer. One day, when he asked, I raised my legs and told him that they were very twisted and were very green. He just said: 'You should be glad to be alive', or something like that. But you could see by the look of him, that it would be very embarrassing to him as a superintendent if ...

– You also mentioned something about a decent physician.

– Yes, the third day after I had been hospitalized, they took me to the X-ray department ... Whenever they put me down somewhere I couldn't help screaming like a slaughtered pig ... They took me to the X-ray department, put me on the floor and kept me waiting in the cold. The radiologist was a captain by the name of Dr Lakatos. He wore a white coat and had a perfectly egg-shaped head and was completely bald. He had the head of a roman senator. While turning the X-ray set downwards he said to the nurse: 'When was this patient brought in, sister?' 'Three days ago', she said. I can clearly recall him, standing still for a second, shocked, while he was turning the apparatus. 'And not until now he has been taken to the X-ray?' The nurse stood on tiptoe and whispered something into the doctor's ear. I don't need to tell you what she whispered, of course. I saw the physician flush red in the face, he became as red as a beetroot. He started to scream: 'Sister, how dare you? You need not teach me a lesson. For me there exist patients only, and nothing else. Have I or have you taken the oath? And fuck you,[23] bloody well get lost now at once!' That is the way he put it, in those terms. He was a man of great distinction and I was surprised to hear such words coming from his mouth. 'And never put one foot in this ward ever again!' When this happened the superintendent and commander was in the Arrowcross, Major Ábrahám. That was the kind of gentleman-like gestures you could experience occasionally. Dr Lakatos was never reprimanded for this, to the contrary, he inspired awe and fear, because he had dared to make a stand. And as far as I know Dr Ábrahám never acted against him. He must certainly have heard something because Lakatos bellowed like a jackal. A Romanian doctor would never have done such a thing; he, too, would have helped, certainly so, but not in that way![24]

Here we see ideal medical ethics and human decency at work. Extreme indecency highlights the surprising fact that some semblance of decency existed. After the unsuccessful attempt by Regent Horthy to settle for a cease-fire led to his enforced abdication, on 15 October 1944, members of the Arrowcross, who had gained control over Budapest, killed thousands of Jews.[25] Yet, soldiers who did not have any scruples in shooting children, women and old people, left children under six alone. Thus, passers-by found one of the witnesses, then three years old, wandering the streets and took the child to the police station. Arrowcross guards had fetched people from the so-called 'International Ghetto' (Jewish safe houses under Swedish, Swiss and Portuguese protection) and drove them to the quayside on the Danube. There they shot everyone (over six) and dumped them in the river, including the witness's grandparents who had been looking after him. Children under six years of age, however, were just chased off.[26] At the same time that barbarism was at its very height, we can still see some remnants of moral codes at work effectively – codes only to be recognized as such in contrast to recent genocides in Bosnia and Rwanda.

After the German occupation of Hungary, on 19 March 1944, the Hungarian administration deported, in just eight weeks, all the Jews from the countryside, with the whole of Budapest, and around 150,000 men in the labour battalions, temporarily exempted. First, the Jews were driven from their houses and concentrated in local ghettos, then, from 15 May onwards, they were put on trains. The marching-off to ghettos and railway stations could not have been totally unobserved by bystanders. The unusual sight of columns of pariahs being driven away by gendarmes was apt to bring out a number of reactions, both positive and negative. What was the prevailing mood in the streets when the Jews were driven from homes? Was it anti-Jewish, indifferent or compassionate?

One observer recalled the deportations:

> The first thing in connection with your questions, that happened to me was in the summer of 1944, in August. My father was hiding in our house because he had deserted. It happened on a Sunday, I think it was 10 August, and we were having lunch. All at once, a long line of carts was coming from the town. We lived along the provincial road; we looked out of the window and saw many carts and horses approaching from the town, but they were still some way off. We thought it was a wedding party. It was a weekend, the usual days for

couples to go to town to get married. When the carts had reached our house, however, it appeared that there were as many as 20 to 30 of them, all crammed with Jewish families, armed German soldiers and Arrowcross men on either side as escorts. I remember the semi-automatic guns they carried and their rolled-up sleeves. They left in the direction of Debrecen. In front of our house there was a well. They stopped there to drink and fetch water for the horses and soldiers. The water supply was just outside our boundary so that passers-by could drink from it. The column came to a halt, many German soldiers and a big crowd before our house. My father was watching, paralysed. He was a deserter and was bound to be killed if caught. The family was under a great strain. My mother went to the well, taking a cup to drink from. She noticed, however, that the people on the carts were not allowed water, whereas the soldiers merrily drank and the grooms looked after their horses. Mother quite spontaneously took a bucket and a cup and was walking toward the first cart when a German soldier roared at her. Mother hesitated for a moment and then walked on. There was a ditch alongside the road, mother being on one side and the German on the opposite side, near the cart. The moment that mother walked on – I shall never forget it: that German soldier, a half-smoked cigarette in his mouth – he shot some bullets right in front of mother's feet, so that little fountains of earth leapt up. To us that looked as if mother herself had been hit! Mother stood stock-still and said something to the soldier and pointed to the water. Then the German walked over to her and prodded her aside with the butt of his rifle. She was a small, delicate little woman; she started back looking completely puzzled. Then another soldier appeared and drove her back into the house ... We were very anxious what would happen next. My father, you knew him, was the kindest of men; he saw that my mother was trembling. If she said something at all it was like: 'There is no God, otherwise he would not tolerate such a thing'. Such was the atmosphere in the room. My father comforted her, saying something like: 'Quiet, we are not people that make history', or so. Her legs were trembling in a mixture of fear, shock and a sense of helplessness. Very gently he was searching for words to try and reassure her. And while he was doing so, something happened in my family that I shall never forget in all my life. Mother got up, grabbed my father by the hair and pressed him to the floor, the stone kitchen floor. There was absolutely no need to reassure her! I think he had said something to her like, 'Let us be glad that you are still alive'; nothing insulting, something quite natural, but my mother reacted to this in a spirit of keen moral resistance. So badly could she cope with a feeling of human helplessness, that she attacked my father. Never had such a thing happened, there had never been a harsh word between them. This was the only time. My mother, too, was taken aback ... They led a wonderfully pure and harmonious life together. Mother walked out of the room, aghast at what she had done, almost in a state of frenzy. She went to the cellar and closed the door behind her. My grandmother came in and told my father to go to her at once lest she might harm herself ... When the carts had left, nobody said a word. We knew something terrible had happened and that mother had almost been killed. What sort of a world did we live in? ... This was my earliest memory of this kind. I clearly recall the faces of the deported. Just imagine yourself, 20 to 30 cartloads full of people, families, stony faces, miserable, desperate people who must have had some misgivings about their destination, certainly not anything very nice. By the look of them they were all poor people. That they were Jews, I did not realize at the time, I did not even know the word. Such a thing had never come up among us. This was my first experience of it.[27]

These recollections, heavily burdened with emotions are, in retrospect, connected with the deportation of the Jews from the countryside either on the way to or from the Nyiregyháza ghetto, or to the train to Auschwitz.

Despite the detailed, graphic character of this testimony, some factual aspects of this recollection give pause. Apparently, neither German soldiers nor the Arrowcross took part in the deportations then (with the exception of internment camps like Kistarcsa and Sárvár, which housed convicts, not families). Some 200 men of the *Eichmann Dezernat* organized the deportations and Hungarian gendarmes carried them out with thousands of Hungarian civil servants and with the enforced co-operation of the Jewish Councils. Jews from the villages were, in fact, often transported on carts to the assembly points, with a small number of gendarmes as escorts. The Arrowcross was not armed until 15 October, long after the deportations of the country-Jews had been completed. The region of Nyiregyháza, for instance, had been cleared between 14 April and 6 June. It is quite unlikely then that the scene described took place on 10 August which, in 1944, fell on a Thursday. The specified destination of the Jews, Debrecen, seems unlikely as Nyiregyháza was the designated internment centre for the Jews in these surroundings.[28] Yet, such details do not necessarily discredit the recollection. The intensity of the experience and many concrete details point to a key event. On the other hand, the child who experienced it could only have understood the event at a later moment, and then may also have filled in certain details.

The recollection shows that anti-Semitic wartime acts were not simply condoned, notwithstanding the fact that blood libel outbursts of hysteria occurred in eastern Hungary as late as the 1960s![29] According to traditional mores, as shown in the story above, strangers had to be given water to drink. To forbid this, was something rather incomprehensible for the local population.

Some citizens dared defy the isolation imposed upon the Jews on their way to the wagons by the authorities, as seen in another recollection:

> – We had been kept one week, maybe one and a half, in Monor, then we were put into the wagons. This road through Monor was memorable to me in an extraordinary way again. Our arrival may have taken place in the early morning, and probably that was the reason why there were few people present, but our departure was in the early afternoon, and this time (as this had been the case before, in Nagykáta) many people stood along the roadside.[30]
> – This time a bigger crowd?
> – This here was already a significantly bigger crowd. I add here immediately that this was one of those peculiarities which I found heart-warming, through which I could keep my humanity or belief in mankind. In the brickyard, as water-provision was already rather difficult, water was carried in big buckets. We were thirsty, it was warm too, and from the rows we called for water ... I don't know who. To bring and give us something was, however, forbidden. But there were people who put enamelled jars of water on

the roadside in advance, before the march column reached them, in order to enable us to drink as we came along. I don't know who did it, nor how many did, yet this meant to me that the community or the public opinion or the people who were standing there were, at least in the majority, not against us.[31]

Yet other witnesses refer to hostile crowds along the streets where gendarmes drove the Jews out of their homes on the way to the wagons.

– The secretary of the Bishop of Veszprém, László Lékai, the later Archbishop, gave in 1984 a speech on the Jewish graveyard in commemoration of the deportations. He started with the recollection of the people standing with bowed heads along the streets when the Jews of Veszprém were deported.[32] I felt like telling him that this was true as – indeed – people were standing along the streets. However, instead of bowing their heads they stood by laughing, mocking us and spitting at us. Nor do I believe that Lékai himself bowed his head. On the way to the ghetto of Sárvár we could see announcements along the streets, in big capital letters, inviting the public to the 'Thanksgiving mass for the deliverance of Veszprém from the Jews', signed: 'Mindszenty'[33] ...
– Can you remember people standing by with tears in their eyes as well?
– Surely you don't really mean this?
– Actually, I do. But obviously you did not see this. Nor anyone protesting?
– Not as far as I am concerned. I saw crowds of people standing on both sides of the road ...
– Crowds of happy people?
– Yes, and these happy people were jeering and making personal remarks and spitting at us ...
– You mean, this was an anti-Semitic town. Didn't you know of anybody who stayed home on purpose?
– Some may have, but I don't know of anyone.[34]

Concerning the mocking and spitting masses on the streets, several witnesses contradict each other.

We have, for example, recollections of another survivor about the atmosphere in the same town:

> – We were put on the trains in Veszprém, attended by the gendarmes we were directed to the railway station.
> – What were your impressions? I mean, people must have seen what happened. Were you marching through the town?
> – Yes, we were, but the town was relatively quiet. We passed by early in the morning and there were few people. It is possible that it was early so few people would be around. Maybe they did not want to see it.
> – Is it possible that the early hour was chosen on purpose?
> – Maybe. In fact, when we were directed from Siófok to Veszprém, this also took place early in the morning, presumably for the same reason.[35]

In the memory of RR, in the streets of the same provincial town, there was no laughing and jeering crowd. They were empty, possibly because of the early hour of the transport. BÁ did not specify the time of the march, so we miss this point of comparison. The witness RR suggested that people deliberately stayed home, embarrassed by the sight of the Jews being driven out of town. However what exactly did their absence mean? Embarrassment? Anger? Indifference? We simply do not know. The fact that the gendarmes scheduled the marches in the early hours could very well mean that they took into consideration that some citizens might express disfavour.

BL, in another interview, mentioned two other villages. He wondered about the reactions of non-Jewish onlookers, interpreting silence, like the jars of water, as a sign of solidarity. What characterized the Hungarian streets during those six weeks? Was the predominant mood one of sympathy or hostility? Probably it varied at different times and places. Certainly there were Nazi sympathizers among the citizens who hailed the spectacle of Jews being driven away; but, for others, the marches were shocking to view. It is natural to expect that different witnesses have drastically different memories of such scenes.[36] Obviously, the attitudes of both bystanders and of the persecuted reflected an ambiguity that can hardly be reduced to a simple trait.

The question of either merry or mourning masses is in a political sense not inconsequential. After 30 years of official silence and denial, substantial symbolic mourning of the murdered Jews began even before 1989. Over 45 years after the Holocaust, the Synod of the Hungarian Reformed Churches pleaded guilty for past sins and for opportunities missed to rescue the persecuted. The Parliament dedicated a special session to commemorating Jewish victims. The symbolic acts of mourning began even previous to the transition from one-party rule to parliamentary democracy. Archbishop Lékai's 1984 speech was one among these. Another contemporary example was the motion picture titled after the prophet Job.[37] Jewish families were shown sitting on carts on their way to the wagons, accompanied by crying villagers. At the border of the village, a gypsy band bid the Jews goodbye by playing funeral music. Although the possibility of such a farewell is not entirely improbable, its historical credibility is questionable. After all, prejudice at the time made it less easy for those who felt like crying than those who hailed the anti-Jewish measures with sardonic laughter.

Even so, some people were not intimidated. In responding to a moral urge, they had courage to speak out. They defied the temporal authorities, at least for a moment. After eight weeks, during which the government cleared the Hungarian countryside of its 450,000 Jews, the erosion of public morality went on at an even faster rate. None of the parties ever recovered from the shock.

NOTES

1. Rudy Kousbroek, 'Gedroomd museum', in *Morgen spelen wij verder* (Amsterdam: Meulenhoff, 1989), p. 207.
2. See Paul Thompson, *The Voice of the Past: Oral History* (Oxford: Oxford University Press, 1978).
3. The first set was collected during the 1970s by Mrs M. Grandpierre-Szegö, the second during the 1980s by Mr S. Szenes, and the third, mainly in the years 1989–90, by myself in co-operation with Mr J. Rékasi and Mrs E. Hetesi.
4. For a review of the literature on Hungarian Jews between World War II and the 1980s, see Péter Várdy, 'The Unfinished Past: Jewish Realities in Postwar Hungary', in Randolph Braham (ed.), *The Tragedy of Hungarian Jewry: Essays, Documents, Depositions* (New York and Boulder, CO: Social Science Monographs, 1986), pp. 133–89. On Hungarian Jewish historiography after World War II, see Randolph Braham, *The Hungarian Jewish Catastrophe: A Selected and Annotated Bibliography* (New York: Social Science Monographs and Institute for Holocaust Studies, City University of New York, 1984). Cf. Péter Várdy, 'A magyarországi zsidóüldözések a hazai történetírásban:

Szemléleti problémák és a kérdés aktualitása', in Péter Kende and András Kovács (eds), *Zsidóság az 1945 utáni Magyarországon* (Paris: Magyar Füzetek, 1984), pp. 181– 220.

5. On these crucial facts, tens of thousands of survivors' testimonies have been collected, and this work is still going on. See Lawrence Langer, *Holocaust Testimonies: The Ruins of Memory* (New Haven, CT and London: Yale University Press, 1991).

6. The questions centred around the following topics: family background; Jewish religious practices in the family; early experiences of discrimination; persecutions during 1938–45; reactions and overall behaviour of the social environment; rescue activities; the fate of other members of the family; new start of life in 1945; the reclaiming and restitution of properties; acts of gratitude; acts of revenge; the 1956 uprising; experiences of anti-Semitism between 1945 and around 1990. Obviously, the recollections are not uniformly distributed over these various topics; rather, their centre of gravity lies in the experiences with discrimination and persecution.

7. A session lasted mostly between one and a half and three hours, occasionally followed by a second, sometimes even a third session. To conclude, I filled out a questionnaire together with the interviewee, that dealt with special arrangements with the respondent concerning the interview, and confidentiality, family background, education, professional career, political preferences, religion, social status and losses owing to persecution. Such an exhaustive list of personal items implies full trust. Although I felt that trust did prevail in my interviews, some interviewees left questions unanswered, particularly those related to political preference. Full listing of family losses was another subject, which, in a number of cases, went beyond what an interviewer could reasonably ask. In contrast, one of my colleagues had to break through occasional distrust owing to the facts of being born both after the war, and being non-Jewish.

8. Richard Ellmann, *James Joyce* (London, Melbourne, Toronto: Oxford University Press, 1966), p. 87:

> The epiphany was the sudden 'revelation of the whatness of a thing', the moment in which 'the soul of the commonest object … seems to us radiant'. The artist, he felt, was charged with such revelations, and must look for them not among gods but among men, in casual, unostentatious, even unpleasant moments. He might find 'a sudden spiritual manifestation' either 'in the vulgarity of speech or of gesture or in a memorable phase of the mind itself'. Sometimes the epiphanies are 'eucharistic' … These are moments of fullness or of passion. Sometimes the epiphanies are rewarding for another reason, that they convey precisely the flavour of unpalatable experiences.

9. A recent assessment and estimates of the Jewish losses at this date are to be found in Tamás Stark, *Zsidóság a vészkorszakban és a felszabadulás után (1939–1955)* (Budapest: MTA Történettudományi Intézete, 1995), p. 74. The estimates of Stark are significantly lower than those given shortly after the war by Zsigmond P. Pach and Vilmos Sándor, *Zsidó Világkongresszus Magyarországi Képviselete Statisztikai Osztályának Közleményei*, Nos 1–14 (Budapest, 1947–49); see esp. Nos 1 and 10–12.

10. See Bernard Wasserstein, *Vanishing Diaspora: The Jews in Europe since 1945* (London: Hamilton, 1996) concerning the lower estimate for 1944. The notoriously blurred notion of what it means to be a Jew in Hungary explains the significantly different estimates of the number of present-day Jewry.

11. By 'guilt on Jewish side', I refer to the aftermath of the persecutions: between 1945 and 1949, trials of the so-called People's Tribunes against war criminals judged many cases of officers, fascists and petty criminals, with subsequent sentences occasionally based on allegations and out of proportion for minor infractions. A number of my interviewees acknowledge today with regret that their indictments were highly exaggerated. Such cases must have occurred quite frequently in the aftermath of the war. On the other hand, I regard what in the nationalist parlance is called 'The Jewish Vengeance' inherent in Stalinist terror in Hungary between 1949 and 1953 under communist leaders (most of whom were of Jewish origin), simply an excuse for extant prejudices.
12. Citations to follow refer, with a few exceptions of personal communications, to documents in my possession, some of them written depositions, the majority of them recorded interviews, cited by the code of the document containing references to the interviewer and the interviewee, the tape number of the interview and the page number of the transcript.
13. Average losses among the labour battalion men were lower than among the deportees. The spring 1944 conscriptions were intended by officials in the Ministry of War to prevent the Jewish men from being deported to Auschwitz, partly in order to strengthen the Hungarian military efforts, partly as explicit rescue operation, implying that some officials had to be conscious of the fate the deportees faced. See Szabolcs Szita, 'A magyarországi zsidó munkaszolgálat' ('The Jewish Labour Service in Hungary'), Randolph Braham and Attila Pók (eds), *The Holocaust in Hungary: Fifty Years Later* (New York: Columbia University Press, 1997).
14. The Jewish labour battalion men could buy certain privileges – food and protection from their commanders, officers and soldier-guards – for vouchers to be converted by the family into cash or jewels. This was a generally accepted practice.
15. VL, 33.
16. For example, until the German occupation in March 1944, barristers refused to exclude Jewish members from their Chamber. See Mária M. Kovács, *Liberal Professions and Illiberal Politics: Hungary from the Habsburgs to the Holocaust* (New York and Oxford: Oxford University Press, 1994), pp. 90ff., 106ff.
17. Personal communication of the late Mrs PB-F.
18. See Randolph Braham (ed.), *The Politics of Genocide: The Holocaust in Hungary* (New York: Columbia University Press 1980), p. 762.
19. After the Trianon treaty of 1920, Transylvania became part of Romania. In September 1940, Hungary marched into Transylvania and occupied Kolozsvár and the greater part of Hungarian-speaking northern Transylvania in accordance with the Second Vienna Award.
20. Sz JZs, p. 18.
21. Béla Zsolt, *Kilenc koffer* (Nine Trunks) (Budapest: Magvetö, 1980). This bewildering and revealing testimony of an outstanding liberal journalist, concerning the ghetto of Nagyvárad, was first published in his magazine *Haladás* during 1946–47. The demonstration of an estimated 500 persons ended in a bloody suppression (pp. 52–6). However, there is no confirmation of this event to be found.
22. 18 May 1944; see an extensive quotation from the sermon in Braham, *Genocide*, pp. 1046ff.
23. 'És most menjen az anyja picsájába', literally: 'Go into the cunt of your mother' – which was, especially in those times, a quite exceptional way for the upper classes to express disapproval.

24. P 316 TI, 49 ssq.
25. The Gestapo kidnapped his only living son, Miklós, and Admiral Horthy himself was arrested by the SS commando of Skorzeny, forced to abdicate and interned in Weilheim, Bavaria.
26. Two independent interviews in my possession mention this fact, both based on personal experience: M 1 MJ, 21, and P 351 BGy, 3.
27. P KF, 8–10.
28. Braham, *Genocide*, pp 547ff.:

> As in Carpatho-Ruthenia, the concentration of the Jews in the north-eastern parts of Trianon Hungary began in the middle of April. The ghettoization of the Jews in the villages and smaller towns of Szabolcs County began on 14 April. After a few days in their local synagogues and communal buildings, the Jews were transferred to Nyiregyháza, the county seat. By 10 May, the ghetto population swelled to 17,580. In preparation of their deportation, the Jews were transferred toward the end of April and during the first half of May to three farm areas in the neighbouring plains of Sima, Nyirjes, and Harangod.

There the Jews were subjected to the usual cruel searches for jewels by the gendarmes and police investigations during which many were beaten to death, including the historian and chief rabbi Dr Béla Bernstein. From 17 May until 6 June, on five different days, the Jews were once more transferred to Nyiregyháza, from where they were transported to Auschwitz.
29. János Pelle, *Az utolsó vérvádak* (The Last Blood Libels) (Budapest: Pelikán Kiadó, 1995).
30. According to Braham, in *Genocide*, p. 639, the Jews of Nagykáta were transferred for entrainment to Kecskemét; meanwhile the Jews of Monor and the surrounding communities (7,500 persons) boarded trains from the brickyard of Monor (p. 673). Even after the halting of the deportations by the Regent, and contrary to his orders, on 8 July, the men of the Ministry of the Interior still continued the deportation of the Jews via Monor from the communities surrounding the capital (p. 763).
31. Sz 2 BL, 15sq.
32. The ghettoization of western and south-western Hungary, of altogether some 30,000 Jews, took place between 15 April and 3 July. Their deportation on ten trains occurred between 4 and 6 July; see Braham, *Genocide*, pp. 666ff., 671.
33. The Bishop of Veszprém in 1944 was József Mindszenty. He was appointed Cardinal-Archbishop of Esztergom soon after the war. In 1976, after the compromise between the Vatican and the Kádár regime, his former secretary, László Lékai, was consecrated as Mindszenty's successor. During the 1980s, Lékai was fully co-operative with the State, condemned conscientious objectors of military duty, tolerated or stimulated the persecution of the reform movement around Father Bulányi and suppressed critical publications. Other Christian Churches played along with the State as well, which included making conciliatory gestures to the Jewish community. Notwithstanding the exception of a few critical dissenters – like father György Kis – see his reminiscences: *Megjelölve Krisztus keresztjével és Dávid csillagával* (Budapest: Private edition, 1986) and the late Tamás Nyíri, one time Dean of the Faculty of Theology of Budapest – see his Foreword, 'Elöszó helyett', in Sándor Szenes, *Befejezetlen mult* (Budapest: Private edition, 1986, pp. 5–23) – the Roman Catholic Church in Hungary has declined up until now all critical self-scrutiny concerning its attitudes during the persecutions.

The role of the one-time Bishop of Veszprém is also disputed. He consented to the thanksgiving Mass under pressure from local Nazis, on the condition that no Arrowcross uniforms be allowed. Apparently, these terms were not respected. That the announcements were made in the bishop's name, is not corroborated. Cf. Braham, _Genocide_, 1047ff., regarding the thanksgiving service, held on 25 July: 'The bishop protested against the plan, arguing that the deportees also included converts, but relented after the _Nyilas_ (Arrowcross) threatened to distribute a flyer about his opposition'.

34. P 215 BÁ, 122sq.
35. SZ RR, 15.
36. Personal communication of the late Dr Teréz Virág, Budapest.
37. _Jób lázadása_; directed by Imre Gyöngyössy and Barna Kabay, 1983.

12

Resisting Fascism: The Politics and Literature of Italian Jews, 1922–45

STANISLAO G. PUGLIESE

Recent scholarship has generated an abundance of literature on the history and culture of Italian Jews, with several fine works in English.[1] Study of the nature and vicissitudes of Jewish identity have coincided with this literature.[2] Self-reflexive writing, by definition, seeks to answer the question of identity. This chapter turns to a particular facet of a larger question: as a people whose entire history and cultural memory has been dependent on the Word, how did Italian Jews define themselves during the fascist regime and what strategies did they develop in response to the dictatorship? Although many bourgeois Italian Jews supported fascism in the 1920s – seeing it as the only viable alternative to a Bolshevik Revolution in Italy – others immediately devoted themselves to the anti-fascist cause. For these Italian Jews, politics and literature fused in creating an identity that was Italian, Jewish and anti-fascist.

Historically, in Italy, the Synagogue existed before the Church, making Jews the 'most ancient minority'.[3] Depending on the time and the place, Italian Jews could expect tolerance, discrimination, persecution, or outright violence. At the end of the eighteenth century, Napoleon's troops had broken down the walls of the ghettos and burned their gates in the public squares of Italy. With the defeat of Napoleon and the restoration of Papal rule in 1814, the ghetto was re-established in Rome. The *Risorgimento* (movement for national unification) found support among the Jews of Italy, prompting Giuseppe Mazzini to write to the royal House of

Savoy that, 'the Jews of Italy have an Italian heart … and are integral members of the Italian nation'.[4]

With the final unification of Italy in 1861, the new nation-state dismantled the legal walls of the ghetto.[5] After an emancipation that they directly associated with the House of Savoy and the constitutional monarchy, Italian Jews actively participated in the political and cultural life of the fledgling nation. Rapid integration and assimilation followed, characterized by the high rate of intermarriage. Because of the very high rate of literacy, Italian Jews were active in the intellectual and cultural professions such as law, medicine, journalism and the academy. Two Italian Jews (Sidney Sonnino and Luigi Luzzatto) became prime ministers and several rose to prominence in the military, including Emanuele Pugliese – the most highly decorated officer of World War I. It would be impossible to conceive of an analogous situation in Germany, France or even England.[6] Lynn Gunzberg has recently challenged this traditional reading of Italian history as devoid of anti-Semitism in her provocative study of latent anti-Semitism in Italian popular culture and literature, *Strangers at Home: Jews in the Italian Literary Imagination.*[7]

When Benito Mussolini became Prime Minister, in October 1922, Italian Jews had no unified position on the fascist regime. With the major exception of Rome, Italian Jews had successfully entered the middle class; therefore, their perception of fascism was determined by socio-economic status, rather than religion. This was only natural, for the early programme of fascism contained no trace of anti-Semitism; indeed, there were Italian Jews among the *san sepolcristi* (first fascists) when Mussolini formed the nucleus of the new movement in Milan, on 23 March 1919. Jews participated at the highest levels of the fascist regime, as evidenced by Aldo Finzi (Under Secretary of the Interior) and Guido Jung (Finance Minister). Anti-Semites like Roberto Farinacci and Telesio Interlandi were kept on a short leash by Mussolini. Il Duce even encouraged the Zionist movement in Italy, not through any sincere desire to further the cause, but because he saw Zionism as a possible counterweight to British influence in the Mediterranean. As late as September 1934, Mussolini criticized Nazi anti-Semitism in a contemptuous speech when he declared that:

> Thirty centuries of history permit us to regard with supreme pity certain doctrines supported beyond the Alps by the

descendants of a people who did not know how to write and
could not hand down documents recording their own lives
at a time when Rome had Caesar, Virgil and Augustus.[8]

However, Mussolini held contradictory poses regarding the Jews;
while he could take the charming, sophisticated and brilliant
Jewish woman, Margherita Sarfatti, as a mistress, he could also
ominously write (as early as 1920), 'Let us hope the Jews will be
smart enough not to incite anti-Semitism in the one country
where it has never existed'.[9]

   Many Italian Jews – as members of the bourgeoisie, not as Jews
– were favourably disposed toward the new regime. Like their
fellow citizens, they too were susceptible to the rhetoric of the
dangers of a communist revolution in Italy. When anti-Semitic
legislation was passed in 1938, approximately 10,000 men in an
Italian-Jewish population of c. 50,000 (or one in three Jewish
adults) were formally members of the Fascist Party. Of course, not
all of these members were ideological fascists; many had joined
the PNF (*Partito Nazionale Fascista*) in order to keep their jobs. A
common sly reference at the time was to the PNF as *Per Necessità
Familiare* ('For Family Necessity'). In addition, Italian Jews sensed
more hostility from the Vatican than Mussolini's early regime;
consequently, they saw fascism's conflict with the Vatican in a
favourable light. Alfredo Rocco, Minister of Justice, and one of the
theoreticians of the Fascist State, pushed for legislation in 1930–31
which gave a coherent national and legal status to Jewish
organizations and their members for the first time.[10] As late as 1933,
the Italian-Jewish scholar, Arnaldo Momigliano, in a review of
Cecil Roth's, *The Jews of Venice* – later echoed by Antonio Gramsci
– could speak of the 'parallel nationalization' in which, 'the history
of the Jews in almost every Italian city is essentially the history of
the formation of their Italian national consciousness, which took
place at the same time as the general Italian national consciousness'.[11] Yet, one scholar has argued that as recently as the 1970s
and 1980s, 'the perceived ambiguous nature of Italian-Jewish
identity still created tension in the lives of Italian Jews'.[12]

   After the unification of the new nation and their emancipation,
Jews' religious observance rapidly declined, especially *kashrut*.[13]
According to Cecil Roth, Italy could count 108 synagogues conducting services twice daily in 1830; a century later, that number
had dropped to 38, and those held services only irregularly.[14] A

study in 1976 discovered that while there had been 87 organized Jewish communities in 1840, that number had dropped to 22 by 1970.[15] Andrew Canepa has argued that Italy's well-known lack of anti-Semitism and willingness to accept Jews into mainstream society came at a price: Italian Jews were expected to renounce the most overt expressions of their Judaism and conform to the dominant social mores.[16] Ironically, by the time the Racial Laws were promulgated in 1938, the rate of intermarriage with Gentiles was nearly 50 per cent. Such demographics, along with the work of Canepa and Gunzberg, suggest that Italian-Jewish assimilation was far more complex than previously thought and that Italian Jews may have been affected by a subtle social dynamic that suggests at least the possibility of a latent anti-Semitism. Italian Jews, in a psychic effort to compensate for this perceived 'difference' were often more patriotic, nationalistic, and fascist than their Gentile neighbours. Hence, patriotism became a 'secular religion'.

One of the most fascinating, and tragic, examples concerns the fate of the Ovazza family of Turin. In 1915, Ernesto Ovazza, at age 50, had volunteered for service in World War I; he brought with him his three sons. Just before his death in 1926, he requested that three words be carved into his tombstone: *Patria, Fede, Famiglia* ('Fatherland, Faith, Family'). One son, Ettore, fanatically dedicated to the fascist regime, founded *La Nostra Bandiera* ('Our Flag') in 1935, as a fascist-Jewish newspaper to counter the influence of the Zionist newspaper *Israel*. In the 1930s, Ettore Ovazza failed to, recognize the signs of coming persecutions and refused to abandon the fascist cause. In 1943, he and his family fell into the hands of the Nazis in Italy; they were shot, hacked to pieces, and their bodies burned in the furnace of a building in Intra, a town near Laggo Maggiore.[17] Although an extreme case, the Ovazza saga clearly indicates that many Italian Jews were unable or unwilling to see the seeds of destruction in fascism's alliance with Nazi Germany. They insistently clung to the belief that Italy was a refuge from the vicious anti-Semitism in other parts of Europe.

While Ettore Ovazza's story can be understood because of his distance from the loci of power, Aldo Finzi's fate was, if anything, even more absurd and tragic. Finzi had been a close confidant of Mussolini's before Il Duce came to power. A fascist deputy of Parliament in 1921, he was appointed Under-Secretary of the Interior (a highly sensitive post in charge of Fascism's secret police and hired assassins) and named to the Fascist Grand Council in late 1922. Although he gained a reputation for corruption, he was also appointed aviation vice-commissioner in January 1923. As Under-Secretary of the Interior, he was responsible for the fraud and corruption that characterized the April 1924 national elections. After the Socialist Deputy Giacomo Matteotti denounced the 'irregularities' in a long speech before Parliament, he was abducted and killed in June; his body was found two months later in the Roman countryside. Finzi privately implicated Mussolini in the assassination, and was forced out of the regime, although no other action was taken against him. When the anti-Semitic legislation was passed in 1938, Finzi used his past affiliation with the regime to escape the consequences. He remained a member of the Fascist Party until November 1942, when he was expelled for 'indiscipline'. With the Nazi occupation of Italy in the autumn of 1943, Finzi had a change of heart and joined the partisan movement in the countryside outside Rome. Early in 1944, he was captured by the Nazis and, in a final ironic twist of fate, was executed along with 334 others in the Ardeatine Caves massacre on 24 March 1944. The massacre was in retaliation for a partisan attack the day before in the streets of Rome.[18]

The positions of the Vatican and the monarchy on the 'Jewish question' in Italy require a separate study.[19] Suffice it to say, that the Vatican oscillated between outright hostility and vague support of the Jews. Italian Jews for their part loyally supported the monarchy. Ironically, it was the same Vittorio Emanuele III who had officially visited the opening of the new synagogue in Rome in 1904 and proclaimed 'Italy is a country without racial discrimination', who 34 years later signed the Racial Laws.[20]

These Racial Laws came as a shock in 1938. Scholars still debate the origin and evolution of fascist anti-Semitism, with some claiming that the Racial Laws were directly influenced by Hitler's Nazi Germany, while others contend that Mussolini himself allowed the anti-Semites to gain power.[21] Ominous signals had preceded the Racial Laws. In May 1936, Hitler visited Italy and was accorded full honours. In 1937, Paolo Orano's book *Gli ebrei in Italia*, appeared, spelling out the regime's official position against Zionist Jews and making the transition from anti-Zionism to anti-Semitism. In July 1938, the country was stunned by the publication of the grotesque 'Manifesto of the Racial Scientists', a document clothed in the language of positivist science. Among other 'scientific facts', the Manifesto concluded: that 'The population of modern Italy is of Aryan origin and its civilization is Aryan'; that, 'There now exists an Italian race'; and that, 'Jews do not belong to the Italian race'.[22] During the same month of July, the name of the Office of Demography was changed to the Office of Demography and Race, and in August a census was taken of Jews in Italy. In addition, fascist newspapers, such as Roberto Farinacci's *Il Regime fascista* and Telesio Interlandi's *Il Tevere*, stepped up their anti-Semitic diatribes, indicating Mussolini's consent. Farinacci, later 'Inspector-General for Race' in the Republic of Saló, had the distinction of publishing the 'Protocols of the Elders of Zion' in Italian. The Vatican, not to be outdone in the sport of anti-Semitism, kept pace with the Jesuit organ, *Civiltà Cattolica*.

Ironically, the Racial Laws were a catalyst: Italian Jews, many of whom were neither observant nor familiar with Judaism, turned to their religious and cultural legacy. The memoirs, diaries and recollections are unanimous on this point: by passing the Racial Laws, the regime in effect pulled Italian Jews out of their assimilated ways, their support for fascism, and triggered a return to a 'cultural memory'. They were now forced to confront the question: who exactly was a Jew? How was identity to be conceived, especially after many Italian Jews had abandoned Hebrew, Yiddish and the synagogue?[23] The answers were often paradoxical and contradictory. One scholar has written that:

> The Italian Jew ... considered his own religious crisis as a personal phenomenon: too profound to be healed by a single reform of ritual ... [he] has found it possible to distance himself from religious observance, but has been firm about leaving intact the faith from which he was departing.[24]

Italian Jews were therefore in an ambivalent position. What was to be their relationship to the State and Italian society? Debates raged within Jewish communities. The question was sometimes framed as a choice between assimilation, a complete absorption into Italian society which demanded an abandonment of traditional Jewish culture and ultimately conversion to Catholicism, or integration, which would allow the Jews to participate fully in Italian society while maintaining their distinct cultural identity. Others argued over the question of Zionism and what it meant for Italian Jews. At the fourth Zionist youth conference in

Livorno, held in November 1924, the two fundamental positions were spelled out by Nello Rosselli, an advocate of integration, and Enzo Sereni, a fervent Zionist.[25] What Sereni and Rosselli agreed on was that Judaism could not be constrained in a narrow definition. It had what might be called a 'polyphonic' character; a single reading or interpretation was contrary to its history and its character. Alternatively, as Sereni himself put it, 'every attempt of ours to define it fails'.[26] Enzo's brother, Emilio, eventually abandoned Zionism in favour of communism, which seems to bear out the point that many Jews found socialism and communism attractive as secular religions promising terrestrial redemption. Enzo never wavered in his beliefs and insisted that the Jews carve out a new state; accordingly, in 1927 he left a secure bourgeois life in Rome, and helped found the Givat Brenner Kibbutz near Rehovot. With the outbreak of World War II, Enzo Sereni enrolled in the British Intelligence Service and carried out missions in Egypt and Iraq. In 1944, he persuaded his superior officers to allow him on a dangerous mission, parachuting behind German lines. Tragically, he was captured by the Nazis, tortured for four days, and perished at Dachau.[27]

Nello Rosselli was the historian brother of the more famous anti-fascist leader, Carlo. The Rossellis were related to the most distinguished Jewish families in Italy such as the Nathans (Ernesto Nathan was mayor of Rome at the turn of the century) and the Pincherle family (the writer Alberto Moravia was a first cousin). While Carlo had become actively engaged in the anti-fascist struggle, escaped from the penal island of Lipari, and established a new movement in Paris,[28] Nello remained behind to carry out the anti-fascist struggle through his scholarly work as a historian.[29] At the Livorno conference, Nello delineated what Judaism meant for him personally, and also what political, social and civil consequences derived from his position.[30] Rising before the Zionist majority, Nello Rosselli gave a speech remembered by all those present and even grudgingly admired by the Zionists themselves as a most succinct and eloquent challenge:

> I am a Jew who does not go to Temple on the Sabbath, does not know Hebrew, does not observe any rituals of the faith … and yet I hold fast to my Judaism … I am not a Zionist … For the Zionists there is only one problem … For me all the problems of life present themselves … as an equal torment

to that of the religious problem ... The Jewish problem is not, and I do not feel it to be, as the only, fundamental problem of my life ... I call myself a Jew because the monotheistic conscience, which no other religion has expressed with such clarity, is indestructible in me, because I have a very live sense of my personal responsibility ... because every form of idolatry repels me; because I consider with Jewish severity the task of our lives on this earth and with Jewish serenity the mystery of the afterlife; because I love all men as it was commanded in Israel. And therefore I have a social conception which descends from our best traditions; because I have that religious sense of the family that, for those who look from the outside, truly appears as the fundamental and bedrock principle of Jewish society. I can therefore call myself a Jew.[31]

For Nello Rosselli, Judaism was not to be closed behind domestic walls but launched into society as the nucleus of collective freedom. Placing Judaism within schematic confines would rob it of its vitality, limit its power and deprive it of its civic potential. This was a definition of Judaism as a collectivity of values, a historical legacy, that was earthly and concrete. Rosselli's definition of what it meant to be an Italian Jew emphasized a civil aspect founded on the principle of liberty and thereby tied his concept of Judaism with Benedetto Croce's theory of history as 'the story of liberty'. It was precisely this dimension of Judaism – paradoxically both particular and universal – that brought together Nello Rosselli's conception of Judaism with his stand against fascism.[32] In March 1925, Nello travelled to Germany to conduct research in the Archives of the German Social Democratic Party; he attended the lectures of Friedrich Meinecke in Berlin, and commented on the death of the Social Democratic President, Ebert, and the election of Marshal Hindenburg. Letters to his mother back in Florence reveal his sensitivity to German anti-Semitism.[33] An intensely personal 'Diario Politico', published 30 years after his assassination in 1967, reveals an unmistakable subterranean current of religiosity in his political thought:

> The problem of freedom from fascism is, first of all, the problem of convincing every Italian of the need for internal cleansing; of acting according to conscience; of having the courage of one's convictions.[34]

Nello Rosselli consciously rejected the idea that only through Zionism could Jews assert their identity as Jews. It was the commitment to universal, timeless values which made one a Jew, not adherence to an 'artificial' construct such as Zionism. When he was stridently criticized by Guido Bedarida for his position, he responded in a letter published in the Zionist journal, *Israel*:

> I did not come to Livorno to put Italian Judaism on trial ... but only *my* Judaism. You have pronounced a severe summation. I do not contest. The sentence? The sentence, unfortunately, does not come from without – we each sentence ourselves, in life, at the cost of torments ... These are the most severe sentences.[35]

The Livorno Congress of November 1924 took place during the only serious challenge to Mussolini's regime – the Matteotti affair mentioned above. Finally, on 3 January 1925, Mussolini appeared in Parliament, took full responsibility for what had transpired in June, and challenged his opponents to remove him from office. Little happened, and within months Mussolini had put in place legislation that was to characterize the fascist regime as 'totalitarian'. Politically conscious men and women were forced to choose and many Italian Jews chose anti-fascism. For the majority of Italian Jews, the questions raised by Sereni and Rosselli in 1924 did not assail them until 1938, yet so many Italian Jews participated in the anti-fascist cause that the question has arisen: was there a strain of 'Jewish anti-fascism', or are we limited to saying that there were simply some anti-fascists who happened to have been Jewish? The foremost Italian historian on the subject, Renzo De Felice, insisted that there was no 'Jewish anti-fascism'.[36] Yet, if we look at the leadership of the anti-fascist opposition we find Umberto Terracini and Emilio Sereni of the PCI; Giuseppe Emanuele Modigliani and Claudio Treves of the PSI; and Eugenio Chiesa of the PRI. All recalled the formative influence of Judaism on their early lives.[37] Other well-known Jewish anti-fascists include Carlo Levi, Leone Ginzburg, Primo Levi, Max Ascoli and Vittorio Foa. Primo Levi, in fact, when arrested in the countryside in November 1943, confessed to being a Jew rather than admit his role in the partisan resistance, thinking this would be the safer course.

To what extent did their Jewish heritage contribute to their political stance? Most did not address the question directly, but all shared the common assumption that the moral life intersected civic concerns. Carlo Rosselli went so far as to insist that the precedents for his heretical conception of a liberal socialism were Greek rationalism and the messianism of Israel. Liberalism had its roots in a Greek rationalism that contains, 'a love of liberty, a respect for autonomy, a harmonious and detached conception of life'; while socialism was the heir of a Judaic tradition stressing a completely terrestrial justice, 'the myth of equality, a spiritual torment that forbids any indulgence'.[38] Yet, neither Carlo, nor his brother Nello, made many more specific remarks concerning their religion. Like many of their generation, they had substituted a secular, civic religion and it was this, combined with vestiges from Judaism, that propelled them into opposing fascism. In a revealing memoir, their mother Amelia, a noted playwright, confessed the extent of her family's assimilation:

> We were Jews, but *first and foremost* Italians. That is why even I, born and raised in that profoundly Italian and liberal environment, saved only the pure essence of my religion within my heart. Religious elements that were solely of a *moral* character: and this was the only religious instruction I gave my children.[39]

That religious instruction was reflected in both the historical works of Nello and the political activism of Carlo. Translated into secular terms it generated an autonomy of thought and stress on free will, and the refusal to accept any truth as absolute. Italian Jews may have lost the desire to follow the rituals and customs strictly, but they clearly maintained a strong desire for social justice in the tradition of the Hebrew prophets. This is borne out if we turn to the many memoirs that have been written since the end of World War II. They are almost unanimous: when the Racial Laws were promulgated in 1938, they generated a fierce sense of pride in being an Italian Jew. Those who had long ago abandoned the synagogue returned and young students began to pore over the ancient books once again. What they found convinced many that they had an ethical imperative to resist and fight. Gianfranco Sarfatti was 22 years old in 1943 when he wrote to his parents seeking refuge in Switzerland, about why he had returned to Italy and joined the Resistance:

Reflect that while it seems that all the world is collapsing and that the ruins must surely cover everything, your children ... are looking toward the future and toward reconstruction, devoting all their forces to it. You are suffering; but millions of parents have been and are still in anxiety; and this must no longer be. And as I have recognized your sorrow in the sorrow of all suffering mothers and fathers, you must recognize your children in all the children and in all the young people who have been born into this world.[40]

It is this universalism and humanism that is evident in the memoir literature of Italian Jews under fascism.

However, perhaps it is misleading to speak of a single tradition of Italian Judaism. Different cities had different Jewish communities; and even within a city, Jews were further divided according to social class, degree of religious observance, place of origin and date of arrival.[41] Among the few Italian-Jewish writers who spoke of their Judaism, Italo Svevo and Alberto Moravia spring to mind. Carlo Levi seemed more touched by the pagan existence of the southern Italians during his period of confinement there in 1935–36.[42] For Primo Levi, it was science rather than Judaism which he turned to for a defense against the bombast and rhetoric of fascism; science was 'clear and distinct and ... verifiable', hence an effective 'antidote to fascism'.[43] His Holocaust memoir, *Survival in Auschwitz* is, after Anne Frank's diary and the writings of Elie Wiesel, perhaps the best-known work to come out of that experience. Natalia Ginzburg, wife of the Russian-Italian intellectual Leone Ginzburg, did not address her Jewish heritage until late in her writing career. Her *Family Sayings* of 1963 was an intricate web of concealment and disclosure; like Carlo Levi, she too remained 'haunted by the ancestral theme of exile'.[44]

Other writers testify to this new consciousness of a lost tradition. Dan Vittorio Segre, cousin of Ettore Ovazza, in his aptly titled, *Memoirs of a Fortunate Jew*, and echoing Amelia Rosselli, recounts that his parents:

... grew up in a climate of obsolete Judaism and of vigorous Italian nationalism and, as a result, shared all the virtues and prejudices typical of a generation of Jewish bourgeoisie sure of themselves, affluent, and respected, and totally unconscious of the dangers that lay waiting for them in the future.[45]

Segre recalls that his father strongly opposed the Zionist movement, which to his mind undermined the patriotism of Italian Jews. Although the memoir sometimes approaches a nostalgic lament for a lost tradition, Segre approvingly and tellingly quotes the Napoleonic King of Naples, Joachim Murat, who once said proudly, 'I am my own ancestor'.[46]

Of all the twentieth-century Italian-Jewish writers, it was Giorgio Bassani who forged the strongest ties with Judaism: 'Jews … in whatever part of the earth, under whatever sky History scattered them, are and always will be Jews'.[47] It may not be too far-fetched to suggest that all of Bassani's writing revolved around the question that he so simply puts at the beginning of his most famous work, *The Garden of the Finzi-Contini*: 'For what on earth did the word "Jew" mean, basically?'[48] That probing question pierced the hermetically-sealed garden of the Finzi-Contini when the Racial Laws of 1938 became a reality. However, the narrator is stunned that the question has to be posed: he and his fellow Jews had become banal in their ordinariness. The existential angst fostered by the Racial Laws remained behind even after the war.

In a small literary masterpiece, *The Tiber Afire*, Fabio Della Seta recalls how the Racial Laws spurred radical questions about Judaism. In the context of persecution it was perhaps necessary, according to the author, to recall, 'the original and proud meaning of the name Israel: "He who wrestles with the Lord"'. Following Martin Buber, Della Seta reminds us that, 'Before each person, whatever his means and situation, the opportunity opens to attempt the absurd enterprise. And it is not only a possibility, but a duty as well'.[49] That 'absurd enterprise', the perennial task of Jews in Italy and throughout the Diaspora, is the creation of a relationship with the Deity and, subsequently, the forging of a sustaining identity in a modern world that seems intent on obliterating all traces of that ancestral consciousness.

NOTES

1. Although published over 15 years ago, the essay by the distinguished historian, Arnaldo Momigliano, 'The Jews of Italy', in *The New York Review of Books*, 24 October 1985, is an excellent introduction. Of the many works that have appeared, see especially H. Stuart Hughes, *Prisoners of Hope: The Silver Age of the Italian Jews, 1924–1975* (Cambridge, MA: Harvard University Press, 1983); Meir Michaelis, *Mussolini and the Jews: German–Italian Relations and the Jewish Question in Italy, 1922–1945* (New York: Oxford University

Press, 1978); Susan Zuccotti, *The Italians and the Holocaust: Persecution, Rescue, and Survival* (New York: Basic Books, 1987; repr. Lincoln, NE: University of Nebraska Press, 1996); Alexander Stille, *Benevolence and Betrayal: Five Italian Jewish Families Under Fascism* (New York: Summit Books, 1991); Nicola Caracciolo, *Uncertain Refuge: Italy and the Jews During the Holocaust*, trans. Florette Rechnitz Koffler and Richard Koffler (Urbana and Chicago, IL: University of Illinois Press, 1995). See the valuable bibliography compiled by Professor James Mellone of Queens College, 'The Jews of Italy: A Select Bibliography, 1996–1999', in Stanislao G. Pugliese (ed.), *The Most Ancient of Minorities: The Jews of Italy* (Westport, CT: Greenwood Press, 2002).

2. Here the literature is, if anything, more vast. Of particular importance are Alain Finkelkraut, *Le juive imaginaire* (Paris: Seuil, 1980); Saul Friedlander, *Memory, History, and the Extermination of the Jews of Europe* (Bloomington, IN: Indiana University Press, 1993); Albert Memmi, *Le juif et l'autre* (Paris: C. de Bartillat, 1995); Michael A. Meyer, *Jewish Identity in the Modern World* (Seattle, WA: University of Washington Press, 1983); Leon Poliakov, *L'impossible choix: histoire des crises d'identite juive* (Paris: Australis, 1994); Linda Nochlin and Tamar Garb (eds), *The Jew in the Text: Modernity and the Construction of Identity* (London: Thames & Hudson, 1995).

3. The phrase is from Hughes, *Prisoners of Hope*, p. 2. In September 1962, while preparing the way for a new road from Rome to Ostia, authorities uncovered the remains of a Jewish temple. See *The New York Times*, 28 September 1962.

4. Maurizio Molina, *Ebrei in Italia: un problema d'identità (1870–1938)* (Florence: La Giuntina, 1991), p. 70.

5. Rome's ghetto was opened a decade later. Guido Fubini, *La condizione giuridica dell'ebraismo italiano: Dal periodo napoleonico alla republica* (Florence: La Nuova Italia, 1974).

6. Although it is true that Leon Blum, a Jew, became prime minister in France, this was not until the 1930s; and large crowds chanted 'Better Hitler than Blum!' in the streets of Paris.

7. Lynn M. Gunzberg, *Strangers at Home: Jews in the Italian Literary Imagination* (Berkeley, CA: University of California Press, 1992); see especially the last chapter, 'Strangers at Home'.

8. Quoted in Renzo De Felice, *Storia degli ebrei italiani sotto il fascismo*, 4th edn (Turin: Einaudi, 1988), pp. 138–9; and Zuccotti, *Italians and the Holocaust*, p. 30.

9. Benito Mussolini, *Il Popolo d'Italia*, 19 September 1920; quoted in Gunzberg, *Strangers at Home*, p. 219.

10. De Felice, *Ebrei italiani*, p. 127.

11. Quoted in Molina, *Ebrei in Italia*, pp. 25–6.

12. Steve Siporin, 'From *Kashrut* to *Cucina Ebraica*: The Recasting of Italian Jewish Foodways', *Journal of American Folklore*, 107 (1994), pp. 268–81; esp. p. 268.

13. Ibid., p. 269.

14. Cecil Roth, *History of the Jews of Italy* (Philadelphia, PA: Jewish Publications Society, 1946), p. 506.

15. Sergio Della Pergola, *Anatomia dell'ebraismo italiano: Caratteristiche demografiche, economiche, sociali, religiose di una minoranza* (Rome: Carucci, 1976), p. 59.

16. Andrew Canepa, 'Emancipation and Jewish Response in Mid-Nineteenth-Century Italy', *European History Quarterly*, 16, 4 (1986), 403–39.

17. For the story of the Ovazza family, see Stille, *Benevolence and Betrayal*, pp. 17–89.

18. On Aldo Finzi, see Alessandra Staderini, 'Una fonte per lo studio della utilizzazione dei "fonti segreti": la contabilità di Aldo Finzi', in *Storia Contemporaneo*, 10 (October 1979), pp. 4–5; and 'Aldo Finzi', in Philip V. Cannistraro (ed.), *Historical Dictionary of Fascist Italy* (Westport, CT: Greenwood Press, 1982), p. 225.

19. See the controversy surrounding the work of John Cornwell, especially *Hitler's Pope* (New York: Penguin, 2000); cf. Pierre Blet, *Pius XII and the Second World War: According to the Vatican Archives*, trans. Lawrence Johnson (Mahwah, NJ: Paulist Press, 2000); Michael Marrus, *The Holocaust in History* (Hanover, NH and London: University Press of New England, 1987), pp. 179–83; Jonathan Steinberg, *All or Nothing: The Axis and the Holocaust* (London: Routledge, 1990).

20. Molina, *Ebrei in Italia*, p. 15.

21. The most exhaustive work on the subject – based on archives in Israel, Italy, Britain, and the US – is the Michaelis book. Because of a lack of any documentary evidence, Michaelis concludes that the anti-Semitic laws were not a result of direct pressure from Hitler. See also Zuccotti, *The Italians and the Holocaust*; Michael A. Ledeen, 'The Evolution of Fascist Anti-Semitism', in *Jewish Social Studies*, 37, 1 (January 1975); Gene Bernardini, 'The Origins and Development of Racial Anti-Semitism in Fascist Italy', *Journal of Modern History*, 49 (September 1977), pp. 431–53.

22. These are points 4, 6, and 9 of the 'Manifesto of Racial Scientists'. For more on the Manifesto, see Stille, *Benevolence and Betrayal*, p. 70; Zuccotti, *Italians and the Holocaust*, p. 35; De Felice, *Ebrei italiani*, pp. 541–2.

23. This is the question that Hughes perceptively raises in *Prisoners of Hope*, p. 2. (Years later, Hughes revealed that 'I derived more pleasure from *Prisoners of Hope* than from any other of my books': 'Doing Italian History: Pleasure and Politics', *Journal of Modern Italian Studies*, 1, 1 (Autumn 1995), p. 100.)

24. Attilio Milano, *Storia degli ebrei in Italia* (Turin: Einaudi, 1992), p. 374.

25. On the role of Enzo Sereni and his wife (later widow), Ada, see Idith Zertal, *From Catastrophe to Power: Holocaust Survivors and the Emergence of Israel* (Berkeley, CA, Los Angeles, CA, London: University of California Press, 1998).

26. Mario Toscano, 'Fermenti culturali ed esperienze organizzative della gioventù ebraica italiana (1911–1925)', *Storia Contemporanea* (December 1982), p. 957.

27. Zuccotti, *Italians and the Holocaust*, pp. 268–70.

28. On Carlo Rosselli, see Stanislao G. Pugliese, *Carlo Rosselli: Socialist Heretic and Antifascist Exile* (Cambridge, MA: Harvard University Press, 1999).

29. Nello Rosselli's first work was *Mazzini e Bakunin: 12 anni di movimento operaio in Italia, 1860–1872* (Turin: Einaudi, 1927); this was followed by *Carlo Pisacane nel Risorgimento italiano* (Genoa: Orfini, 1936); his *Saggi sul Risorgimento e altri saggi* was published posthumously in Turin by Einaudi in 1946. See also Zeffiro Ciuffoletti (ed.), *Nello Rosselli: un storico sotto il fascismo* (Florence: La Nuova Italia, 1979).

30. A valuable study is Bruno Di Porto, 'Il problema ebraico in Nello Rosselli', in *Giustizia e Libertà nella lotta antifascista e nella storia d'Italia* (Florence: La Nuova Italia, 1979), pp. 491–9. See also Zeffiro Ciuffoletti, 'Nello Rosselli: storico e politico', in the same volume, pp. 439–82.

31. The entire speech was reprinted in the Zionist newspaper, *Israel*, 20 November 1924 and later in *Il Ponte*, 13, 1957, pp. 864–8; now in *Nello Rosselli: uno storico sotto il fascismo*, pp. 1–5. A partial English translation appears in Zuccotti, *Italians and the Holocaust*, p. 246.

32. On Nello Rosselli, see Zeffiro Ciuffoletti, 'Nello Rosselli: A Historian Under Fascism', *Journal of Italian History*, 1, 2 (Autumn 1978), pp. 287–314; and Alessandro Galante Garrone's 'Introduction' to Nello Rosselli, *Saggi sul Risorgimento* (Turin: Einaudi, 1980).

33. The letters from Germany can be found in Carlo Francovich (ed.), *Epistolario familiare: Carlo, Nello Rosselli e la madre (1914–1937)* (Milan: Sugar Co., 1979; repr., Milan: Mondadori, 1997), pp. 268–92.

34. Nello Rosselli, 'Diario Politico' in the Archivio Rosselli, Istituto Storico della Resistenza in Toscana; reprinted in *Il Ponte*, 23 (1967), p. 737.

35. Nello Rosselli to Guido Bedarida, published in *Israel*, 7 January 1925; reprinted in Ciuffoletti (ed.), *Nello Rosselli: Uno storico sotto il fascismo* (Florence: La Nuova Italia, 1979), pp. 5–6.

36. De Felice, *Ebrei italiani*, p. 433.

37. Terracini speaks about his Judaism in an interview found in Gina Formiggini, *Stella d'Italia, Stella di Davide: Gli ebrei dal Risorgimento alla Resistenza* (Milan: Mursia, 1970), pp. 414; on Emilio Sereni, see Ruth Bondy, *The Emissary: A Life of Emilio Sereni*, trans. Shlomo Katz (Boston, MA: Little, Brown, 1977); for Modigliani and Chiesa, see Guido Ludovico Luzzatto, 'La participazione al'antifascismo in Italia e all'estero dal 1918 al 1938', *Gli ebrei in Italia durante il fascismo: Quaderni del Centro di Documentazione Ebraica Contemporanea*, 2 (March 1962), pp. 32–44.

38. Carlo Rosselli, *Liberal Socialism*, ed. Nadia Urbinati and trans. by William McCuaig (Princeton, NJ: Princeton University Press, 1994), p. 6.

39. Amelia Rosselli, 'Memoriale', unpublished manuscript in the Archivio Rosselli, deposited in the Istituto Storico della Resistenza in Toscana, Palazzo Medici, via Cavour, Florence, Italy. Emphasis in the original; partially quoted in Nicola Tranfaglia, *Carlo Rosselli: dall'interventismo alla Giustizia e Libertà* (Bari: Laterza, 1968), p. 13.

40. Zuccotti, *Italians and the Holocaust*, p. 269.

41. The point is made by Hughes in reference to the Jews of Rome, *Prisoners of Hope*, p. 36.

42. Out of that experience came one of the greatest books of twentieth-century Italian literature and a masterpiece of amateur anthropology: Carlo Levi, *Christ Stopped at Eboli*, trans. Frances Fenaye (New York: Farrar, Straus and Giroux, 1947).

43. Hughes, *Prisoners of Hope*, p. 74.

44. Ibid., p. 112.

45. Dan Vittorio Segre, *Memoirs of a Fortunate Jew* (Bethesda, MA: Adler & Adler, 1987), p. 23.

46. Ibid., p. 10.

47. Giorgio Bassani, *The Garden of the Finzi-Contini*, trans. William Weaver (San Diego, CA: Harcourt Brace Jovanovich, 1987), p. 14.

48. Ibid., p. 22.

49. Fabio Della Seta, *The Tiber Afire*, trans. Frances Frenaye (Marlboro, VT: The Marlboro Press, 1991), p. 83–4.

Index